IMPROVEMENT DRIVEN GOVERNMENT:

Public Service for the 21st Century

David K. Carr
Ian D. Littman
John K. Condon

Coopers
&Lybrand

Coopers & Lybrand L.L.P.

a professional services firm

Washington, DC

Coopers & Lybrand L.L.P., 1530 Wilson Blvd.
Arlington, VA 22209

David K. Carr, Ian D. Littman, John D. Condon

Improvement Driven Government: Public Service in the 21st Century

Library of Congress No. 95-070309

ISBN 0-944533-20-5

Bulk quantities of this book may be obtained from:

Bookmasters Inc.
Distribution Center
1444 State Rt. 42
RD 11
Mansfield, Ohio 44903
Telephone: 1-800-247-6553
Fax: 419-281-6883

OTHER BOOKS AND MONOGRAPHS PUBLISHED OR DISTRIBUTED BY COOPERS & LYBRAND'S PUBLISHING DIVISION

Managing Project Expectations, 1995

Benchmarking: A Manager's Guide, 1995

Activity-Based Management in Government, 1995

Managing Change: Opening Organizational Horizons, 1994

Innovation: The Creativity Jogger, 1994

Customer Service Measurement, 1994

Survey Assessment, 1994

Excellence in Government: Total Quality Management in the 1990s, 2nd Edition, 1992

Process Improvement: A Guide For Teams, 1993

BreakPoint Business Process Redesign, 1992

(For more information on these titles, see Appendix A)

Table of Contents

Organizational Process Alignment

PART V: DEVELOPING IMPROVEMENT DRIVEN ORGANIZATIONS

Preface

Our original intent for this book was for it to be the third edition of *Excellence in Government: Total Quality Management in the 1990s*, which was written in 1990 and updated in 1993. However, in reviewing the critical issues governments are facing as America moves into the 21st century, it was clear that a simple update or revision would not be enough. By the time this book was finished, it included 60 percent totally new material, 30 percent of the information found in *Excellence in Government,* and additional examples from *Activity-Based Management in Government.* (See Appendix A for abstracts of these books.)

Considering the sharp, continuous upward trend in America's management learning curve, we suspect that in a few years we will once again have to start afresh in preparing a management book that meets the needs of government leaders and managers. We sincerely hope that it will not be a book that focuses on contract management. That could happen, if governments fail to heed citizen demands for management reform. Then, we expect, there could be wholesale privatization of many functions now handled by career civil servants. Frankly, we do not think that business has any particular patent on good management.

Government managers can do the best possible job for citizens, if they are enabled to do so with good management, training, responsibility, and accountability.

Acknowledgments

We express our appreciation to the organizations that contributed the time, information, and examples that made this book possible. They include organizations first described in *Excellence in Government: Total Quality Management in the 1990s*. These include:

U.S. Department of Agriculture

    Forest Service
    Ochoco National Forest

U.S. Air Force

    Aeronautical Systems Division
    Air Force Development Test Center
    Air Force Systems Command
    Electronic Systems Division
    Rome, New York Air Development Center

U.S. Army

    Sacramento, California Army Depot
    Watervliet, New York Army Arsenal

U.S. Customs Service, Miami Airport Operations

State of California

> Department of Motor Vehicles

U.S. Coast Guard

> Headquarters Division

U.S. Department of Commerce

> Patent and Trademark Office

U.S. Department of Defense

> Defense Commercial Communications Office
> Defense Industrial Supply Center
> Defense Logistics Agency

U.S. Department of Education

> Division of Quality Assurance

U.S. Department of Energy

U.S. Environmental Protection Agency

Federal Quality Institute
U.S. General Accounting Office

> General Government Division

U.S. General Services Administration

Office of Physical Security and Law Enforcement

City of Indianapolis, IN

Department of Capital Asset Management

Internal Revenue Service

Cincinnati, OH, Fresno, CA, and Ogden, UT, Service Centers

State of Michigan

Department of Commerce

National Academy of Public Administration

National Aeronautics and Space Administration

Lewis Research Center, Cleveland, OH
Johnson Space Center, Houston, TX

U.S. Navy

Cherry Point, NC, Jacksonville, FL, and
    Pensacola, FL, Naval Aviation Depots
Combat Systems, Field Operations, and Ordnance
    Support Group (NAVSEA 06G)
Crane, IN, Naval Weapons Support Center
Naval Air Systems Command
Naval Facilities Engineering Command
Naval Sea Systems Command, Shipyard Directorate
    (NAVSEA 07), Washington, DC
Naval Publications and Forms Center
Norfolk, VA, Public Works Center
Charleston, SC, and Norfolk, VA, Naval Shipyards

State of Oregon

> Department of Transportation, Region 4
> Oregon Progress Board

City of Phoenix, AZ

> City Auditor's Office

U.S. Postal Service

County of Riverside, CA

> Information Services Department

U.S. Social Security Administration

> Dallas Regional Office

Sweden Post

U.S. Department of Veterans Affairs

> Veterans Affairs Regional Office and Insurance
> Center, Philadelphia, PA

Executive Office of the Vice President of the United States

> National Productivity Review

County of Volusia, FL

City of Wilmington, NC

We especially wish to thank the following people for sharing their experiences with us and otherwise helping us develop this book and its predecessors: George Allen, Ernst Becker, Michael Beha, J.T. Benn III, Peggy Bianco, Ken Biddle, Theresa Brelsford, Carolyn Burstein, Dennis Cronin, Gregory Conway, Patrick Cummings, Martha Curry, Jodi Davenport, Patsy Davis, Scott Dillon, Richard Engel, James Flanagan, Kenneth Fletcher, Matt Frymire, Dale Geiger, Jim Hamilton, Richard Hankinson, Maureen Hlavacek, Charles Hooper, Janice Hopkins, Tom Kelly, Richard Kesteven, Ken Kittridge, Paul Koons, Edward Kubasiewicz, Betty Ledewitz, John A. Leitch, John Loh, Merline Lovelace, Jeffrey Manthos, Paul Michaels, John Scott McAllister, Marilyn Mozingo, Lee Pollock, RADM Thomas Porter, Ken Staten, Barbara Shatto, Wayne Simpson, David Steigman, Michele Steinhauer, James Stevens, Dan Stewart, Greg Stoddard, Leslie Sullivan, the UNITY team, Noel Wall, Clif Williams, and James Wright.

We appreciate the fine technical insights of our Coopers & Lybrand advisors Charles Brown, Jim Dillard, Dan Hayward, Lisa Miller, Bill Rossello, David Wilkerson, and Tracy Wilkerson.

Finally, this book would not have been possible without the superb work of project manager/editor Steve Clyburn, and graphic artist Kim Farcot, cartoonist Keith Braxton, production chief Mike Clover, word processors Ana Fano and Lucia Gladschtein, and the copyediting and proofreading of Grammarians, Inc.

Introduction

American government budget cuts are perhaps the greatest shell game of all time. In the "now you see it, now you don't" razzmatazz of soundbite pseudo-policy, lawmakers shift taxpayer money from department to department, from one level of government to another and back again, and into and out of duplicative programs. The result, for the past few decades, has been mounting deficits and bankrupt treasuries, despite gradual but relentless tax increases.

Program Cuts Are Only Part of the Answer

In the future, are taxpayers doomed to get less for more? Yes, if elected officials continue to attempt major cost savings just by eliminating programs. It is true that some programs should be eliminated or at least cut back drastically; they have either outlived their purpose or private companies can provide the same services for less money. But all too many programs threatened by the budget cut meat ax, such as basic science and medical research, environment, education, health care, public safety, infrastructure, and other important areas, are critical to the future of the nation and often to everyone on this planet. Even if the President and the Congress succeed in cutting or reducing funds for the programs targeted in Fiscal Year 1996 federal budget proposals, the savings—even though adding up to tens of billions of dollars—will not be enough to balance the budget or reduce the deficit within the time spans being ballyhooed about.

Saving More Through Better Management and Operations

We know how to save at least an additional $100 billion per year in federal taxes, without eliminating a single program. This is about 20 percent of the federal operations budget, or the cost of administering programs such as labor, materials, equipment, facilities, utilities, travel, and so on. For some federal, state, and local agencies, these constitute the bulk of their budgets. Imagine the opportunities that would emerge in your organization if 20 or 30 percent of the operations budget was available for increased programming, or the appreciation of citizens if you could simply return this money to the treasury for tax relief.

How can this happen? The answer is better management of the operations of government. Only recently have governments started to understand the opportunities available to reduce these costs while increasing, not reducing, the effectiveness of public services. As private business learned over the last decade, improvements in operations, often made possible by modern technology, can quickly and easily reduce operations costs by 20 percent, and by upwards of 50 percent with hard work and a few major breakthroughs. This is one reason for the downsizing of corporate America: It is now possible —indeed, imperative—to do more for less.

This is a hard notion for most civil servants to accept. After all, they have already been through many downsizings or hiring freezes, and feel the stress and strain that comes from fewer people trying to do the same amount of work the same way as before. But there is another group of government managers and employees, those who work in progressive organizations with true commitment to continuous improvement, whose jobs are better, less stressful, higher paid, and more fulfilling—and who produce more for the money than their colleagues in private industry. Here are examples that will illustrate these lucky people's happy situation.

Government Operations Can Be Better Than Those of the Private Sector

You can find world-class management in every level of government; many of the examples in this book will testify to that. For example, city employees in Phoenix, Arizona and Indianapolis, Indiana routinely outperform private companies when competing against them for municipal contracts. As we go to press, yet another such case appeared in the May 29, 1995, issue of *Business Week:* the U.S. Social Security Administration had the best rating in a Dalbar, Inc., study of telephone customer service, beating out customer-focus legends like Southwest Airlines, Nordstrom, L.L. Bean, Xerox, and Federal Express, the last two of which won the Malcolm Baldrige National Quality Award a few years ago. Such performance is great news for citizens, because most Americans do not want to see public programs put on hold. Instead, they want those programs run more effectively. The examples in this book show that government can be managed more effectively, and that it can be improved in leaps and bounds, just like the private sector.

The bad news is that examples of world-class excellence are still fairly rare in the public sector, about the same as in the private sector a few years ago, when American industry first got serious about competing in world markets. We are not talking about governments that have improved operations by 5 or 10 percent, but those whose performance equals or exceeds the quantum leaps of newly streamlined, innovative private companies. In fact, most governments are falling behind industry in their ability to manage the many changes involved in the transition into the Information Age, the new global economy, and 21st century realpolitik.

World-Class Management is the Same Everywhere

A few years ago, the CEO of a *Fortune* 50 corporation wanted know our qualifications for helping him to radically transform his company from a slow-moving dinosaur to a fast, flexible modern operation.

Our credentials included dozens of successful consulting engagements, but what won the job was our work in helping public sector
clients make the same transformation. Since then, the company has
been singled out by *Fortune, Business Week,* and dozens of other business periodicals as the prime example of corporate transformation.
The company also blasted past its competitors and saved $100 million
in operations costs in three years.

We're not telling this story to brag. Instead, our point is that world-
class management is the same in business and government. Its value
is measured the same way: better quality, faster cycle time, lower
costs, enhanced service, and, most of all, highly satisfied customers
— the results everyone wants. And top leaders go about creating
world-class organizations the same way: with an integrated approach
to which they give their full commitment.

All governments can operate better than they do now. What they
need is: (1) leadership and (2) a management approach that drives
improvement. We discuss and provide examples of both in this book.
Almost all of our examples are government, because we want you to
see that "good enough for government" can once again mean world-
class. Also, the tools and methods we discuss have been used with
equal success in government and business, so you can be assured of
their effectiveness in the public sector.

Who Should Read This Book?

This is a book for public sector executives and managers, including
elected and appointed leaders. It will be particularly valuable in the
following situations:

- Your organization has tried several new approaches, such as quality management, but has failed to realize the required results;

- You have consolidated operations with one or more organizations, and want to create a new management structure and approach;

- You are faced with increased competition from private contractors or other agencies;

- Your budget has been slashed, and you need to greatly improve operations in order to meet your mission; or

- You want to create an organization that can continuously improve operations.

We hope you enjoy reading this book as much as we enjoyed writing it. As former government workers ourselves, we get a real kick in discovering just how good some public sector organizations can become when they put their minds (and hearts) into it. The potential is there, bound up in yet-unreleased abilities of millions of public servants. The opportunities abound, because today there are so many new and better ways to work more productively. And the imperative is there, because the true mark of a nation's excellence is its government. If we as a nation are to survive and thrive in the next century, it will be because all our many and diverse governments rose to the many challenges that face them today, in order to create a better tomorrow.

David K. Carr
Ian D. Littman
John K. Condon

Coopers & Lybrand L.L.P.

How to Use this Book

We divided the book into five major sections, four of which follow the structure of the Improvement Driven Organization^{SM}, our framework for integrating all aspects of managing for continuous improvement.

Part I—Introduction to the Improvement Driven Organization

Chapters 1 and 2 introduce you to the Improvement Driven Organization, including the need for a comprehensive, integrated approach to management. Chapter 3 is a background chapter on the basic concepts of customers and processes, which are all key aspects of the Improvement Driven Organization approach.

Part II—The Leader Driven Phase

The Improvement Driven Organization approach has three phases: Leader Driven, Process Driven, and Improvement Driven. Chapters 4 and 5 discuss the leader-driven tasks of assessment, planning, and preparing for comprehensive process and organizational improvement. Chapter 6 focuses on change management at the process improvement level.

Part III—The Process Driven Phase

The Improvement Driven Organization approach uses the tools and methods from a wide variety of process improvement practices. Chapters 7 through 11 of this section are detailed discussions of how and when to select and use tools and methods such as those commonly applied by process improvement teams: reengineering, activity-based costing, cost-of-quality, simultaneous engineering, quality function deployment, statistical process control, privatization and competition, and others. Chapters 13 through 15 discuss the changes to infrastructure that must accompany major process changes, such as performance measurement systems, organizational structure, management information systems, and internal controls. Chapters 16 through 18 focus on organizational transformations that accompany process changes, such as the role of individual employees, managers, and teams; rewards and salaries; competition; and culture.

Part IV—The Improvement Driven Phase

Achieving continuous process improvement is a major goal—perhaps the most critical goal—of the modern organization. Chapter 19 discusses how continuous improvement is built into the Improvement Driven Organization's processes and how it is enhanced over time.

Part V—Developing Improvement Driven Organizations

Chapter 20 provides a road map for transforming your department, agency, or office into an Improvement Driven Organization. It includes guidance on whom to include in the initiative, the steps to take, and the issues you will need to address throughout the transformation.

Appendices

Appendix A lists a selection of readily available books, periodicals, and other materials on the many tools and methods for improvement discussed in this book. In addition, the appendix lists Internet sites, networks, groups, and organizations that can provide valuable information and assistance to government organizations interested in continuous improvement.

Several chapters of our book mention the Coopers & Lybrand Survey of Best Practices in Management, conducted in summer 1994. Appendix B shows the survey's results, and compares those of private companies to those of government organizations.

PART I

INTRODUCTION TO THE IMPROVEMENT DRIVEN ORGANIZATION

Chapter

1

THE COMPELLING NEED FOR IMPROVEMENT IN GOVERNMENT

■ Governments everywhere face crises in finances, effectiveness, and citizen trust. The situation is so bad that even being a world-class government is not enough; citizen expectations are set by performance in the private sector, not the public sector.

■ Most governments have exhausted all the alternative solutions to these crises, save one: taking a comprehensive, committed approach to management improvement.

■ Citizens overwhelmingly believe that government can be better managed in order to produce results that are more effective.

■ Only one management approach is comprehensive enough to do the job right: the Improvement Driven Organization. This approach operates on all levels of change: processes, people, organizational structure, infrastructure, and culture. It is designed to produce high performance results in missions, operations, and finance.

The system we have inherited needs a searching reexamination, and where it is yesterday's government and not tomorrow's, it ought to be changed.

— President Bill Clinton, March 27, 1995

A half-century ago, in 1945, the Allied powers emerged victorious from a harsh struggle to defeat fascism. The United States of America played an extraordinarily key role in World War II by sacrificing the blood of its people and contributing the wealth of our natural resources, industrial might, and productivity. But American participation in the twentieth century's fulcrum event was not a foregone conclusion. Inside our country, many resisted U.S. entry into that war. Others overseas doubted our will to face down the dark forces of totalitarian rule. However, as British Prime Minister Winston Churchill, whose mother was an American, said in 1940: "You can count on the Americans to do the right thing—*after* they have exhausted all other alternatives."

In 1995, government organizations have about exhausted all the alternatives for providing better, more cost-effective services to citizens. Most federal agencies follow some (usually limited) form of quality management, as do the majority of state governments and many local jurisdictions. Some government technology investments would beggar the world's largest companies, but their full benefits are seldom realized. Reengineering, the current cure-all for what ails government operations, is an increasingly hot topic in the public sector even as its failures have caused it to lose luster in private business. Narrow-minded downsizing, rightsizing, and delayering are producing the same results in government as in industry: organizations that are lean, but made up of meanly treated, overworked, and demoralized managers and employees. Privatization, the latest prescription for productivity, makes promises that it cannot possibly keep, given how lawmakers and agency chiefs approach it.

Governments persist in choosing only one or a few management alternatives, using them halfheartedly, and yet wondering at citizen skepticism and distrust of the public service. Integrated and used with commitment to gaining results, these alternatives, along with others discussed in this book, make a valuable toolbox for improving government operations. Using these tools is the right thing to do and *that* is what you will be able to do after reading this book.

An Improvement Driven Organization: the California Department of Motor Vehicles

Just to survive, every state agency in California must become an Improvement Driven Organization because the old sources of revenue growth just aren't there anymore. Natural catastrophes and economic slumps have strained the state's treasury, while anti-tax movements by citizens block the easy way out of the state's fiscal woes. Fortunately, those agencies have a mentor readily at hand: the California Department of Motor Vehicles (DMV).

The DMV serves more drivers (twenty million) who own more vehicles (twenty-five million) than any other state, and the numbers increase daily. With a comprehensive approach to improvement that combines entrepreneurship, advanced technology, and quality management, the DMV continually reduces the time it takes to serve citizens and business, while holding down costs.

A good example of this, according to the American Society for Quality Control (ASQC), is the DMV's process for registering new rental vehicles. In the old process, a rental car company handed over registration papers to the DMV, which keyed in the data, collected the fees, and issued the necessary documents, license plates, and stickers. The three to five days it used to take the DMV to handle this process often meant its customers—the rental companies—were deprived of hundreds of dollars in revenue for each new vehicle that sat idle. One company estimated its losses at well over $1.5 million per year.

To improve this process, in a pilot project the DMV and rental car companies formed a partnership and redefined the role of the customer. From their offices, the participating companies now handle registration fee payments through direct access to the DMV data base and electronic fund transfer (EFT). Registration cycle time has dropped from days to minutes, and new cars hit the road as soon as the companies attach pre-issued license plates and stickers kept in their own garages.

Benefits to the DMV (besides *very* happy customers) include the elimination of two data entry clerk positions (a savings of nearly $50,000), plus additional interest earnings from fees deposited faster with EFT. And let's not forget the increased revenues to the state from taxes on millions of dollars in new earnings by the rental companies. All these benefits will rise as more companies enter the partnership.

Although technology enabled this process improvement to occur, the more basic change was the formation of a trusting partnership between the DMV and car rental companies. Another such partnership enables automobile clubs to provide some vehicle registration services to their members, and still another allows court-appointed vehicle vendors to update court abstracts on-line.

Even more fundamental is the DMV's comprehensive approach to improvement, which starts with executive leadership and strategic planning, then deploys process improvement goals and methods throughout the department. By creating a comprehensive infrastructure to drive its pursuit of quality, the DMV assures California citizens of continuous improvement in government service.

THE IMPROVEMENT DRIVEN ORGANIZATION

We call this comprehensive approach the *Improvement Driven Organization.* Such an organization constantly makes changes in its operations, because *improvement* comes from doing the right things in ways that are different from before. Improvement *drives* an organization to make these changes because the alternative is a death-spiral of continuously diminishing relevance and effectiveness. By *organization,* we mean that everyone involved in your enterprise, from suppliers to employees to customers, must be part of improvement; otherwise you will not gain powerful, comprehensive results. Let's examine the *driven* aspect of this definition, to establish that the only alternative for satisfying customers and meeting your mission is to create an Improvement Driven Organization.

mprovement — Change in the right direction.

**riven — Compelled to improve,
because there is no other choice.**

**rganization — Your executives, managers,
employees, customers,
stakeholders, suppliers, and
partner organizations.**

Figure 1-1
The
Improvement
Driven
Organization
Defined

Why Be Driven by Improvement?

In this world, in this age, people stop buying things that do not improve. You would not buy a five-year-old personal computer because its technology is too primitive to handle today's most advanced applications; in fact, most computers are obsolete within two years. Why, then, should citizens buy, with their tax dollars, a government service that is either obsolete in the way it operates or simply no longer needed? If there is one thing you can depend on, it is that the way you provide services now is already, or will soon become, obsolete.

Even those things that we do not want to see changed, like Coca-Cola Classic or the friendly neighborhood police officer who walks a beat, have to undergo change simply to remain as they are. For example, old-fashioned Coke may have the same ingredients and taste as before, but how the soft drink gets mixed, bottled, and distributed must change in order to keep it competitive with Pepsi. The officer on the beat needs advanced training in community relations, a mini-radio instead of a call box at every corner, and sometimes even a bicycle to do his or her job as effectively and efficiently as in the old days.

In the private sector, when people no longer buy a product or service, the people responsible for that product or service lose their jobs and their companies eventually go out of business. Governments are not immune to this market-driven truism, which in its mildest form causes the demise of individual political and civil administrator careers, as citizens "spend" their votes to put another party in power. Government overthrow is the strongest form of customers/citizens taking a stand, and we can readily see the results of that in the recent collapse of the Soviet Union.

HOW COMPELLING IS THE NEED FOR GOVERNMENT IMPROVEMENT?

In an Improvement Driven Organization, you would answer that question by posing it to your customers. Although we do not want to belabor the key point made by nearly every public poll in the past decade, government's citizens/customers are pretty disgusted. A good example of government's customers' views of both the problem and the solution is found in a March 1995 survey of 1,000-plus citizens by the nonprofit Council for Excellence in Government, of which Coopers & Lybrand is a member. Conducted by Democrat Peter Hart and Republican Robert Teeter, it is a bipartisan look at what citizens want from their governments.

According to this survey, 56 percent of citizens think government programs and policies do more to hinder than to help them achieve the American dream. In fact, the survey shows that most people think that federal and state governments create more problems than they solve.

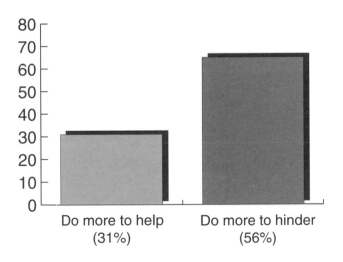

Do government policies help or hinder you in achieving the American dream?

Figure 1-2: Citizen Views of Government Performance

Figure 1-2
Continued

Percentage agreeing that government creates more problems than it solves.

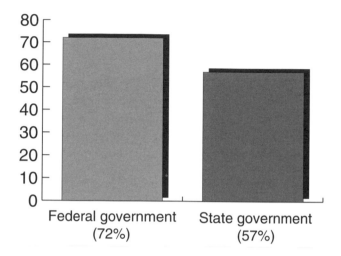

Federal government
(72%)

State government
(57%)

Percentage who say they have a great deal or quite a lot of confidence in their federal, state, or local government.

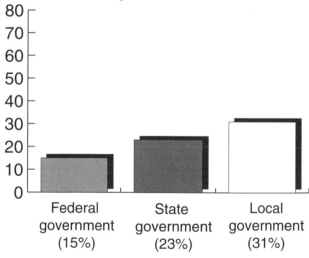

Federal government (15%)

State government (23%)

Local government (31%)

Source: The Council on Excellence in Government, Washington, D.C., April 1995

Such results are more than simply a reflection of the distrust of government that has always been an American cultural trait. They are the latest point on a downward slide in citizen confidence in government. According to Vice President Al Gore, speaking at a 1994 Harvard commencement ceremony, analysis of public opinion poll data shows that in 1965, more than 60 percent of citizens thought that government generally tries to do the right thing. By 1994, only 10 percent agreed that the statement is true. In 1975, a Gallup poll showed that 47 percent of Americans had a great deal or quite a lot of confidence in their state and local governments. The 1995 Council of Excellence survey registered only a 23 percent confidence level for state and 31 percent for local government. In the same period, confidence in the federal government fell from the mid-forties to 15 percent.

Given these dismal, long-term figures, the 1992 presidential election was not necessarily an endorsement of the Democratic Party platform, nor should the 1994 federal, state, and local victories by Republicans be labeled a sanction for that party's philosophy. More likely, those results reflect a general "throw the rascals out" mood by an electorate that is irate about plunging public service performance. Unless the trend is reversed, we suggest that newly elected officials of any party get only short-term leases for their homes in state and federal capitals.

BETTER MANAGEMENT IS THE KEY TO CITIZEN SATISFACTION

We are management consultants, not policy pundits, and so we will not debate in these pages whether government, or which level of government, or which kind of government, should or should not provide any specific type of service. However, we have come to the conclusion that the public is less concerned about *what* governments do than with *how* they do it. For example, when asked in the Council of Excellence survey about the message they would most like to send to the federal government, 49 percent of respondents said, "Be more effective through better management," versus only 9 percent who said, "Make government smaller by cutting programs." About two-thirds of those surveyed felt that the federal government spends too much money on the wrong things and that it could reduce spending considerably and still take care of essential needs if it were better managed. Nearly three out of four said that better management would make the federal government more effective.

Figure 1-3
What Citizens
Want from
the Federal
Government

Do you think the federal government could be more effective if it were better managed, or do you think it is bound to be ineffective no matter what?

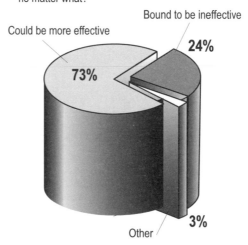

Bound to be ineffective

Could be more effective

24%

73%

Other

3%

Source: The Council on Excellence in Government, Washington, D.C., April 1995

Thus, *effectiveness,* by that or any other name (value, quality, results), is what the large majority of citizens want to buy with their tax dollars. Democrats, Independents, Libertarians, Republicans, liberals, conservatives, the far right, the far left, and those in between may all disagree on *what* government should do, but all want value, quality, and results from *how* the public service operates.

An Improvement Driven Organization: Miami's U.S. Customs Service

Although it may be true that governments have too many regulations, it is often how those rules are administered that makes the difference to citizens and businesses. Consider the U.S. Customs Service, an agency as old as the Constitution, and whose North American predecessors operated over one hundred years before that. Lately, the agency has taken a new look at its rules, especially those dealing with fresh flowers and other perishables that enter the United States through Miami, Florida.

Flowers and fruit don't last long in the South Florida heat, so it is no wonder that shippers went ballistic when customs delays caused their imports to wilt and spoil on Miami runways. Customs officials decided to dispose of their old crime-and-punishment attitude and begin treating shippers like customers. Among other changes, they began to work with the shippers to build computer systems and other facilities, and to teach them how to help with enforcement. Today, many shipments clear Miami customs before leaving their point of origin, exporters help the Customs Service identify high-risk shipments, and enforcement rates are higher than ever before.

What was the missing ingredient in the old way of doing business at Customs? Customer focus, the bedrock of a comprehensive approach to process improvement.

FEDERALISM DOES NOT MEAN EFFECTIVENESS

Much has been said lately about devolving national programs to state and local governments through block grants and other means, which is a federalist approach. Three out of four citizens support devolution, according to the Council on Excellence survey. A sizable minority would make that the main message they would like to send to Washington, D.C. (after better management, of course).

Proponents of devolution believe that, somehow, government will be more effective at the local and state levels. However, where is the evidence that simply passing federal tax dollars down to states and communities will radically improve the effectiveness of government services? We regularly consult at all three levels of government and find no indication that this is true. And, as Figure 1-2 shows, even where people are most confident in their government—the local level—nearly 70 percent are less than enthusiastic in this confidence. Also, state and local government is where the greatest growth in public employment has been occurring—the federal work force has held steady for the last decade and is beginning to shrink. Although rising numbers of employees are not necessarily a bad thing, these numbers should arch the eyebrows of citizens when they realize that state and local work force growth has exceeded general population growth, at a time when private industry is producing more and more with fewer and fewer people.

A tax dollar is a dollar, whether it goes to a federal, state, or local government. Federal law makers need to consider their fiscal stewardship responsibilities before simply dumping money on other jurisdictions—and good stewardship starts with demanding good management.

On the other hand, state and local governments should not be too thrilled about this potential federal windfall. The money is not likely to be sufficient for meeting the responsibilities that come with it, and, if past is prologue, the contents of the pipeline from Washington, D.C. eventually will slow to a trickle. The only way to prepare for the unpleasant, belt-tightening aftermath of federal largess is to become world-class managers—because that's how you will win back the confidence and respect of citizens who control long-term funding (and thus, your agency's future).

WORLD-CLASS GOVERNANCE IS NOT ENOUGH TO SAVE AMERICAN GOVERNMENT

Now for the kicker: we think American government at all levels is about as good as government gets in this world. Anyone who has had to deal with foreign bureaucrats knows that customer service is an alien concept to them. Most foreign government taxes exceed those of the United States, as does the cost of postage stamps and other basic public services. Unfortunately, being the best of a bad lot is not a great endorsement. "Good enough for government" used to be an honorific given to products that met the ultra-high standards of the American military services; today, it has a completely different meaning.

One reason is that, except in a few areas, government performance has fallen far behind that of private companies. It may not be fair, but like it or not, citizens make these comparisons and ask of government, "If they can do it, why can't you?" Thus, it is foolish for government managers to applaud many of their improvements, or say "We're the best public service around," when they have been far surpassed by private organizations.

Evidence of the root cause of this disparity between public and private sector performance can be found in a survey we conducted of three hundred organizations in 1994. To qualify for the study, all participating organizations had to have active quality management initiatives. Our purpose was to identify the management practices that were most closely associated with gaining positive results in improvement, innovation, and customer satisfaction. These included promoting a customer focus in all operations, strategic planning, measuring process performance, involving employees, teamwork, and change management (see Appendix B for a more detailed description of the study).

Most of our sample consisted of private companies recognized as being the best in their industry in terms of productivity, profit, and innovation. The government organizations had each received high awards for their quality management initiatives and the resulting successes they had had in customer service and cost savings.

With only one exception (training), the government organizations reported that they were less likely than the private companies to carry out the best management practices described in the survey. The public agencies used less teamwork, their people were less likely to understand the reasons for major changes, leaders showed less support for improvement projects—the list goes on through over fifty different practices. Not surprisingly, the private companies were more likely to report positive results than the government organizations.

For those who would argue that the private companies had the advantage of a profit motive, we point out that none of the management practices had anything to do with profits. Teamwork is teamwork, whether aimed at making money or making babies healthier, and strategic planning works as well for meeting public needs as it does for gaining market share.

So, along with base-line continuous improvement, governments need the quantum leaps that have propelled many American industries back into leadership positions in the global marketplace. Otherwise, government will stay back-of-the-pack and eventually become little more than a contract manager for a privatized public service. Effective management is the way for any organization to become world-class in every class of industry.

An Improvement Driven Organization: the City of Phoenix, Arizona

Like every municipality, the city of Phoenix, Arizona charges fees for permits, inspections, and licenses. The customers for these services range from real estate developers to dog owners. In 1980, however, cost analysis showed that the fees the city collected were only about 40 percent of the cost of issuing them and providing related services. "In effect, taxpayers were subsidizing the people who received these services," said the Phoenix city auditor.

Before 1980, appropriations supported the city offices that provided user fee services. "With appropriations, you are better set up to absorb things like higher overhead costs, so you don't think too much about them," said the city auditor. "There's not as strong a motivation to look for cost savings, because you do not need them to survive."

Shocked by the information of the cost analysis, the Phoenix City Council issued a new policy of full cost recovery for user fees. Going further, the council decided that the offices that provided user fee services had to be supported by the fees, not by appropriations.

Managers had two ways to go: fee adjustments and process improvement. For many, charging higher fees was not an option, because of pressure from user groups. To reduce costs through improvements, these managers were able to use process information developed along with cost analysis.

One example of improvement was in the process for planning plats for new real estate developments. Analysis of the process found that the city's aviation department (which runs the Phoenix airport) was always included, although it seldom really needed to be. By making this step optional, the city saved money, and plans were approved faster for service users.

As a result of improvements and fee adjustments, Phoenix now recovers almost all of the costs of its user fee services. "Another result is that the managers are much more sensitive about costs," said the city auditor. "For example, now that they're fee-supported, they cannot easily absorb increased overhead costs. They go over their overhead cost rates very carefully, and question them. They'll say to a city support or administrative department, 'Do you really have to do that?' That's a key question in the improvement process, one that the user fee offices are continually asked by their customers. It changes the way you think about your business."

How Will You Succeed?

All organizations across the country—not just those in the public sector—are undergoing fundamental change, for several reasons:

- Their capacity to process information and to make decisions has been greatly enhanced by technology;

- They have come "out of the box" of functional or departmental thinking and instead look at how work gets done as a cross-functional process; and

- Because their environment has become extremely dynamic, they must continually form and reform teams from different parts of their operations to address emerging problems and opportunities.

The result is a distinct movement away from the old command-and-control organizational hierarchy to a flatter, more flexible structure. This arrangement is guided not by strict rules and several layers of management, but instead by goals, objectives, and organizational culture.

Like it or not, this is one of two alternative futures for your organization. The other is not to survive as an independent operation, because your mission will be handed over to an organization that fits the description just given.

So how do you get there? First, understand that making the transition will not be easy. Three challenges face the government organization that wants to follow this path to improvement.

- **Leadership.** Progress in improvement will not happen until the top leaders in government get serious about leading management reforms. Although leadership and management are different things (the former is about getting people to do the right thing, and the latter is about doing things right), they have to come together to create progress. Unfortunately, most government leaders *still* do not understand their role in management reform; perhaps we should give them signs that say, *It's the Management, Stupid.* You will have to educate them —but most are fast learners.

- **Untangling multiple improvement initiatives.** Most governments of any size already have had several recent improvement and reform campaigns. Although individual initiatives may have been technically sound and even well supported, they have not been coordinated, and often have lacked the direction that could be provided by an integrated, strategic management and operations improvement approach (some leadership would help, too). One of your challenges will be to sort out these initiatives into a comprehensive framework.

- **Internal and external competition.** Within many governments, agencies and offices will be vying for a shrinking pool of discretionary funds, both for improvement and even for basic services. At the same time, they will be pressured to outsource internal functions to contractors and other agencies. In short, securing funds to invest in improvements is going to be increasingly difficult—so you had better be ready to guarantee major savings from your improvement proposals, as well as better service to citizens.

Given these very real constraints, what is the magic formula for success? Well, there is none. You have to work out your own formula, after reading this book and many others, visiting world-class organizations, and studying your own organization very, very hard.

About the most valuable thing we can offer you is the Improvement Driven Organization's principles and framework, which, though not magic, show you the elements of success and how to mix them. This framework will show you how to obtain success in three key areas:

- **Mission performance.** Results, measured in terms that are meaningful to customers, taxpayers, and law makers.

- **Operating performance.** The quality, efficiency, productivity, and effectiveness of processes, or how work gets done.

- **Financial performance.** The return on investment of taxpayer dollars and the effective use of scarce resources.

Because the three areas are intertwined and interdependent, the results of applying narrow solutions have at best been suboptimal and at worst cause major operations problems.

IMPROVEMENT DRIVEN PRINCIPLES

Improvement Driven Organizations adhere to the following five principles:

Listening

Improvement Driven Organizations have an external orientation, both for improvement direction and specific ideas for individual improvements. These organizations consider that listening to customers, employees, and others in their enterprise is perhaps the most important thing that they do. It is why they regularly survey customers, employees, and suppliers; why they benchmark their performance against best-in-class practices in other organizations; and why they are learning organizations, committed to continued expansion of corporate and individual knowledge and understanding.

Involving

An organization that truly listens to its managers and employees will quickly want to involve them in seeking solutions to problems and taking advantage of opportunities. Improvement Driven Organizations constantly seek ways to increase employee and supplier involvement in improvement through teams, individual suggestions, and special campaigns to gain the benefit of that most valuable resource: people power.

Focusing on Process

Improvement Driven Organizations focus improvements on core business processes. Core business processes are those that directly produce the services that customers want and value. Such an organization aligns its administrative and support processes with these core processes, not the other way around, as so often occurs in "stovepipe" organizations structured around narrowly defined departments and functions. This core process focus is key to an Improvement

Driven Organization's flexibility, because it removes teams from the artificial constraints of department and functional boundaries.

Promoting Evolutionary *and* Revolutionary Change

Dismissing the argument that one type of change is better than the other, an Improvement Driven Organization uses both gradual and radical improvement to achieve its goals, depending on the circumstances. However, such an organization *always* builds into its processes the capability for process operators to make evolutionary improvements, because without these smaller gains, the positive results of revolutionary change will soon be lost.

Managing All Aspects of Change

An Improvement Driven Organization's leaders understand that change in any one of five factors—-technology, people, organization, culture, and, in government, politics—-can lead to change in the other four. Thus, through active and aggressive change management, these leaders ensure comprehensive improvements that last.

How, then, do you manage all aspects of change? The IDO framework offers a solution.

THE IDO FRAMEWORK

Figure 1-4 presents the IDO framework, a structure you will see repeated many times throughout this book. The framework has two applications. First, you can use it when planning and executing a major process improvement that requires more change and coordination than can be handled by simpler frameworks such as the Shewhart/Deming Plan-Do-Check-Act cycle (PDCA, see Chapter 9). Second, you can apply the framework to completely transform your entire organization so that it is improvement driven in all of its parts.

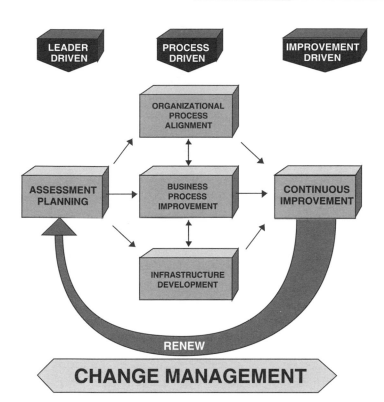

Figure 1-4
The
Improvement
Driven
Organization
Framework

As a structural guide to improvement, the framework will show you what areas to consider during the various phases of improvement. We call these phases Leader Driven, Process Driven, and Improvement Driven.

Leader Driven

This is an assessment and planning phase. Using tools and methods we discuss in Chapters 4 and 5 of this book, an organization's leaders get actively involved in doing the following:

• Taking a baseline look at customer satisfaction and determining the gap between what customers expect and what they actually get from a process;

- Forecasting trends that may affect a process, such as in customer demographics, politics, economics, and other factors that influence their business environment;

- Surveying employees to determine their readiness for change and their organization's culture and climate; and

- Benchmarking the performance and methods of internal processes against those of other organizations in order to identify performance gaps and possible improvements.

Armed with this information, leaders prepare strategic plans that will guide improvement. A process or an entire organization is then ready for a solid, results-producing launch of process change and performance improvement.

Process Driven

This phase deploys the plans made by leaders. By operating on three levels—process, organization, and infrastructure—-Improvement Driven Organizations develop solutions that produce results, will last, and will continue to improve over time.

Business process improvement tasks include:

- Forming teams of managers, employees, suppliers, stakeholders, and customers to enhance and sometimes completely redesign processes, products, and services;

- Using different methods, such as PDCA, and reengineering, to carry out improvement projects;

- Training managers and employees in new ways of managing and working;

- Adding new capabilities to an infrastructure, such as better management information systems, internal controls, and communications systems; and

- Building continuous improvement capabilities into processes.

Organizational process alignment tasks focus on the human issues of change and seek to ensure ongoing effectiveness by generating:

- **High involvement.** All executives and managers, and many employees, directly participate in assessing and planning for change, which ensures that their good ideas are heard and that they feel part of the improvement process. Managers and employees belong to the teams that create change, ensuring their ownership of the results.

- **High motivation.** People in Improvement Driven Organizations *want* to improve, because there are no barriers that get in their way, and they are rewarded for making things better.

- **High innovation.** People are trained, given resources for, and encouraged to make creative improvements.

- **High alignment.** Leaders understand the need to change the culture of their organizations in order to support new ways of thinking, acting, and working.

Organizational process alignment follows a conscious, deliberate plan that has been prepared by leaders and is constantly monitored by them. This planned change management is a major part of the work of executives in an Improvement Driven Organization.

Infrastructure development. An organization's processes are supported by a multi-faceted *infrastructure,* which includes the following elements:

- The organization's structure, which can be hierarchical or flat, open or compartmentalized, top heavy or bottom heavy;

- Support systems, such as physical facilities, and written policies and procedures;

- Financial management and internal control procedures and systems;

- Information systems, including MIS, customer data bases, and feedback systems that provide people with information on the performance of their processes; and

- Human resources, including HR planning, personnel, rewards, and training.

Improvement Driven Organizations understand that they must adjust these elements every time they make a moderate to major change in their processes. Otherwise, their infrastructure will become a barrier to progress, not an enabler for success.

Improvement Driven

Each time an Improvement Driven Organization changes a process, it builds in certain features that promote continuous improvement. These include the following:

- Systems for measuring process performance, for gathering internal and external customer information, for determining the quality of external suppliers, and so on;

- Operations plans that include time and resources for investing in ongoing improvements; and

- Appropriate training and retraining for people whose improvement efforts work them right out their jobs.

On a larger scale, the IDO framework curves back on itself, so that each major process that was improved once is again *renewed* with assessment, planning, and more improvement. This is the true cyclical nature of continuous improvement: everything can and should be done better.

Change Management

Change management underlies every phase of the IDO framework. Leaders prepare plans for change management during the Leader Driven phase, while managers fine tune and apply those plans during the Process Driven phase. Because the Improvement Driven phase is characterized by hundreds, even thousands, of small changes, managers spend much of their time determining how to align operations to ever better work processes.

Summary

So what is the formula for becoming a world-class government? It all starts with making the commitment to become an Improvement Driven Organization. This commitment leads to continual improvement in mission performance, finances, and operations—the measures of organizational effectiveness.

Hard work? Sure is, but with excellent leadership your people will enjoy doing it—and customers will appreciate and reward you for the results. And it is a job that must be done, because the success of a nation rests with the effectiveness of its governments.

Chapter
2

SYNERGIZING THE NEW MANAGEMENT APPROACHES

■ Traditional management poses barriers that must be overcome to create the Improvement Driven Organization.

■ These barriers have been surmounted by the most basic of government services, which poses a challenge for those government services that view themselves as more sophisticated.

■ Improvement Driven Organizations adopt and adapt new management approaches to create a synergistic management style. These include:

- Quality management
- Cycle-time reduction or time-based management
- Business process redesign/reengineering and information technology
- Activity-based costing
- Privatization and competition
- Change management

However, the above list is not exhaustive. Improvement Driven Organizations have a framework for adopting other management approaches that meet their unique needs.

An Improvement Driven Organization doesn't just happen. It has two challenges. The first is to overcome past management practices and organizational culture to introduce new practices and culture. The second is to understand, integrate, customize, and synergize the many proven approaches to improvement that are now available. We will look at both in this chapter and, in the process, issue a challenge of our own.

TRADITIONAL MANAGEMENT

For the past decade, organizations both public and private have been pushing decision-making authority down to front-line operations. Also, having come to see the problems inherent in managing through boxes in an organizational chart, many organizations now follow the concept of the cross-functional operation that traverses the boundaries of departments and functions. New technology enables decentralized decision making, which is faster, more flexible, and more responsive to customers. The message is clear: in a world that is changing, management approaches too must change.

Yet, initial attempts to introduce new management practices always collide with powerful barriers to change. It would be easy to blame these barriers on individuals who want to maintain their place in the status quo (the human nature argument).

Instead, the barriers are structural and cultural and have strong historical roots. Let's take a look at "Taylorism," one of those roots.

High-Priced Man and the Railroad Organizational Model

Efficiency expert Dr. Frederick Taylor's time-and-motion studies in the late nineteenth and early twentieth centuries are the foundations of so-called scientific management, which is the study and measurement of how work is done in order to make it more efficient. The regional commissioner for the Social Security Administration in Dallas illustrated the impact of this approach on organizations with a story about coal shovelers.

"In 1897, managers at a Baltimore coal yard asked Taylor to help them become more efficient," the commissioner said. "He observed and measured the work of the 500 shovelers, learning that the ideal weight of each shovel load was twenty-one and one-half pounds and that the workers needed different shovels for different types of coal. He also charted the most efficient movement of coal in the yard. The yard cut back to 140 shovelers, who could each shovel fifty-nine tons of coal versus sixteen tons. This reduced the cost of moving a ton of coal from seven cents to three cents. To do this, the coal yard needed a special staff for shovel inventory, planning, and management information. Before, this was the job of workers and foremen."

With results like these, cadres of planners, analysts, and efficiency experts schooled in Taylorism grew up in most large industrial organizations. Many aspects of Taylorism also were applied, by design or osmosis, in white collar and clerical administrative and support functions and eventually in service companies and government organizations.

A few years before Dr. Taylor began his studies, American railroad companies created a multi-tiered management reporting system for corporate communications. In this system, local managers collected, summarized, and telegraphed information on the locations of engines and cars to another set of managers, who in turn summarized and sent the data up the hierarchy to corporate decision makers. The decision makers developed plans and orders for relocating the moving equipment and sent it back down the hierarchy for implementation. This was an excellent system for dealing with complex issues of a national and regional scope at a time when communication was slow.

Most complex national organizations adopted Taylorism and the railroad organizational structure for sound reasons: they reduced costs and improved control and communications. Simple, local organizations did so because everyone thought this was the best way. Throughout the nation, and eventually the industrialized world, the job of line supervisors became making sure that workers followed the dictates of specialists and higher-level management. Someone needed to ensure that the supervisors were doing their jobs and to coordinate all the specialists with the line departments. Several layers of middle managers emerged to handle these functions as well as the job of passing information up and down what was fast becoming a top-heavy hierarchy. Management centralized authority at higher and higher levels and in increasingly specialized departments. This is how most large organizations manage today.

What is the good side of this management approach? Taylor's finest legacy to modern organizations is the idea that work should be studied systematically and objectively to improve how it is carried out. Nearly all the tools and techniques you will read about in this book are grounded in this concept, and several were actually used, if not developed, by Taylor himself. The centralized model of organization developed by the railroads made it possible for many organizations to expand their operations throughout the country, yet still maintain control of them.

For individual workers, there was a dark side to Taylorism. What were employees supposed to do in this new management system? In his *Principles of Scientific Management*, Taylor said, "A high-priced man does just what he's told and no back talk.... When [your supervisor] tells you to walk, you walk; when he tells you to sit down, you sit down...." This "high-priced man" was motivated only by money and did not need any other incentives to do his job, such as the intellectual challenge of managing and of doing the job better than before.

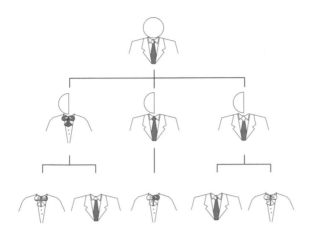

Figure 2-1
Traditional
Management
"Command-
and-Control"
Hierarchy

Traditional organizations assume the smarts are always at the top and that employees leave their brains at home when they come to work.

Today, the railroad organizational model inhibits instead of enhances communication. Modern information technology allows data to be captured at their source and to be instantaneously analyzed and communicated throughout an organization. Likewise, orders from on high can be quickly transmitted to everyone who needs to know them. This drastically cuts back on the need for managers to send and receive reports up and down the hierarchy. Organizations that rely on the nineteenth-century management reporting system actually slow down and often garble key messages to and from front-line workers. Besides being expensive, this outdated method can be dangerous for an organization's health and survival.

A New Way to Run Government's Business

We have a modern, relevant contrast to that dismal, soul-dulling coal yard: self-directed highway maintenance teams in Oregon. In the central part of the state, two hundred employees of the Oregon Department of Transportation (ODOT) go to work on the roads every day without a supervisor. Trained and working in teams, employees learn how to use decision-making tools and guidelines that empower them to run their operations based on ODOT's mission, values, and goals. On a regional road maintenance budget of $19 million, ODOT estimates that its team system has:

- Reduced the region's one-manager-to-seven-employees ratio to 1 to 27, for gross savings of $1.2 million in supervisory costs;

- Cut overtime by 58 percent, saving $135,000 a year; and

- Enabled employees to reduce annual equipment repair costs by $60,000 and develop improved road surfacing procedures that cut unit costs by 25 percent.

Dollar savings were not the only gains. Crews meet with local officials and hold town hall gatherings for citizens to discuss road maintenance issues. Employees are quick to follow up personally on customer complaints because they feel responsible for customer satisfaction. Sick leave and absenteeism is down, and three out of four workers say that the system has improved the quality of their work lives.

Up-ending the organizational chart

Taylor would have appreciated this part of our story. Late in his life he came to regret that many organizations built top-heavy, complex bureaucracies based on his approach to management. At the district level, ODOT's self-directed team approach turned the traditional organizational chart upside down (as seen in Figure 2-2), in recognition of the fact that there are brains at work where the rubber meets the road: on the front line, in direct contact with customers, every day. According to one crew member, "Our maintenance team can out-think and out-perform our previous supervisor, and he was one of the best supervisors a crew could have."

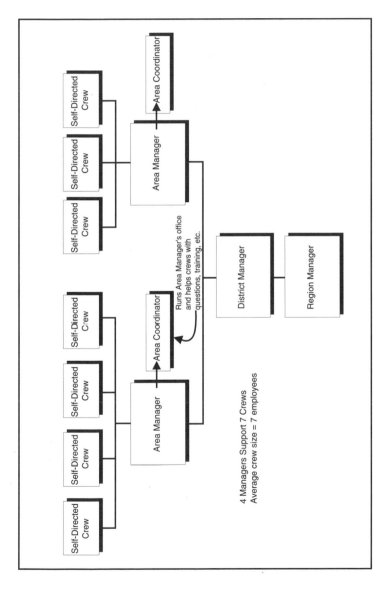

Figure 2-2
District Level
of the Region
4 Highway
Maintenance
Organization,
Oregon
Department of
Transportation

This new organization operates more smoothly with three management layers instead of the previous five because information moves more quickly up and down the hierarchy. Old "turf" problems are all but gone because the crews freely share information, knowledge, and resources. No longer having to worry about supervising the supervisors, managers can focus on higher-level decisions tied to the ODOT mission. Where once employees viewed managers as adversaries, they now see that managers knock down barriers so that everyone can work better.

If They Can, Why Can't You?

With all respect to the road crews and managers of ODOT, we ask, "If they can do it, why can't you?" The crews are not made up of civil engineers with MBAs, yet they manage and improve the way that millions of dollars are spent maintaining public roads. In attempting to make the change to self-directed crews, leaders of ODOT challenged seventy-five years of old-style management tradition and a highly bureaucratic, hierarchical, and union environment. Yet they prevailed and were vindicated.

If ODOT were a private company, one could understand how profits might motivate this change. Yet ODOT is a government agency of the most basic kind. It is subject to myriad rules and regulations, powerful political pressure, and the closest possible scrutiny by the media, interest groups, and a public that daily inspects the results of its work, because the public drives on the roads it builds and maintains.

If the crew's improvements and ability to manage had been due to major investments in new technology, then resource-poor organizations could claim that they cannot afford the price. Yet not a penny was spent on new technology to achieve the gains we listed. All the credit goes to management—new, modern, leading-edge management thinking, backed by strong leadership.

For the rest of this chapter, you will get a quick overview of this thinking, as we briefly describe several management approaches that help achieve comparable results. Later in the book, we will discuss most of the approaches in detail and offer you criteria for selecting the best parts of each for your purposes. Why this degree of freedom in a type of management book that usually is prescriptive? Because every organization is unique, and you must choose the best path for your own. There is a path for you. If Oregon can, why can't you?

OVERVIEW OF LEADING-EDGE MANAGEMENT

Most federal, state, and local government organizations have or are attempting to introduce new management methods and approaches. The most frequent of these are quality management (QM) or total quality management (TQM), and cycle-time reduction or time-based management (TBM). Recently, business process redesign or reengineering (BPR), which is used to radically change processes, has been added to the list. Also included are benchmarking and activity-based costing (ABC).

Applied correctly, each of these methods and approaches is a powerful driver of improvement. Unfortunately, most organizations do not apply them correctly, which leads to major problems and a feeling that "these things just don't work!" Through this review and later in the book, we will show how to avoid this outcome.

Quality Management

QM is a set of principles, tools, and procedures that guide the practical affairs of running an organization. QM has become the leading new management approach in government. In 1992, about 68 percent of federal organizations had quality initiatives.[1] Many state and local governments

---

1. U.S. Government Accounting Office, *Quality Management: Survey of Federal Organizations*, GAO/GED-93-9B2 (Washington, DC, October 1992).

(including Arkansas, under the leadership of then-Governor Clinton) have done the same.

We define QM as:

> Involving everyone in an organization in controlling and continuously improving how work is done, to meet customers' expectations of quality.

Quality means everything of value to a public service organization and its customers. This includes the physical quality of the products and services, productivity, efficiency, ethics, morale, safety, and use of resources.

Figure 2-3 shows QM's distinguishing characteristics. Practitioners of all the other management approaches discussed in this chapter draw their customer focus emphasis from QM and use many QM tools and procedures.

Ensuring quality

Traditional management tolerates errors and waste if these do not exceed set standards and specifications. *Quality control*, or inspecting things after they are made, is the chief means of ensuring that products and services meet the old quality standards. Cadres of quality control inspectors wait at the end of production lines to examine products for defects. In white collar organizations, managers and many employees spend most of their time checking and correcting documents prepared by others.

TRADITIONAL MANAGEMENT	QUALITY MANAGEMENT
Needs of users of products and services defined by specialists	Customer focus, where users of products and services define what they want
Errors and waste tolerated if they do not exceed set standards	No tolerance for errors, waste, and work that does not add value to products and services
Products and services inspected for problems, then "fixed"	Prevention of problems
Many decisions governed by assumptions and gut feelings	Fact-based decisions using hard data and scientific procedures
Short-term planning based around budget cycle	Long-term planning based on improving mission performance
Product or service designed sequentially by isolated departments	Simultaneous design of total product or service life cycle by teams from many functions
Control and improvement by individual managers and specialists	Teamwork among managers, specialists, employees, vendors, customers, and partner agencies
Improvement focused on one-time breakthroughs, such as computers and automation	Continuous improvement of every aspect of how work is done
Vertical structure and centralization based on control	Horizontal and decentralized structure based on maximizing value added to products and services
Short-term contracts awarded based on price	Vendor partnership of long-term buyer/seller obligations, based on quality and continuous improvement

Figure 2-3
Traditional
Versus
Quality
Management

More conscientious traditional organizations also use *quality assurance* to help guarantee quality. Quality assurance is a system of audits and other procedures, usually done by specialists, to make sure products and services are made as planned. The key flaw to this approach? The way things are planned may not be the best way. The plans allow for errors, so you still need quality control.

Anticipating errors, traditional organizations devote substantial time and money to "planned rework." These resources are formal parts of cost estimates and budgets, or simply informal "fudge factors."

QM focuses on improving the processes that make products and services to the point that they are defect-free and yield no scrap or waste. This approach eliminates the need to inspect for defects afterward, except in critical products and services such as nuclear fuel or aircraft maintenance. Advanced QM organizations have either put most of their quality control or quality assurance personnel back into line departments or retrained them to help workers and vendors use QM methods.

Focus on systems improvement

Perhaps the key difference between traditional management and QM is how individual performance is viewed. Traditional management focuses on the behavior of individuals, measures their performance through periodic appraisals, and rewards or punishes individual results. Management by objectives (MBO) and employee performance standards are natural outgrowths of this approach.

QM says that 85 percent of the problems in an organization arise from systems, or the way in which management sets up work to be done. Only 15 percent of problems arise from mistakes by employees. This is the "85/15" maxim. Some government organizations take this perspective a step further. Israel's government-run military industries audited 900,000 worker decisions over twenty-seven months and found that only two hundred five were wrong decisions. In other words, workers were right *99.9998 percent of the time.*

Does this mean that the *results* of worker decisions are nearly always right? No, because such decisions are based on instructions that may be wrong. Nor does it mean that all workers are always on time, never abuse sick leave, or are never lazy or irresponsible. It simply means that if well-planned systems do what they are supposed to, most problems will be prevented.

Another way of looking at the 85/15 maxim, according to a general in charge of Air Force logistics, is that "85 percent of your gains are within the realm of the manager [who is responsible for systems]. The implication is that you can get 85 percent of the gain by managing harder. But the real answer is managing differently. Managing harder tends to add bureaucracy and reports. This impedes progress rather than improving it."

Continuous improvement

QM places the most value on the small but regular gains made by daily attention to enhancing how work is done, or *continuous improvement.* This type of improvement is within the grasp of the individual employee or teams of workers. Taken together, these small gains often exceed the level of improvement brought about by some technical innovations. An organization can buy new technology but not continuous improvement, which comes from training and enabling all its people to explore innovations.

The value of continuous improvement has been recognized in several federal executive orders dating back to the administration of President Ronald Reagan and is a prominent feature of the National Performance Review. In 1993, governors from twenty-one states submitted to the National Governors' Association *An Action Agenda to Redesign State Government*, which states that success in reform depends on "a process of change that embodies a culture of continuous improvement." Part of the new management philosophy of hundreds of local governments, from Wilmington, North Carolina to Austin, Texas to Portland, Oregon, continuous improvement is a fundamental and widely accepted goal of government.

A brief history of quality

QM has its roots in the early work of Taylor and Dr. Walter Shewhart. Taylor, as we said earlier, established the value of objective and systematic study of work. Shewhart, a scientist at Bell Laboratories in the 1920s, developed two innovations that helped do this for the manufacture of telephone equipment. One was *statistical process control* (SPC), a mathematical approach to measuring variance in production systems. QM uses SPC to help monitor consistency and diagnose problems in a work process. Shewhart also created the Plan-Do-Check-Act (PDCA) cycle, which applies the scientific method to improve how work is done.

During World War II, quality control and SPC were such critical elements in the war effort that they were classified as military secrets. The War Department hired Shewhart's student, Dr. W. Edwards Deming, a mathematical physicist and U.S. Department of Agriculture and Census Bureau researcher, to teach SPC to the defense industry. Yet, during the postwar period, almost all U.S. companies stopped using this powerful approach to quality control and improvement.

After the war, U.S. occupation forces in Japan faced the problem of a devastated nation. How could this resource-poor island country "boot strap" itself back to self-sufficiency and thus avoid being a burden to its conqueror or a victim of communist expansion? The only answer was to sell Japanese goods on the world market; at the time, however, "Made in Japan" was a synonym for cheap, shoddy products.

As early as 1946, armed American military police rounded up Japanese industrialists and forced them to attend lectures on SPC and quality control (and you thought *your* agency strong-armed people into training on improvement methods!). Deming was invited to Japan, where he lectured on SPC, PDCA, and other quality improvement ideas. Other American experts, such as Joseph M. Juran and Dr. Armand V. Feigenbaum helped Japanese companies expand these methods from factory lines to all their departments and functions.

Juran also taught that quality should be defined as "fit for customer use." This changed the idea of quality from simply "products that met technical specifications" to how the entire product life cycle met customer expectations. Japanese companies expanded Juran's customer concept to include internal customers, that is, those people within an organization who depend on the output of other workers. Dr. Kaoru Ishikawa extended the responsibility for quality improvement to include all employees, not just department managers.

About this time the Japanese began to study the work of American behavioral scientists, such as Dr. Abraham H. Maslow (the hierarchy of needs) and Dr. Douglas N. McGregor (Theory Y). Basing his work partly on Theory Y, Ishikawa helped to create quality circles. These were small teams of managers, workers, and supervisors trained in SPC, PDCA, and group problem solving; they are the original model for all QM teams. If first-line supervisors and employees can improve how work is done, they must know enough to control it. Companies using quality practices began to give more authority to employee teams to plan and carry out their daily work.

If SPC and PDCA drive improvement, and teams at every level of an organization use them daily, then the result is continuous improvement, which the Japanese call *kaizen.* Some have said that kaizen is based on unique Japanese cultural characteristics that compel a never-ending striving toward perfection. However, closer study shows that the compelling reason was desperation: to enter world market competition, Japan had to depend on many small improvements because after the war it could not afford huge investments in new technology and factories. Today, Japan invests heavily in technology to maintain competitive advantage, but kaizen has become such a habit that it continues to be a major management goal. It *is* part of Japanese work culture now, but by plan, not chance. Executives and managers who think American culture is not receptive to continuous improvement should tour Japanese factories in the United States, as well as such organizations as Motorola, Federal Express, and the ODOT.

To guide people in making continuous improvements, almost all major Japanese companies developed top-down/bottom-up systems called *quality policy deployment* or *hoshin* planning. In it, executives develop a five-year plan that includes two or three goals labeled "critical." Managers develop one-year plans that show the actions they will take to help meet the goals. Supervisors and employees are educated in the executive and manager plans and directed to focus most of their improvement actions on achieving them. Plan achievement progress is reviewed monthly at all levels. In this way, everyone from top to bottom marches to the same drummer.

Other Japanese enhancements to the quality movement included Dr. Genichi Taguchi's application of experimental design techniques to product design and production. The

Japanese also added better and faster methods of product planning, including the quality function deployment technique. Finally, they redefined their relationships with their suppliers into what QM calls "vendor partnerships."

By the 1970s, most large Japanese companies had adopted most of these practices in one form or another. The effect this management style had on Japanese products is obvious: "Made in Japan" now stands for world-class quality.

The quality and low cost of these goods sent American manufacturers scrambling to find the secrets of Japan's success. In 1980, a television program entitled "If Japan Can, Why Can't We?" spotlighted Deming as a key reason. But U.S. companies were puzzled by his message. John A. Betti, former Undersecretary of Defense (acquisitions), was an executive at Ford Motor Company then. He recalled: "I distinctly remember some of Dr. Deming's first visits to Ford. We wanted to talk to him about quality, improvement tools, and what programs would work. He wanted to talk to us about management, culture change, and senior management's vision for the company. It took time for us to understand the profound cultural transformation he was proposing."

What Deming was talking about went beyond the principles and techniques of quality management. In fact, shortly before his death, we attended one of his lectures, where he read a note passed to him that asked, "What do you think of TQM?" His typically brusque and gruff reply, as he tore up the note, was, "I don't know what that is." Deming was interested in profound knowledge: understanding the fundamental nature and causes of how things work in organizations. His search for improvement did not stop with QM, nor does ours.

Cycle-Reduction or Time-Based Management

Time-based management (TBM) is one of several names for an improvement approach that focuses on reducing cycle time by eliminating waste. Cycle time is the amount of time it takes a unit of output to travel through a process from start to finish. TBM has its roots in QM and also in the Just-In-Time (JIT) production management approach, which aims at supplying each process in a production stream with no more than the exact quantity of what is needed to produce immediate needs.

TBM focuses on eliminating *waste,* which is defined as:

> Anything other than the minimum amount of equipment, materials, parts, space, and worker's time that is absolutely essential to add value to the product.

TBM methods include work simplification and the reduction of non-value added steps in processes. In TBM, a task or process adds value to a product or service if it meets the following conditions: the customer recognizes the value, it changes the product being made, and it is done right the first time.

TBM is favored by organizations to which speed in production is important. However, the TBM approach to decreasing cycle time always reduces costs because there is less waste in the system. Quality also improves, because to eliminate waste you must improve outputs so that they no longer need quality control inspection—which means the products are made right the first time.

Several government organizations use TBM methods of looking at time information. As one U.S. Internal Revenue Service manager said, "Cycle time is one of our most important indicators of whether we are satisfying our customers. Taxpayers don't want to be put on hold on the phone for several minutes to get an answer to a tax question, and they want their refunds promptly."

Business Process Redesign/Reengineering and Information Technology

While kaizen aims at making small increments in improvement, BPR focuses on achieving quantum leaps in speed, cost effectiveness, quality, and customer service performance. The difference, according to the CEO of Alcoa, lies with your situation: "Continuous improvement is exactly the right idea if you are the world leader in everything you do. It is a terrible idea if you are lagging in the world leadership benchmark. It is probably a disastrous idea if you are far behind the world standard. In too many cases, we fall in the second and third categories. In those cases, we need rapid, quantum-leap improvement."

Many of these gains are made possible by new technology, especially in the field of information systems. For example, the IRS has redesigned its process of filing 1040EZ forms from a paper operation to one in which taxpayers use touchtone telephones to enter information directly into IRS computers. Riverside County, California used reengineering methods to enable county law enforcement agencies to have instant access to information on stolen cars, suspects, and other information by integrating dozens of older systems using wide-area network (WAN) technology, FM transmission, and personal computers installed in offices and police vehicles.

As the words *redesign* and *reengineer* imply, BPR's approach is to virtually eliminate all parts of old, outmoded, or dysfunctional processes and replace them with newer technology and methods. Newer often means fewer, both of work steps in the new process and of people who work in the process.

BPR arose due to a lack of integration in information technology, process engineering, and the management of organizational change. In automating existing processes, information technologists and systems engineers did not consider that they were simply "paving the cow paths" of meandering, redundant, and inefficient processes. On the other hand, the capabilities of information technology were not being exploited, because operations managers and process engineers did not understand them. Neither group fully grasped the effect of major change on people inside and outside the organization.

Figure 2-4
BPR
Integrates
Three
Aspects of
Radical
Change

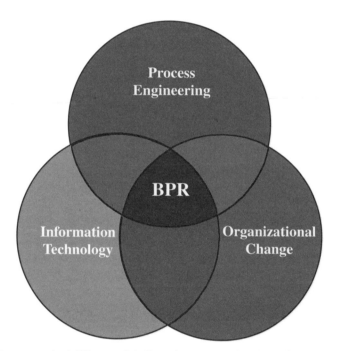

As a result, billions of dollars in new technology investments were wasted when the investments did not return comparable benefits in higher performance. At the same time, many private companies suffered severe losses in profits and market share to competitors who had pulled ahead of them through kaizen-type improvements and better use of technology. Caught behind the eight ball, these companies were forced to look for quantum leaps in performance. BPR provided the methodologies for these leaps.

Ideally, BPR begins with strategic decisions about where to invest in major process improvements. These decisions are based on extensive research about customer expectations, competitors, technology capabilities, and future environment. Usually, the focus of improvement is a cross-functional process, so that reengineering the process is the job of a team that includes people who work in the different functions, along with information technology professionals. The target set for new performance often is 100 (or more) percent better than current performance.

Some organizations take a "green field" approach to BPR, which means totally scrapping the old process and building a new one from scratch. Others use a less extreme system of mapping the as-is process, then modifying its major parts. All reliable approaches install new process infrastructures, such as process performance measurement systems and continuous improvement practices.

Interestingly, BPR is new to the Japanese, and they are enthusiastically studying it. One of the authors of this book wrote another one on BPR in 1992 called *BreakPoint^{SM} Business Process Redesign*. It has been published by Japan's leading business publisher under a title that roughly translates as *Hyper-Performance.*

Activity-Based Costing

Right now, cost savings is a primary survival goal of most businesses and all governments. Make no mistake: with tight home budgets, consumers today shop for price. With tight public budgets, so do governments. Costs count, as they must when making process improvements. Improvement is *not* free: its benefits must exceed costs.

Unfortunately, the manner in which QM, TBM, and BPR *most commonly have been applied* in government largely ignores cost. This is because existing systems of cost accounting are at best marginally relevant to management decision making, often misleading, and a barrier to progress. Such systems are structured around the *spending* of resources in line-item budgets and departments, rather than being focused on how processes consume resources or what it *costs* to run a business or a government.

Activity-based costing (ABC) was originally developed to trace the cost implications of business decisions and to arrive at accurate product and service costs. In this latter application, companies frequently discovered that products they thought were highly profitable in fact lost money. Often, the reason was that they consumed more than the average amounts of indirect or overhead costs (i.e., for administrative and support services) yet were allocated the average amount. The resulting distortions hid the actual cost of these products.

Figure 2-5
Perceived
Versus Actual
Cost

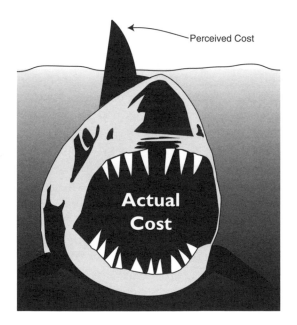

Perceived Cost

Actual Cost

Today, ABC has become the major new addition to process management and improvement in such organizations as the city of Indianapolis, Indiana and the U.S. Internal Revenue Service. Indianapolis Mayor Stephen Goldsmith has said that ABC is the fulcrum for levering city managers into competitive thinking, while at the IRS it gives managers flexibility in how they invest resources.

More than simply an accounting system, ABC enables an organization to create business, cost, and operations models based on processes. It links into process measures related to speed, quality, and customer satisfaction, permitting a balanced-scorecard view of total organizational performance. And, at the risk of repeating ourselves, it is the *only* cost accounting system that is fully compatible with other process-based management approaches.

Benchmarking

Reinventing government does not mean reinventing the wheel, but it is surprising how few public agencies have well-planned procedures for adopting and adapting the best practices of other organizations. In the private sector, where they are considered highly valuable, these procedures are collectively called *benchmarking.*

Benchmarking's objective is to discover and imitate processes outside an organization that do what internal processes do, except much better. For example, an agency that issues user permits may look at others that do the same, for purposes of adopting all or part of their issuance process. Going a step further, some private companies look for outside processes that do the same generic procedures but on different products and processes in a completely different industry. Adopting these types of processes usually lets a company leapfrog past competitors who look for improvement ideas only within their industry. This is a good practice for public agencies that face competition from the private sector.

As with the other approaches and methods just discussed, benchmarking starts out by a thorough understanding of the operations of the internal process to be benchmarked. QM and other tools are used to reach this understanding.

Competition

When it comes to government reform, the most popular word on people's lips today is *privatize.* Privatizing, from selling off public assets to outsourcing of services, must remain as an alternative to be explored in improving government effectiveness. There are well-established methods for doing this exploration, and we include them in this book.

However, many public services are already being run by private companies and nonprofits, and the results are not uniformly good. For example, the majority of child and family services in local government are contracted out to nonprofit community organizations, yet few jurisdictions report improvements in this area, and costs continue to go up.

There is nothing that says that a government organization cannot be as cost effective as a private one. Perhaps one reason that the reverse seems true is lack of competition for many public services. In a capitalist society, competition is considered the invisible hand that improves products and services. Some governments are making this basic economic force more visible within their agencies.

For example, cities like Indianapolis make their street maintenance districts compete with private companies for work, while Phoenix, Arizona does the same for its garbage collectors. Seeing a better deal outside its organization boundaries, the U.S. Treasury Department lets the U.S. Department of Agriculture handle its payroll functions. This practice of competition for support services among federal agencies will likely increase with the government's new emphasis on franchising. In franchising, program managers are more free to choose which agency they will contract with for such support services as personnel, procurement, security, and training—a situation that will certainly motivate their internal service organizations to start improving.

Competition needs guidelines and ground rules, too. Among these are gaining a good understanding of what, precisely, is being put up for bids. Process mapping and analysis, along with ABC, are the modern tools for this analysis.

Change Management

Douglas McGregor put it succinctly: "The decision which achieves organization objectives must be both (1) technologically sound and (2) carried out by people. If we lose sight of the second requirement or if we assume naively that people can be made to carry out whatever decisions are technically sound, we run the risk of decreasing rather than increasing the effectiveness of the organization." All of the above approaches have much in common, but the strongest similarity is that they all mean *change*. For example, continuous improvement does not mean doing the same things better or working harder; it means doing things differently. BPR and restructuring an organization mean making major changes in operations and often result in many people losing their jobs. Even ABC, which may seem to some like a mild-mannered innovation, requires managers to make significant changes in their decision-making processes. In addition, each of these methods does not simply discover ways to change. They promote—indeed, compel—a never-ending series of changes that alter an organization's operations from static and stable to dynamic and fluid.

This continuous stream of change runs dead into the greatest barrier to progress in government and industry: people don't much like to change. This is as true in the executive suite as it is out in the field. Given this fact, organizations that adopt new management practices are wise to make change management one of them.

Change management is *the process of aligning the human, organizational, and cultural elements of an agency with new ways of doing business*. It is a conscious process, involving careful assessment of how improvements will affect people and planning interventions that will maximize acceptance and minimize fear and discomfort with new ways of working.

There is a larger, long-term, and critical purpose to change management, and that is to facilitate the transition from a traditional management culture to a new, more resilient, improvement-driven culture. Like continuous improvement, this purpose has been recognized at all levels of government, based on an understanding that technical change is the easy part of reform and "people-change" the hard part.

PULLING IT ALL TOGETHER

There is nothing intrinsically wrong with any of the improvement approaches discussed in this chapter—indeed, there is everything right about them. The problem is that each addresses only part of the operations and management challenges facing government today. QM lacks the important cost accounting features of ABC and is more geared toward gradual improvement than are the radical changes of BPR. However, if BPR is not followed by continuous improvement, then gains that were once quantum leaps soon become scrap heaps. Organizations that fail to use change management to introduce these approaches are doomed to failure, as are the misguided agencies that have tried to change their cultures without adopting new management methods or altering how people do their daily work.

You cannot simply bolt together the methods and approaches we have just discussed, because then you lose their synergy. Improvement Driven Organizations have discovered how to make that synergy happen. Through the IDO framework, they adopt and *adapt* the best aspects of all management approaches, especially those reviewed in this chapter. And, because the best management is always a work-in-progress, these organizations are continuously improving how they manage.

Chapter
3

BASIC CONCEPTS—CUSTOMERS AND PROCESSES

■ Every government has customers. They include:

- External customers: end users of public services
- Internal customers: people inside an agency who depend on fellow workers

■ All customers are also suppliers, and all suppliers are customers.

■ Only customers can define quality.

■ Customer satisfaction should be the prime focus of government.

- An Improvement Driven Organization takes a systems approach to control and improvement. This approach provides a handy framework for viewing how work is done in core business processes and in supporting processes.
- The foundation of the system is the individual work process. A process has boundaries, suppliers, inputs, transformation components, outputs, and customers.
- Every organization has a hierarchy of processes that are interconnected and interdependent. Improving one process without considering the others often will sub-optimize total organizational performance.

In this chapter, we give you an overview of two basic concepts that are central to the rest of this book: customers and processes.

WHO ARE GOVERNMENT'S CUSTOMERS?

Call them clients, stakeholders, users, beneficiaries, or John Q. Public—the government has customers just like private companies. If this surprises you, you are not alone. Many public organizations do not have this view when they start to use process management.

Your customer is anyone who receives or uses what you produce—or whose success or satisfaction depends on your actions. For most people, that user will be an *internal customer*, or other unit or person in your agency, whose part in a work process comes after yours or who uses your output to do his or her job.

At the Crane, Indiana Naval Weapons Support Center, the internal customers of the procurement office are all the line units that work on weapons systems. These units depend on the procurement office to order parts and materials to get their jobs done right and within deadlines. If buying problems put them behind schedule or over budget, they are the ones who hear from angry external customers and managers.

In most public agencies, middle managers developing policies or budgets for their units are the customers of administrative officials and upper managers who develop and communicate agency-wide policies and objectives. Department heads need clear direction and feedback from the top to create effective policy directives for their staffs.

In justice and law enforcement systems, litigators are customers of investigators. Litigators need a sound investigative memo to develop legal strategies and adjudicate cases successfully.

"On a day-to-day basis, cooperation among internal customers is what management is all about," noted the chief of statistical methods at Watervliet Army Arsenal in New York State. "The more we understand the needs of our 'downstream' internal customers, the better the whole process works."

Government Program	External Customers
IRS Service Center Ogden, Utah	Tax attorneys Tax preparers Taxpayers
Norfolk Naval Shipyard Norfolk, Virginia	Fleet commanders Type commanders Ship commanders
Johnson Space Center Houston, Texas	Congress & the administration NASA headquarters Other government agencies Scientific community Private businesses Foreign governments
U.S. Patent & Trademark Office	Engineers, scientists, and inventors Patent and trademark attorneys Private businesses Industrial information specialists Students
Defense Commercial Communications Office	Whole Department of Defense
Office of Physical Security & Law Enforcement, General Services Administration	All federal agencies that lease space from GSA (6,800 buildings) Building managers Federal employees Visitors to federal offices
Social Security Administration	Beneficiaries Congress

Figure 3-1
Government
Has Varied
External
Customers

At the ultimate level, the final product or service user is an *external customer*. External customers can be direct, such as the retirees who receive benefits from the U.S. Army Accounting and Finance Center in Indianapolis and the naval commands that send ships for overhaul to naval shipyards.

They also can be indirect. For example, the Federal Deposit Insurance Corporation works directly with financial institutions, but the ultimate customer is the individual bank account holder. Figure 3-1 gives additional examples of agencies' external customers.

Stakeholders include those individuals or organizations who have an interest in or who are affected by a program or organization, but are not the direct recipient of its services. However, they have a major impact on program effectiveness and, consequently, their opinions and recommendations matter. For example, the U.S. Coast Guard's Office of Marine Safety, Security, and Environmental Protection includes the following organizations in its list of stakeholders:

- Environmental response groups
- Federal, state, and local government
- Maritime unions
- Maritime training interests
- Classification societies
- Key congressional representatives
- Advisory committees
- Trade associations
- Foreign flag operators
- U.S. Department of Transportation representatives
- U.S. Environmental Protection Agency

The office surveys and interviews these stakeholders for their advice and opinions on its policies, programs, and effectiveness.

Everyone Is Both a Supplier and a Customer

It is important to note that *supplier-customer relationships for internal and external customers and stakeholders are reciprocal*, as shown in Figure 3-2.

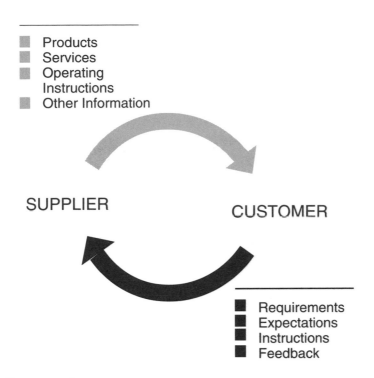

- Products
- Services
- Operating Instructions
- Other Information

Figure 3-2
The Customer-Supplier Relationship

SUPPLIER   CUSTOMER

- Requirements
- Expectations
- Instructions
- Feedback

For example,

- Although the line departments at the Crane Naval Weapons Support Center are the customers of the procurement staff, the buyers are also the customers of the line departments: for timely advance requests for materials, clear and accurate specifications, and external customer feedback on needed improvements.

- Taxpayers are customers of the Internal Revenue Service, but the IRS is a customer for the information that taxpayers give in their tax return forms.

- Managers are customers for employees' reports, but employees are customers for managers' instructions on how and when to prepare those reports.

In short, you are both a customer and a supplier for everyone you deal with. Treat your suppliers like customers, and
you will have better suppliers. Make sure your customers
give you the right information, and you will be a better supplier.

WHY DOES AN IMPROVEMENT DRIVEN ORGANIZATION EMPHASIZE CUSTOMERS?

In business, understanding customer requirements has obvious importance: if customers are not satisfied with products
or services, they won't buy them—and profits will reflect
their disaffection. Although government doesn't usually sell
its products or services, a customer-driven process is equally critical in the public sector.

In quality management, reengineering, and other process
management approaches, customer needs and expectations,
not agency-established standards, define quality. Take a
moment to read the example in the box below.

No matter how fast the VAROIC processes loan applications
in its offices, the veterans measure turnaround from the time
they mail an application to the time they receive a check in
the mail. Which is the better definition of performance in
turnaround time: veterans' perceptions or internal cycle
time?

Customers Define Quality at VAROIC

The Philadelphia Veterans Affairs Regional Office and Insurance Center (VAROIC) handles veterans' GI life insurance loan applications. A top executive there said, "We had a standard of processing 95 percent of the applications within five work days from the time we received them until the Treasury Department issued the check. We were proud we averaged 3.3 work days per loan.

"But when an improvement team asked veterans about our service, they heard complaints that it took up to two weeks to get a check. The team realized the veterans counted time from the calendar day they mailed an application to the day they got the check. So our standard did not meet our customers' expectations.

"The team added a special post office box number, which saved time that the applications spent in the mail getting to us. We added a dedicated fax machine for emergency requests. We worked internally and with Treasury to streamline the application approval and check-mailing processes down to a 1.7 work day average.

"The immediate payoff was more satisfied customers. We also saved money by eliminating or reducing work that added little value to the application process—including time answering complaints—since our improvements have cut them by more than half.

"This taught us to tie what we do into customer expectations. We have to ask, have we aligned what we consider good service with what our customers really want?"

The commanding officer at the Cherry Point Naval Air Depot in North Carolina recalled, "For years, some of our operators made a component for a larger part. One of the operators asked the workers who used the component about its quality. 'Quality's fine,' said these internal customers. But could it be any better? 'Well, we have to open it up, drill an alignment hole, and then reassemble it. Takes us about an hour to do that.' Checking the component's plans, they found that the hole had been left out of the drawings. Now, the operators who make the component put the hole in it, which takes six minutes. We make hundreds of these a year; think of the time we had wasted by not finding out what the internal customers really needed."

No matter how good you think products and services are, they cannot be considered high quality unless they meet your customers' needs and expectations. You cannot "do it right the first time" unless you know the right thing to do.

Do Customers Know the Right Thing to Do?

"Right" is relative and is best defined through customer/supplier interaction. You have no doubt had the experience of customers asking for a product or service that is partly or totally wrong for their needs. You have to talk with these customers to help them better define what you are to deliver; often you are more of an expert on the subject than they. But ultimately the customer validates your mutual decision on what is best.

Also, customers may not realize that it is often possible to go beyond their expectations. *Customer satisfaction,* shown in the lower right-hand corner of the matrix in Figure 3-3, comes when customers expect a product attribute (physical quality, timeliness, cost, and so forth), and the attribute is present in the product. *Customer dissatisfaction* comes when they expect an attribute, but it is not present.

Opportunity for Delight	Delight	Attributes Not Expected by Customer
Dissatisfaction	Satisfaction	Attributes Expected by Customer
Attributes Not Present in Product	Attributes Present in Product	

Figure 3-3
Product
Attributes
and
Customer
Satisfaction

Now, it is possible to go beyond simply satisfying customers by including attributes they do not expect in a product. This is doing that special "something extra." For example:

* The fax machine that the VAROIC added to its loan processing permitted veterans to get quick service in emergencies.

* The Oregon Department of Motor Vehicles found that drivers were intensely irritated by unflattering photographs on their licenses. Now, Oregon uses a video system that allows drivers to choose from among several pictures.

When you add these types of attributes, you are *delighting* customers (the upper right-hand corner of Figure 3-3). The greatest challenge is to work on the *opportunities for delight* (the upper left-hand corner), whereby you find new ways of pleasing customers. This is one of the chief goals of government organizations that want to stay competitive with customer-focused private companies.

Customer Dissatisfaction

Most organizations measure customer satisfaction by how well they avoid customer dissatisfaction. A common mistake is to think that if few customers complain, most are happy. Let us say that only 5 percent of your customers complain to you. Does this mean that 95 percent are satisfied? How would you feel if you learned that 96 percent of your unhappy customers will not complain and that all customers with unresolved gripes will tell them to nine or ten other people? That was one finding of a federal consumer products study.

Multiply the number of complaints you get by ten, and you may have a more realistic picture of customer satisfaction. Multiply unresolved complaints by one hundred, and you have an idea of how many people out there have heard bad things about your organization. Think about that the next time you have problems getting your budget approved or when voters fail to support your bond issue.

WHAT ARE PROCESSES?

Processes are what organizations do—the activities done by people, equipment, or software to produce products and services. Traditional management in the public sector focuses on managing employees, clients, and budgets. Improvement Driven Organizations focus on ensuring that processes meet customer expectations and operate as intended and that the organizations constantly improve process performance. In particular, an Improvement Driven Organization gives top priority to core business processes—those that make the products and services valued most by customers.

Process management is based on systems theory. Systems are discrete operations with inputs, transformation components, outputs, and feedback. Systems are made up of networks of sub-systems, each with its own suppliers, boundaries, inputs, transformations, customers, outputs, and feedback. Another name for a sub-system is a *process*.

Processes within a system are interconnected and interdependent. Some processes are in charge of finding outside *suppliers* of material and information to be used by the system. Others take in these *inputs* across the *boundaries* that separate an organization from the outside world and distribute them to internal processes that *transform* the inputs into interim or final services, or *outputs*. Another set of processes distribute the outputs to *customers* on the other side of the boundary between them and an organization. Together, all these processes make up a system.

By taking the systems view that processes are interconnected and interdependent, you avoid *sub-optimizing,* or improving a single part of a system while inadvertently lowering performance in other parts. For example, an agency's system for acquiring outside goods and services starts with line departments recognizing needs and sending requisitions to a purchasing department. The purchasing department may improve its processes by requiring line departments to fill out long, complex requisition forms. However, this requirement creates extra work and delay in the line departments, which is not an optimal solution for the entire system of acquiring.

Also, a systems approach means that a process is capable of generating feedback information on its performance. With the feedback, a process' suppliers, operators, and customers can adjust operations to control process performance. In the short run, such an adjustment allows a process or system to be self-correcting, because its operators know whether it is on or off course. In the long run, such feedback, when combined with external information on customer expectations and other factors, provides information for process improvement.

Finally, a systems view gives you a logical way to classify and organize all the parts of your organization. Without this logic, it is difficult to understand how things operate in an organization, to find solutions to problems, and to ensure that those solutions actually solve the problems.

PARTS OF THE PROCESS

Figure 3-4
Components
of an Activity

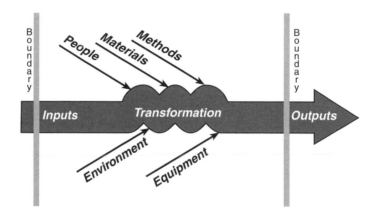

All processes and systems, whether large or small, simple or complex, have the same basic characteristics, which are shown in Figure 3-4. Every process has *inputs,* or material that comes from outside its boundaries, such as bills that must be paid by an accounts payable office, vehicles to be repaired by a municipal garage, and raw data that a clerk enters in a data base. *Information* may be included with this material, such as an authorization to pay a bill, a job order for a repair, or instructions on coding the data. The people or organizations that provide these inputs are called *suppliers.* The process that receives the inputs is called the *customer process.*

Boundaries separate one process from others. The input boundary is the point where a supplier process loses control of inputs and a customer process gains control of them. An output boundary is where a process loses control of its outputs and other customer processes gain control of them. In paying bills, the input boundary is the point where bills are handed over to the check-writing process, and the output boundary is where the checks are handed over to the process that mails them to creditors. Understanding boundaries is important, because they define the starting and ending points of a process. As you will see in later parts of this book, organizations run into major problems if they do not define process boundaries correctly.

Inside the process, a *transformation* occurs to the input. It is changed from its original input form to a new output form. For example, in a vehicle repair process, a vehicle that has worn brake pads is transformed into a vehicle with safe brakes. Transformations include all the *tasks* and *steps* involved in writing a check, fixing a car, and entering data. Sometimes this is called "throughput." *Tasks* are smaller parts of processes. For example, paying a bill may include the tasks of reviewing the paperwork that accompanies it, ensuring that payment is authorized, and the physical act of writing a check. *Steps* are the smallest parts of a process, such as lifting the pen that signs the checks, turning a wrench, or keying in data on a computer keyboard.

Internal components of the transformation include *people, equipment, methods, materials,* and *environment.*

- *People* are the employees and supervisors who directly work in a process. They are the process *operators.* Sometimes, process customers can be operators. For example, citizens in Arizona who file for uncontested divorce can use the state's QuickCourt system, which allows them to use computers located at public kiosks to fill out the needed forms. Thus, they are simultaneously suppliers of input (they provide information for the forms), operators in the transformation (they key in the data and take the printed forms to the court clerk), and customers (they receive the service). However, transformation does not include administrative, middle and upper management, or support personnel who do not have hands-on work to do in the process. These latter people are seen as working in other processes that affect a specific process, but they are not part of it.

- *Equipment* includes the machines and hardware used in the transformation, such as equipment used to receive materials and information from upstream suppliers, transform them, and send them to downstream customers. Examples might be personal computers, scientific instruments, or printing presses.

- *Methods* means the way that work is done. It includes operation manuals, rules and regulations, software, training, formulas, algorithms, and other procedures used in transformation.

- *Materials* are supplies or tools, already at the transformation site of a process, that are used to add value to input. They are not the inputs themselves. They include chemicals, forms, printer toner, ledgers, cleaning supplies, repair tools, and audiovisual aids.

- *Environment* includes air temperature, noise levels, location, decor, and maintenance and other physical conditions of the area in which the process is located. Environmental factors may affect the physical properties of a product or service (e.g., dust in a paint shop) or the people working in a process (e.g., office decor). It can also mean decreasing physical distance to customers by, for example, decentralizing operations to the field.

Transformations produce products or services, which are process *outputs*. Outputs might be bills and checks to mail, a repaired car, or data entered in a data base. An output is called interim or work-in-progress when it goes to another process within the same system or organization. This receiving process is called an *internal customer.* Final output goes to an *external customer* outside the system or organization.

Bills   Bills verified,   Bills to   Checks   Checks   Checks   Bills
    payment   pay   written   to mail   mailed   paid
    authorized

Figure 3-5
Diagram of
Linked
Processes

Most processes in an organization are strictly internal and have no contact with external suppliers or customers. So, as shown in Figure 3-5, most of the time the output of one process becomes the input of the next, and so on, until a final product or service is delivered to the external customer. This linked flow of work is the *production stream.* In the figure, the process "checks written" is the *downstream* internal customer of the "bills verified and payment authorized" process and the *upstream* supplier of the "checks mailed" process. This upstream/downstream concept is important, because often the performance of a process is governed by the quality and timeliness of output from processes that are upstream from it.

In general, it is more effective and less costly to correct a problem in an upstream process than to try to solve the problem with inspection and rework in a downstream process.

Figure 3-6
Feedback in
Linked
Processes

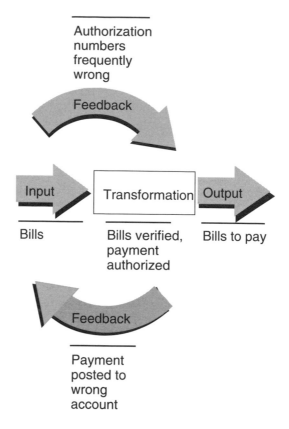

All customers and suppliers, both internal and external, give each other *feedback,* or such information as problem reports and suggestions for improvement. Figure 3-6 shows feedback between the processes "bills verified, payment authorized" and "checks written." Parts of the process may give feedback to process operators on problems and performance. For example, some telephone systems (equipment in a transformation) have software that records the number of incoming calls in a period, how many were answered by the third ring, how long callers spend on hold, and other information. This information can be used to evaluate the performance of a customer service process that uses the phone system and to spot problems in the process. In Chapter 8 you will see tools that translate this type of internal feedback into formats used to monitor and improve performance.

The beauty and utility of the conceptual framework just described is that it applies to all processes and systems, no matter what their size, complexity, or location in the process hierarchy.

THE PROCESS HIERARCHY

In process management there is a pyramidal hierarchy of operations, illustrated by Figure 3-7. Executives and elected officials focus on the top parts of the pyramid in order to understand the big picture of an organization's operations, while supervisors and employees focus on the lower parts. Each level is an aggregation of the ones below it, so there is a direct link between high-level views of operations and more detailed examination of how work is done. Let's look at each level now.

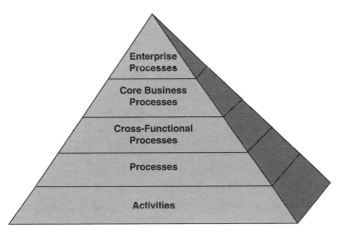

Figure 3-7
The
Operations
Pyramid

Simple Processes or Activities

In its simplest form, a process is a segment of work usually done by one or more persons belonging to the same office, branch, or other small group. Organizations that use activity-based costing label these types of simple processes as *activities.*

Processes

Linked in sequence and having identifiable boundaries between them, a group of simple processes form a complex process. The outputs of one simple process become the inputs of the next, until a final process output is produced. For example, the process of qualifying people for public assistance might include the five processes of (1) collecting information from them (external input), (2) reviewing the information to see if they qualify, (3) verifying the information, (4) reporting the names of eligible persons to another process that arranges for assistance (a final output of this series of simple processes), and (5) notifying ineligible persons that they do not qualify (another final output).

Processes such as these are the usual focus of employee process improvement teams, self-managed teams, and natural work groups. Typically, these teams keep their daily operations or improvement efforts within the boundaries of one or a few simple processes in which they are operators.

Cross-Functional Processes

When a process is done in several different functions or departments in an organization, it is called a *cross-functional process.* The cross-functional process of procurement involves (1) a line department, where a need is recognized and reported to (2) a purchasing department that arranges to buy a product or service to fill the need and then sends the seller's invoice to (3) an accounting or finance department that pays the bill.

There can be dozens and even hundreds of cross-functional processes in an organization, ranging from making the products and services customers value the most, to support operations such as arranging and paying for local travel expenses. One of the key objectives of process management is to make these cross-functional processes visible to executives and managers.

This enables an organization to introduce changes that will optimize an entire cross-functional process and the entire system, not just one or two processes.

Core Business Processes

Core business processes are cross-functional processes that are "get right, keep right, or die" operations that are essential to your organization's mission. These operations almost always directly produce the goods and services your external customers value the most. All other processes are secondary in importance to them. Some examples include fighting fires by a fire department, recruiting qualified enlisted personnel for a war-fighting organization, and preventing the outbreak of communicable disease by a public health department. A few support processes qualify for this category, such as ensuring the safety of employees who handle explosives or nuclear fuels.

Core business processes are also called strategic business processes because they are the engines of an Improvement Driven Organization's long-term strategy to survive and continually improve to meet changing customer expectations. Strategic planning focuses on these processes and considers other processes only insofar as they support strategic processes.

Ideally, an organization focuses its initial reengineering projects on core business processes and makes it clear that most continuous improvement projects should support the strategic goals set for such processes.

Enterprise Processes

For some government operations, these processes are at the top of the pyramid and flow through several independent or quasi-independent organizations. For example, some parts of law enforcement can be seen as enterprise processes. One such process may start with investigating a crime (done by a police agency), then go on to issuing a warrant (done by a court), arresting a suspect (police agency), trial (public prosecutors, public defenders, and a court), and finally ending with incarceration (a prison or jail) or probation (a probation office).

Whether you need to consider enterprise processes in your organization depends on the types of services you produce. If these services are essential to a larger, multi-organization operation, then the enterprise process is a handy concept for understanding where your organization fits in the big picture. For elected officials and city and county managers, the enterprise process concept provides perhaps the most accurate and revealing view of this big picture.

A Process Example Hierarchy

Major division chiefs at the U.S. Internal Revenue Service (IRS) identified their five core business processes at the start of an Activity-Based Management initiative: Managing Accounts, Informing and Educating, Ensuring Compliance, Resourcing, and Value Tracking. In Figure 3-8, the Ensuring Compliance core business process is broken down into four smaller, cross-functional processes: "identifying," "compliance planning," "determining," and "collecting."

"Collecting," in turn, is disaggregated into three complex processes that occur mostly in field offices. The IRS defines the three as follows:

- **Contact with Taxpayer.** This process has as its boundary those activities that *begin* when a taxpayer has a balance due and *end* either with full and immediate payment of the balance or with referral to the Alternative Action or Enforcement Action processes.

- **Alternative Action.** This process begins when a taxpayer acknowledges that he or she will not pay the full balance due immediately. It ends when the taxpayer pays the balance due in full or with case closure or referral to the Enforcement Action process.

- **Enforcement Action**. This process begins when a balance due cannot be resolved through Alternative Actions and ends with full payment, case closure, or when the taxpayer proceeds with an Alternative Action.

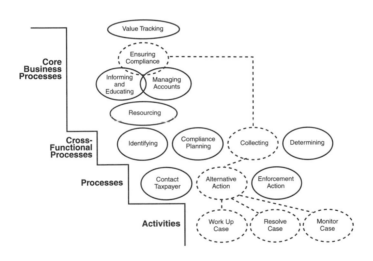

Figure 3-8
IRS' Ensuring
Compliance
Core
Business

Finally, the Alternative Action breaks down into three simple processes or activities: work up a tax case, resolve the case, and monitor the results of the case. Each of these processes has its own boundaries. Below this last level are tasks, and underneath them are steps. Usually, this last level of detail is shown only in flow charts and procedures manuals used by process operators.

THE TOTAL SYSTEM

Groups outside a process influence the way work is done. Inside an organization, a line process (one that produces the products or services sent to external customers) may be influenced by supplier and customer processes or by administrative and support processes such as those of the agency director, personnel department, comptroller office, or supply department. In a government organization, all operations are also influenced by external suppliers, customers, and stakeholders, such as elected officials, oversight agencies, special interest groups, unions, and voters. Taken together, all internal processes and these other elements constitute the organization's *total system*, as shown in Figure 3-9.

Figure 3-9
The System

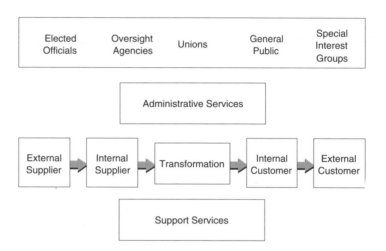

This total systems view is important for government organizations, which are more subject to outside influence than private companies. Often, problems in processes may be due to demands from outside groups that have nothing to do with producing an organization's primary products and services.

Customers and processes are at the core of all sound improvement approaches. Customers define requirements, while processes produce what is required. Throughout the rest of this book, we will return frequently to these concepts.

PART II

THE LEADER DRIVEN PHASE

Chapter
4

ASSESSMENT

■ Building and sustaining an Improvement Driven Organization begins with a comprehensive assessment that compares current operations and results with the requirements of customers and stakeholders. Without this assessment, an organization will be clueless and directionless in its efforts to improve.

■ Part of assessment focuses on current customer and stakeholder requirements. Equally important is the ability to predict future requirements that will be driven by competition, demography, technology, politics, and other forces of change.

■ The objectives of assessment are to provide executives and managers with a profound knowledge of their organization and its current and future environment, to inform strategic decision making, to motivate change, and to set baselines for measuring performance improvement.

■ Assessment can focus on customer opinion, gap analysis, cost effectiveness, and management practices and culture, depending on an agency's situation.

■ Assessment is a team activity, with team members drawn from executive and management ranks.

I have become a fanatic about quantifying—but a new sort of quantifying. I insist upon quantifying the 'soft stuff'— quality, service, customer linkups, innovation, organizational structure, people involvement. . . .

—Tom Peters

All too many public organizations that set out to reinvent themselves do so without understanding the following fundamental factors. As a result, they fail in the attempt and, eventually, will fail in the eyes of their constituents.

- **What they are**—that is, their mission, structure, customers, and customers' expectations

- **How they do things**—that is, their processes, their culture

- The **results** of what they do compared with customer expectations or outside best practices

- What must **change** so that they can improve

- How **ready** they are to change

Understanding these factors is a continuing job. Over time, the environment in which you operate changes; assessment allows you to anticipate and plan for changing, too. As you reach one level of understanding about your operation or customers, you must strive to reach the next level; assessment is, by itself, a form of continuous improvement of your understanding. Finally, no closed system ever survives for long; assessment keeps your decision-making system open by feeding it new information. By extension, because decisions control your entire operation, if you do not conduct routine assessment activities such as those discussed in this chapter your organization will eventually veer off course.

FOUR PURPOSES OF ASSESSMENT

Knowledge

Deming said that his life's work was not to develop better ways to introduce quality management but rather to seek profound knowledge. Profound knowledge goes far beyond superficial, external, and obvious information. Instead of being narrowly focused, it has broad significance. The result of profound knowledge (and reflecting on it frequently) is good decisions that address the right issues, in the right way, and that not only improve operations now, but also set the stage for further improvement.

In the Improvement Driven Organization, the search for profound knowledge begins with understanding "hard" data about performance: dollars, errors, cycle time, and customer satisfaction. It also means quantitative measures of the "soft stuff": leadership, culture, and readiness to change. Both are important, because the soft stuff drives performance as much as—and perhaps more than—anything else.

Simply knowing where you stand does not produce results, but if you act without knowledge, then improvement is a crap-shoot. Anyone who has rolled the dice at a casino craps table knows that you hope a lot to win but lose most of the time. That's no way to win the trust of workers and the public.

Informed Decision Making

What is the result of profound knowledge? "Ye shall know the truth, and the truth shall make you free" (John 8:32). Assessment information frees you in many ways. It removes the subjectivity from management decisions, guides them in the right direction, and provides the means to validate their results. That takes a big burden off executives who often have to rely solely on experience, rules of thumb, and general guesswork when they plan for action. One side effect is shorter meetings: you don't have to debate long on the status quo when it leaps off the pages of a good assessment report.

Leverage

Equally important, assessment is a tactic for motivating people to change. Assessment information results help convince them that the as-is state is no longer acceptable and that the need for change is compelling. However, this is true only when the assessment itself is credible; if it is not, the normal penchant is simply to deny bad news.

So how do you gain this credibility? We think that involving your people in assessment tasks is the best way, through methods such as the following:

Assessment is a team exercise. Depending on the subject you are assessing, the teams that do the work of gathering and analyzing information can include executives, managers of key work processes, unions, employees, suppliers, customers, and stakeholders.

Have top leaders select the methods you will use. If they do not select the methods, then you cannot expect them to accept the results. To guide them in this decision, brief leaders on the alternative methods, who will be involved, and how they can use the results during strategic planning and afterwards.

Brief all managers. They frequently will need to help collect the data. Also, managers often are frightened by assessments—they need to have the big picture of how your organization will use the results. Managers should play active roles in collecting and analyzing data, which gives them a sense of ownership of the results.

Baselines

Assessment information documents your as-is performance and so creates baseline measures for monitoring progress. By looking at improvement trends in your initial areas of focus and analyzing successes and failures, you will gain insights about your organization's learning curve, acceptance of change, and other issues. Such information gathering is a continuation of your quest for profound knowledge.

ASSESSMENT QUESTIONS

Before starting assessment, your executives should frame a set of questions that will help take stock of your organization. Which questions they develop will depend on your mission, environment, and other factors. Figure 4-1 is a list developed by a government agency that provides a service to other agencies. This agency has competitors both inside its government and in the private sector, which explains why the list has questions normally found in industry. Given the current emphasis on competition in government, it may be a good list for most agencies.

TOPICS	ISSUES/QUESTIONS
Customer Analysis	Who are our major customer groups?
	What results are our customers looking for?
	Regarding our customers' needs and expectations: What are they, what is their relative importance to the customers, and how are we doing in meeting them?
	What are our customers' unmet needs and expectations?

Figure 4-1
Assessment
Questions

What criteria do our customers use to judge the quality, timeliness, cost, customer service, and other factors of the goods and services we give them?

How accurate are our internal measures of these criteria?

Market Analysis

What is the size of the market for our goods and services?

What is our core market? What are our secondary markets?

What are the key trends in the industry in which we work? Is it:

- Growing or shrinking?

- Using more technology?

- Opening up to new competitors?

- Experiencing breakthroughs in operations?

Competitor Analysis

What are the critical success factors for being competitive in this industry?

What are the sources of competitive advantage?

What goods or service do we provide to customers?

Who else provides them?

How and where are we allowed to compete?

What competitive discriminators exist in our market, such as cycle time, cost, quality, customer service, location, and so on?

How do we compare with competitors in these discriminators?

Self-Analysis What is our current performance when compared with our objectives?

What has been our strategy?

What are our assets? Skills? Weaknesses? Strengths?

What are the structural, people, cultural, and systems characteristics of our organization that will affect strategy?

What is our cost structure?

What is our existing business portfolio (i.e., the goods and services we offer)?

What are the requirements we must meet to serve our core market?

What are our strategic problems, constraints, questions? How do we compare with our competitors?

What is the normal and peak size of demand from our core market? What capital and human resources do we need to meet core market requirements?

What capital and human resources do we have now, and where are they located in relation to the sources of core market requirements?

METHODS FOR ASSESSING AS-IS STATUS

There are dozens of ways to assess your as-is status, forecast future trends, and compare your performance with internal and external standards of excellence. We will discuss what experience shows are the most important methods for a government organization. Afterwards, we give you some guidance in selecting the best ones for your situation. The methods discussed include the following:

- **Customer opinion.** What do your customers think about your services, and how do they want you to improve results?

- **Gap analysis.** How well are your core business processes delivering the results customers expect?

- **Cost effectiveness.** What do your processes cost to operate, and what is their potential for cost savings?

- **Management.** What are your current management methods compared with generally accepted standards of excellence?

- **Culture.** Do you have a culture that will support the changes needed to make improvements?

Each method overlaps the others somewhat. You need to select among them according to your resources, time available, and the information that leaders want to see. Do not use all five at once; this is too expensive and unnecessary. Over time, however, try all the methods, because each reveals a different dimension of your organization.

Customer Opinion

In Chapter 3, you saw the importance of obtaining customer opinion on quality, timeliness, cost, customer service, and other issues. During your initial assessment, focus groups and surveys often are the best methods to query customers about their expectations and levels of satisfaction.

Focus groups. These are small groups of customers (twelve maximum) who are typical of all or a subset of your customer population. Such groups are led through discussion agendas by a qualified facilitator. The agenda includes questions about customer perceptions of issues critical to the organization, such as quality and cost. Group members talk among themselves, not to the facilitator or to executives or managers (who should not even be in the same room). Notes from the meetings are typed and summarized for executives. Sometimes, group discussions are audio- or videotaped and transcribed. The notes prompt executives and managers to investigate issues raised by the group and are used to help develop survey questionnaires.

When you have a large constituency, focus groups are best at giving you qualitative information on the broad range of customer concerns and perceptions. In this case, you cannot—indeed, should never—use the results of focus groups as reliable measures that can be projected to the total population of customers or even subsets of it. A focus group is never intended to be a statistically valid random sample, and usually it is too small a group to be representative of your total customer base.

It's a different story when you only have a few dozen customers. If you can recruit representatives from all or most of them into one or more focus groups, then a simple technique—administering a survey questionnaire at the start of each group's session—will give you statistically reliable information on the customers. Then, you can begin a guided discussion that will give you more insight into the results of the survey.

Surveys. Chapter 12 describes a simple system of surveying customers and analyzing the results. This system works with small numbers of customers, but it has grave limitations when you try to use it with thousands. If you plan to interview more than a few hundred customers, get professional help from a consultant, local college, or other agency with experience. You will need the help to create a useful, reliable questionnaire, draw a valid sample of the customer population, administer the survey, and analyze the results.

There are other sources of customer opinion, such as information on their complaints, customer service cards, and anecdotes from customer-contact employees. Although you should review these, don't rely on them for your initial round of assessment. Such sources tend to represent outliers, or extremes in good (or poor) customer perceptions. Later on, however, you can introduce systematic means of using these tools.

Preparing executives for customer opinion. Most governments and their agencies have surveyed citizens and customers at some point. The problem is that few of the results were ever used. Instead, they were reviewed, reviled, filed, and forgotten. The exception was when an executive used the results to "beat up" a colleague or a work group for poor performance (and political gain).

If you want the results of these methods to be useful and used, then have executives help prepare the agendas and questionnaires. They can do this by listing the types of information they need for their decisions and by agreeing in advance on the format in which you will present the results. Then, be prepared to show executives with some specificity and detail how they can apply the results to planning and process improvement.

Gap Analysis

Gap analysis shows the distance between what you do and what you need to be doing. Customer expectations and satisfaction levels learned during customer opinion assessment give you starting points for establishing process requirements, but they are only the beginning. As you will see, there are many other requirements.

Customer requirements. You can compare as-is process performance with requirements developed from customer opinion data in order to identify gaps. In Chapter 9, we discuss how to do this for a process while measuring its performance during the Plan-Do-Check-Act cycle (PDCA). PDCA is a method for assessing and planning process improvements. One of its first steps is to interview process customers on their expectations, then contrast the expectations to actual performance.

The same principles apply to measuring the performance of core business processes that deliver an agency's products and services. To do this organization-wide, you first have to identify the outputs external customers use, then map the processes that make the outputs. Usually, these are your core business processes. This is high-level mapping, so don't sweat the details until later. Next, you measure the performance of each core business process as it relates to a customer requirement. By contrasting actual performance to required performance, you begin to understand the extent to which you are not meeting customer expectations.

Key questions to ask during this investigation include the following:

- What is the time length between a customer's request for a service and the receipt of every part of that service?

- Do customers receive the services they requested? If not, what is the difference between what they wanted and what they got? How often do customers return products to us, recontact us for more information, or find errors in our work?

- What must a customer invest to receive a service, by way of time, money, distance traveled, or other resources?

- Does service delivery produce the results desired by the customer or stakeholders?

Only meeting today's customer requirements is dangerous. There is good reason to not limit your gap analysis to the distance between current customer requirements and how you have met them. Customers may not expect very much from your processes, given their experience with your and other government agencies. Also, customers may not know about the latest advancements in your field or in process technology—but that is true only for right now. Eventually they will learn that the citizens in a jurisdiction next door or across the country enjoy a much higher standard of performance from private companies or government agencies similar to yours. New technology may radically raise the standard of performance in some areas. Finally, demographic and other trends may strain your existing processes past the point of keeping up with demand.

So there are standards you must *plan* to meet in the long term, as well as those you should be meeting right now. Just drawing even with customer requirements today will put you behind the curve tomorrow. Below, we discuss why you should use benchmarks and forecasting to determine tomorrow's standards.

Performance benchmarks. Using methods discussed in Chapter 19, you may want to look for outside benchmarks of process performance. These include the results measures of comparable processes or outputs from other public and private organizations. Sometimes, these benchmarks are better measurement standards than customer expectations.

Oregon's state government has an extensive system of future-oriented performance targets it calls benchmarks. As discussed in Chapter 12, these are results targets, not necessarily performance measures of processes. The targets include raising Oregonians' real per capita income from 92 percent of the national average in 1990 to 110 percent in 2010, reducing the miles of rivers and streams that flunk water quality standards from 1,100 miles in 1990 to 75 in the year 2000, and so on. Oregon had two hundred fifty-nine such benchmarks by the end of 1994, developed by agencies and citizen groups. The value of the approach is that it forces you to consider how your agency's performance will contribute to meeting one or more of the state's benchmarks.

Forecasting demand for existing and future process outputs. Yesterday is done, and it is too late to plan for today. That leaves only tomorrow, so your assessment has to include forecasting what the future may bring. Forecasting tools useful for setting performance standards and doing gap analysis include the following:

- **Trend projections.** All governments study demographic, crime, environmental, and other trends related to their missions. For example, the violent crime rate (number of violent crimes per one hundred thousand people) may increase for several years. You can plot this trend on a chart and project what the curve will be in five, ten, or twenty years. You can make the crime trend forecast more accurate by factoring in demographic projections of population growth, socioeconomic status, and other factors. Some governments are keeping an eye on trends like the number of homes with PCs and modems, because this will influence some of their process design decisions now and in the future.

- **Scenarios.** Scenarios are descriptions of future states based on trend projections and other assumptions. They are useful for understanding what may happen, given alternate trends, new developments, and shifts in the political environment. We will discuss them more in this chapter, under strategic planning.

- **Consulting other people and organizations.** Executives frequently consult with experts to learn about future possibilities and leading-edge process operations. Consulting citizen, special interest, and business groups, other governments, and academics is a good practice when assessing future requirements.

- **Modeling and simulation.** If you can construct a model or simulation of how your core business processes operate now, then you can test different assumptions about the volume and frequency of demand. This allows you to ask "What if?" questions based on trends, scenarios, and input from outside people and organizations. There are many process simulation software systems available that you can use to look at large, cross-functional processes. The simplest are based on spreadsheet software geared mostly to financial modeling, while others allow you to map actual operations, then test them against different assumptions. These also are tools for planning how to improve processes.

Preparing executives for measuring process performance. In most agencies, executives "own" a major function or department. However, few own (or own up to owning) a cross-functional core business process, and they may not even have a clue as to what one is. Before measuring process performance, executives need a little education about customer requirements, processes, and their measurement. Next, they should identify the core business processes that produce outputs that are most important to customers and stakeholders. They may need help, so be sure to arrange it. Also, work with the chief executive to ensure that the results will not be used for finger pointing or laying blame.

Cost effectiveness

One of the easier ways to assess cost effectiveness is through cost-of-quality (COQ) analysis, which we discuss in Chapter

13. COQ is a method of identifying money spent to prevent, find, or correct errors, plus the cost value of products and services that fail. During the assessment phase, you can focus COQ on specific core business processes, and use line-item budget information and interviews to estimate the amount of money you are spending in each of the four COQ categories: prevention, appraisal, internal failure, and external failure.

Value analysis done with activity-based costing (ABC, see Chapter 13) is another good cost effectiveness assessment method. It provides all the information you would find in a COQ analysis, plus it allows you to calculate resources going to value added and non-value added processes. Value processes change the form of work-in-progress in ways that customers would value and, if fees are involved, would pay for. Non-value added processes do not change work-in-progress, but still add costs. For example, inspection is non-value added. ABC is more costly and takes longer to implement for a whole organization than COQ, so you have to weigh its costs against the near-term benefits. However, ABC is almost imperative for assessment if you face the following situations:

- Your organization recently merged with another, or you acquired several major new programs, along with their support staffs. In both cases, process mapping and ABC will help you sort out who does what for how much so that you can develop a logical organizational structure.

- You are under a clear mandate to cut costs and maintain tight control over budgets. ABC will show you how to streamline your process to cut work as well as budgets.

- You have decided to introduce a new managerial cost accounting system geared to helping managers make process improvement decisions. In this case, you might as well start out with the ABC approach, which is the only one based on processes.

Preparing executives for cost effectiveness analysis. In an initial assessment, both COQ and ABC are "shock therapy." We have yet to do a COQ analysis for U.S. government organizations in which less than 30 percent of the operations budget goes to the four categories (in one case, this was 85 percent). Often, we find that two-thirds of a government's resources goes to non-value added processes. What you must convey to executives before doing COQ or ABC is that the results portray the legacy of a century's worth of management theory about how organizations *should* be run. That theory *used to be valid*, and all executives grew up with it. Added to this is a government environment with too many rules, regulations, and redundant or unnecessary control procedures. All the more reason to explain carefully the theories that underlie COQ and ABC and to gain executive buy-in to them.

Management practices, quality, and results

Leaders often ask, "How do we manage now?" and "How does this compare with organizations recognized as having the best management practices?" Internal management assessments answer those questions. Many private and an increasing number of public organizations use the criteria of the Malcolm Baldrige National Quality Award or ISO 9000 quality guidelines as their tool for management practices, quality, and results assessment.

Government and industry established awards programs like those we list below to encourage organizations to review and revise their management practices to become more competitive. Management and business experts developed the awards' criteria based on what it takes to succeed in a global economy and excellent corporate citizenship. The criteria address issues such as the following:

- **Leadership:** Executives' personal commitment and involvement in creating and sustaining organizational vision, customer focus, and quality values, and how these are integrated into the management system, labor relations, and external partnerships.

- **Information and analysis:** The scope, management, and use of information and measurement systems, and how they are used to drive quality and improvement in processes, products, services, and customer satisfaction.

- **Strategic planning:** Short- and long-term planning processes, including how plans integrate customer and process improvement requirements, and how these are deployed throughout an organization.

- **Human resource development and management:** How managers and workers are enabled to reach their full potential and to pursue excellence goals, and building and maintaining an environment conducive to involvement and personal and organizational development.

- **Management of process quality:** The systematic processes used to design and manage process quality, internal customer-supplier relations, supplier and intermediary quality, and quality assessment.

- **Results:** Trends and quality levels for products and services, operational performance, business and support services, and supplier and intermediary quality, and associated comparison or benchmark information.

- **Customer satisfaction:** Knowledge of external customer requirements, how an organization establishes and maintains customer relationships, the methods used to determine customer satisfaction, and trend data in customer satisfaction.

How the awards work. First, you fill out an extensive application detailing how your organization handles the criteria just listed and the results. At the organization that administers the program, a panel of reviewers scores and comments on your application. This is excellent feedback. If you score high enough, a team of judges will visit your agency to document and evaluate its management practices; this is even better feedback. If you are among the highest scoring organizations, you may be selected as one of the winners. As a winner, you are entitled to display the emblem of the award in facilities, material, and advertising. Also, you must prepare a case study or other description of your organization, management practices, and results, speak at an awards ceremony, and help others to achieve the same success.

However, winning is not the purpose of these programs. They are designed to help you learn about your organization, so self-assessment and self-scoring are more important. Answering all questions in the award application forms points out specific things you can do to improve operations. Even if you happen to win an award, the greater prize is the improvement you make, so choose your program based on how it will help you improve.

Different types of awards. Appendix A has information for obtaining information on the Malcolm Baldrige Award, which is the basis for the other programs and guidelines listed below:

- **The Malcolm Baldrige National Quality Award.** This is the most rigorous and broad self-examination of any of the awards programs and takes the broadest view of quality. Most of the questions are about internal management, but many address how you manage quality with your enterprise partners (other agencies, vendors, and distributors of your funds). They also ask how you respond to community concerns and contribute to community development. Only private companies are eligible for the Baldrige award, but do not let this stop you from using it. A few questions may at first seem unrelated to government service, but if you have read this book you will quickly make the translation. Baldrige administrators may add a category for government in the future. One advantage to the Baldrige is that it is well documented. There are hundreds of articles, books, seminars, and training courses about the Baldrige process, so you will not want for background and how-to information.

- **Federal government awards programs.** The federal Quality Improvement Prototype award and the President's Award for Quality and Productivity Improvement are good examples of government pro-grams. Today, they are almost identical to the Baldrige. In fact, the federal government may soon start to use the Baldrige award criteria with no modification. There are published profiles of both types of federal award winners, who will willingly talk with you about their experiences.

- **State quality awards programs.** Several states have adapted the Baldrige criteria and system into awards programs for business, government, nonprofit organiza-tions, educational institutions, or all four. These include Connecticut, Maine, New York, Virginia, Minnesota, Michigan, North Carolina, Texas, and California. To obtain information on state awards programs, contact the State Quality Awards Network listed in Appendix A.

- **ISO 9000 quality standards.** If your main business is to provide products and services to other government agencies or to sell them to the public, then these inter-national quality standards may be of interest. We dis-cuss them in detail in Chapter 11.

Conducting a quality management assessment using awards criteria. We suggest a six-step approach, as follows:

- **Preparing.** Brief leaders and help them choose the award program, set the scope of assessment, select the people to be involved, allocate the resources, and make a schedule. Then train data collection and scoring teams and identify data sources. The teams should be managers from the key functions of your organization.

- **Collecting information.** Collection teams assemble the information needed: qualitative data (rules, procedures, policies) and quantitative data (budgets, incidence of poor quality). Before starting, the teams identify the types of trend data and external benchmarks needed for comparison; doing this helps guide the selection of internal measures and how they will be displayed.

- **Comparing.** The teams compare the performance of your processes, products, and services, using trends and external benchmarks.

- **Scoring.** Most awards programs assign points to general areas of quality management. Your scoring team can use benchmark information to help to do this. Even without benchmarks, a well-trained scoring team can arrive at a fair rating. The results make an excellent baseline for future comparisons.

- **Analysis.** The teams review the findings and decide what steps they might take to improve organizational performance.

- **Reporting.** The teams report to leaders on their findings and recommendations.

How long this assessment process takes depends mainly on data availability. Estimate about one to three months, using part-time manager assistance, for a small- to medium-sized organization (up to four thousand personnel). The first time you conduct the process, however, do not let it go on for more than three months. You are much better off doing a partial assessment quickly. Although the resulting score probably will be low, it is an accurate reflection of an organization's status. If an agency had the requisite data and documentation readily at hand, it could do this type of assessment in a couple of weeks. The CEO of one small business wrote a Baldrige-winning application by himself in one weekend, because the data and documentation were ready to go. Just having the information available on demand means that an organization already pays attention to measuring and improving its management practices.

Culture

Culture surveys of your employees and managers are a way to give you feedback on the "soft things" Tom Peters talks about. As the chief of management analysis at the Johnson Space Center in Houston, Texas pointed out, "As engineers, we didn't understand our corporate culture because we didn't have the data. Our surveys helped to give us this data and to point the way for improvements. It identified the parts of our working environment we needed to change."

Selecting a survey. All organizations interviewed for this book that used culture surveys acquired them from outside groups and modified them to fit their needs. Never develop employee questionnaires from scratch. They require careful construction and validation by experienced survey and human resources researchers. If surveying is new to you, consider this advice from the *Federal Total Quality Management Handbook:* "Private contractors often provide an entire service, rather than just the survey tool itself. The ability to purchase the data analysis and interpretation is a distinct advantage over public sector surveys. Analyzing hundreds of survey responses is far more labor intensive than many organizations anticipate. An automated results processing system becomes more valuable as the size of the survey increases. Purchasing a service improves interpretation of results as well. Most contractors have staff experts who assist an organization in determining what the responses indicate. These experts also help define a plan for improvement."

If you already use a survey, make sure that it covers the

types of information needed to show areas of potential improvement to processes, products, services, and customer satisfaction. Surveys that deal only with morale and employee satisfaction issues usually do not do this, but can be modified.

Aggregate figures for your entire organization will not show you where you need to improve; look at individual units and make inter-unit comparisons. You also need to compare your survey's results with those of previous surveys or of similar organizations.

Below, we present an example of a comprehensive culture assessment system, the Culture Climate Survey.

The Culture Climate Survey (CCS). The CCS is Coopers & Lybrand's system. The Air Force Leadership and Management Development Center created the original model for the CCS. It has been validated by experts from Harvard, the Massachusetts Institute of Technology, the University of California-Los Angeles, and industry. About three hundred seventy thousand employees in three hundred government and private organizations have participated in the survey. Their results are stored in a national computer data base and used to make comparisons. To ensure confidentiality, the names of the employees and organizations are not in the data base.

The CCS has about 110 questions answered on a Likert scale of one to seven. You can add or subtract some questions, but core questions remain the same. The survey is given to samples of employees, supervisors, and managers from different work units.

Results are used to answer these questions:

- Do your workers understand what the organization wants from them now that things have changed? Are they getting the kind of training and direction they need? How involved and committed are they? How well do they function as a team?

- Are your supervisors giving the right kind of feedback and evaluating performance in a constructive way? Are they promoting a shared sense of responsibility? What bureaucratic obstacles are holding things back?

- Are your managers giving only lip service to change? Do they have the skills to lead and direct necessary innovation? How customer-oriented are they?

Results analysis begins with external and internal comparisons. You compare your results with selected components from the three hundred seventy thousand-respondent data base, that is, with groups whose characteristics are similar to those in your organization. You can compare results from your clerical workers, engineers, senior managers, and others with those of people in the data base with similar job descriptions. Also, you can make comparisons with the organization in the data base that has the highest positive scores in functional areas similar to yours.

When you make internal comparisons, you often will find that units and groups of managers and employees have different perceptions about your organization's culture, ability to innovate, and other issues important to introducing quality management. This helps you determine where you will focus your attention during planning and implementation.

Taking action. Taking action on CCS or other survey results is a multi-level procedure. During the planning approach discussed in Chapter 5, the data are used to describe organization-wide obstacles and opportunities for introducing new management practices or other changes. They also may cause leaders to focus attention on specific units or types of managers or employees.

During the Process Driven implementation phase, different units and groups review their results in a team setting. They form action plans to overcome any obstacles shown. This procedure is repeated at lower levels until the entire organization is actively pursuing changes that lead to a better working environment.

SELECTING ASSESSMENT METHODS

How you get there depends on where you want to go. Most agencies start out with a compelling need to find out how they should improve. This need may be driven by budget cuts, a crisis in service delivery, merger of several programs, or a management and work force that resist change. Understanding why you want to improve your organization is the first step in choosing an assessment method that will produce information to address that need. The best way to do this is to have executives write down the need and agree on it.

Next, consider your resources. Some methods take longer and cost more than others. Don't be afraid to trade cost for time; the sooner you finish assessing, the sooner you can plan and execute cost-saving improvements. Finally, think hard about what will motivate your organization to take action. If customers are satisfied right now, you may need shock therapy methods like COQ and value analysis. Finally, look at assessment as a long-term activity. Which methods would be best for you to repeat over time? Which lend themselves to the development of an internal performance measurement system suitable for managers and employees?

Here are some general guidelines about choosing methods appropriate to your areas of greatest interest:

- **Customer satisfaction and requirements.** Use customer surveys and focus groups to obtain information on satisfaction levels and requirements. Hold meetings with stakeholders or interest groups who represent your constituency to obtain added information.

- **Cost.** If you must reduce costs, then use COQ or ABC, including value analysis. Also, benchmark your costs against similar operations in the public and private sector.

- **Cycle time.** If you need faster turnaround in delivering products and services, use gap analysis methods to determine your current performance in moving them through your core business processes. Value analysis will give you an idea of the extent of waste in your processes, and waste slows down cycle time.

- **Product or service quality.** Interview customers about specific products or services, then use the measurement system described in Chapter 12 to link their requirements for quality to the processes that make these outputs.

- **Customer service.** Interview customers for their reactions to interactions with customer service personnel, the ease of use of your agency's services, and other issues. Observe these personnel in action to record potential problems that could be solved by process improvement, better training, or other interventions. If you do a culture survey, ask employees what they think of customer service and what they see as the barriers to excellence in this area.

- **Management practices and their results.** Use one of the quality award programs' criteria to guide you in documenting and scoring current management practices.

- **Culture.** Use culture surveys and employee focus groups to gather information for management review.

Any and all of these are good methods, and there are others we have not mentioned. As we said earlier, doing them all at once is too expensive (and probably too confusing) to be worthwhile. In general, you will want to maintain one or two as permanent assessment methods; some form of customer feedback must be one of them. But we encourage you to try all of them over time.

Chapter
5

STRATEGY

■ At the heart of every Improvement Driven Organization is a customer-driven strategic planning system that includes:

- **Long-term goals and strategy**, which show how the organization will transform itself over the next five to ten years to meet changing customer and stakeholder requirements
- **Short-term objectives and plans** that, if obtained, will achieve the long-term goals
- **Vertical and horizontal deployment** of goals and objectives throughout the Improvement Driven Organization
- **Action by everyone**—executives, managers, employees, customers, suppliers, stakeholders, teams, and individuals—to achieve the goals and objectives
- **Monitoring** of progress toward goals
- **Periodic and routine renewal** of the plan to adjust it to an ever-changing environment

■ The strategic plan is an Improvement Driven Organization's chief means of top-down control, steering everyone in the right direction. This guidance helps to empower managers and employees to take charge of the daily operations and their improvement.

If you simply want to write a strategic plan, please refer to some other book. We are going to show you a *system* of long-term planning that stretches from executive offices to front-line employees, that guarantees action and results. This system is more critical to your success than any written plan, because it is at the heart of enabling all the people in your organization to control and improve their processes daily. You can see the system in graphic form in Figure 5-1. In a moment, we will examine its parts, but first, here is some background on strategic planning.

Figure 5-1
Strategic
Planning
Framework

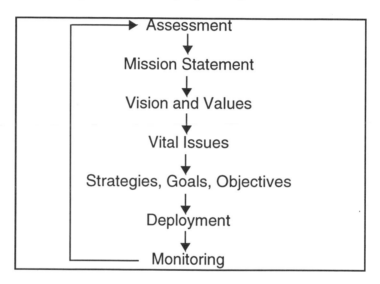

ABOUT STRATEGIC PLANNING

One way to look at a government strategic plan is as a community master plan for future growth and development. The master planning system starts with a vision of what a community wants to become. The vision is based on community values: what is important to citizens, what they want to see promoted and prevented in their neighborhoods. To obtain this information, planners survey citizens and employers, hold community meetings, and consult stakeholders and interest groups. This is exactly what Oregon did for its

Benchmarks program, which guides executive, legislative, and agency decisions about promoting the state's growth and quality of life.

The master plan translates vision and values into community goals for quality of life, environment, education, safety, recreation, and jobs. These documents transform the goals into requirements: plans and maps that show the direction and type of growth that will achieve the vision, the types of construction encouraged in certain places and discouraged in others (zoning, building codes), and the infrastructure that will be needed to support growth (roads, schools, utilities). As a system, it also has rewards and sanctions for adhering to or violating the plan, a process for modifying and updating every part of the system, and a budget for maintaining plans and the planning system.

By publishing and holding public meetings about the master plan, community officials educate people about its purpose and contents. This way, local government managers, developers, employers, and citizens can make informed decisions about investments in the community. By monitoring progress, planners and citizens alike ensure that development is happening as planned.

Similarly, when an agency's leaders plan together, they have to agree on vision, values, and goals. This unity permeates an organization and keeps it going in the right direction. The prime objective of planning is, according to the chief of management analysis at the Johnson Space Center, "to enable all people in an organization to make day-to-day decisions about improvement, equipment, work processes, training, and personnel based on tomorrow's needs as well as today's." To do this, a strategic plan sets forth corporate priorities and strategies—those that apply to the entire organization. It becomes a frame of reference for decision makers, employees, stakeholders, suppliers, and customers.

Strategic Planning in Government

Today, almost every federal organization does some form of strategic planning, as do states and communities that follow the quality management approach. For example, a recent U.S. General Accounting Office report on state governments with results-oriented performance measures noted that the seven most advanced states in this area all had strategic planning systems. The federal Government Performance and Results Act requires strategic planning, while all the awards programs described in the previous chapter emphasize its importance to continuous improvement.

This was not always so, even for public organizations that thought they had advanced well along the road to continuous improvement. Eventually, they realized that efforts to improve operations were rudderless. True, their managers and employees invested heavily in process improvement and achieved solid results. However, improvement in priority areas was not happening as fast as was needed. This was not necessarily a case of rearranging the deck chairs on the Titanic, but when the ship of state began to list, those areas needed concerted, concentrated efforts to right it. That's why these agencies, many of whom won quality awards several years ago, have gone back to the beginning and introduced strategic planning.

Goals of Strategic Plans

Usually, you can divide a government strategic plan into two sets of goals. The first set is directed at achieving specific mission-related targets. These include achieving specific results important to customers and constituents, being prepared to handle customer demands, expanding the scope of operations to include new services, and meeting competitive challenges. Such goals might include the following:

- Increase the number of students who score above average on national tests;

- Develop the capability to support new types of customer requirements, such as for technical support in client/server computer technology; and

- Reduce costs and cycle time in a public service to become competitive with private companies that offer the same service.

Another set of goals may relate to how an organization intends to transform its structure, management style, and culture. These goals may include the following:

- To become an Improvement Driven Organization by introducing the practices described in this book;

- To improve the education, skills, and quality of working life of employees and managers; and

- To develop a work force that operates in self-managed teams.

Both sets of goals fulfill the requirements of being high priority, valuable for guiding manager and employee decisions, and important to customers and stakeholders. Both require significant investment of agency resources and executive time and attention, so they belong in a strategic plan.

Not suitable for a strategic plan are goals that simply say, "We're going to keep doing the same things." This is not to say that you should not continue to do the things that already produce superior results and are likely to continue to be superior in the future. Strategic planning is not about maintenance, though. It is about developing new capabilities, reaching new targets, doing new things. That's why most of an organization's activities are not addressed in a strategic plan. Instead, such plans focus on priorities for change. So one rule of thumb for goals is that they must compel you to do something different.

Strategic Time Frames

Typically, a government organization's strategic plan covers at least a three- to five-year period. That's how long it should take to achieve a goal or to make serious progress toward it. Depending on the nature of your organization's work, this could extend to ten or twenty years. For example, the Oregon Benchmarks program sets some final result targets fifteen years in the future, and at least some agency planning has to stretch over that period. However, the program has interim goals at five- and ten-year intervals. Some municipal governments also have ten- to twenty-year goals, mostly tied to long-term capital investment. Finally, several defense organizations must do forward planning that looks at least a couple of decades ahead.

No matter what the time frame, strategic planning is an iterative process. Thus, the actual "plan" evolves over time; as situations and forecasts change, some goals are achieved, and others set.

Who Does the Planning?

Improvement Driven Organization strategic planning begins with leaders; they cannot delegate this responsibility to anyone. This is top-down planning and control. Yet leaders' planning must reflect the ideas of customers, stakeholders, managers, and employees, who know their requirements or processes better than anyone else. Strategic planning should combine all inputs to create a future-oriented organization with realistic, comprehensive plans.

We call the group of leaders who conduct the top-level planning sessions the executive steering committee. It includes the chief executive and other top executives, supported by staff. As discussed later in this section, other groups may participate in the planning process in several ways.

CONDUCTING STRATEGIC PLANNING

You need a structured planning method such as that shown in Figure 5-1, and you should use trained facilitators. Facilitators help move the meeting along and help the committee handle group dynamics. We advise using outside facilitators for executive planning sessions, because even the most objective internal manager or employee will be quickly overpowered by executives.

Environmental Assessment

This phase begins before the assessment activities discussed in the previous chapter. In a meeting or individually, executives develop sets of questions that will help their organization take stock of itself. Figure 4-1 in the previous chapter is a good example of these questions. The next part of the phase is assessment itself, when you gather and analyze information from customers and other sources, forecast future events, and benchmark your performance against that of other organizations, processes, or standards. The last part is when executives review the information, comparing its findings with the corporate mission statement, which we will discuss in a moment.

Using assessment information, the executives review the strengths, weaknesses, opportunities, and constraints they face in meeting customer expectations if they make no changes to your organization. The product is an agreed-on estimate of the factors that influence the direction of the organization. Although an organization can control some of the factors, seldom will it be able to control the external environment in which it operates. For this reason, an agency must anticipate what the external environment will mean to its chances for success and plan accordingly. If there are alternate futures for the external environment, *scenario building* is a way to explore them.

Scenarios. A scenario is a description of conditions and events that define a possible future operating environment. Because the past often is an inaccurate predictor of the future, it is misleading to simply project past events with straight-line trends and create a plan around the projections. Scenario building allows you to use the results of assessment to create alternate futures that describe factors that must be considered in strategic planning.

Two or three alternative scenarios usually are enough to stimulate thought about how they can be addressed. One uses the most realistic set of assumptions and expectations about the future, given current knowledge. Another presents an extremely pessimistic view of the future, while another may be very optimistic. The latter two help define the outside boundaries of possible realities and alert executives to the need to consider contingency plans.

Discussing the scenarios helps an executive steering committee understand their corporate strengths and weaknesses in the context of potential external events. It also makes those events more vivid and life-like, sparking concern in what might be a complacent group. Combined with other assessment data, mission, and vision, the scenarios become the basis from which evolve strategic goals, objectives, and strategies. Periodically, executives can review the "realistic" scenario to see if it still is accurate. If so, they can then focus attention on monitoring the progress of a strategic plan. If not, the plan itself may have to change. This type of review highlights events over which people responsible for meeting goals have no control and focuses on correcting the goals, not admonishing the people.

Mission Statement

A mission statement summarizes an organization's reason for being. It clarifies an agency's purpose, products, services, and customers served. Many organizations already have a mission statement, but we advise reviewing it in the light of assessment information and these criteria:

- The statement should say why the organization exists.

- It must be consistent with formal requirements and guidance from higher authority.

- It must reflect the needs of an organization's customers and stakeholders, products and services, and factors unique to its business.

- Everyone should be able to understand and relate to the statement, including internal personnel, customers, and suppliers.

The box below shows mission statements from three government organizations. You might assume that your leaders know the mission already, that it is actually written down somewhere, and that it reflects what you are supposed to be doing. Usually, none of these assumptions is correct.

Mission Statements of Government Organizations

Department of Veterans Affairs, Philadelphia, Pennsylvania

Our mission is to accurately and efficiently provide benefits and services to veterans and their families in a manner recognized as fair and responsive.

U.S. Department of Labor, Wage and Hour Division, San Francisco Region

To enforce the nation's employment standards to serve and protect the present and future workers of America.

U.S. Tank-Automotive Research, Development, and Engineering Center, Warren, Michigan

To conduct research, development, and engineering to achieve global superiority in military ground vehicles and to stimulate the transition to a growing, integrated, national industrial capability that provides the most advanced, affordable military systems and the most competitive commercial products.

Vision

Your leaders need to develop a "vision of excellence" to give your organization direction. This vision should be a description of the desired outcome of the strategic plan—the to-be state of your organization at some point in the future. Creating the vision for change—and then empowering your staff to achieve it—is management's most important contribution. Visions are broad, but they point where to go. Developing a vision includes writing specific statements about desired results, which leads to identifying internal and external barriers to success and framing general strategies for overcoming the barriers. All strategic plan actions should contribute to making the vision a reality. Some of the essential elements of a good vision statement are shown in Figure 5-2, and sample vision statements from government are shown in the box on the next page.

Figure 5-2
Elements of
Vision

Joel Barker, futurist	Tom Peters, management expert
Powerful visions are:	Effective visions are:
Leader driven and focus diverse inputs and interests into a coherent statement	Inspiring
Shared and supported by the team, which creates agreement on direction	Clear and challenging, about excellence
Comprehensive, so others know their place in the vision	Those that make sense in the marketplace, and stand the test of time in a turbulent world
Positive and inspiring, a challenge, a stretch	Stable, but constantly changing
	Aimed at empowering your people
	Those that prepare for the future but honor the past

Vision Statements from Government

Department of Veterans Affairs, Philadelphia, Pennsylvania

Our vision is to be the finest provider of services in the VA and to be recognized as such; to have a culture which respects both our customers and our staff and which earns the trust of veterans and their families.

City of Wilmington, North Carolina

We want Wilmington to be recognized as a great place to live, where our customers receive high-quality services, our employees work in an environment of respect and support, our leadership stimulates cooperation and innovation in our community, and our gift to future generations is an even better city than was given to us.

Values

Values are principles and standards that describe how an organization wants to operate and what it stands for. They are meant to guide daily decisions by everyone in an agency. The box below has samples of government statements of values and guiding principles.

Statements of Values and Principles

U.S. Department of Labor, Wage and Hour Division, San Francisco, California

Values

Integrity – We believe in being ethical, keeping commitments, and adhering to the letter and spirit of the law.

Continuous Improvement – We believe that we can always do better, and work toward that end. We achieve this through understanding our processes and making them work better.

People – We believe that each employee is empowered and expected to act, to treat everyone with respect and dignity, and to grow.

Electronic Systems Center, Air Force Materiel Command, Bedford, Massachusetts

Guiding principles

Integrity and mutual trust are the foundation of our interactions.

Constructive communications are the life blood to our success.

We keep our minds open to all people and ideas.

Everyone has the responsibility to challenge business-as-usual.

Our fullest potential is realized through teamwork and cooperation.

Our leaders nurture our people and empower them to excel.

We are dedicated professionals who take pride in our work.

Values and principles must be more than words posted on a bulletin board, though. They are a reflection of how executives intend to lead and manage an organization, and executives must make it clear that they expect the same behavior from managers and employees. Ultimately, executives are accountable for their corporate values and must take as much care in managing them as any other valued asset.

Vital Issues and Key Accomplishments

A strategic plan can dissipate the energy of an organization if it attempts to address every issue identified during assessment. That's why identifying the vital few strategic issues is so important. Strategic issues represent the most critical challenges to fulfilling a mission and reaching a vision. Often, they are interrelated, continuing, and chronic. If you can address and improve the problems or opportunities presented by the issues, then you will reach your goals.

To do this, executives list all issues, then collapse them into common categories. They rank categories by importance to achieving the vision and rate how well they are doing on each. The categories with highest importance but lowest performance scores become the vital issues.

Then, the committee reviews each vital issue to decide what the organization has to do to address it successfully. They develop and reach consensus on "mini-visions" of the to-be state for each issue, set five to ten years in the future. These are called *key accomplishments*. Here are some examples:

- We formed partnerships with education and business to create school/work programs for potential high school dropouts.

- We introduced the technology necessary to make our services available to citizens through on-line access.

- We have the management and accounting information

needed to support sound decisions in improving our processes and services.

- Our personnel use the tools and procedures necessary for continuous improvement.

- We have the right mix of labor skills to do our mission.

Having established where they want to go for each strategic issue, the committee can develop strategies, goals, and objectives for getting there.

Strategies, Goals, and Objectives

In this planning model, a strategy is a narrative description of how an organization will move from the as-is state of today to a future state described in a key accomplishment. A goal is a three- to five-year milestone of the strategy; it is time-bound, specific, and measurable. Objectives are one- to two-year milestones for gaining a goal. They have the same features as goals, with one addition: they specify the manager responsible for their execution. All three elements of the plan specify targeted results or outcomes of taking action, not outputs. For example, an output might be the number of people trained in a job training program. A result or outcome would be the number of trainees who found appropriate jobs and maintained them for one year.

Most strategies address one of the following:

- **Opportunities.** These are the actions that your agency could take—but is not yet taking—that would make it more competitive or yield some other positive result. They include introducing new products, services, processes, markets, technology, and marketing approaches. A strategy addresses how to exploit the most valuable and realistic opportunities.

- **Barriers.** These are things that stand in the way of achieving a key accomplishment. They can include processes that are incapable of meeting future requirements; rising costs of labor or materials; resistance to change by managers, employees, or customers; or a shift in politics that will preclude following normal professional practices. A strategy identifies these barriers and how they can be overcome.

In some cases the leaders will establish the strategies, goals, and objectives themselves. In others, managers will draw up these plans, because lower echelons may have a better idea of how to proceed toward a key accomplishment. The champions and issue management team, discussed shortly, usually do this, or coordinate efforts by departments to flesh out more detailed plans.

Situation Audits

Throughout the planning process, it is important to review both the plan and its needs. We call this a *situation audit*. For example, one or more times during the planning process, executives should discuss the events and the draft products of the effort with managers, employees, customers, and stakeholders. Through this dialogue, executives gain insights and new ideas for strategies. The nature of the dialogue should be, "Here is what we have to do," with the response, "Here is how to do it." Everyone is involved in the process, has a better understanding of its intent, and thus is more committed to it. Also, during the planning process new information needs will surface, requiring further assessment activities to collect more data on the environment, customer requirements, or new technology.

Consensus and Ratification

Our experience is that reaching consensus on a strategic plan is critical to its success. Consensus does not mean the majority rules or that everyone agrees that the chief executive is right. Neither does consensus mean that every member of the executive steering committee is wildly enthusiastic about every strategy, goal, and objective. Instead, it means that everyone agrees to dedicate him- or herself to supporting the entire plan. To gain consensus, often the executives have to negotiate and make compromises, both among themselves and with others.

Finally, executives need to ratify the plan with their signatures and through public discussions with their staffs. This shows their commitment to making the plan a central, guiding part of decision making in all parts of the organization.

DEPLOYING THE PLAN

The vision and plan give your organization direction. Now, leaders must structure the transition from the as-is to the to-be state. This structuring, much harder than preparing the plan, is a daily task for executives and managers.

The more stable your organization, the more difficult it will be for your normal management structure and system to make the complex changes mandated by a good strategic plan—a fact that has more to do with inertia than resistance. Usually you need to create a new system for plan execution. Below, we suggest a system for plan management that is both horizontal and vertical; it is also the beginning of restructuring your organization around core business processes.

Horizontal Deployment

Champions

Horizontal deployment refers to taking cross-functional action. It is necessary because most vital issues, strategies, and goals cut across department and function boundaries. Because no single executive is automatically responsible for a cross-functional issue, each vital issue needs a *champion,*

someone who will take the lead. The champion is the spark
plug, energizing everyone in the organization to help
achieve goals related to a vital issue. He or she should be a
member of the executive steering committee, because this
creates a direct link between corporate planing and corpo-
rate-wide execution. If most of the work on a vital issue
will be done by one of your major units, that unit's leader is
a natural choice to champion the issue.

A champion needs to have these characteristics:

• The power, influence, and resources to get things
  rolling and maintain momentum;

• The respect of the leaders and of the groups that will be
  part of the change; and

• The interpersonal skills needed to persuade people to
  take action.

In other words, you want your best leaders to be your champions. When issue champions do not have these qualities,
their issues remain, but no progress is made.

Figure 5-3
The
Champion is
the Spark
Plug and
Leader of
Improvement
Initiatives

The improvement champion. You also may want an "improvement" champion. Ideally, this will be your chief executive. In reality, the job often goes to the second in command or another leader. For example, Vice President Al Gore is the improvement champion for the federal government. The improvement champion works with the other champions and with functional managers to promote the use of new improvement methods and practices. As with Vice President Gore, this champion must always have direct, regular access to the chief executive.

Issue teams

Each champion needs a small team of people to work on the vital issues. Team members come from the departments, functions, and key processes involved in an issue. This permits cross-functional and inter-unit teamwork. Depending on the issue, you may want to include representatives from unions or your enterprise partners on these teams. Team members need not be assigned full-time to improvement work, but do not hesitate to do this if you need quick action.

The job of issue teams is to make change happen and manage it. They may continue the strategic planning process for their issue, if the executive steering committee assigns them this task. They also make more specific plans, appoint improvement teams, and monitor progress on the key accomplishment. These plans include the following:

- Narrative, schedule, and budget;

- Evaluation criteria for success;

- Investment strategy;

- Cost/benefit analysis;

- Marketing strategy (if appropriate);

- Training requirements and plans for meeting them;

- Recommendations for organization change, if needed; and

- Outline of how change will be managed during improvement.

The organization-wide improvement team

The improvement champion also needs a team and a plan. In many organizations, this team is called the executive quality council and includes executives and senior managers. The council may have its own support staff, which includes managers and employees whose job is to provide training and technical support for the improvement initiative. When continuous improvement becomes the normal way of doing business, this support staff no longer will be necessary.

Preparing vital issues and improvement plans and making them happen is hard, time-consuming work for busy executives and managers. That's why champions must meet regularly with the chief executive to report on the progress of their team's plans. If chief executives delegate this oversight responsibility, they will be sending a signal that strategic planning is not important enough to warrant their personal attention. When that happens, you might as well shelve the strategic plan, because it is dead.

Vertical Deployment

In the book *Managing Change: Opening Organizational Horizons* (co-authored by David Carr, see Appendix A), a consultant reported, "Whenever an executive tells me his vision, whether he wants market dominance or increased market share, quality improvement, or a team-based organization, I ask him if I can do a little experiment. Let me run down the halls, up and down a few floors, and over to the next building and ask 10 to 15 people at random what they are going to have to do differently as a result of this new vision. In about 45 minutes, I find out that most people don't see the impact that a change in vision, strategy, culture, or technology is going to have on them. When I talk with suppliers and customers, I get the same responses: 'We didn't even know they were up to that. We've heard some vague comments, but we haven't seen any change and aren't sure what it will be, if any.'"

As the warden told prisoner Paul Newman in the film *Cool Hand Luke*, what we have here is a failure to communicate. More than that, it is a failure to establish a system that motivates and enables everyone in an organization to help achieve corporate goals and make the transformation into an Improvement Driven Organization. This transformation will not occur if you only use issue champions and teams to work on vital issues. That's because the teams include only a small percentage of your total organization.

Deployment to managers

Issue teams deal mostly with cross-functional improvement. To deploy strategic improvement vertically into departments, our planning system requires managers to prepare plans for how they will contribute to reaching corporate goals and objectives. Some planning systems, most notably Japanese *hoshin* planning or policy deployment, requires every manager to prepare individual plans. Our approach has managers in a department or major work unit become a team.

Besides encouraging teamwork, this approach gives the improvement champion an opportunity to conduct management training in process improvement practices. The training is somewhat similar to the executive steering committee's planning process. It begins with a review of the corporate strategic plan and assessment information. Next, managers identify their internal products, customers, suppliers, and create top-down flow charts of their processes. They use the maps to establish process boundaries and identify links to cross-functional and core business processes. Managers survey or meet with their unit's internal customers and suppliers to learn their requirements and levels of satisfaction. They also gather other assessment information similar to that developed for corporate planning but focused on their own operations.

These management plans concentrate on the three or four activities in a work unit that tie into corporate goals and objectives. Such plans also address nonstrategic improvement issues important to the work unit. In either case, managers set clear, measurable, time-limited objectives for improvement, and monitor progress in achieving them. Work units send their management plans to department executives for approval.

Managers have many options to execute their plans, including:

- Removing barriers to progress identified in the strategic plan and their own plans;

- Forming improvement teams to address specific issues and opportunities within their work units;

- Working with other managers on cross-functional improvement;

- Focusing the improvement efforts of individuals and self-managed teams on specific issues that tie into organizational and unit goals and objectives;

- Educating themselves and employees in improvement tools and methods;

- Soliciting suggestions for improvement from employees, suppliers, and internal customers;

- Developing and installing performance measures that track progress in strategic areas;

- Reading books and professional/technical journals and attending seminars related to corporate vital issues;

- Constantly searching for opportunities to steer budgets, investment, and action toward achieving corporate goals; and

- Forwarding suggestions and insights to vital issues teams and to executives.

Does all this sound like too much planning and improvement and not enough managing of daily operations? In an Improvement Driven Organization, solving systems problems and guiding employees are a manager's most important tasks.

Deployment to workers

As shown above, employees learn about strategic goals from their managers and then begin to work toward them. Also, the executive steering committee promotes awareness and action on the entire strategic plan through the following types of activities:

Corporate communication. Regularly and often, executives must educate the work force about subjects such as mission, vision, values, and strategies by using methods such as these:

- Articles in internal newsletters, videotapes, posters, wallet and desk cards, and other media;

- Work unit meetings in which the chief executive or other executives discuss with employees the meaning and importance of these subjects; and

- Special campaigns aimed at generating suggestions for improvement in specific vital issue areas. They work best when the issue is common to the entire organization, such as reducing cost, cycle time, and errors.

During the campaign, workers receive training in recognizing opportunities for improving the targeted issue.

Reward and recognition. Wise executives will take every opportunity to publicly praise and reward individuals and teams who contribute to corporate goals, successfully master new improvement methods, and personify corporate values. Occasional elaborate ceremonies aren't necessary. An equally powerful effect is when a chief executive routinely drops by offices and shops to shake someone's hand and thank that person.

Monitoring management improvement activities. Executives need to routinely ask managers, "What did you do this week to promote improvement by your staff?" Also, executives should expect documentation from managers on this type of activity.

Deployment to external suppliers and customers

Wise suppliers who know a customer must reduce cycle time or errors will start looking for ways to help. This means you must educate suppliers about your corporate priorities and help them align their services with your goals and new approach to managing operations. Otherwise, suppliers will go about business as usual, and you lose the benefit of their contributions to improvement. Eventually, they lose, too, when you decide to find another supplier better suited to your needs.

Briefing customers and stakeholders on your strategic plan makes sense when there is a direct relationship between their requirements and your goals. This is especially true when you need their cooperation to meet the goal. However, our experience is that most customers and stakeholders are at best only mildly interested, if at all, in your mission, vision, and values or in goals that do not relate to them. Managers in several organizations tell us they are getting a bit annoyed with the parade of public and private suppliers who want to brief them on the nitty-gritty details of their strategic plans. So, keep things pertinent.

OTHER PLANNING ISSUES

Repeating the Planning Cycle

The executive steering committee repeats the planning procedure periodically. Many agencies follow a two-year cycle. Year One is a "ground-up" structuring of the plan. Year Two efforts are less intensive and focus on validating and updating the Year One scenarios, strategies, goals, and objectives. Issue and management plans need to be updated at roughly the same intervals. If you adopt the *hoshin* system of individual manager plans, managers must develop them anew annually.

Training During the Planning Phase

If your organization has never used the strategic planning system we just described, your executives and managers will need training in it before they begin. A good facilitator who knows the system can do this training, both before and during planning sessions—just-in-time training applies to executives and managers, too.

Before you begin executing the plan, your executives may need more in-depth training in the Improvement Driven Organization or other similar approaches to corporate control and improvement. They must learn to use the tools and methods of the approach, both to improve how they manage and to model appropriate behavior. The best outcome of this training will be that your leaders teach these skills to their direct subordinates and lead by example.

Champions and issue management teams need general awareness training followed directly by just-in-time training involving their new work. Your improvement champion will need thorough training in all aspects of the approach and its implementation. You may wish to send him or her to an extended off-site training course for this purpose (just be sure that the course agrees with the approach you take).

Assessment and Planning are Iterative

As you execute your strategic plans, every goal reached creates a change that customers and stakeholders will appreciate. However, this also elevates your goals to higher standards. Reaching them requires more assessment, planning, and execution. That's why assessment and planning must be constantly repeated leadership tasks—it's the only way to stay ahead.

Chapter
6

MANAGING CHANGE

- In government, change has five dimensions: process (or technical), human, organizational, cultural, and political.

- Our experience in working with hundreds of government organizations is that 95 percent of the problem in introducing innovations is due to poor management of the nontechnical dimensions of change.

- Change management is the process of aligning the human, organizational, and cultural dimensions with the process or technical dimension.

- What makes change management different in government is the political dimension; managing it requires collaboration of many outside groups: elected officials, interest groups, and other stakeholders.

Fundamental change is threatening to everyone who works within the system, and the need for real change can be difficult to explain to those outside it. It is critical to develop a comprehensive strategy for building and maintaining support across all lines early on.

> — An Action Agenda to Redesign State Government, National Governors' Association

It is hard for an organization to introduce innovations to its operations, because affected groups—executives, managers, employees, customers, and suppliers—have invested their lives in creating the status quo, and will resist changing it. Consequently, many improvements fail to produce the intended results.

Figure 6-1
The Five
Dimensions
of Process
Change in the
Public Sector

Process or Technical. Process inputs, outputs, and transformation elements, except process operators

Human. Process operators, managers, customers, and suppliers

Organizational. Structure, infrastructure, and management

Cultural. Formal and informal norms, values, and beliefs

Political. Influence of politicians and interest groups

FIVE DIMENSIONS OF PROCESS CHANGE IN THE PUBLIC SECTOR

The key cause for resistance is a myopic, single-dimension focus on the process or technical aspects of innovations, instead of the multi-dimensional focus shown in Figure 6-1. We define the process dimension as follows and will discuss the others shortly.

- **Process or technical.** Changes to the design of a process's inputs, outputs, transformation elements (i.e., equipment, supplies, methods, and environment, but not people), information feedback, and customer, supplier, or stakeholder requirements.

We use the terms *process* and *technical* interchangeably throughout this chapter and the rest of the book in discussions of change management.

Management pioneer Douglas McGregor emphasized the importance of managing the human dimensions of change, as well as the process or technical: "The decision which achieves organization objectives must be (1) technologically sound and (2) carried out by people. If we lose sight of the second requirement or if we assume naively that people can be made to carry out whatever decisions are technically sound—we run the risk of decreasing rather than increasing the effectiveness of the organization." *Our experience in working with hundreds of government organizations is that 95 percent of the problem in introducing innovations is due to poor management of the nonprocess dimensions of change.*

Change Management: The People Dimensions

Change management *is the process of aligning the human, organizational, and cultural elements of an agency with new ways of doing business.* These three dimensions focus mostly on people:

- **Human.** How people accept the new way of working, its effect on their lives, and their capabilities to operate under the new way, including skills, rewards, attitude, and motivation.

- **Organizational.** How an organization is structured to accommodate new ways, including authority levels, lines of communication, and infrastructure.

- **Cultural.** How an organization's culture—its people's norms, values, and beliefs—fosters or hinders change in the right direction.

Organizations find that including these dimensions in a process of *planned change* will produce the desired outcome: new ways of doing business that are both technically sound and that are carried out in the way intended by their people. This process has become increasingly important to all sectors of our economy because we are undergoing major—some would say wrenching—change as the economy adjusts to the Information Age, other new technology, and global competition.

Politics: The Fifth Dimension

In the private sector, management makes most of the operating rules. In government, legislators and council representatives often micromanage routine operations and demand a role in planning special efforts. That's why we added a fifth dimension to managing change in the public sector:

- **Political.** How an agency influences or is influenced by elected and appointed officials to take appropriate action to allow change in the desired direction.

The political dimension can be critical when proposed changes conflict with legislative rules or will affect public employees, suppliers, or customers' benefits. Then, unions, interest groups, and beneficiaries can be powerful political forces that resist or compel positive change. Another aspect of the political dimension is time. Major changes can take years, but agencies are accountable to elected and appointed officials whose tenure may be much shorter. Because of external influence and shifting political leadership, the success of an agency's change initiatives often depends on political activities like forming partnerships with other agencies, elected officials, employees, and outside groups. This is why the change advocate role we discuss later may be more important in the public sector than in industry.

AN OVERVIEW OF CHANGE MANAGEMENT

Under Coopers & Lybrand's change management methodology, organizations work concurrently on all five dimensions of change. The three phases of the Improvement Driven Organization's framework—*Leader Driven, Process Driven,* and *Improvement Driven*—integrate the process or technical dimensions of change with the other four dimensions (shown in Figure 6-2).

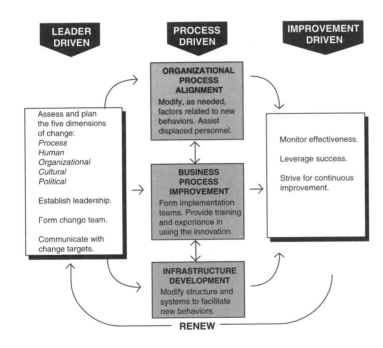

Figure 6-2
Improvement
Driven
Organization
Framework
Applied to
Change
Management

Agencies that are adept at innovating integrate all the dimensions of change; such a holistic (and realistic) approach to managing continuous change is characteristic of an Improvement Driven Organization. Integrating the five dimensions is not easy to do at first, but it soon becomes a habit, reinforced by the ability to transform process and whole organizations when success requires you to change.

KEY CONCEPTS OF CHANGE MANAGEMENT

Change management has its roots in the theories and practices of extension services, organizational development, communication, education, and social sciences, such as sociology, anthropology, and psychology. Although practitioners of change management may differ slightly in their concepts and terminology, they have the following ideas in common:

Innovation

An innovation is something new that people consciously introduce into their processes or systems. Examples of innovations include the following:

- Technology, such as introducing personal computers to an operation or work unit.

- Information, such as providing process operators with feedback on process performance.

- Processes, such as changing an authorization process from serial to parallel approvals.

- Rules, such as authorizing work units to order supplies directly from vendors instead of from a central supply unit.

- Structure, such as introducing self-managed teams.

- Management, such as introducing strategic planning.

- Culture, such as changing leadership styles.

Rarely does an innovation include only one of the factors just listed. More often, innovations are "bundles" of two or more of the factors, which explains the need for careful change management.

Change versus Planned Change

Change is a verb that means the transformation that occurs when shifting from one state to another. Change happens whether or not you manage it, and so it is not always, by itself, a process. In physics, this unplanned change is called entropy, or random transformation that ultimately leads to chaos. When a system undergoes entropy, less and less energy is available for carrying out critical functions; the same is true for an organization that does not manage change. Planned change is the conscious process of developing an innovation along the five dimensions outlined earlier. Change management is planned change, and it is absolutely essential for avoiding chaos and maximizing the controllable energy and resources of a process or organization.

Change Targets

Change targets are the individuals or groups who must accept and use an innovation. They may include managers, employees, suppliers, customers, stakeholders, and others. For minor changes, there may only be one change target, such as a small group of employees who operate a single process. Beyond such simple changes, change targets vary during the life of a change management project. Typically, the progression follows this sequence: executives, middle managers, employees, and suppliers, with each group being won over before going to the next. Customers are change targets when you need to change their behavior to fit into a new process or system; this is especially true for public services in which customers are part of the process of service delivery.

Resistance

Resistance is any overt or covert conduct by people that serves to maintain the status quo when you try to change it. A natural phase in the process of adopting an innovation, resistance is a function of fear and resentment. Much of change management is focused on reducing resistance.

Fear

People do not accept or resist an innovation. Instead, they accept or resist the way that they perceive it will change their lives. For some people, the consequences of an innovation will be positive, and for others, negative. Negative consequences are at the heart of any fear of change you encounter. Whether the fear is real or imagined, you must always treat it as real. A major, visceral fear of all human beings is of loss of control over their lives. Ambiguous situations where people do not know what the future holds for them produce a paralyzing sense of loss of control. This terrifying feeling is most apparent in organizations that mishandle major restructuring and downsizing by keeping plans a secret and drawing out the process. When people are let go after a prolonged bout of such ambiguity, they actually feel a sense of relief because now they can get on with planning and controlling the rest of their lives.

Resentment

People resist change imposed from without. Nobody likes to be ordered to change, especially if the change means radically altering how one's work is done. There can be sound reasons for managers and employees to feel this way. Perhaps, in the past, top management has ordered them to do things that just did not work. Most organizations have a legacy of failed management initiatives such as quality circles, management by objectives, or zero-based budgeting. Remembering these failures, people resist new approaches that they anticipate will have the same results.

Resistance as feedback

When people resist your attempts to introduce an innovation, do not think that they are being unreasonable. Accept their resistance as a natural thing, and learn to interpret it. By resisting change, people give you vital information. They are revealing who they are—their resources and limitations and their attitudes toward new ideas and the sources of those ideas (i.e., you and top management). More specifically, they are telling you what you need to do to introduce change successfully.

Compelling Need

In any technical project, you begin by identifying and defining a problem that must be solved or an opportunity to be gained. In change management, the reason to address the problem or opportunity becomes the *compelling need* for change that must be communicated to everyone. Here are some examples of compelling needs that drove many organizations mentioned in this book to adopt major changes:

- Oregon is not a rich state, yet it has rich natural resources that are a prime part of the quality of life of its citizens. The state's government needed a unifying focus for investing tax dollars in appropriate development and for bringing on board the many private organizations that could make a difference in maintaining and enhancing that quality of life. The Oregon Benchmarks program provides that unifying theme, along with hard, objective measures of progress.

- Deep budget cuts, major Navy fleet reductions, and base closures caused many naval shipyards to restructure their operations and introduce new management processes aimed at continuous improvement.

- The Indianapolis Department of Public Works had to start competing for business with the private sector, but it lacked the means to understand and reduce its costs.

- The Phoenix, Arizona, city council required that user fees finance 100 percent of the resources needed to issue permits, so that many fee-supported offices had to find ways to cut costs or justify fee increases.

Ironically, these examples indicate that the more trouble your organization is in, the more you can expect people to rally around an innovation. But do you have to be on the brink of disaster before people will innovate? Not if you understand about "pain" and communication. Let's start with pain.

Pain. The more pain people feel with the status quo, the more likely they are to accept a reasonable remedy for the pain. A sharp pain, such as a sudden budget cut, is like appendicitis: the sufferer knows it's there and wants to do something about it. Unfortunately, many management ills are more like cancer: people do not realize they have it until too late. In that case, you must plan a careful communication campaign to educate people on the need to change.

Communication. "Selling" the compelling reason to your people, customers, suppliers, and stakeholders is one of the most critical challenges of public sector change management. If they understand why you must introduce an innovation, and if the reason is sound, those who will be affected by change will be more likely to support it.

In summary, the key concepts of change management are the innovation itself, planned change, change targets, resistance, and compelling need. Everything that follows now will describe methods of working with those concepts.

CHANGE MANAGEMENT APPROACHES IN THIS BOOK

Because change management is essential to improvement, we have integrated it into four other improvement approaches discussed in this book: individual suggestion programs, PDCA, reengineering, and cultural change.

Suggestion programs. Most minor changes in an Improvement Driven Organization come from individual or team suggestions. Usually, these changes do not require formal change management action by employees and managers. However, starting and maintaining a high-powered suggestion program such as that discussed in Chapter 12 requires the type of cultural change outlined in Chapter 18.

Plan-Do-Check-Act (PDCA). An Improvement Driven Organization achieves most changes of moderate significance by following PDCA. In Chapter 9, we discuss the role of change management in the Act phase of PDCA, indicating the need to identify and address the people elements of change. Usually, PDCA projects do not need special change management plans such as those discussed below, although managers should be alert to the need for some planning if an improvement will involve significant change. Most innovations of this type are below the political horizon, and they rarely require attention to the political dimension of change.

Business process redesign or reengineering. BPR *always* requires careful change management. Our BreakPoint BPR approach discussed in Chapter 10 shows the key points in a redesign at which you engage in change management.

Cultural change. Attempts to change an organization's culture require careful, meticulous change management. We devote Chapter 18 to applying the Improvement Driven Organization framework to managing cultural change.

The change management framework we will now discuss applies mostly to BPR and other major changes. Successful changes to basic organizational systems also require careful change management. These systems include: performance measurement, accounting, rewards and compensation, and continuous improvement approaches.

A BASIC FRAMEWORK FOR MANAGING CHANGE

Earlier, we gave you a basic Improvement Driven Organization framework for managing change (see Figure 6-2). Now we will discuss each phase of the framework.

The Leader Driven Phase

As you recall from Chapters 4 and 5, the Leader Driven phase is divided into two parts: assessment and planning. Assessment leads to an understanding of what must be done and the reasons for doing it. Planning determines how an innovation will be implemented.

Assessment

During assessment, you collect and analyze information needed to understand the people dimensions of a process change, so that you can develop a sound change management strategy. Also, you begin to win support for the process change from various groups in your organization.

Understand the process dimension of the innovation and of the transformation required for its success. This task starts with a thorough review of the process innovation, including its purpose and methods of operation. Then, consider the process changes needed to operate the innovation: inputs, outputs, transformation, information, and requirements. Next, map the as-is process or processes that will be altered because of the innovation and the to-be process that will result from the innovation. Pay particular attention to where the as-is and to-be processes reside in your organization, because your primary change targets will likely work there. Also, consider how a change in one process will affect others, such as providing different inputs to or requiring different outputs from other processes.

Understand how the process dimension affects the other dimensions. At this early stage, you may not be able to grasp the full extent of how the process dimension interacts with the others. However, you can learn about this interaction by asking the following questions:

- **Human dimension.** Several of these questions may apply to customers and suppliers, as well as to employees and managers.

  - What knowledge, ability, and skills will people need to use, operate, or continuously improve the innovation? How will they obtain new knowledge, ability, and skills?

  - Will new personnel, or new types of personnel, be needed?

  - Will people be displaced by the innovation? Who are they?

- **Organizational dimension**

  - How will people operate under the innovation? As individuals? In teams?

  - What will be the relationship between supervisors and employees? Coach? Inspector? Team leader?

  - What new tasks will managers and supervisors need to do, and what new management skills or abilities will they be required to have?

- **Cultural dimension.** What cultural norms will be affected by the innovation? For example, if the norm in your organization is to adhere rigidly to rules and regulations and avoid risks at any cost, will the innovation require a new norm of questioning rules that do not make sense and taking reasonable risks?

- **Political dimension**

    - Will the innovation cause real or perceived negative consequences to outside groups with strong political influence?

    - Will the innovation's success depend on collaboration with other government entities, customers, or stakeholders?

    - Will the innovation produce results that are in keeping with the expectations of politicians?

Answering questions also helps you identify the members of your change team: the internal and external people and groups who will guide, facilitate, and sustain the new way of doing business.

Form the change team. This team consists of the people who will manage the change and includes the roles of sponsor, agent, and advocate. Usually, you identify people to serve in these roles during the Leader Driven phase after, for example, answering the just-listed questions. Although all three roles are important to planned change, we find that the sponsor role is most critical.

Change sponsors are the individuals or groups who lead the way to change. They have *power,* or the organizational position and influence to champion and legitimize an innovation. A work unit's manager may be the change sponsor for an innovation within that unit, while presidents, governors, mayors, and other elected executives are the key sponsors for government-wide reforms. The sponsor must have a personal stake in an innovation's success that commits him or her to invest the time, energy, and political capital that may be needed for change.

In some cases, a change management project starts out with an initiating sponsor, such as a chief executive who starts the ball rolling by appointing members of the change team and giving them their mandate and his or her guaranteed support. Then, one or more *sustaining sponsors* take over the daily work of leading the change initiative. A good example of this is President Bill Clinton, the initiating sponsor of the federal National Performance Review, and Vice President Al Gore, who is the very active sustaining sponsor and who has been joined in this role by many Cabinet-level secretaries.

Change advocates are individuals or groups who want to see an innovation succeed but do not have the power to make the change happen. Often, change advocates stimulate an organization to initiate an innovation. They may include legislators, advisory groups, internal managers or employees, external customers, regulatory groups, and other stakeholders. Effective change advocates may provide information and technical assistance, testify to elected officials about the effectiveness of an innovation and an agency's need for resources to introduce it, or prod recalcitrant agency executives to speed up and improve their progress in adopting an innovation.

Change agents are the individuals or groups, mostly middle managers, who do the detailed work of developing and introducing an innovation. Usually, they are identified in the Leader Driven phase and go into action during the Process Driven phase. Often, they are middle managers responsible for such tasks as working with technical staff to identify an innovation's nontechnical dimensions, collecting assessment information, and developing communication strategies and tactics. Change agents work directly with change targets and act as their advocates to top management.

External change agents can be professional consultants who specialize in change management or special representatives from another part of a government who provide the same service. For example, the Federal Quality Institute (FQI) is a government office that helps arrange for external change agents to assist federal agencies that are introducing quality management. Some are professional consultants (we fall into this category), and others are government executives on loan to the FQI.

Determine the readiness of people for change. A group's *readiness for change* relates to their willingness and ability to adopt a specific innovation. Several factors determine readiness. First, for example, most organizations have recently gone through many changes, as they apply new technologies, enter the Information Age, and face tougher competition. Many people are exhausted from all these changes and not eager for more. Second, people may be preoccupied with other issues. For example, one of our clients who wanted to introduce ABC had to first clear the air about an impending layoff. Until managers and employees could reconcile themselves with the layoff, they were in no mood to work on ABC. Third, employees, customers, and stakeholders may distrust management's ability and intentions. Often, this is a legacy of past mishandling of major changes.

- **Probing for reasons.** Change sponsors and change agents learn about readiness from the change targets. However, simply asking, "Are you ready for this innovation?" is not enough. Probes are needed, such as:

  - Do you think the existing process or system is adequate for your needs? If so, why? If not, why not?

  - If you already know there is a problem with the existing system, did you ever try to do anything about it? If so, what happened, and why? If not, why not?

  - Do you need the type of added capability the innovation will give you? If so, what would you, personally, do with it? If you don't need it, why not?

- Do you see any barriers or problems in introducing the innovation and using it to do your work? What would be the cause of those barriers or problems? How and why did they come to exist? Why do you think they have not already been removed?

- What would help you use the innovation? Why would this help? Who are you most likely to turn to for this help, and why?

- Do you see yourself as gaining or losing any personal benefit under the innovation? If so, why? If not, why not?

By asking questions like these, you avoid what Harvard professor Chris Argyris calls single-loop learning. This happens when you ask a one-dimensional question (Are you ready for the innovation?) that elicits a one-dimensional answer (yes, no, maybe). Double-loop learning asks follow-up questions about initial answers and probes the reasons and motives behind the answers. Also, asking about personal behavior forces individuals to reflect on their own responsibility for the success or failure of innovation.

How to ask the questions. In some cases, the just-listed questions can be asked in an informal conversation with change targets. It is important to talk with opinion leaders, the people to whom others go for advice about the worth of an innovation. Whether the opinion leader is a manager or employee, he or she generally has been around for many years and is recognized as having excellent technical competency and, above all else, wisdom. Opinion leaders also are ideal candidates for teams you form to introduce an innovation.

If the change is going to be major and affect many people, you may want to use the focus group and survey methods we discussed in Chapter 4 to obtain information from change targets, including customers and your work force.

For a change that involves the political dimension, checking with oversight or advisory groups and even holding public hearings may be advisable.

Analyze assessment information. Analyzing for change management begins by listing all issues discovered during assessment, collapsing the issues into categories, and then classifying them into a useful framework. For example, complaints that process operators have about the as-is system can be categorized as "pains," while their concerns about job displacement can be categorized as "fears." It is possible to rate the strength of these pains, concerns, and other issues if you have used methods such as the Culture Climate Survey discussed in Chapter 4.

Using tree diagrams like those discussed in Chapter 8, you can analyze the root causes of issues. Tree diagrams are graphic tools that start with an outcome, such as fear of new ways of working, and, through an analysis of sequences of cause-and-effect relationships, lead you to understand the underlying cause of that fear.

Force field analysis provides a useful framework for classifying the issues you identify. In this analysis, you write the forces or issues for and against an innovation. We discuss force field analysis in detail in Chapter 8 on process improvement tools. Figure 6-3 shows an example, with the forces for change listed in the left column and forces against in the right column. During the Leader Driven phase, you develop strategies that emphasize the positive forces and eliminate or minimize the negative forces.

Figure 6-3 Force Field Analysis Applied to an Example Innovation

Dimension	Forces for the Innovation— Take advantage of these:	Forces Against the Innovation— Eliminate or minimize these:
Process or Technical	The innovation requires only minor changes in the existing procedures of most of the processes it affects.	A few processes will have to make major changes to their procedures, and their operators may resist the changes.
Human	The innovation will remove several "pains" that were mentioned by managers and employees during assessment.	Fewer quality control inspectors will be needed, resulting in displacement of some inspectors, which will create fear among the inspectors.
Organizational	The innovation will not require significant structural change.	The innovation requires much more cross-functional teamwork than is usually found in our organization.
Cultural	It is a high-tech innovation that fits our cultural value of being on the leading edge of technology.	Managers will have to turn over daily control of routine operations to employees, and some may see this as a threat to their power.
Political	The innovation is aligned with legislative intent to reduce costs in government operations.	The innovation will require a major change to a rule that some legislators feel is important.

Communicate about the innovation during assessment.
Your careful assessment has not gone unnoticed. The
rumor mill may already be grinding out misinformation
about "What will happen to me?"—the most frequently
asked question in today's turbulent work environment. To
quiet the rumors and start selling the compelling need to
your change targets, use newsletters, memos, and discussions with them to cover the following topics:

- Why we need the innovation to accomplish our mission
  and satisfy our customers;

- How it will change the way we work;

- Who will need to change, and in what ways;

- How the innovation will affect job security; and

- The milestones and time frame for introducing the innovation.

Invite response, and make an iron-clad rule to get back to
people within twenty-four hours, even if only to say that
you are working on a reply. You will win people over with
this respect for their opinions, including those who are
ambivalent or initially negative about an innovation.

Planning

The key objectives of planning are to develop the change
management plan, remove barriers, assign roles, and establish a means of monitoring progress.

The change management plan. A change management
plan spells out the actions management will take to introduce, sustain, and continuously improve an innovation during the Process and Improvement Driven phases. The plan
addresses all or most of the topics listed below.

- **Training.** Improvement Driven Organizations devote more resources to formal training than do traditional organizations. As Deming said, if you rely on informal training, you always end up with nonstandard operations, which tend to deliver poorer quality at higher cost. Formal training plans always state behavioral objectives for an innovation: the precise types of actions and behaviors people will use when working in or with the innovation. Most organizations have technical training systems that translate these objectives into curricula and training courses. Work with your training specialists to develop the appropriate training plan for an innovation, and make sure the plan is followed.

- **Planning for sustained use of the innovation.** Most training systems overlook critical behaviors needed to sustain the innovation. For example, what if an innovation's success depends on managers regularly reviewing a performance measurement report? Technical training may have shown them how to interpret the report, but how can you make sure that they actually read and act on it? Some methods might include the following:

  - Include a discussion of the report on management meeting agendas;

  - Have superiors read the report, too, and ask managers about it;

  - Tie promotion and compensation to superior results on the performance measurements;

  - Give special recognition to managers who regularly improve their measures using the desired methods and techniques; and

  - Schedule periodic assessments of the use and benefit of the report, to ensure that it and all the actions just described do not become meaningless ritual.

By asking a critical question about each behavioral objective—"How can we make sure it happens now and in the long run?"—change agents develop strong foundations for innovations. Including the answers in the overall process and change management plan leads to institutionalizing desired behavior: it becomes part of the normal way of doing business.

- **Communication.** You must continually communicate with change targets about the innovation during its implementation, including progress, issues raised by the targets, and management response to those issues.

- **Pilot tests and demonstrations.** If appropriate, you may want to conduct pilot tests or demonstrations of the innovation, which allow change targets to watch it in action. This helps calm concerns about the technical difficulties of using an innovation and promotes acceptance because people can readily see its benefits.

- **Displacement.** If people are going to be displaced by an innovation, you need to plan for either transferring them to other parts of your organization or government or providing assistance if they are to be let go. Actions in this area can include retraining for new positions, early retirement packages or attractive separation benefits, out-placement assistance, and personal and family counseling. For example, we helped one government organization establish a temporary labor pool for 450 displaced employees, where they were assigned short-term jobs as needed and received out-placement assistance. During the year they were permitted in the pool, nearly all employees found permanent positions inside or outside the organization. This type of plan also helps to avoid "bumping," when senior employees take over the jobs of junior employees even if the juniors are excellent and the seniors are less qualified.

Displacement plans can become political issues because of

government-wide civil service rules and union pressure. It is wise to plan early on how you will address these issues by consulting with legislators, stakeholders, and union representatives.

- **Survivor assistance.** An innovation such as privatizing an in-house operation can result in major layoffs. The people who remain often face psychological problems, such as survivor guilt—they are collecting pay checks while former colleagues are out of work. According to researchers at the University of Michigan (Kim Cameron, Sarah Freeman, and Aneil Mishra), the survivors also feel that the attributes traditionally valued in good employees, such as loyalty, hard work, and personal competence, no longer count in their organizations, because people with these qualities were laid off anyway. The researchers identified several ways that organizations could help people deal with survivor guilt, including:

    - Special efforts by management to communicate the reasons and circumstances of the layoffs, including frequent formal and informal meetings with employees and managers;

    - Management's reaffirmation of the value it places on remaining employees, and assurances that neither the survivors nor the displaced were the cause of the layoffs;

    - Involving employees slated to remain in the organization in the front-end planning of new operations; and

    - Special events to mark the end of the old era and the beginning of the new.

Let's be frank about displacement and survivor assistance. Most of the working world—and we mean world-wide—is undergoing major transformation, and whole categories of managers and employees have been and will continue to be displaced. Even if you do not have to deal with layoffs in your first change management initiative, eventually you will. That's why you need excellent forward planning at handling displacement and survivor assistance issues.

- **Rewards and compensation.** If the innovation requires totally new ways of working, then you may need to alter reward and compensation systems to reinforce these new behaviors. For example, what if the innovation is a self-managed team system such as that used by the Oregon Department of Transportation (see Chapter 2)? If the existing reward and compensation system puts a premium on individual performance only, you may need to tie bonuses to team performance. Also, you might tie salaries to individual contributions to the team, such as paying extra for workers who cross-train in skills used by other team members, because this increases team flexibility.

  In another example, a private company evaluated its customer service workers on the average time they spent answering customer service telephone queries. Customers, the company discovered, had to call several times to solve a single problem. When the company introduced a case management system in which customers dealt with one employee, it started evaluating the number of queries answered in full. The calls were longer but fewer, which increased customer satisfaction.

  Sanctions are the reverse of rewards: they punish undesired behavior. Sanctions can be as mild as an executive refusing to listen a manager's proposal for an innovation until the manager addresses change management issues. They can be as strong as firing or reassigning a manager who balks at forming employee teams in his or her work unit. If you identify undesired behavior, you may need to develop sanctions against it.

Tasks, assignments, schedules, milestones, and budget.
A change management plan should be part of the technical
plan to introduce an innovation, so it requires written tasks,
people who are responsible for the tasks, a schedule, milestones, and a budget. Without these items, the change management plan cannot be communicated or implemented,
much less monitored for progress. Worse, without specific
assignments, no one can be held accountable for the change
management tasks.

Removing barriers. Barriers are technical and social, formal and informal road blocks that prevent or inhibit change
targets from adopting desired behaviors. During the Leader
Driven phase, you identify and remove these barriers, or at
least minimize their effect on the innovation.

Process barriers include outmoded rules, regulations, and
policies. For example, some years ago a Ford Motor
Company executive sent a memo to managers telling them
to, whenever possible, change from short-term to long-term
contracts with suppliers. However, he forgot to eliminate a
policy that required a detailed written justification for long-
term contracts. Faced with a mountain of new paperwork,
the managers stuck with short-term contracts. The policy
was a process barrier to the innovation of long-term contracts. (When he discovered the problem, the executive
switched the policy to require written justification for short-
term contracts and got the results he wanted. This action
was a sanction against short-term contracts.)

Behavioral barriers include all the issues raised earlier
about resistance, fear, and culture. Unlike many process
methods, they cannot be overcome simply by executive
order. Pronouncements that an "undesired" behavior is no
longer, well, "desired" are not credible until executives and
managers begin modeling the new behavior. Also, these
leaders must reward the new way among other managers
and employees and penalize those who do not follow it.

The Process Driven Phase

The prime objectives of the Process Driven phase are to maximize involvement, stay flexible, carry out the change management plan, and stabilize the innovation.

Involve change targets in implementing the innovation. Whenever possible, involve change targets in introducing innovations that will affect them. You can do this by including change targets on implementation teams and by acting on other change targets' comments, complaints, and suggestions for introducing the innovation.

During this phase, change agents become the most important change team members. They meet frequently with the technical members of the innovation team and work with change targets to help them adopt new methods and behaviors. The greater the change, the more time change agents must devote to the Process Driven phase, so be sure that they have sufficient relief from normal duties to do their innovation work.

Implement the change management plan. The more an innovation changes basic operations, the more concerned executives must be with progress in the change management plan. A small technical problem can be fixed, but failure to do even a small task in change management can cause major harm to a project (Ford's change to long-term contracts is a good example). That's one reason why progress in the change management plan should stay ahead of the process or the technical change plan's execution. Being ahead of the game ensures that when the process innovation finally arrives in a work unit, managers and employees are prepared for it.

Stay flexible. Technical planners like to think that they can anticipate every event in introducing an innovation. That's impossible with change management. Resistance *is* going to happen, and sometimes it will come in unexpected forms and from people you thought were not even concerned about the change. Keeping communications lines open with everyone is the best way to at least get early warning about problems.

In practice, good communication can mean many late night meetings of the change team, as they develop ways to address the problems. Again, including change targets and stakeholders in the meetings helps promote solutions. You may find that you have to modify the innovation to meet the concerns raised; don't hesitate to do this if it will not harm the effectiveness of the innovation.

Stabilize the innovation. Any complex innovation is bound to have a few technical glitches, both during its introduction and immediately afterwards. These situations are ideal opportunities to form small, glitch-fixing teams made up of the managers and employees working with the innovation. Also, you must take care that people start out on the right foot when they use the innovation, which is a prime reason for conducting formal training and monitoring the results.

Communicate with change advocates. Stay in touch with political allies and other change advocates during this phase, and keep them informed of progress and problems. Ask for their help when you need it, and praise their support whenever possible.

The Improvement Driven Phase

Due to entropy, an unmonitored, unmanaged innovation soon decays in its performance, or it develops a tendency to grow, spread, and mutate. Instead of trying to maintain the status quo, however, an Improvement Driven Organization builds continuous improvement into an innovation, so that both the innovation and the organization are constantly renewed.

Continuous improvement of the innovation. There are process performance measures that can be built into an innovation to provide continuous feedback on its effectiveness. They focus on quality, cost, cycle time, and customer service, and we discuss these measures in detail in Chapters 8, 12, and 13. Part of change management is to ensure that these measures are built into the innovation and that the information gained from them is available to process operators. The operators also must be trained and enabled to use the information for process improvement. Such use of information by operators may itself be an innovation as may be management's interest in having workers act to enhance their operations.

Thus, no change management plan or project is complete until it addresses how an innovation will be continuously improved. Although individual process improvements are usually technical, the *process* of process improvement is a function of the human, organizational, and cultural dimensions of change. Chapters 7 through 19 discuss the methods for putting these dimensions into practice.

Renewing the organization. As an agency or government becomes better at managing the process and human aspects of innovating, more of its internal managers and employees become change advocates. When a certain percentage of personnel (sometimes as few as one in ten) become advocates, this shift in attitude creates a critical mass of acceptance for most planned change. Such advocacy helps to make an organization resilient, or capable of rapidly adjusting to changes in its environment.

Improvement Driven Organizations promote resilience in three ways. First, they involve as many people as possible in innovation projects, because this participation imparts the principles and methods of planned change, including change management. The more of its people who can apply planned change, the more an organization becomes capable of changing.

Second, they improve the process of planned change and, by doing so, develop a resilient culture, which we talk about in Chapter 18. Such a culture accepts change as a normal part of doing business.

Third, an Improvement Driven Organization consciously uses every innovation project to increase resilience of processes and their operators. Thus, the success of an innovation initiative should be measured by how it (1) achieves its specific objectives, (2) creates resilience in the processes that are changed, and (3) contributes to the total resiliency of the organization.

PART III

THE PROCESS DRIVEN PHASE

Chapter
7

SELECTING THE RIGHT
IMPROVEMENT APPROACH

■ There are many approaches to improving processes; success depends on choosing the right one for a specific situation. In broad categories, the alternatives include quick fixes, gradual improvement, design/redesign, privatizing, and eliminating.

■ Before choosing an approach, you must understand the different points at which a process or system can be improved and the customer-driven objectives for improving it.

■ Which approach to use also is determined by the following factors:

- Strategic goals
- Understanding of current process configuration and levels of performance
- Capability of a process to perform at the required level
- The value of a process to an organization and its operations
- Benchmarks that compare a process's performance with that of best-in-class processes that fulfill similar purposes

■ No matter what approach is selected, it should be followed by continuous improvement.

When you only have a hammer, everything looks like a nail.

— Anonymous

It's a major problem: people learn one improvement method, then apply it to every problem and opportunity. Here, in broad strokes, are the results of forty years of this misguided practice:

- Since the 1960s, organizations have been using information technology to automate tasks that should not have existed in the first place. The result, as we explain later in this book, is like paving the meandering cow paths in a pasture.

- Having learned about employee quality circles and their role in gradual improvement, many organizations in the 1970s and 1980s tried to apply the circles in the wrong way to totally inappropriate problems. The only thing gradual about this was the demise of almost all quality circles.

- In the early 1990s, organizations rushed to reengineer their way out every conceivable difficulty, even those they just imagined. Most early projects that followed the lead of Michael Hammer and James Champy's best-selling book, *Reengineering the Corporation,* have failed, according to all surveys on the subject. Both authors now admit that there were some significant shortcomings in their original approach, but we believe that many failures came from using reengineering when another approach would have been more appropriate.

- As we write this book, many legislators, economists, and pundits believe that privatizing government services is the taxpayers' panacea. As some governments have learned, though, privatizing does not guarantee improvement and cost savings—contractors can end up costing taxpayers much more than public employees.

Also, some agencies mistakenly privatize the very processes that define them to customers and citizens; without such processes, there is no longer a reason for these agencies.

The only true thing you can say about all of these improvement methods is that each is right for some types of problems, opportunities, and organizations, but none is appropriate in every case. Given the many alternative approaches to improvement we present in the next several chapters, which will be best for you to use in a particular process, problem, time, or place, and how do you apply them comprehensively? In this chapter, we provide you with guidelines.

WHAT GETS IMPROVED, AND WHY

Depending on the problem or opportunity, a process can be improved through some change in the process itself or through changes in the larger system in which it exists. The operative word is change: something must be done differently for the process to improve. The following examples show how to make improvements at ten different points in a process or system. Chapter 3 outlined these points.

1. Inputs and suppliers	6. Environment
2. People	7. Outputs
3. Equipment	8. Internal administrative or support functions
4. Methods	9. Other external groups
5. Materials	10. Feedback

Figure 7-1
Ten Points of Process Improvement

Inputs and Suppliers

Changing inputs may mean finding better raw materials or components for an industrial process, more accurate work orders in a service process, or more reliable performance reports for an administrative process. It may also include making sure that the right amount of material or information is delivered on time.

Altering the packaging of input can bring improvements. For decades, lawyers wrote court documents on legal-sized paper. When federal courts mandated letter-sized paper a few years ago, they reduced the need for separate legal-sized file cabinets and folders. This change saves money for the courts, lawyers, and everyone else in the country.

Changing suppliers may produce better inputs, but only if the customer for the inputs specifies and enforces accurate requirements. Altering the relationship between supplier and customer from one of distrust to a compatible partnership in planning and delivering inputs is another way of improving this part of a process (See Chapter 11 on vendor partnerships).

Changing inputs can also involve customers. The external customers of the U.S. Patent and Trademark Office include people who apply for patents. Clerks were spending hundreds of hours a month matching up different parts of patent application documents. An improvement team of clerks recommended having the applicants put their application numbers on documents they submit after their original applications. This idea was carried out, there were no complaints from applicants, and now fewer than a dozen documents have to be matched each month.

Transformation

Process transformation components are people, equipment, methods, materials, and environment. Changes in each of these process components are possible.

People

The Navy Public Works Center in Norfolk, Virginia reorganized its single-trade maintenance crews into cross-trained, multi-trade crews with plumbing, carpentry, electrical, and other skills. No more time is wasted waiting for one single-trade crew to finish before another can begin. This change also eliminated the need for job coordinators and some third-level supervisors. Most organizations that use process management eventually reorganize their work forces into fewer job classifications and more cross-trained personnel, a structure that allows for increased flexibility, especially in cross-functional processes.

Equipment

The Key Team, made up of guards in the Volusia County, Florida correctional facility, documented that the use of radios for officer-to-officer communications meant that inmates could eavesdrop on the conversations. A security breach could result. Based on team recommendations, the facility installed telephones at key locations, including the watchtowers, dormitories, and central control areas.

Methods

An improvement team at the Ogden, Utah IRS Service Center found that the method that the center used to put addresses on taxpayer notices caused Postal Service equipment to misread the information. The team recommended changing these procedures, and the change decreased the volume of undelivered mail.

Materials

An improvement team of maintenance workers at the Volusia County public airport looked for ways to speed up the cleaning of aircraft parking areas. Team research identified a degreaser that is more effective and faster in removing oil spills than the one the airport had been using.

Environment

As you recall, environment can include the physical location of a process. The Defense Industrial Supply Center transferred many of its financial analysts from a central office to internal customer divisions. The analysts now work closely with customers to identify projects that lead to cost savings.

Outputs

Altering the form or distribution of an output may also cause improvements. An example of such a change would be giving customers draft documents on computer disk as well as hard copy. When most of their potential vendors have computers and modems, many agencies advertise requests for bids via electronic bulletin boards as well as through paper notices. Vendors can check the bulletin board daily and download entire requirements packages from it. This cuts lead times, mailing costs, and errors inherent in paper communications.

Internal Administrative or Support Functions

Improving internal administrative and support functions often has a direct effect on line function processes. Improvements may mean eliminating unnecessary reports from a line function or improving a support function process. Engineering departments at one government agency had a shortage of qualified workers, although positions were available. Process improvements in the personnel office shortened the length of time needed to hire an engineer from one hundred seventy-eight to forty-five days.

Other External Groups

Government agencies must comply with rules formulated and administered by other agencies. Often these rules are seen as immutable, particularly by field operations staffs.

In fact, the external agencies will usually accept reasonable arguments for change, particularly in today's push for improved public sector performance.

For example, Navy public works centers had streamlined their administrative and support functions by eliminating unnecessary work, which caused several hundred people to lose their positions. The centers wanted to place these people on temporary assignments in line functions, where more staff were needed, and gradually train and transfer them to permanent line positions, but civil service rules would not allow temporary assignments for more than one hundred twenty days. The centers persuaded the U.S. Office of Personnel Management to extend this period to one year, as an experiment with a special transition staffing pool to which they assigned the employees. Within the year, nearly all workers found permanent jobs in the centers or elsewhere. While waiting, they did needed work. The experiment led to a permanent rule change, so that this approach is now used in many federal organizations.

Feedback

Improving feedback is key to process improvement. When organizations aggressively seek internal and external customer and supplier complaints and suggestions for improvement, they are improving feedback.

Another form of feedback is performance measurement information. The procurement chief at the Crane Naval Weapons Support Center in Indiana gave an example of this form of feedback: "We had an extensive system for measuring performance, but most of the information flowed upstairs. This was like police having radar guns and cars not having speedometers. We decided to stop worrying so much about the bosses' numbers and focus on giving buyers the feedback they need to do their jobs right. Doing this allowed buyers to spot and solve problems early, as well as manage their work-in-progress better."

THE SEVEN OBJECTIVES OF PROCESS IMPROVEMENT

Figure 7-2 lists seven expectations of customers and measurement indicators for each. These are the objectives of process improvement. Note that each relates to the *ability* of the process to meet customer expectations, not necessarily to physical output.

Figure 7-2
The Seven
Objectives of
Process
Improvement

	Expectation	Indicator
1.	"Rightness" of output	Feedback from customers that product or service is the right type for their needs
2.	Consistency of output	Variation in characteristics of output, such as some of those listed in items 3 through 7 below
3.	Timely delivery of output	Degree of variation from normal, average, or scheduled delivery time
4.	Appropriate cost, or resources required for the process	Degree of variation from normal, average, or scheduled cost, time, or materials required to produce, physical space required, etc.
5.	The safety and well-being of those involved in the process	Accident rates; morale and comfort as measured by interviews, surveys, or complaints
6.	Effect of the process itself on society and the environment	Risk of danger, poll of neighbors, measurement of pollutants
7.	Customer perceptions of how work is done	Customers' feedback on confidence they have in processes or outputs, and their view of how service gets delivered

Rightness of Output

By now you have heard the phrase, "Do it right the first time." It is possible to do it right the first time, but you may be doing the wrong thing. So the first question to ask in looking at any process is whether the output is right for the customer. If it is not, then all decisions about improvement are grounded on sand.

For example, if no one needs the output of a process, why do it? One government manager noted: "We used to distribute stacks and stacks of computer reports throughout the organization. Then we found out that half the people receiving these reports threw them away, and the other half didn't use them but kept them 'just in case.' We don't have as many reports anymore."

Output may be generally of the right type, but not be totally right for the customer. The example of the veterans' loan applications in Chapter 3 is an example of internal requirements not being suitable for customers.

Rightness of output is also determined by the core mission of an organization. When Volusia County public safety department deputies respond to non-police-related calls, they duplicate the services of other agencies and reduce the time available for police priorities. The department's SALT III improvement team examined the problem and recommended emphasizing non-deputy responses to nine categories of calls for service. The team then met with local service providers to ensure that they, not officers, would handle the calls.

In the long term, strategic planning determines the right things for an organization to do to satisfy customer expectations. Thus, strategic plans focus on future customer requirements and how to develop new capabilities to meet them.

Consistency of Output

Keeping output consistent makes sense, but it is one of the more difficult concepts for people new to process management. Consistency has obvious benefits. If you are buying a part for your car, you want it to fit exactly. If you are paying bills, you want all the checks to go out exactly on time: if they are late, you will have penalties; if they are early, you lose interest payments at the bank.

Nothing is absolutely consistent; everything varies at least a little bit. But even a minor amount of variation can lead to at least some extra cost, defective products, late deliveries, and so on, so an important objective of process control is to produce consistent output.

Consistency does not mean that you do everything perfectly or that you are meeting any of the other categories of customer expectations. In fact, you can produce the wrong thing consistently or make the same mistake over and over again. Consistency simply means that output always has the same characteristics and that processes operate the same way each time they produce output. We will discuss measuring consistency and diagnosing reasons that it varies in the next chapter.

Timely Delivery

Everyone understands the need to deliver output on time to external customers, but most people give themselves a little slack when it comes to internal customers. This is a major cause of cost overruns in many agencies, because the internal customer's meter is running during this delay. Late deliveries cause an internal customer to do expensive workarounds and to issue poor output.

Late delivery also encourages customers to stockpile expensive parts and supplies, because they cannot depend on their suppliers to deliver these when needed. This practice, in turn, takes up space and ties up capital—and both are scarce resources. How serious can this be? In one government facility, we found $150 million in unrecorded inventory of components and supplies, in part because unneeded items were squirreled away instead of being returned to the supply system. Why? The internal customers could not depend on the supply system to deliver these items when they were needed. Multiplied across all government agencies, the problem runs into billions of dollars.

Should you be pleased when something is delivered ahead of schedule? Not necessarily, because early delivery can cause its own problems. For example, resources used to produce and deliver some products and services ahead of schedule may have been needed to prevent others from being late.

Early delivery also may force customers to devote extra storage space to products that arrive before they are needed. For example, in the past many manufacturers stockpiled raw materials and parts in warehouses, made their products in large lots in long, uninterrupted production runs, and stored finished goods in warehouses until customers ordered them. This approach tied up scarce capital in inventory and storage and often resulted in products sitting unsold in warehouses. Today, some factories use a form of process management called Just-In-Time (JIT), which makes products in small lots in short production runs to meet immediate customer orders. Raw materials and parts often are delivered daily in quantities that meet one day's production needs and go directly to the factory floor, not to a warehouse. Finished products move from the assembly line to a loading dock and are shipped immediately to customers. The savings to manufacturers and their customers is enormous.

In process management the performance measure of timely delivery is its variation from the planned dates of delivery. The goal for delivery is "just-in-time": all inputs to a process should arrive exactly when scheduled.

Appropriate Cost

Improvement in this area is aimed at maximizing the value of output while minimizing costs. Often costs can be reduced by technology, by using a new type of input, or even by buying a product or service instead of producing it internally. Technology also may increase the value of an output by improving precision and decreasing errors. These are the easy ways to reduce cost, though. Organizations that have concentrated improvement projects on them while ignoring everything else run into major problems.

The harder way to lower costs requires the removal of non-value added steps and the introduction of new value added steps. Typical non-value added steps that increase costs include:

Unnecessary sign-offs and approvals: According to a manager at the Johnson Space Center, "When people want something signed off on, they may not understand the time this might require. That's why some organizations get things done in days, while others need weeks."

Unnecessary paperwork and documentation: If nobody needs them, they do not add value.

Inspection: Inspecting output for errors does not add value to it.

Reworking: Doing something over because it was not done right the first time does not add value to output.

Storage: The only things that get better when stored are wine, whiskey, and fruitcakes. The time, money, and space needed to store any amount of input or output beyond what is needed immediately do not add value.

Transportation: Any engineer will tell you that no value is added to a product by moving it from one point to the next in an assembly line. Likewise, a document does not necessarily gain value when, during its production, it moves from one desk to another. Often, you can save money by having all work done at one desk or office, rather than moving work around to several different ones.

Ping-Ponging: Very often a document will "Ping-Pong" back and forth between two offices, with slight revisions occurring each time. If the revisions can take place all at once, every Ping-Pong beyond that point is unneeded effort and delay.

Treating different things the same: This situation often occurs in procurement functions, when large and small purchases are treated the same. The small purchases should require less effort and a lower level of sign-off authority. The same thing happens when planning departments treat simple jobs in the same way as more complex ones.

Outside coordination: Often a coordinator is simply someone you have to go through to get to someone else. It is better to have two offices do their own coordinating than to put someone in between.

Expediting: If you have to make frequent special efforts to get something through the system quickly, the system probably is not working right. Signs of expediting include frequent use of expensive overnight delivery services, "walking papers through the system," and lots of overtime.

Fragmented responsibility: The responsibility for seeing that a job gets done may be divided among several units. The result often is that no one is really responsible, a process is delayed, and costs go out of control.

Some people think that *streamlining* means removing all non-value added steps in a process, system, or organization. This is a dangerous misconception that will cause you to focus on cutting, not improving. The streamlined organization is not "lean and mean." Instead, it has minimized non-value added steps *and* maximized valueadded steps.

Safety and Well-Being

The importance of focusing on the safety and well-being of people involved in a process varies with the nature of the process. Obviously, inherently dangerous processes need extra attention to safety aspects. Creative solutions to these types of problems come from good teamwork and have beneficial side effects. For example, some workers at the Norfolk Naval Shipyard did not always wear safety shoes. The two reasons they gave for not wearing the shoes were the limited selection at the shipyard shoe store and complicated, slow reimbursement procedures. An improvement team recommended moving the safety shoe store to a better location and increasing its inventory and styles. Accidents from slips and falls dropped 45 percent. The team also suggested a new, streamlined reimbursement procedure, which eliminated the processing of five thousand checks a year.

Effect on Society and the Environment

Governments are very aware that their policy decisions and how they work can have a tremendous effect on society. The effects of even the simplest change in a law or regulation can cause financial loss and even death for some citizens. For example, changing the laws and procedures for regulating savings and loan institutions in the 1980s had tremendous negative consequences for taxpayers, who had to bail them out.

The side effects of a process also may affect the environment. Varying some component of the process can alleviate this. For example, defense operations are sometimes allowed to use chemicals and paints prohibited to private industry for environmental reasons. The Navy's ordnance facilities are researching substitutes for these materials and recommending the substitutes to weapons systems program managers.

Recycling is a way to prevent the negative side effects that can result from a waste disposal process. Governments have started to require residents to separate newspapers, glass, and plastic from garbage, so that these items can be recycled instead of dumped in bulging land-fill sites. Many governments have a policy of buying recycled paper and plastic to help create a market for these products.

Customer Perceptions

The quality of a process also must be judged by the customer's perceptions of its ability to deliver the desired output. It may matter little that a process is the best available and that the output cannot be matched anywhere. If customers have no confidence in it, they will complain or go elsewhere. For example, a research report may be technically accurate and useful, but customers may not have confidence in the report until a specific outside expert "blesses" it.

One major weakness of government organizations is their inability to communicate high performance to customers in a believable way. A root cause of this problem often is failure to measure performance. For example, the opinion that building tenants had of maintenance services provided by the Navy's Norfolk Public Works Center was biased by "worst case" examples. A new performance measurement system measured all jobs done for each individual tenant. When they saw the whole picture, tenants agreed that the center's services were satisfactory and that problems were more the exception than the rule. The tenants thus gained confidence in the center and its processes.

Another problem for government is presenting budget information in ways that citizens can understand and judge. The city of Indianapolis's budget for street repairs and maintenance shows how many linear feet of deteriorated curbs will be repaired or replaced in 1995 (one thousand five hundred feet, at $23.50 per foot), that the city will make fourteen thousand road signs averaging $30.24 each, and so on. To arrive at accurate figures for these budget items, the city introduced a new budget process that uses ABC. In budget discussions and negotiations, the city's executives now can tell elected officials, "You can get this much of this type of service for this amount of dollars"— and both parties understand exactly what is on the table.

Customers also must perceive that a process is fair. This is particularly true for government functions such as regulation, law enforcement, benefits calculation, tax assessment and collection, and health and safety inspection. Inside an organization, employees must see that performance appraisals and decisions about office space, complaints, and similar issues are handled fairly.

This sense of fairness will not come from explanatory pamphlets, published reports, and documentation. On a daily basis, it will result from polite, concerned, and informative communication with internal and external customers. The same is true with how services are delivered. An indifferent attitude by a government employee can do more to damage an organization's reputation than anything else.

Now that you know the general types of improvements you can make to processes, we will present a few concepts that will aid you in selecting the appropriate improvement approach for a specific problem or opportunity.

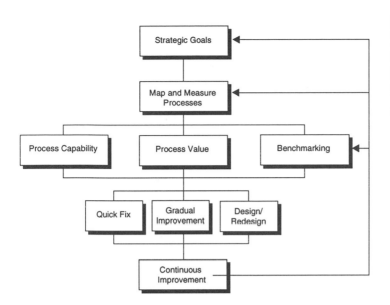

Figure 7-3
Framework
for Selecting
Process
Improvement
Approaches

A FRAMEWORK FOR SELECTING
IMPROVEMENT APPROACHES

Figure 7-3 shows a broad framework for selecting an appropriate approach for improving a service, operation, or process. We will discuss the parts of the framework now.

Strategic Goals

As discussed in Chapter 5, strategic goals shape improvement strategy. The more important a process is to achieving a strategic goal, the more attention and improvement resources it should receive. Given the choice between investing in redesigning a strategic or a nonstrategic process, the strategic process should win. In choosing processes to outsource, nonstrategic processes are the more likely candidates.

Mapping and Measuring

To understand and improve a process, your first have to map and measure its parts and performance. Otherwise, you will not understand what is involved in improvement, or even if improvement is needed.

Chapter 8 discusses the type of high-level process maps you would use when choosing improvement approaches, while Chapter 12 shows ways to measure process performance. More detailed mapping and measuring is done during improvement projects.

Process Capability

Process capability is a technical term referring to the long term performance level of a process once it has been controlled. As you will see in Chapter 8, *control* refers to re–ducing or eliminating abnormal variation in a process. Abnormal variation is caused by one-time events such as equipment breakdown or a key worker's absence due to illness; these events cause performance to vary. Correcting an abnormality is not process improvement; it simply returns the process to normal operations.

Once it is controlled, you can measure the actual level of performance in a process, in areas such as accuracy, cycle time, or cost. If the measured level of performance falls below the desired level, then the process needs to be improved.

If simply changing a few elements in a process will deliver the required level of performance, then the process is said to be capable of that level. Such minor or moderate changes usually are made through quick fix and gradual improvement methods. However, if such changes will not achieve the desired performance levels, then the process is said to be incapable. Then, the process has to be completely redesigned to the extent that it bears little or no resemblance to its original form.

Now, here's the secret to major improvement of many public sector operations, especially in administrative and support functions: they have surprisingly high potential for increased capability *without* redesigning. For example, in conducting value analysis (see Chapter 14), we routinely discover that 50 percent or more of the resources devoted to many administrative and support processes go to non-value added activities. *Eliminating* these processes, or at least purging the non-value added activities from them, always reduces cost and nearly always reduces cycle time and errors; substantial increases in process capability inevitably result.

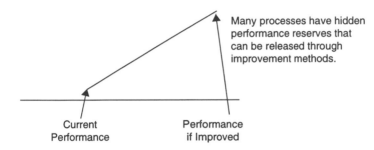

Many processes have hidden performance reserves that can be released through improvement methods.

Figure 7-4
Hidden
Process
Capability

Current
Performance

Performance
if Improved

Thus, before you set about improving a process, measure its actual performance and its capability to deliver the desired level of performance once it is improved. In general, if the gap between actual and desired performance is lower than 50 percent, then there is a strong case for using gradual improvement. There are exceptions to this, but it is a good starting point for discussion and decision making. Among the more important exceptions are the following:

- **Planned, maintained processes.** These are operations that were originally planned using formal process engineering or design methods and that have been regularly upgraded by engineers, management analysts, and other specialists. Well-planned and maintained processes always function at a higher level of efficiency than unplanned processes. You will be lucky to gain more than 25 percent improvement in such processes without radically altering them. (There are some exceptions even to this rule; see the case study of the Jacksonville Naval Aviation Depot in Chapter 19 on continuous improvement.)

- **Major technological breakthroughs.** When competitors suddenly surge ahead because they scrapped their old processes for a new breakthrough technology, you may have no other choice but to do the same.

Process Value

How do you make improvement decisions about processes that are not necessarily related to strategic goals but are still central to daily operations? How do you apply valid subjective judgment along with objective data on process capability? The answer is that you can classify most processes according to their value to your organization: *asset, liability*, or *value neutral* (neither an asset nor a liability).

Usually, you want to keep asset processes inside your orgnization, which means using gradual improvement and redesign methods to improve them. If you cannot change a liability process into an asset, then it is often a good idea to eliminate it or outsource it to another organization that can. Value-neutral processes can go either way: in-house improvement, or outsourcing/elimination.

There are several dimensions of value, each of which may be more or less important for a specific type of process. These dimensions, several of which may apply to a single process, include *identity, priority, background, mandate,* and *ritual.*

Inspecting restaurants for health code violations	Process	Obtaining reports on sexually transmitted disease (STD) from private physicians
Identity and priority. Public expects protection, and results are published. Serious incident could cause deaths.	Process Classification	**Priority and background.** Reporting is critical to preventing STD outbreaks, but is invisible to public
Asset. No serious illness or deaths reported in last three years.	Process Value	**Liability.** Several STD outbreaks could have been prevented with prompt reporting by private physician.
Now inspect 90% of restaurants annually. Could do 100% with minor scheduling changes.	Process Capability	All local primary care physicians find several STD cases a year, buy only 30% reported a case last year. Unlikely that current process can improve much on this.

Figure 7-5
Process Value
Classifications
and Capability
Estimates in a
Health
Department

Identity

Some processes define your organization to customers, stakeholders, or the public, and others do not. Those that do are related to your central mission, business strategy, or core business processes. Federal Express's guarantee of next day delivery is central to its identity with customers; processes that directly cause next day delivery to happen are the company's *identity processes*. Investigating crimes and apprehending criminals are identity processes in a local police department, while preventing contagious diseases from spreading is part of a health department's identity.

If these processes perform according to customer and stakeholder expectations, they are assets. If not, they are liabilities, especially if they consume large amounts of resources needed in other processes. Processes that customers don't see or care about, and that do not turn other processes into identity assets or liabilities, are value neutral in their effect on your identity.

Now, there may be a sound political or economic case for outsourcing or privatizing an identity process that is a strong asset or liability to your organization. However, if you do this often, your agency will become a shell of its former self, staffed by contract and oversight officers. The public will come to identify your mission with your contractors, even though you fund the work. There is nothing intrinsically wrong with that; most local governments run many and sometimes all their human services programs through contracts and grants with nonprofit organizations. However, this may not be the best solution for serving *your* customers.

Priority

A process can be classified by the way that it directly affects your organization's daily operations. If the increase or degradation of a process's performance has a fairly immediate, visible affect on total operations, then it is a priority process. For example, if your operations depend on an up-to-date data base, then maintaining that information is a *priority process.* If such a process is stable, capable, and continuously improving, it is an asset; if the opposite is true, then it is a liability.

In Chapter 11 on competition, we mention that Alaska's public health department decided to keep its medical test processes in-house instead of contracting with an independent laboratory for them. This is because, to the department, medical testing is a priority process that must be closely monitored to ensure its stability and capability.

Background

These processes operate in the background, invisible to most customers. Improvements in them usually do not affect core business processes—unless the background processes break down. If such processes are very inefficient and breakdowns are frequent, then they are liabilities. Normally, the highest rating for a background process is value neutral. This is why many background processes are good candidates for outsourcing if this will save money or greatly increase efficiency.

However, you can change some background processes into identity or priority assets. For example, preparing and distributing printed copies of draft legislation, hearing minutes, and reports is a background process in law making, takes weeks or months, and is costly. Putting this information online on the Internet can transform this into an identity process, winning public praise for prompt service and more open, visible legislative processes.

Mandate

This type of process is done because it is required by oversight organizations, regulations, or some other mandate. It does not add value to an agency's main products and services. Depending on your mission, examples may include complying with federal, state, and local regulations concerning procurement, work place safety and environment; labor laws; and financial audits. If noncompliance puts your funding, operations, or public image in jeopardy, or compliance diverts large amounts of resources, then such processes are liabilities. Rarely do they become assets, and usually the most you can hope for is value neutral.

Although there may be some exceptions, your best bet is to try to eliminate the mandates that cause these processes to exist. One quick way to do this is to ask people for documentation that such mandates are really from the outside, instead of internally imposed tasks you can safely eliminate. At the least, you can reduce to the absolute minimum the resources devoted to these tasks.

Much of the work involved in such tasks consists of collecting information and documenting events (for example, publishing a notice, conducting a test, or investigating a case). Often, these tasks are treated as separate processes done for outside organizations. As discussed in Chapter 15 on internal controls, one improvement approach is to use information technology to automatically capture, analyze, and distribute this data during the normal operation of the processes that create the outsiders' need for information. However, this ought to be a side product or minor priority of improving other processes, not a separate effort. Few, if any, such mandated operations are worth the investment of more than a minor amount of improvement resources—and a job not worth doing is not worth doing well.

Ritual

Ritual processes are those processes that are carried out because they always have been part of operations but that have no real purpose. Continuing to produce reports that no one reads, maintaining documents for commissions that do not meet, and conducting inspections for problems that no longer exist are good examples. If no one admits to being a customer to a process, or if you just can't seem to map its parts, then it probably is a ritual. All such processes are liabilities and can never become assets. Just eliminate them.

You can use subjective judgment to determine how a process should be classified in the just-described value system, but sometimes people will squawk about the results (especially those who learn that you think they manage a low priority, ritualistic liability). However, there are objective ways to justify your choices, such as the following:

- Survey customers and citizens about what defines good service from your organization (identity and priority processes);

- Ask internal and external customers to list the "pains" they get from your organization or operation, such as major errors, delays, or poor service. These reported pains point the way to liability processes;

- Measure the capability of processes and compare it with demand (also good for spotting current and potential liabilities); and

- Demand documentation of mandates or of requirements for rituals.

Benchmarking

In benchmarking, you compare a process's performance to the highest levels attained by other processes that operate in the same way. Although you do not have to do this to decide on the appropriate improvement approach, making such comparisons shows the magnitude of the gap between your current performance and that which is possible. If the gap is small, then gradual improvement may be the best approach. If it is large, then you may have to redesign a process.

In Chapter 19, we discuss best practices benchmarking, which allows you to learn the reasons for exceptional performance in outside processes. Then, you can adjust your approach to fit the task of adopting and adapting these external best practices to your internal process.

Process Improvement Approaches

Although we use three broad classifications of process improvement, these are not mutually exclusive categories. First, they may overlap, such as when several quick fixes result from the findings of a Plan-Do-Check-Act (PDCA) or redesign project, or when privatizing an operation causes major internal redesign. Second, the timing of one method may cause it to resemble another. For example, PDCA projects ordinarily produce gradual improvement; if accelerated, some become virtually the same as redesign initiatives.

Quick fix

Quick fixes fall into two categories: minor changes and barrier removal. Minor changes include low-risk modifications to a process and its components, the side-effects of which (if any) will be confined within that process.

Usually, these changes simplify a process by removing an unneeded or non-value added work step. Quick fixes do not require elaborate research, but they are best made when a process has been mapped and understood by its managers and operators.

A high volume of minor but sound quick fixes indicates that an organization promotes a healthy environment for improvement. Managers should be routinely making quick fixes based on the suggestions of employees and their own continued monitoring and study of processes (see Chapter 17). In addition, the initial phases of gradual improvement and redesign projects invariably identify many obvious improvements that can be made immediately, without waiting for the completion of these initiatives.

Figure 7-6
Quick Fix
Process
Improvement
Approach

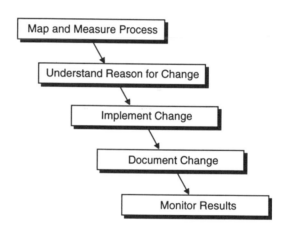

Quick fixes to remove barriers are management actions to eliminate rules, regulations, and policies that get in the way of process improvement. For example, a management decision to rescind a requirement for multiple sign-offs on purchase requisitions of less than $100 may enable the use of electronic ordering of minor supplies.

There are two often-overlooked aspects of quick fixes that can cause problems. First, *every change to a process, no matter how small, should be documented and incorporated into relevant process maps, flow charts, procedures manuals, and formal job training lesson plans.* Otherwise, the change often will not become standard operating procedure. If nobody follows such an improvement, then it is useless. If some people do and others don't, then the quick fix will have introduced nonstandard procedures, which cause abnormal variation, loss of process control, and eventual performance decay.

Second, all quick fixes—indeed, all changes of any type—should be monitored for at least a short time after they are made. This will ensure that their desired results have been achieved and that they have become standard operating procedure.

Gradual improvement

By *gradual improvement* we refer to carefully planned and executed improvement action aimed at achieving spelled-out objectives, such as a 30 percent decrease in cycle time or cost. When applied to a specific process, an approach such as PDCA is used. PDCA employs many of the tools discussed in Chapter 8 to rigorously study a process to discover the root causes of its failure to perform up to expectations. By repeating the PDCA cycle over time with different problems and opportunities in the same process, performance is raised in increments in all its parts, until the process reaches the limits of its capability.

PDCA can be applied to cross-functional and core business processes, under the control of a team of managers from the processes involved. The management team conducts some improvement tasks themselves and charters employee teams to use PDCA for other tasks.

Although not yet widely practiced in the United States, some companies combine PDCA with employee suggestion programs and management quick fixes for gradual improvement aimed at specific, measurable, organization-wide improvement objectives. These initiatives take the form of company campaigns where everyone is trained to recognize such problems as things that waste time, money, space, or other resources. Lasting one to a few years, such campaigns help focus attention on corporate priorities.

Design/redesign

Process design refers to the planning and installation of a new process. Most approaches to process design follow classic production engineering methods, many of which are sound. However, as you can see in our discussions of simultaneous engineering and Quality Function Deployment (QFD) in Chapter 9, leading-edge approaches combine product and process design and emphasize the importance of determining customer expectations and using cross-functional design teams. These practices ensure that your products and services will meet customer requirements and that the processes that produce them are properly aligned, thus avoiding postproduction problems.

Redesign, also called reengineering, is used to radically change existing processes (see Chapter 10). Organizations use this approach for several reasons. As noted earlier, when a process reaches its maximum capability, the only way to gain higher performance is to redesign it or outsource it to another organization with higher capability. As a strategic approach to improvement, redesigning a process can raise performance to such a degree that an organization leapfrogs past its competitors.

Finally, *major new technology almost always requires major changes in the processes that use it.* Therefore, every large information or systems engineering project you undertake will require process redesign. If your systems engineers say otherwise, then you have strong reason to suspect that they plan to simply automate existing processes, instead of creating a technology/process synergy that will transform your operations.

There is no hard and fast dividing line between process design and redesign, but here are some general distinctions. If you are developing new products or services or making radical alterations to existing ones, use combined product/process design approaches even if you do not anticipate major changes to existing processes. If major process changes are required, then also consider using redesign techniques.

If your products and services are going to remain about the same as before, but you need a quantum leap in performance in the processes that make them, then use a redesign approach. However, the basic process design principles of simultaneous engineering and cross-functional teamwork apply to process redesign, as well.

PRIVATIZING OR OUTSOURCING PROCESSES

Privatizing is an option in process improvement, but by itself privatizing is not enough to guarantee improvement. If you simply contract out for the same process as before, your results will be the same, too. This is why wise organizations improve their processes before contracting them out.

As discussed in Chapter 11, there are many forms of competition, including selling public assets to private companies, public/private competitions for work, and restructuring an agency into a private or semipublic organization. As noted in that chapter, we think it important to introduce competition wherever possible, because it generally motivates people to improve.

In this chapter, though, we refer to the practice of outsourcing a process, or contracting out for the products and services it delivers. As noted in Chapter 11, outsourcing may be a good alternative for nonstrategic processes when you want to raise their performance by more than 10 or 20 percent. Any less than this and you will probably do better with an internal gradual improvement approach.

In general, just saving money is not sufficient cause to out-source or otherwise privatize a process. Some additional reasons include gaining better quality, service, or speed, or the fact that contractors have proprietary resources you need, or that you want your organization and leaders to spend more time focusing on strategic core business processes instead of on nonstrategic support functions.

ELIMINATING PROCESSES

To eliminate means to remove a process from your organization, with no intention of replacing it. Eliminating processes improves the performance of other processes, by reducing cycle time and hand-off errors, and by redirecting resources to value added activities.

Mandates, rituals, and all other non-value added processes are prime candidates for elimination. One approach to identifying such processes is through value analysis, which we discuss in Chapter 14. Also, you may want to consider eliminating products, services, and their related processes that are peripheral to your main mission. These can be transferred to other agencies whose missions are more aligned with them. If there is a viable market for the products or services, you may want to abandon them and allow private companies to take over their production.

Getting rid of processes is the most radical approach you can take to improvement. It is not always easy, especially when jobs will eliminated, too. However, if you are faced with major budget or staff cuts, jobs are going to disappear, anyway. Then, the best thing you can do for your organization's health is purge it of unnecessary work. At the least, this will decrease stress, and increase morale and productivity among the managers and employees who survive the downsizing.

Once Again, Continuous Improvement

Every improvement to a process, with the exception of elimination, should be followed by continuous improvement. Chapter 19 clearly explains the reasons why: (1) unless you continually improve a process, its performance will begin to decay, and (2) constant improvement means less need for radical approaches such as redesigning and privatizing.

As we show in Figure 7-3, continuous improvement loops back to earlier parts of our framework for selecting improvement approaches—strategy, performance measures, capability, value, and external benchmarks. You will see the same type of renewal loop in the Improvement Driven Organization framework. This is because these earlier parts change over time; often, this change is driven by the results of continuous improvement. Because of this constant change, you have to reassess process performance and begin again the healthy renewal cycle of process improvement.

Chapter

8

TOOLS FOR PROCESS CONTROL AND IMPROVEMENT

■ Process management is an analytic approach to process control and improvement.

■ Process management tools include:

- Charts, graphs, matrices, and other methods of collecting, organizing, and displaying information
- Statistical methods for revealing underlying patterns of process performance
- Root cause analysis methods
- Techniques for generating, reviewing, and agreeing on ideas

■ People at all levels have learned to use these tools effectively.

If it ain't broke, don't fix it: "So what if it can be done better? Nobody's complaining."

Live with it: "We don't have the power to make it better."

We've always done it that way: "We never think about doing it better."

It's state-of-the-art: "We'll wait until someone else discovers a better way."

We're no worse than anybody else: "We'll never try to be better than anybody else."

We'll correct it in the field if there's a problem: "We won't take the time to anticipate and prevent all possible problems."

It's good enough: "We can get away with it."

99.9 percent is good enough: "We're complacent."

Good enough for government work: "Nobody expects us to be any better."

Each of these phrases effectively prevents improvement in systems. The attitudes they reflect are the reasons for problems and for the eventual stagnation and ruin of an organization. Process improvement is about getting to the root cause of a problem and preventing it from occurring again. More than that, according to a maxim of the Air Force Development Test Center, continuous improvement means "Even if it ain't broke, make it better!"

Well, what tools do you use to make things better? In this chapter, we will introduce a variety of tools used for process control and improvement. Besides helping solve problems, these tools have two added benefits. First, they give your organization a common language to discuss process management. Even better, they offer a common set

Tools and Techniques Discussed in This Chapter

Tools for Data Collection, Analysis, and Display

Process maps

Flow charts

Cause and effect diagrams

Check sheets

Bar charts

Pareto charts

Histograms

Scatter diagrams

Run charts

Control charts

Experimental design and Taguchi methods

Tools for Generating, Reviewing, and Agreeing on Ideas

Brainstorming

Challenging assumptions

Force field analysis

Multi-voting

Nominal group technique

Pairwise ranking

of management concepts, such as using objective data for making decisions, variation, and consensus.

TOOLS FOR COLLECTING, ANALYZING, AND DISPLAYING DATA

Every form of process management benefits from logical and proven methods of gathering, analyzing, and displaying information. The tools discussed below are among those most frequently used in government organizations. We do not have the space in this book to describe in detail how to apply each tool, so we offer an overview. If you would like more details on the tools, please read Coopers & Lybrand's book *Process Improvement: A Guide for Teams* (see Appendix A).

Process Maps and Flow Charts

Process mapping is a procedure used to list and organize the tasks of a process or, on a larger scale, to do the same for all simple processes in a core business process or even an entire organization. There are many mapping tools available, depending on your need for information.

For example, let's say a process's operators want an initial map of all the tasks in the process. One tool they can use is the *top-down flow chart*. After establishing the process boundaries, the group then lists and defines four to eight major tasks that flow in sequence through the process. Next, they break each task into three to eight steps and list the steps under the corresponding tasks. Figure 8-1 is an example of a top-down flow chart of the process of responding to a request for proposals from a government agency.

| Plan for Proposal | Organize Proposal | Draft Proposal | Produce and Deliver |

- Review RFP
- Develop Strategy
- Develop Milestone Chart
- Assemble Team

- Identify Milestones
- Outline Proposal Questions
- Make Assignments
- Identify Resources

- Gather Data
- Draft Proposal Sections
- Assemble and Edit
- Incorporate Graphics
- Final Review

- Design Layout
- Typeset
- Paste-Up
- Proof
- Reproduction and Building
- Delivery

Such charts also can be used to lay out the flow of a cross-functional process or all the critical segments of a core business process. Doing this is one of the first steps in reengineering these types of processes. Organizations that practice ABC create similar maps for all processes in every department or function. By giving each process or activity a unique code number, the ABC users can apply computer data base technology to reconfigure their process maps into core business process and
organizational, business, and cost models that provide different views of the same operation.

Figure 8-1 Top-Down Flow Chart of the Process of Responding to a Request for Proposals (RFP)

Process Steps	Clerk	Supervisor	Input Operator	Scheduler
Log in document	X			
Sort	X			
Review for corrections		X		
Data entry			X	
Assignment to purchasing team				X
Review		X		
Distribution	X			

Figure 8-2 Deployment Chart for Receiving and Assigning Requisitions Process

Like a top-down flow chart, a *deployment chart* such as that in Figure 8-2 lists in sequence the tasks or steps in a process and also shows where or by whom a task is done. Such charts are handy for identifying all process operators and the points at which work might temporarily flow out of and back into a process. For example, Process A, which writes regulations, may send its draft rules to Process B for review, then receive back the comments and incorporate them in a final document. If you want to improve Process A, a deployment chart would show that you might want to include someone from Process B on your team.

A *detailed flow chart* shows the sequential steps of a process along with their relationships and contingencies. It has symbols that show process flow, decision points, delays, and rework. People use detailed flow charts such as those shown in Figure 8-3 to identify problems and opportunities for improvement in a process. Note that there are several opportunities in Figure 8-3: the squares that indicate inspections and the points marked R for rework and D for delay. If the causes of inspection, rework, and delay can be removed, then this process will be faster and will cost less.

Detailed flow charts help identify critical points for process performance measurement. For example, in Figure 8-3 the process operators might want to measure the percentage of invoices and purchase orders that are not on file when needed (the decision box labeled with a D after it).

Process operators use detailed flow charts to standardize their work, write procedures manuals, and train new operators in process operations. The charts also are used to develop information systems that can help reengineer processes. For example, if you can eliminate the need for the "inspect material" task in the process in Figure 8-3, the entire process can be done with a computer, including paying vendors with electronic fund transfers instead of checks.

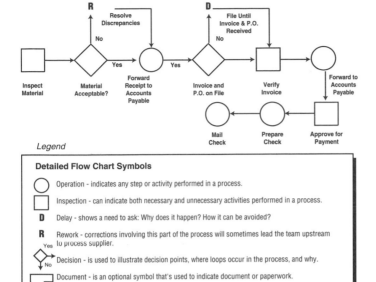

Figure 8-3
Detailed Flow
Chart of
Receiving
and Paying
for Materials
Process

In the past, some organizations have tried to develop detailed flow charts for all their processes at once. This is a mistake, because creating such charts consumes so much time. We recommend that you wait until process operators need detailed information, such as when they conduct an improvement project or install performance measures within their process.

Cause and Effect Diagrams

Cause and effect diagrams help teams to organize information, identify knowledge gaps, and clarify relationships among process elements and possible problem causes. They can be used to study any issue and are simple to apply.

Tree diagrams such as that shown in Figure 8-4 can be used to identify the root causes of a problem. In the figure, the problem is inaccurate orders from a supply warehouse. Possible causes of the problem are shown going from left to right and branching into possible root causes. This is an important concept in process improvement. In the figure, what initially appears to be a cause of a problem, such as a "wrong item code" on a requisition form, usually is a symptom or outcome of another problem. In this case, the problem is "outdated supply lists," which is in turn caused by the frequency with which those lists are updated and distributed. This tree diagram also branches into other causes, indicating that the initial problem will require a multi-faceted solution. People who "shoot from the hip" with their solutions tend to miss these multiple causes, then wonder why things did not get all that much better. Tree diagrams can be used for other purposes, such as functional and decision analyses, or linking customer expectations to current process performance to problems in performance and their causes.

**Figure 8-4
Tree Diagram**

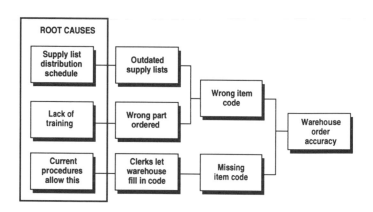

Another type of cause and effect tool is called the fishbone or Ishikawa diagram. In the fishbone, the effect is shown in a box to the right of the diagram (the head of the fish). In Figure 8-5, the effect is "Late Payment of Invoices." Possible causes of this effect are shown as branches off the spine of the diagram and are categorized under some part of the process. Smaller branches off the main branches indicate possible root causes. Fishbones are useful during a team brainstorming session to organize possible causes of problems or opportunities for improvement. Many teams start by categorizing the causes according to the process elements we discussed in the last chapter: inputs, people, equipment, methods, materials, environment, and so on.

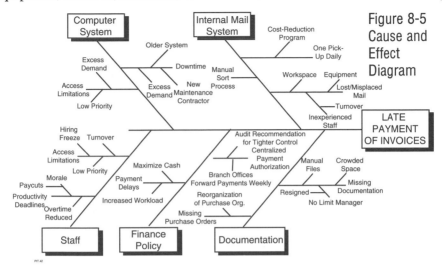

Figure 8-5 Cause and Effect Diagram

Five-Whys

One way to develop the information needed for cause and effect diagrams is the five-whys technique. Five-whys uses the rule of thumb that you must ask a "why" question up to five times before you arrive at a root cause. For example, excessive cost in a process that writes purchase orders may be related to the number of orders that must expedited or rushed through the system with special handling. Questions to ask about this include:

Question: "Why do we expedite these purchase orders?"

Answer: "Because the operations units that need purchases tell us to."

Question: "Why do they tell us to expedite?"

Answer: "Because normally we take ninety days to make a purchase."

Question: "Why do we take ninety days to make a purchase?"

Answer: "Because we have a large backlog of requisitions."

Question: "Why do we have a large backlog?"

Answer: "Because many of the requisitions we receive are incomplete or full of errors, and we have to correct them."

Question: "Why are they incomplete or full of errors?"

Answer: "Because the requisition forms are too complex and operations people do not know how to fill them out."

This series of questions produced several potential causes: average number of days to make a purchase, backlog, number of requisitions with errors, complexity of forms, and skill level of requisition writers.

Check Sheets

Check sheets are forms used to collect data on the frequency of an event or problem. These data can be used by nearly all the quantitative tools of process control and improvement, so expect to use lots of check sheets.

Figure 8-6
Check Sheet

Problem	Month			
	1	2	3	Total
A	III	II	IIII	9
B	II	I	III	6
C	ЖІ	II	ЖҐ	12
Total	10	5	12	27

Bar Charts

A bar chart is an easy way to organize, summarize, and display data collected with a check sheet or other source.

Figure 8-7 is a bar chart of the time that different departments take to develop materials for employee training workshops. If your objective is to reduce the cycle time of the materials development process, you might start by studying how the information systems department shown in Figure 8-7 develops its material.

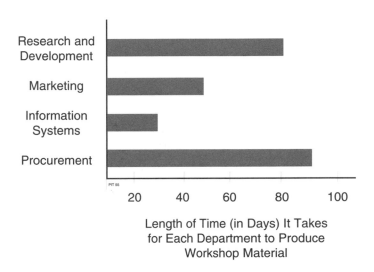

Figure 8-7
Bar Chart

Length of Time (in Days) It Takes
for Each Department to Produce
Workshop Material

Pareto Charts

Pareto charts are a form of bar chart used to rank order causes according to their contributions to an effect. In the pareto chart in Figure 8-8, the greatest cause is shown on the left side of the chart; the lesser causes are displayed in descending order to the right. Usually, you start improvement by working on the greatest cause, then go to the next, and so on. For example, faced with four causes of customer complaints, you may want to start with the one that causes the most complaints.

Figure 8-8
Pareto Chart

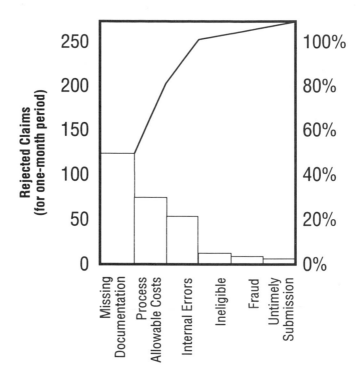

You can't create pareto charts through guesswork. They require objective, quantitative data to be accurate and useful. This is why a pareto chart is a wonderful tool to use in a political environment where competing interests demand that you focus on their pet problem or solution.

Histograms

All repeated events will produce results that vary over time. If you record results, you will have the data to build a histogram, a bar chart that shows the distribution of this variance. Histograms show measures of central tendency—the clustering of values found in a statistical distribution. These include the mean (the arithmetic average), median (a midpoint in the data), and mode (the value that appears most frequently). Histograms also show the range of variation and whether the distribution curve of data collected is normal or abnormal (more on this later, when we discuss process variation). All this is essential information for understanding process performance and possible causes of problems. You also use histograms to determine the type of control charts or experimental designs you will use to study a process.

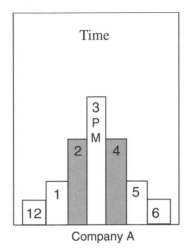
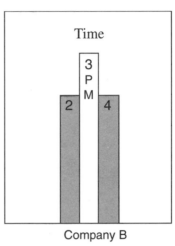

Figure 8-9
Histograms

As mentioned in Chapter 6, one objective for process improvement is consistency of output. For example, let's say you want to choose between two courier service companies for your office. You try both out, asking each to deliver your material to another location at 3 P.M. every day. On a check sheet, you record the results for both companies and use the results to construct the histograms shown in Figure 8-9. Looking at these charts, you will see that Company A's couriers often arrive considerably before or after 3 P.M., while Company B's couriers tend to arrive on time. Which company will you hire? Company B, which has the least variation in arriving exactly on time.

Scatter Diagrams

Scatter diagrams or charts, also called scattergrams, help show the correlation between one variable and another. This might be, for example, whether deliveries (variable one) are made later as the volume of transactions (variable two) increases or whether work performance increases with more training. Correlation does not mean that one variable necessarily causes another to change; intervening variables may remove the apparent relationship. Statistical formulas and experimental designs will adjust for this. In Appendix B, you can see how we used correlation to learn which process management practices were most associated with customer satisfaction, innovation, and employee participation in improvement activities.

Figure 8-10
Scatter Chart

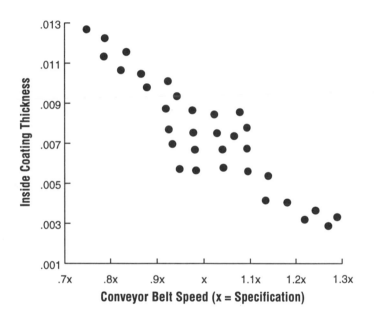

Run Charts

A run chart is a line graph that shows data related to a variable such as time, cost, or productivity. It plots this over time—yearly, monthly, weekly, daily, or hourly—and lets you see trends, cycles, and other patterns in a process. Run charts can be used along with histograms to help you understand process variation. For example, the run chart in Figure 8-11 shows the variation in daily travel time of a commuter. It is easy to see that this person's commuting time is increasing in a nonrandom way, which in statistical parlance is called abnormal variation (more on abnormal variation in the next section of this chapter). The cause of trends like this should be investigated, and action should be taken to remove the cause. For example, the commuter could take a different route to work or start earlier or later than normal; any of these variations would constitute a change in his or her commuting process.

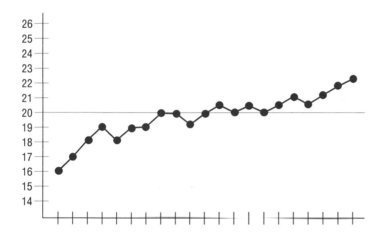

Figure 8-11
Run Chart of
Commuting
Time in
Minutes

Although run charts are good preliminary tools, *control charts* give you much more information. We'll discuss them in a moment, after you read about the principles behind them in the next section on process variation.

All statistics needed for the tools just discussed and for control charts can be calculated by hand, but personal computers make this unnecessary. All spreadsheet software can be used for the statistical calculations and to generate most charts and graphs. Special statistical process control (SPC) software is available that handles all the calculations and charts just discussed, plus many more. For example, the book *Process Improvement: A Guide for Teams* comes with a computer diskette of statistical software programs for the tools discussed in this chapter (See Appendix A).

Anybody can use the basic tools of process management. As the county manager of Volusia County reported: "Some people in our mosquito control programs can't read very well, but when they are working on a problem like hitting power lines, they sound like management analysts."

MEASURING PROCESS VARIATION

Everything in life varies: your phone bill is different from month to month, crime rates go up and down, and reports come in early, late, or on time. In traditional organizations, people label variation either "bad" or "good." Bad variation is when this month's results are "worse" than last month. Good variation is when the results are "better."

There is a lot more to variation that just "good" or "bad." When a process varies, it is talking to you, telling you reasons for variation. But without control charts, most of the time you cannot understand what the process is saying.

Types of Variation and Their Causes

If you calculate the average performance of a process over a year's time, you will find that each month there is some variation in performance. Sometimes performance will be higher than average and sometimes lower.

Abnormal variation occurs when performance suddenly shoots much higher or lower than average. You cannot predict abnormal variation, because it is due to *special causes*. For example, errors may have increased because a new and untrained employee is working in a critical process. Other special causes may be a flu epidemic that keeps employees away from work, a sudden surge in demand, or the one-time breakdown of equipment. If a problem appears only once or very rarely, then it probably has a special cause.

Normal variation is the routine fluctuation of performance. Over time, process performance may go up or down, but you can predict with a reasonable degree of certainty what the range of variation is going to be within a few percentage points. Normal variation occurs because of *common causes.* These may be the design of the process, the level of training of all employees in a process, the reliability of equipment and methods normally used, or simply minor random events. When everyone has the same problem or makes the same error in working in a process, then you should look for common causes.

Now, here's the interesting part: *common causes account for about 85 percent of the variation in a process and special causes for 15 percent.* This is in line with the 85/15 maxim discussed in Chapter 2: managers are responsible for 85 percent of process variation because they design and oversee the system, so reducing most variation is a *management* responsibility. Unfortunately, many traditional managers devote most of their time to solving special cause problems; this is "fire fighting." Process managers in Improvement Driven Organizations work on discovering and preventing common causes. Which type of manager do you want to be?

Fixing, Improving, and Tampering

When you remove a special cause of abnormal variation, you are *fixing* the process. This does not mean the process is any better. When you fix a flat tire on your car, you do not have a better car. It simply means that the car will function normally again.

If you remove or reduce a common cause of normal variation, you *improve* the process. The normal operations of the process will be better.

Now, intuitively, you may know the difference between special and common causes—sometimes. But even the best managers and employees can fail to distinguish between the two. When this happens, they start *tampering* with the process. They may or may not gain their objectives, because the approaches to reducing abnormal and normal variation are different.

Stability, Capability, and Reducing Normal Variation

Whenever you work on a process, you need to know what you are shooting for: stability, capability, or a reduction of normal variation.

If a process frequently shows abnormal variation (outcomes cannot be predicted), it is out of control, or *unstable*. You cannot improve an unstable process. If you try, you will not see the improvement, because it will be masked by abnormal variation. Your first objective is to make a process *stable* (outcomes can be predicted). Employees, first-line supervisors, and technical experts usually can solve these types of problems quickly and easily.

However, a stable process may not be *capable* of meeting customer expectations. Say, for example, you can predict that, on average, your output is going to be delivered two days late—but your customer wants it on time. Satisfying your customer may require fundamental changes in the process. If you try any quick fixes, though, you will be tampering with the process.

Let us say you have a stable, capable process. On average, you deliver output on time, although normal variation still makes some deliveries late and others early. You now want to *reduce normal variation* until all deliveries are exactly on time. This, too, will require permanent changes to the process. Your end goal is a stable, capable process that has minimal variation.

Statistical Process Control

Process management uses statistics to show you the types of variation in processes. These statistics are best understood not by their formulas but by the information they give you when put into charts. Taken together, these methods are called SPC. SPC is simply a way to communicate. It is the "voice of the process," telling you what is going on.

One frequently used SPC tool is the control chart. The solid middle line of the chart in Figure 8-12 marks the average performance of the process over the period measured, and the line connecting the dot points tracks the performance variation during the period. The control limits, shown as dashed lines, define the expected amount of variation, based on the process's history. In this chart, the process experiences abnormal variation when the line spikes up and out of the upper control limit. With the exception of certain trends and patterns, we say that when the line stays inside the dashed lines of the upper and lower control limits, the process is experiencing normal variation.

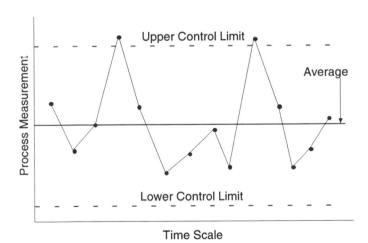

Figure 8-12
Control Chart

Maintaining process control

Control charts serve an additional purpose: they help *keep* a process in control. Organizations that use SPC regularly measure samples of their work-in-progress and use the data to build control charts. People grow adept at spotting negative trends in the charts and can take steps early to avoid problems. Processes with long cycle times might view these trends once a month. Those with high-speed, repetitive processes might look at control chart data several times a day.

Other statistical tools

There are about a dozen different types of control charts, each of which has its special application. Probability papers and analysis of variance (ANOVA) are other examples of statistical tools. If your processes are very high volume and repetitive, these techniques can be helpful (see the books listed in Appendix A for more information on these methods).

SPC in white collar organizations

Most government organizations are white collar operations. Can they use SPC? According to a former commanding officer of the Defense Industrial Supply Center, which is a white collar group, "Administrative and other white collar processes have output, the same as manufacturing or commercial functions. Products such as documents can be sampled, and their variation charted and evaluated. A manager, employee, or work unit can take action on the basis of this analysis." He compares the objectives of improvement in white and blue collar functions to show they can be measured and are therefore amenable to SPC:

Objectives

Blue Collar Functions	*White Collar Functions*
Reduce reject rates	Reduce document errors
Limit rework	Limit reprocessing
Minimize scrap	Minimize wasted time
Shorten	Shorten
manufacturing cycles	turnaround time

As noted earlier, even when work is nonstandard, SPC can help monitor processes. For example, a comparison of the labor hours and budgets forecast for a series of jobs with the actual hours used will show variations in the job-planning forecasting process and lead the way for improving that process.

EXPERIMENTAL DESIGN AND TAGUCHI METHODS

Potential process improvements often go through an experimental stage during which they are tested and the results are compared with previous performance or some desired outcome. Generally, these are very simple experiments involving one independent variable. With more than one independent variable, or potential intervening variables, you need more rigor in your method. When you suspect that only one or two variables are the cause of an effect, experiments that involve a few variables are a good approach. But what if you have only a general idea of what the causes are, or you have a complex process with many inputs and transformation steps?

Experimental design methods are useful in such situations. For example, *Taguchi methods* of experimental design can be used to solve complex production problems and to design new products and services. Their advantage is that employees and supervisors can run most types of Taguchi experiments with a minimum of expert guidance, because the methods are straightforward and the results clear. More-traditional experimental design is equally valuable but requires more intense help from experts (see Appendix A for reference books on this subject).

TOOLS FOR GENERATING, REVIEWING, AND AGREEING ON IDEAS

Some tools of process improvement and management help teams think creatively, while other tools enable teams to logically examine all facets of a solution. Another set of tools allows teams to reach consensus on issues and solutions.

Brainstorming

Brainstorming is a technique for using the subconscious—the most creative part of the brain—to generate ideas. It is a structured exercise in which all members of the team suggest causes in a round-robin fashion, then discuss the merits of each. The power of brainstorming lies in its ability to bring about synergy, when the total effect of team thinking is greater than the sum of each member's individual thoughts. Let's say that one team member suggests an idea that seems vague and unworkable. This idea triggers a thought in another member, a thought that yet another member modifies and builds on. Soon, this team will develop an innovative idea that no one member could have devised alone.

Brainstorming also can be applied to generating ideas about potential causes of problems. Cause and effect diagrams help classify these causes according to process components. After collecting data on the potential causes, a team can use pareto charts to rank them by the magnitude of their effect on the issue addressed.

Challenging Assumptions

Success in innovation often requires you to look at problems from many points of view. To do so, you have to escape the self-imposed constraints of traditional assumptions about processes, what customers want, and the causes of problems. One technique for challenging assumptions is to have everyone on a team write down all the assumptions they have about a process or problem. Then, team members transform their assumptions by doing the following:

Reversing, or changing the assumption to its opposite. If you now assume that a department head has to approve all transactions, then try assuming that this approval is no longer required. What effect would that have on your solution?

Modifying an assumption. Revise your assumptions slightly to make them better or easier to deal with. Suppose your immediate supervisor could approve all transactions?

Viewing from a different perspective. Try looking at an assumption from the point of view of someone outside your process, organization, or profession. For example, what would Federal Express say about an assumption that it takes three days for requisitions to move through your internal mail system?

Perhaps the most powerful challenge is: *"What if we simply did not do this entire process at all?"* Exploring the answers could lead you to a profound understanding of the reasons (or lack of reasons) for existing activities. Challenging assumptions sparks lively discussions and deep reflection. Be prepared to switch to brainstorming to capture the creative thoughts that spring from this spark.

Force Field Analysis

This versatile tool helps teams reality-test ideas and solutions. For example, suppose you want to pay invoices ten days after receipt instead of thirty days, which will reduce administrative costs and late payment penalties, plus improve customer satisfaction. A few invoices are very large, and paying them so quickly conflicts with cash flow policy. You can lay out such issues in a force field analysis chart like that shown in Figure 8-13, which shows the forces working for and against an idea. With this information, you can look for ways to modify an idea to overcome the forces working against it. In the figure example, you might make an exception to the ten-day payment schedule for large invoices.

Figure 8-13 Force Field Analysis

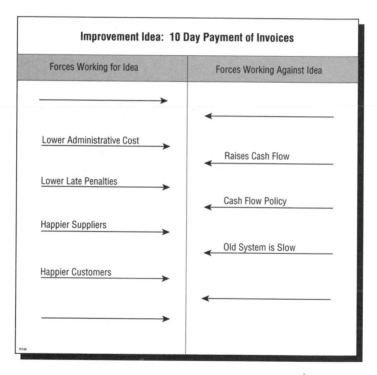

Force field analysis is an especially useful tool when you plan to introduce fundamental changes in operations. Different groups in your organization, and even suppliers and customers, may resist these changes, or they may be your allies in introducing them. Some forces you might want to examine include management commitment, existing accounting systems, your organization's culture, and the political environment. Figure 6-3 in Chapter 6 is an example of applying force field analysis to the five dimensions of change.

Multi-voting, Nominal Group Technique, and Pairwise Ranking

These three tools allow team members to vote their preferences during different parts of an improvement project. All allow more or less anonymous voting, so that employees on a team have equal say with managers. Each lets a team compare alternatives in order to zero in on those alternatives that members collectively feel offer the most potential. In addition, a team can use the nominal group technique to generate ideas as well as choose from among them.

For example, pairwise ranking forces individuals to contrast each alternative on a list to all the others. In Figure 8-14, there are five alternatives labeled A through E. You would ask a team, "Who prefers A over B? A over C? A over D?" and so on until you contrast the last pair of alternatives, which is "E over D." In the figure, alternative A is preferred over the rest, D over B, C, and D, and so on. The zero in the E-C cell indicates a tie vote; another round of voting might remove the tie.

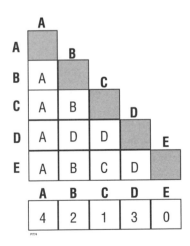

Figure 8-14
Pairwise
Ranking

TRAINING AND TEACHING THE TOOLS

Many people initially resist process management tools, especially those that involve statistics. Based on interviews for this book, we can divide these reactions into three categories: simple nervousness about how to use the tools, resentment of added work, and fear about what the tools will reveal.

The only way to overcome nervousness is to use the tools. "The tools of process management often seem intimidating, but once people have some basic training they see how easy they are," noted a manager at the Philadelphia Veterans Affairs Regional Office and Insurance Center. "Some of our teams stick to the basics, but some enjoy getting into more advanced concepts."

Some people see using the tools as an added burden. A quality assurance director in a private company told us, "What you're teaching is going to, at first, seem like extra work. Neither managers nor employees will automatically see the connection between SPC data and the work they do. The challenge to training people in the tools is to 'prove it' with examples everyone can understand, such as a project or process in which the trainees work. This means using real data, from real processes, collected before and during training."

The third cause of resistance is more insidious. "The problem with control charts," said the chief of statistical methods at the Watervliet Army Arsenal, "is that they show problems. Lots of them. Managers and workers may believe that these problems are going to be blamed on them and that they will be 'beat up' as a result. But SPC and any other measurement tools are not about individual performance. They are about *system* performance. If you use the results of process analysis to punish people, process management and improvement will fail in your organization."

Teaching Why and When is More Important Than How

Training is more than simply teaching people *how* to use
the tools and methods we have described. Teaching *why* and
when is the more important challenge. People can always
refresh their how-to knowledge from a manual, but unless
they learn why-to and when-to, nothing productive will
result from their tool-wielding ability.

The world is full of horror stories about organizations
investing millions of dollars to train their work forces in
process tools, only to see this investment go to waste when
people do not immediately and effectively apply the lessons
learned. The best solution is just-in-time training. In this
approach, you train people immediately before they are to
apply the tools, and, as discussed earlier, you use examples
and data drawn from processes similar to theirs. Even better, use the processes they work in as your source. Best of
all, combine training with an actual improvement project
that is focused on your trainees' processes—nothing is more
real than reality.

Team Training Always Works Best

These are team tools, often best applied by a team of people
who work together daily in the same process. If you train in
such teams, you don't have to worry if part of the class
doesn't have an in-depth understanding of a particular tool,
because someone else on the team will understand it. The
challenge is to identify team members who show a talent or
interest in a specific tool. As with organizations, it's the
sum of the team's ability, not the separate knowledge of
individual members, that is most important.

There Are So Many Tools. . .

Although the tools just described are sufficient for most situations, it is always good to have others. Some we left out
for lack of space include simple tabular lists, pie charts,

idealized redesign, time-to-time analysis, why-why diagrams, defect concentration diagrams, solution maps, glossaries.... We could spend several more pages just listing them.

In most organizations, everyone learns to use a few tools. We won't be prescriptive about which to choose, but, at a minimum, we suggest that you consider using some form of flow chart, check sheets, bar graphs, tree or fishbone diagrams, histograms, run charts, pareto charts, and brainstorming.

Chapter
9

DESIGNING AND IMPROVING PRODUCTS, SERVICES, AND PROCESSES

■ Traditional methods of design often result in major flaws in products, services, and the processes that make them.

■ Simultaneous or concurrent engineering is a procedure for designing a service and the processes that create it at the same time.

■ Quality function deployment is a method for listening to the voice of the customer when designing a product or service.

■ The basic procedure for improving processes is called Plan-Do-Check-Act. Besides developing sound improvement ideas, PDCA ensures that they are implemented correctly.

■ Continuous improvement comes from repeating the PDCA cycle on the same process.

*When the ancients said that a work begun was half done,
they meant that we ought to take the utmost pains in every
undertaking to make a good beginning.*

— Polybius, Greek historian,
c. 202-120 B.C.

Good, better, best

Never let it rest

Until the good becomes the better

And the better becomes the best.

— Elementary school rhyme

The views expressed in these quotations are at the heart of
the Improvement Driven Organization's operations philosophy. Designing a new product, service, or process is not
something to be taken lightly. Decisions made during the
design period will influence process performance—and the
ease of process improvement—for decades to come. We
start this chapter with design approaches that produce products and services that delight customers, while drastically
cutting the time and cost required for their development.
Even the best process, product, or service, however, must be
improved at some point, so we also present the most frequently used process improvement procedure, Plan-Do-
Check-Act.

PRODUCT OR SERVICE DESIGN

Below is a cartoon that nearly everyone in business and
government has seen at one time or another. Depending on
your line of work, the labels underneath the trees may vary,
but the message does not: different groups in a traditional
organization do not plan in teams, much less understand
customer expectations.

**As Marketing
Requested it**

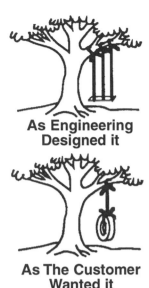

**As Engineering
Designed it**

Figure 9-1
Typical
Outcomes of
the
Traditional
Design
Process

**As Manufacturing
Produced it**

**As The Customer
Wanted it**

Over-the-Wall Design

Consider for a moment all the departments or functions
involved in introducing a new commercial product. They
include, in sequence, marketing, product design, production
design, production, distribution, and customer service.
Typically, the marketing department develops the product
concept without consulting the other departments, then toss-
es it over the wall that divides marketing from the product
design department. The product designers work out a
design, then toss it back over the wall to marketing, which
orders some changes and lofts it back. Once the product
design is worked out, the product is tossed over to production design. Production design, which plans the processes
that make the new product, immediately throws it back, saying, "We can't possibly build this thing without breaking
the bank. Make these changes, and we can build it afford-
ably." Product design has to go back to work, checking its
output with marketing and then shooting the product back
over the wall to production design.

The real fun starts when the product goes into production. Then, the production department discovers flaws in both product and production design that cause problems in quality, cost, and cycle time. Often, these problems require more changes in the product design. Once the product is made, the distribution department may find that it won't fit into the available packing crates, so special ones must be ordered at extra expense. Finally, when the product is in the field, the customer service department often discovers that it is hard to maintain and repair, and warranty costs shoot through the ceiling.

Governments actually do a better job of design than do product manufacturers. That's because most government outputs are services. Once specifications are set for a service, it becomes a process in its own right. Modifying a service process is much easier and less costly than changing a factory assembly line, so downstream errors are easier to handle. Also, government customers and stakeholders readily express their opinions, either directly or through representatives or interest groups. Public service tradition and political pressure ensure that agencies hear these vocal opinions, which are passed on to service designers in document form.

However, private industry's design problems are frequently evident within the walls of a public agency. An agency's service planners must balance many internal and external interests while striving to provide what is best for the direct customer. At the same time, they must ensure that several internal groups understand their role in the service delivery process.

Two process management methods have developed over the years that help to speed up the new product or service development process as well as to improve the eventual design of both product and process: simultaneous or concurrent engineering and Quality Function Deployment (QFD).

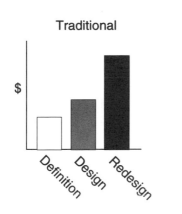

Traditional

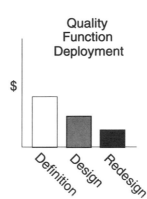

Quality
Function
Deployment

Figure 9-2
Distribution
of Effort in
Product
Development

Simultaneous or Concurrent Engineering

If you gathered in one room a representative from every process that is in a service's design and production stream, then you would have the beginnings of a simultaneous engineering project. In manufacturing, the objective of this approach is to merge the design of a product and the processes that make it. In government, it is to ensure that all relevant people and processes in a supplier agency, from field staff to auditors, understand the new service, contribute to its design, and agree on how it should be operated to maximize customer satisfaction.

This cross-functional team works together to set the standards for operating the service, while at the same time creating a process map of operations, including necessary equipment, material, skills, and other process components. This is the best possible opportunity to conduct value analysis on the process under design (see Chapter 14). Sparks can sometimes fly during these meetings, as each group questions the assumptions and value added content of the other groups' proposed work steps. However, it is better to have this happen with all parties in the room than to wait for problems later on. In addition, the team develops performance measures for both process operations and the results of the service.

Depending on the type of service, it is a good idea to include outside suppliers and customers (or their representatives) on the team. This is especially true if the supplier or customer is actually part of the service delivery process, as is often the case. For example, involving local Internet users is a must when you design a municipal or public university-based computer bulletin board and gateway access system. Speaking of computers, nowadays it is almost always a good idea to include an information technology specialist on the team.

One last thing. At the opening of this section we said that getting different groups to a meeting was the *start* of simultaneous engineering. To ensure that the meeting works, you may need a results-oriented agenda and a good group facilitator. If you already use facilitators in process improvement teams, make sure that they review and understand simultaneous engineering issues, tools, and methods.

In addition, you may need a system for gathering, analyzing, and reporting on the expectations of both external and internal customers and stakeholders. We will discuss one now.

Quality Function Deployment

In Chapter 8, on tools, we said that SPC is sometimes called "the voice of the process," because it translates process performance into understandable form through control charts and other tools. *Quality Function Deployment* (QFD) is called "the voice of the customer" for the same reason. As with the PDCA procedure, you gather objective data on the expectations of internal and external customers and stakeholders, often through surveys, and use QFD matrix tools to translate these into the desired characteristics of the service. For example, prospective users of a community health clinic may want extended clinic hours, waiting times of less than one hour, comprehensive services, an on-site pharmacy, and a nearby bus stop. Doctors and nurses who staff the clinic may want regular business hours, an extensive drug formulary, and a security guard on duty during clinic hours. Neighbors of the clinic may want it to have off-street parking, no evening hours, and health education programs. Third-party payors (Medicare, Medicaid, and private insurance companies) will certainly have an extensive list of requirements on cost control.

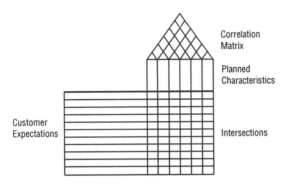

Correlation
Matrix

Planned
Characteristics

Customer
Expectations

Intersections

**Figure 9-3
The House of
Quality**

As you can see, these characteristics can be long laundry lists with many conflicts among the expectations of different customer groups. In QFD, therefore, customers are asked to rate the importance of each of their reported characteristics. Next, you develop supplier performance variables, which are the planned characteristics of the service, including those that will meet customer expectations. Using a QFD matrix, called, because of its shape, *the house of quality* (see Figure 9-3), you list the customer characteristics on the left side and the planned characteristics at the top. At each intersection or cell of the matrix, you indicate how each planned characteristic will help meet a customer characteristic, usually with a rating such as weak, strong, or very strong.

Now, you start experimenting by changing the planned characteristics, to see how this would affect customer characteristics. Often, this is done by putting a "roof" matrix on the house, which allows a two-way comparison among all characteristics. Through adjustments, you eventually develop service performance characteristics that maximize satisfaction of different groups of customers and stakeholders. Next, you translate the characteristics into objectives for each process involved in providing the service. The process objectives are based on what downstream internal customers expect of their upstream suppliers, if the organization is to meet external customer expectations. Later, people from each process develop these into more specific objectives. Attaining these objectives may require that some processes speed up their operations and others add equipment and steps that will save money and time downstream. Making these changes is the job of people working in each process, not the QFD team.

Agencies that compete with each other or with the private sector for the privilege of providing a service will especially benefit from QFD analysis. Additional matrices can be tacked onto the house of quality to make competitive performance assessments, including the degree to which an agency's current services offer advantages to customers over those of competitors.

QFD is ideal for complex organizations and services, where the probability of meeting customer expectations and holding down costs decreases in proportion to the number of processes that lead to a final output. The reason? A gap often exists between the goals for a complex service and the views, values, and goals of individual process managers and operators. QFD also can be used to investigate the performance of an existing service to improve or completely redesign it to better meet customer expectations.

PLAN-DO-CHECK-ACT

Although it is called by many other names, the basic procedure for continuous improvement is Shewhart's Plan-Do-

Check-Act cycle. PDCA is simply the scientific method applied to improving processes; it substitutes objective analysis for gut feelings. All Improvement Driven Organizations use some form of PDCA, even if they do not call it that or if their models are less rigorous.

The four steps of the PDCA cycle are:

- *Plan* what you are going to do;

- *Do* an experiment based on the plan;

- *Check* the results of the experiment; and

- *Act* on the results of the experiment.

To achieve continuous improvement in a process, you repeat the cycle working on different problems or opportunities, usually in order of their importance.

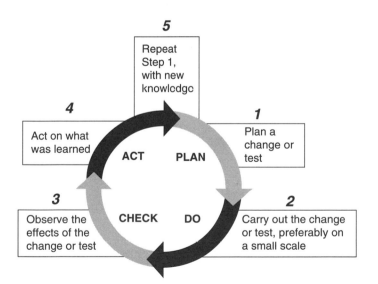

Figure 9-4
The Plan-Do-
Check-Act
Cycle

Using PDCA

PDCA sounds like ordinary common sense, but it is not. Common sense is based on assumptions—we *think* we know what is going on and what the effects of our actions will be. Most people assume their way past PDCA's steps for improving a process. They assume they know the expectations of customers, how a process is behaving, and the causes and solutions of problems; they also assume that, after corrective action, they will, in fact, have improved the process. All too often, they are wrong. That's why *challenging assumptions* (see Chapter 8) is an important tool of PDCA.

Some organizations have had dismal results using PDCA. There appear to be three reasons for such failures: impatience, resources, and results. First, managers and employees become impatient with the procedure, because it seems to take too long to apply. This is certainly true for many of the initial improvement projects in an organization that is experimenting with quality management. Generally, such organizations have never before mapped their processes, collected appropriate performance measurements, or learned what customers expect. In this situation, teams that use PDCA must spend the bulk of their time in basic tasks that would already be done in organizations with more experience in process management. The lesson from this is that the more you use PDCA, the less time it takes. That's why a certain amount of patience is in order the first few times an organization uses this procedure.

Second, others feel that PDCA consumes too much staff and other resources. Experience is again the culprit. When process improvement teams are working on their first projects, they require special training, team facilitators, and other special project supports. Once trained and experienced, employees and managers move through the steps of PDCA with less outside support.

Third, there is the very grave problem of managers who fail to implement the recommendations of teams that use PDCA. In part, this is due to management's lack of familiarity with the benefits of the approach, which affects their confidence in its results. More insidious is management's rejection of the notion that employees can, in fact, develop successful innovations that lead to process improvement.

Finally, highly successful organizations understand that PDCA is, more than anything else, a state of mind. It promotes scientific thinking about problems and opportunities both great and small and is the procedural foundation for continuous improvement.

So, in reading the following step-by-step PDCA procedures, do not become bogged down in the details. Understand that each activity can take hours or weeks, depending on the problem, the size of the process, and the availability of hard, objective data. If you are a manager and think that PDCA will take too much time, ask yourself, "What takes up *most* of my time?" Your answers are likely to be "Things that go wrong" and "Convincing people to change." PDCA prevents things from going wrong. Also, it involves people in making changes to their operations, so they will more readily accept the changes.

Step 1: Plan

The objective of the "Plan" step is to arrive at a workable plan for improvement. Often organizations do not give this step the attention it deserves, and their attempts at improvement bog down or fail. The step's heavy emphasis on a clear purpose statement, conducting objective research, and involving the right people is characteristic of all process management methods. This emphasis saves time and money later and helps ensure workable solutions. Actions that lead to good plans include:

Select the process or issue

A team of managers or process operators selects the process or issue to receive attention, based on priorities: Which issue is most important to customers? Which problem or opportunity requires attention now? Which will yield the greatest return on improvement resources? The team can use available data to construct pareto charts to rank potential improvement projects by importance.

Create a purpose statement or charter

Every improvement project requires a clear purpose statement, sometimes called a charter. Managers or the team write the statement so that the results of the project can be measured in numbers: percentage of improvement, dollars, time, error rates, and so forth. Saying "improve customer service" is too broad and not readily measurable. The statement "reduce the number of customer complaints about late delivery of reports X, Y, and Z" is much better.

Define the process

An important initial task is to define the process or processes that affect the issue being addressed. This definition includes listing suppliers, process inputs, transformation components, outputs, process managers, and customers. The team may do high-level flow charts on the process at this point (usually top-down or detailed flow charts, described in Chapter 8) showing the scope of the process.

During definition, very often a team discovers the unexpected: that what they thought was a single process is in fact several, that there are more levels of authority involved than they anticipated, or that a process has many outputs, not one or two. When this happens, the team may wisely decide to decrease the scope of their improvement project, plan several sequential projects, or add new members to expand team capability to work on all parts of a problem or issue.

The major reason for delays and failed efforts in improvement projects is that their scope is too broad. As a facilitator from the Fresno IRS Service Center recounted, "One team I worked with was charged with reducing undeliverable mail. Sounds simple, doesn't it? It turned out that there were many types of undeliverable mail, and many causes that required action and authority beyond the ability of team members. The team spent a year and a half just narrowing down the possible actions they could take."

Conduct interviews

Next, the team interviews customers, managers, and other stakeholders about their expectations for process performance. Key questions to ask of customers and managers include:

- **What do they expect from the process? Which of their expectations are most important?** You will want to focus on their priorities.

- **How are we doing?** This gives you the current level of performance, from the point of view of customers and managers.

- **How do you measure our performance?** Your measures should include theirs.

- **In your opinion, what causes the problems you have with our process or its outputs?**

- **How could we improve the situation?**

Based on these interviews, the team may develop lists of management and customer expectations, such as this example:

What do *managers* expect from the process?	**What do *customers* expect from the process?**
Minimum rework	On-time deliveries
Average unit cost of $15	No errors
No overtime	

The team may write process objectives at this point, which are simply restatements of these expectations, such as "the unit cost of the output should be no more than $15."

Measure process performance

Based on customer and manager expectations, the team defines performance measures of operations inside the process and of the results of the process's output. Then, the team develops a plan for collecting the measures and gathers the necessary data. How long this will take depends on the cycle time of the process or its tasks. For very long cycle times, teams may want to look for interim measures of performance.

In addition, the team measures process or output variation, with a special focus on discovering abnormal variation. As you recall from Chapter 5, if abnormal variation in a process is too great, then it can be impossible to measure the results of improvements aimed at reducing normal variation.

Identify improvement opportunities

This activity begins with removing abnormal variation from the process. The team uses its data on variation to investigate and control abnormal variation. Fortunately, most causes of abnormal variation can be quickly remedied, but only if they are known. After making these adjustments, the team will have a better idea of the capability of the process.

Next, the team charts current performance and compares it with customer expectations. Based on this analysis, a team can develop lists such as the following:

What do *customers* expect from the process?

What do they get?

On-time deliveries

Half of deliveries are late

No errors

10 percent of units have errors

What do *managers* expect from the process?

What do they get?

Minimum rework

25 percent of units are reworked

Average unit cost of $15

Average unit cost of $20

No overtime

Average of two hours of overtime per day

Finally, the team sets priorities: which areas of the problem will they work on first? Pareto charts are useful for doing this. Afterwards, the team may create a detailed flow chart of the process, so that they will understand all its intricacies. The chart will be most detailed in those areas that relate to team priorities.

Develop solutions

Using the facts they gathered, the team defines clearly the problem they will address. This definition may be built on answering the following questions:

• Why is it necessary to solve this problem?

- What benefits can we hope to realize by solving this problem?

- What do we know about the problem? What is it that we do not yet understand?

- Can the problem be divided into parts?

- How long has the problem existed? Is it persistent? Chronic?

- Can we solve the whole problem or only parts of it?

Having done this, the team can start looking for causes and root causes of the problem. They may ask whether the problem begins inside or outside the process or whether it is upstream or downstream within the process flow. Examining the detailed flow chart, they look for delays, rework points, redundancies, bottlenecks, and other potential causes. Using tools and techniques such as five-whys, cause and effect diagrams, and others, they look for root causes. During this time, the team may gather and analyze additional information on the process.

Having arrived at root causes, the team can start generating ideas for solutions. This can involve brainstorming, challenging assumptions, investigating operations outside the organization, and consulting with technical specialists. The team evaluates potential solutions based on how well they will meet customer and manager expectations and their feasibility in terms of cost and other factors.

Finally, the team writes a plan detailing its findings and suggested actions. The plan includes the estimated costs and benefits of the solutions and schedules, budgets, and other supporting information. In most cases, the team seeks approval for the plan from management.

This completes the "Plan" step. The outcomes include a sound plan and commitment to the plan by the team members who developed it. Both outcomes are equally valuable.

Step 2: Do

The objective of the "Do" step is to test the proposed solutions through a trial or experiment. For example, the test may be conducted as a temporary change to a process. If an organization has several processes that do the same thing, then the test might be pilot tested in one of them. This reduces the risk of making changes before they are proven effective and allows for adjustments. Performance data are collected during the trial according to the measurement plan developed earlier.

Is the "Do" step always feasible or cost effective? Sometimes a process improvement can be very expensive, involving the purchase of new equipment. In such cases, process simulation can help remove some of the risk. In process simulation, you create a computer model of a process, showing its various parts and their relationships. You then test the model under different assumptions—such as larger or smaller volumes of work flowing through it or different configurations—to see the effect on performance. We discuss simulation more in Chapter 4. If managers decide to implement without a pilot, they still collect data on performance and work through the "Do" and "Check" steps, even if they have done a simulation.

One important outcome of "Do" step pilots is that personnel who will be affected by a change have the chance to test or observe others testing it. This involvement increases their acceptance of change.

Step 3: Check

"Checking" the validity and worth of the solutions is the objective of this step.

Verify improved performance

Data collected according to the measurement plan are analyzed to determine if improvement has occurred. If the improvement objectives have been met in a pilot, it is usually safe to introduce the change permanently or roll it out to other similar processes. If little or no improvement has occurred, the team may decide to modify the changes made or to start again at some stage of the "Plan" step.

Validate costs and benefits

Based on the data collected, the team recalculates the potential costs and benefits of introducing the change. If the "Plan" and "Do" steps have been conducted well, the team will probably be in for a pleasant surprise. More often than not, the results will exceed expectations and point the way to further improvements.

Step 4: Act

Installing a permanent change is more than simply "rolling out" process improvements. The "Act" step considers the other changes that are often required and the potential for maximizing return on resources invested in improvement. The other changes fall into various phases of the Improvement Driven Organization framework.

Standardize the improvement

The procedures initially used are not always the final form of the permanent change to be introduced. The procedures may need adjustment based on the suggestions of people who used them during the pilots or in the first few weeks after full implementation. The permanent procedures also may require policy changes. Most of the time the policies in question can be altered within the organization, but outside permission may be needed for some.

The permanent changes must be made standard operating procedure. This means recording them in operations manuals and training people to use the new procedures. The data collection method used earlier must be adapted to the normal performance measurement system (or vice versa). Finally, the higher level of performance achieved should be established as the new baseline for further improvement.

Install the improvement

Even small changes in a process have ripple effects. The team should make sure that their improvement does not create problems for suppliers or other processes; they will need to make adjustments if it does. Also, the improvement must be communicated to the parts of the system that affect or are affected by the process. For example, people working in support functions such as planning, inventory, and facilities management may need to know about the new methods, cost savings, or faster cycle time of the improved process. Human resources offices and perhaps unions will need to know about new skills and job descriptions employed by the process.

These actions address the technical aspects of introducing change but not the social aspects. Simply ordering people to follow new procedures does not mean all of them will do so. They often have what are to them valid reasons for resisting change, or they may simply be afraid of it. As noted earlier, some of this resistance and fear will be overcome by involving people in the improvement cycle and by using pilot projects to demonstrate the change. However, this is not enough when the change is complex or has negative consequences for some people. Then, you must use the change management strategies outlined in Chapter 6 to successfully introduce an improvement.

Leverage improvement

There may be other operations or processes that can benefit from the improvements just made. Management should look for opportunities to "leverage" the resources thus far invested by transferring these improvements to other parts of the organization.

Organizations with weak inter-unit communication or strong "turf" barriers often fail to realize the leveraging potential of single improvements. Improvements in one area must be advertised to others, and top leaders must ensure that managers in all relevant units consider adopting these changes.

Taking Short Cuts

The PDCA approach to process improvement has a rigor that is absent from traditional management. By following all the steps in the cycle, any employee can contribute to excellence. However, everyone who uses PDCA eventually is tempted to take short cuts. You and your employees may grow impatient and want to get on to results. Be aware that skipping steps along the way increases the chance that you will assume your way past a critical point. If you take short cuts, keep a record of them to find out if they work.

Is completing the "Act" step the end of the PDCA cycle? Can you relax and go back to business as usual? Read on to discover the secret of continuous improvement.

Repeating the PDCA Cycle

After successfully going through the PDCA cycle once, you are not "done." There are always other improvement opportunities within the same process or issue. You can go back to the pareto chart created during the "Plan" step and work on the next most important item. Also, during your first time through the cycle you may discover other opportunities.

Available resources and potential return on investment put limits on repeating the cycle. However, Improvement Driven Organizations should have a bias toward repetition, which is continuous improvement in its most fundamental (and powerful) form.

Chapter
10

REDESIGNING BUSINESS PROCESSES

■ Many organizations use business process redesign or reengineering (BPR) when they need to quickly and radically improve operations.

■ Process redesign can be done through two approaches: classic engineering or value analysis.

■ Most BPR projects focus on core business processes.

■ Coopers & Lybrand's BreakPoint BPR℠ approach follows six principles:

- Base redesign on strategy
- Make the business and political case
- Involve the right people
- Use information technology wisely
- Manage change
- Ensure continuous improvement

*We realized that we were trying to operate with a business
structure that was designed in the 1960s. To break out of
that we knew we had to have a radical change—so we
embraced business reengineering in a big way.*

— Chief information officer,
U.S. Internal Revenue Service

Many Improvement Driven Organizations are using *business
process redesign* or *reengineering* (BPR) to make
major changes to large, cross-functional processes. They
find that a combined BPR/continuous improvement
approach causes breakthroughs to occur in the short term
and sustains and increases these gains over the long haul.

Government organizations that use BPR attest to its power
to improve. Citizen demands for better service, looming
budget cuts, and the opportunities offered by modern information technology are causing other agencies to follow.
Consider, for example, the quantum leaps in service now
provided by Riverside County, California.

Giving a new twist to the word *digitize*, suspects arrested in
Riverside County press their fingers against a digital scan-
ner instead of an ink pad when getting fingerprinted. The
prints are quickly analyzed and compared with others in a
bi-county data base. If the prints are on file, officers know
immediately.

That's only a small part of Riverside's reengineered law
enforcement information system. All criminal justice and
law enforcement agencies in the county can quickly access
a unified data base that includes their own information, plus
everybody else's. Soon, when a suspect is booked, information on that person will be sent right on to the courts and all
other criminal justice agencies. This will save between $1
million and $1.5 million annually just in the cost of keying
and rekeying in data.

But there is more. Police officers in their patrol cars use laptop computers to acquire critical information instantly, from license plate numbers to arrest records. Back at the old dispatch offices where officers and clerks spent much of their time looking up paper records, 911 calls can now receive the quick attention they deserve. The unexpected plus for officers in the field? If their voice radio goes down, they can still communicate.

Riverside has reengineered other public services, too. Through computerized public access information kiosks, citizens can use touch screens to call up county board agendas, personnel openings, waste disposal sites, and property assessments and tax information. "Pretty soon," said the county's Data Networks chief, "we're going to put a 'card swipe' on the kiosks so people can pay their taxes with credit cards."

"Our first kiosk cost $10,000," he noted. "The rest cost less. And for each one, we can transfer someone working behind a counter—which citizens have to drive miles to get to— into a more critical job."

WHAT IS REDESIGN?

If existing processes are reasonably close to customer expectations, then often they require only minor modification in order to raise performance to an acceptable level. In these cases, the Plan-Do-Check-Act cycle discussed in Chapter 9 is more than adequate for the job.

But what if a process is completely outmoded or no longer can be improved to the desired degree? Then, redesign may be your only option: you must completely reconfigure the process, changing nearly every component of it. The result often bears little resemblance to the original process.

Figure 10-1
BPR: The
Breakthrough
Maker

Continuous Incremental Improvement Provides Small, Ongoing Change	Business Process Redesign Creates Rapid, Revolutionary Change
■ Current Processes Are Reasonably Close to Customer Requirements	■ Exising Processes Are Broken Down or Outmoded
■ Accepts the Status Quo as the Basis for Improvement	■ Challenges the Fundamentals
■ Uses Technology Incrementally	■ Views Technology as a Process Transformer
■ Less Risk Because Impact Usually Is Narrow	■ More Risk Because Impact Is Large, Cross-Cutting
■ Cost of Making Change Usually is Small, Often "Free"	■ Often Very Large Cost to Make Change

Making smaller improvements does not always require challenging the underlying assumptions about the purpose and structure of a process. In redesign, you completely reassess fundamental assumptions and question whether a process is worth keeping.

Two Basic Approaches to Process Redesign

Process redesign can be done with two approaches that often are combined. In the first approach, you apply classic work planning, systems engineering, or industrial engineering techniques also used in process design. You aim toward pre-specified target levels of performance, under given assumptions and design criteria.

The second approach is value analysis, discussed in Chapter 14. Here, you streamline a process by removing all non-value added steps and adding other value added steps as needed. The resulting changes may be so great that a true redesign comes about.

These approaches can be used for individual and linked processes. However, often your scope may be wider: to redesign major cross-functional processes, or even an entire organization. Under these circumstances, the concept of the core business process becomes extremely useful.

Redesigning Core Business Processes

Most BPR projects focus on core business processes that are vital to the success of an organization. Such a process often begins with an external customer requirement and ends with meeting that requirement and is critical to an organization's mission. Rapid redesign of these large, cross-functional processes is much more complex and costly than smaller improvement efforts, and thus riskier. This is especially true when the project includes expensive new information technology. Also, major redesigns nearly always eliminate the need for significant amounts of work and change the skills needed for the work that remains. The result is near-term employee and manager displacement, which can cause major resistance to change.

For this reason, the decision to conduct a BPR project nearly always is (or should be) made by top executives, who also coordinate and directly support the effort. Decisions about smaller improvements usually are made by line managers and employees, guided by strategic goals and objectives.

SIX PRINCIPLES OF SUCCESSFUL BPR

A close look at successful government BPR projects will show that they follow six key principles: strategy, building a business and political case, involving the right people, using information technology to transform operations, change management, and continuous improvement.

Base Redesign on Strategy

BPR begins with strategic assessments of several aspects of major process improvement:

Customer expectations. Seeking direct customer input through surveys, focus groups, customer advisory councils, and other types of research creates an external vision of performance and value that guides the BPR effort. Some BPR projects proceed without taking this step, and they may achieve considerable cost reduction or cycle time improvement. But such gains have marginal value if they mean nothing to customers.

Understanding the external environment. With the increased practice of outsourcing and privatizing public services, some government organizations face direct competition from business (see Chapter 11 on competition). It is wise to study these competitors' strengths and weaknesses before beginning a BPR project, if you hope to succeed. It is also important to understand the economic and political environments, because they affect an agency's mission and resources and thus its plans for major improvement. Benchmarking, discussed in Chapter 19, is another essential tool for external assessment. With benchmarking you compare your current process with processes in outside organizations that have leading-edge excellence in the same generic application.

Capabilities. Is your organization capable of making radical changes to business processes? What are the barriers to major improvements? The following assessments, some of which are discussed in more detail in Chapter 4, help answer these questions:

- Financial/budgetary review, to understand trends in costs and resources available for investment;

- Operational review, to understand the current efficiency

and effectiveness of the existing business process and other processes that support it;

- Information management review, to assess the current and future role of information services and how they can provide support to redesign efforts. Such a review includes investigating the quality and coverage of management information flows of key performance indicators; and

- Cultural assessment, to understand how your organization's values, norms, and beliefs will help promote, or perhaps resist, the major changes brought about by BPR.

Cost/benefit analysis. The expense of many BPR projects requires careful cost/benefit review. Such analysis is repeated several times during a BPR project to confirm that planned improvements continue to be worth the investment.

Based on all the above types of assessment, executives are able to set the goals and objectives of a successful BPR project. Also, they can plan for every aspect of the redesign effort, including the people they will involve in it.

Make the Business and Political Case

Using the same information, executives must present both a business case and a political case for redesign. The business case focuses on cost savings or potential new revenues (always welcome in today's environment), the capability of achieving targeted goals and, in some cases, the competitive advantage this capability will give an agency.

To most politicians, however, cost savings pale in comparison with other results, such as better constituent service or major reductions in chronic problems. According to a 1994 study of federal, state, and local government reengineering by the National Academy of Public Administration (NAPA), successful agencies examine redesign and reengineering proposals with an eye toward political implications, ensuring that the proposals address the agendas and concerns of major stakeholders. Also, success depends on putting plans in decision-making packages with narrow windows of opportunity that fit legislative or council calendars. By focusing on specific progress and results targets in the short, medium, and long term, an agency increases its chance of receiving authorizations and positive decisions at periodic checkpoints.

Involve the Right People

Staffing plans for successful BPR projects have three things in common:

The highest executive has a leadership role, and senior managers play prominent parts. A Conference Board survey of private companies ranked "obtaining executive involvement/support" as by far the most important factor in instituting BPR. This conclusion is understandable, because only the highest levels of executives can make the wide-ranging decisions that BPR requires. Their involvement also sends signals to middle managers and employees that an organization is serious about dramatic change. Often, the top executive acts as the champion for redesign; at the least, he or she sits on the steering committee that oversees BPR projects.

The organization's "best and brightest" people must participate. Dramatic change requires people with creativity, vision, and openness to innovation. Often, they already will be some of the busiest people in your organization because everyone recognizes and respects their talents. But because BPR projects are mission-critical, involving these activists is a must. This involvement often will require a full-time commitment for several months; without your best people, however, such projects can take years to complete and still may not achieve your goals.

The BPR team leader should "own" the process targeted for redesign. Because BPR often is technology-intensive, some organizations choose the head of their information resources management (IRM) department to be the BPR team leader. However, the industry periodical *Information Week* makes a strong case against this choice, noting that IRM executives seldom have a broad enough constituency to influence change. Instead, *Information Week* recommends choosing the head of the organizational unit that "owns" the process to be redesigned. This manager will have the authority to make things happen and will be committed strongly to success because he or she will have to live with the results.

Use Information Technology Wisely

As discussed in Chapter 2, too many organizations use information technology (IT) to simply automate existing processes, an approach that often results in doing the wrong thing faster. On one level, process redesign helps ensure that new technology is applied to better work methods that produce the right product or service. On a higher level, conducting process redesign and information systems reengineering as parallel tasks completely transforms processes. In this section, we will focus on this transformational effect.

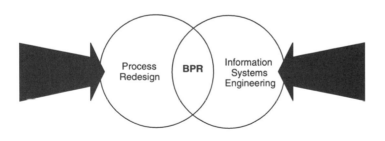

Figure 10-2
Strategy and Leadership From the Top are Necessary to Coordinate Process Redesign and Systems Engineering

Tapping into IT's transformational potential. The traditional way of filing a federal tax return was to fill out and mail a paper form to the Internal Revenue Service, where the information was keyed into a computer. Optical scanning technology improved this process, because many forms could then be read electronically. Scanning saved the time and labor costs of manually keying in tax data but left in place many components of the old process.

A few years ago, the IRS redesigned the process to accept electronic returns filed via computer modems. In another redesign, citizens, prompted by a voice-response system, use their touch-tone telephones to file simple returns. Similarly, in Oregon, people can use a computer kiosk to tap into the state employment office's jobs data base, while in Minnesota, automated teller machines dispense welfare payments.

These redesigns eliminated major parts of older processes (paper forms, the mail, and keying operations) through modern information technology (electronic data transmission). In essence, they *transformed* existing processes, as opposed to simply making them faster by automating manual work steps.

By understanding the full capabilities of IT, you increase the chances of gaining this transformational effect. This means your IRM or IT group must stay current on the latest developments in their field. However, many such groups are mired in the mainframe, batch-process paradigms of the 1960s and 1970s. If that is the case with your group, either they will have to update their knowledge, or you will have to seek outside expert advice.

Using process design to facilitate the application of IT. A large, federally chartered institution planned an organization-wide reengineered information system, using a team of information engineers and process redesign specialists. The project focused on a business process that annually handles hundreds of thousands of transactions worth over $1 billion. This process was not scheduled to receive the new information system for at least two years.

"The process had many manual operations that could definitely be redesigned to exploit the full potential of information technology," said one of the team leaders. "The question was, should every one of those operations be included in the new system? What about unneeded work steps, unread reports, redundancies, rework, expediting, and so on, all of which add time and money, but not value, to the final products? We needed to streamline the process before completing the planning and installation of the system."

The team found that many manual work steps could be eliminated or collapsed by new technology. But there were also new steps needed to feed information into the redesigned process. Identifying them allowed the team to do a better redesign job. This also alerted information engineers to potential problems that might not emerge until after the new information system started up.

There were nontechnical benefits, too, according to a team member: "Many redesign changes can be made now, because they do not depend on the new information system. Also, we know what the new process will look like, in terms of people and how they relate, resource requirements, and interface with other processes. This means our client can begin work immediately on the organizational and human change management tasks needed to make a smooth transition from the existing to the future process."

Using process simulation to facilitate process redesign.
Process modeling software is a major tool in advanced applications of BPR. It allows you to test different process configurations under a variety of assumptions, which speeds process redesign and reduces the risk of errors. For example, the above mentioned team began its analysis by using simulation software to map out a model of the as-is opera-

tions of the business process. This involved gathering data for the model by interviewing process personnel, reviewing procedures manuals, looking at performance results, and constructing work-flow diagrams.

Next, the team simulated new process configurations and test assumptions. As a team member noted, "Without computer simulation, this procedure could have taken many months or even years. With simulation, we did it quickly and in much more detail than usually is the case. The added benefit was that we could afford to ask many more 'What ifs?' without incurring major time delays or costs." The result of these creative exercises was a to-be model of the future process that was ideal for information systems planning.

Strategy and leadership: bringing it all together. To gain the full transformational effect of IT, executives can't turn the whole redesign job over to IT specialists, who may lack the training and understanding of process operations. Nor can they tell the specialists, "Wait outside until we get through planning this breakthrough, then we'll tell you what we need." To truly transform a business process, you have to create a synergy between process redesign and information technology.

Unfortunately, in most organizations the groups that handle process redesign and information systems engineering rarely talk with each other, much less cooperate. Getting these groups to cooperate is a job for executives—it requires strategy and leadership from the top.

Systems reengineering opportunities. Many government organizations are engaged in major information systems reengineering projects that together will cost hundreds of billions of dollars over the next few years. Right now, the lion's share of this investment is slated for new hardware and software, converting old computer code into new languages, and ensuring better communications among system components. But unless some of that money goes into process redesign, these reengineered information systems will simply end up "paving the cow paths" of inefficient, outmoded ways of working.

Thus, every systems reengineering project is a candidate for process redesign, and vice versa. This approach is the only way to maximize returns on both types of investment.

Manage Change

Chapter 6 outlines the basics of change management, which apply both to all forms of process improvement and to changing an organization's culture. However, the often radical nature of BPR raises a critical issue we discussed earlier: job displacement. This means that, in every phase of BPR, you must examine the impact of change on your work force. With this information, you can make transition plans that minimize both organizational disruption and personal suffering by some employees and managers. Key areas that require attention are the following:

Dealing with employees' fear of or resistance to major change. This is discussed at length in Chapter 6. However, if redesign does mean reducing your work force, it is important to quickly identify those people who will be affected and to take steps to accommodate their needs through early retirement, retraining, or outplacement assistance. Unless this is done, your entire work force can become paralyzed with fear of the unknown.

Obtaining the skills needed to operate new processes. Some of your redesigned processes will require skills that are now scarce or lacking in your work force. This area is one in which your human resources and training groups can be extremely helpful. Early on, they need to identify the required skills; they then need to recruit people with these skills and retrain your employees in them.

Ensure Continuous Improvement

An unwatched, unimproved process soon deteriorates in its performance. Without good performance measures and management attention, you will see your breakpoint gains unravel slowly until you are once again behind the eight ball. There are two ways to address this problem: strictly maintain the status quo of the new process, or encourage continuous improvement.

Doing the former is like coasting, and the only way to coast is downhill. You will be far better served to continue the uphill climb (albeit on a milder slope) to long-lasting excellence. Redesigning a business process provides an excellent opportunity to introduce continuous improvement and build in or enhance the type of quality infrastructure needed for long-term success.

BREAKPOINT BPR℠

Coopers & Lybrand's redesign methodology is called BreakPoint BPR, and it incorporates the six principles just discussed. In this section, we will provide an abbreviated overview of this methodology. For more details, see the BPR books listed in Appendix A.

BreakPoint BPR has three phases: *Discover, Redesign,* and *Realize.* We will outline each in sequence.

Figure 10-3
The
BreakPoint
BPR Process

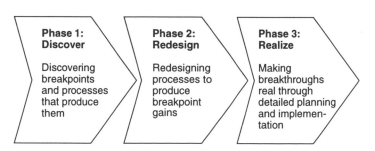

Phase 1: Discover

Discovering breakpoints and processes that produce them

Phase 2: Redesign

Redesigning processes to produce breakpoint gains

Phase 3: Realize

Making breakthroughs real through detailed planning and implementation

Discover

This first phase is carried out by executives and senior managers, with staff assistance. It leads to discovering *breakpoints:* levels of performance that, when achieved, produce extraordinarily positive responses from customers. *Discover* also identifies the processes that can help gain breakpoints and results in a high-level redesign of a strategic business process.

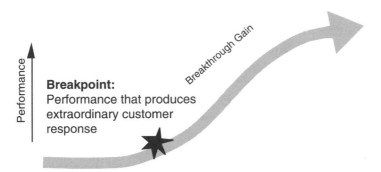

Figure 10-4
Breakpoints
and
Breakthrough
Gains

Setting the breakpoint. In keeping with the engineering aspects of BPR, establishing the breakpoint precedes identifying the processes that require redesign. Using the assessments discussed earlier under "Base Redesign on Strategy," you determine the target level of performance for a specific product or service. These targets may have one or more dimensions, but usually revolve around increased customer satisfaction, time, physical or service quality, or cost.

These are ambitious targets, but grounded in reality. Some example breakpoints include:

• Reducing two-week turnaround time for existing service to one day;

- Developing a single point of contact for all customers;

- Cutting costs of producing service by 50 percent; and

- Collapsing a three-year R&D process into one year.

Identifying processes. Next, you determine which processes in your organization will contribute directly to gaining the breakpoint. Together, these form the strategic business process that will be the focus of the BPR project. Having done this, you create a high-level "quick map" of the as-is business process, showing the relationship between each activity in it (see Figure 10-5). You collect performance measures on the as-is process, to provide a baseline for improvement.

Developing the to-be process. The next step is the most creative: developing a high-level quick map of the to-be business process. To ensure maximum synergy, we encourage clients to involve key operations and IT managers in this activity. Following this exercise, you research the feasibility of the proposed solutions and arrive at one that best fits your organization. Later, a redesign team will use this information in developing a full and workable solution. For now, executives use it as a basis for developing budgets and time schedules for the BPR project.

Setting design parameters. These parameters govern the operations of the to-be process and become the policy basis for how it will be developed. Some examples include:

- Centralizing (or, alternatively, decentralizing) operations whenever possible;

- Shifting responsibility for some types of activities to customers or suppliers;

- Minimizing the employee supervision needed in the new process;

- Using information technology to guide employee decision making;

- Designing flexibility into all parts of the new process; and

- Building continuous improvement into the new process.

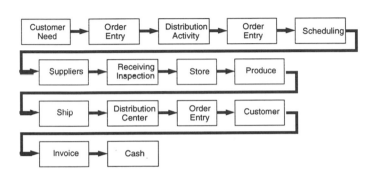

Figure 10-5
As-Is Quick
Map of
Order-to-
Payment
Process

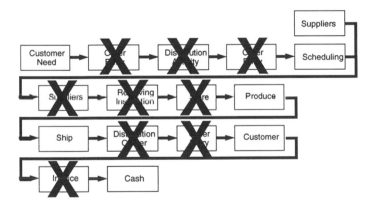

To-Be Quick
Map After
BPR

Modeling information. Because of the cost and complexity of information technology, it is important to develop a high-level information model of the to-be process during this first phase. The model is used for initial cost/benefit analysis and to guide later IT and process redesign work.

Managing change. The final step in *Discover* is to develop an initial change management plan, which would include a communication plan for informing managers and employees about the changes to come and the reasons for them. Also, at this point you start to develop policies and procedures for employee displacement.

Redesign

The objective of this second phase is to arrive at a redesign solution that will ensure reaching the breakpoint.

Managing the redesign effort. Redesign teams are composed of key managers and specialists who have the skills and background needed to handle all practical aspects of a BPR project. Building a good team is important, because in modern design and redesign projects, many development tasks are conducted in a parallel relationship, as in simultaneous engineering (see Chapter 9). This means redesign team members can address many different parts of a process, such as information technology, work flows, and human resources, at the same time.

This parallel approach reduces cost and lead time and ensures against hand-off errors and miscommunication inherent in sequential development. It also encourages synergy among team members, which produces transformational results. Your keys to success in this parallel approach are excellent communication among all members of the team and a master plan for development that integrates changes as redesign progresses, not when it ends.

Expanding the as-is process model. More detailed mapping during this phase helps break a business process down into manageable units. It also provides details for exploring to-be alternatives and for showing the relationship among activities, as was discussed earlier in this chapter.

If you take the activity and value added analysis approach to redesign, you will need quite a bit of detail in this map. In addition, if you want to set priorities for streamlining existing activities, you will need to calculate their cost.

Generating redesign ideas. Now you know the status quo, and it is time to decide how to change it. Although part of this decision may have been made during the *Discover* phase, *Redesign* is when you add the details. Benchmarking, technical advice, trade literature, and other outside sources of information can help at this stage. After digesting this information, you need to add your own creative ingenuity to the design options available.

At this point, challenging fundamental assumptions about the as-is process, "blue skying," team brainstorming, and asking "What if?" take outside concepts to much higher levels of potential performance. Only when all ideas are out on the table should you begin to analyze their feasibility and value.

In government agencies, "blue skying" should include ignoring existing rules and regulations. If the results of doing this appear significant, then proposing that these rules be eliminated should be part of the redesign proposal. At the very least, according to the NAPA report mentioned earlier, the promulgators of such rules should be asked about their original intent, which may be met even better by a redesigned process.

Testing design alternatives. For the mostly likely candidate solutions, you can use simulation to test their assumptions and refine plans for them. The next step includes cost estimating, cost/benefit analysis, and technical feasibility review. The information gained from this step will narrow the solutions down to the best one or two.

Sometimes, you can operate a scaled-down pilot test of a redesigned process in one area of your organization even without the support of planned new information technology. This helps spot the "bugs" in a redesign, lets customers evaluate it, and demonstrates its value to your work force.

Developing the detailed information model. Having arrived at a solution, you develop a detailed information model, which is an overlay of the redesigned process. The model indicates the type of information flow needed to support the new process and often includes components that automate previously manual tasks. The model will guide subsequent information systems engineering work and also govern some of the very detailed process redesigning done in the *Realize* phase.

Managing change. We keep coming back to the matter of managing change, because it is so critical. During the *Redesign* phase, the team develops a more detailed change management plan, which will guide the implementation of the new process. This plan identifies the types of skills needed in the future and the perceived obstacles to implementation.

Realize

This phase develops final refinements on the redesign and installs it in your organization.

Organizing new teams. It is a good idea at this point to set up implementation teams made up of people who will be working in the to-be process. You will be able to clearly identify them now, so including them in the transition period is logical. The more people you can involve in this phase, the better; this involvement encourages acceptance of change. At least some of the redesign team members should stay with these new teams, often as their leaders.

Detailed planning. You will need to flesh out the to-be process and information models with input from the new team members. This includes confirming resource requirements, technical fine-tuning, communications with other processes, and all the other details of putting the final touches on a new operation. Having done this, you should confirm the cost/benefit analysis done during the *Realize* phase.

Implementation planning. This phase involves creating a detailed plan to make the transition from the as-is to the to-be process. Our experience is that most organizations' existing planning systems are adequate for this task (with the exception of change management, discussed below). However, some consideration must be given to the cross-functional nature of the redesigned business process. Because the process will operate across departmental boundaries, superior coordination is needed when it is introduced. The logical focal point for this coordination is the new process "owner," who will be supported by implementation team members.

Managing change. A major part of change management during this phase is communicating the vision of the new process to your organization's people. This is best done face-to-face with managers, then with employees, in sessions that explain the rationale for the change, its benefits to them, and steps you are taking to assist those who will be adversely affected by the change.

Installing the new process. Technically, process implementation means simply executing implementation tasks according to plan. However, any complex change is bound to have a few glitches, both during installation and immediately after. Also, other processes that are connected with the new one may require minor modification or enhancement to adjust to the new level of performance. These problems can be opportunities to further involve people in perfecting the new way of working, such as through teams that follow the PDCA procedure.

Also, take care to ensure that people start out on the right foot, by using the process as intended. Formal training followed by close management attention helps ensure that they do.

Following installation, start measuring the resulting increased performance. As quickly as possible, you will want to confirm the cost/benefit calculations done earlier. And get set for a pleasant surprise: your attention to all the details—technical, organizational, and human—almost certainly will deliver even better results than you anticipated.

BPR AND CONTINUOUS IMPROVEMENT: THE LONG-TERM QUICK FIX

A *Wall Street Journal* cartoon showed one executive saying to the other, "What we need is a long-term quick fix." Although neither BPR nor continuous improvement is as easy as we would like "quick fixes" to be, an improvement strategy that combines both is as close as you can come to them. BPR catapults you way ahead of current performance, while continuous improvement sustains and increases your quantum leap toward excellence.

Chapter
11

COMPETITION AND CONTRACTING

■ Competition increases the effectiveness and flexibility of government services.

■ There are many alternative forms of privatization and competition in government:

- Abandoning or selling off assets or services
- Contracting out or outsourcing for services
- Revolving funds or enterprise funds
- Forming private or semiprivate organizations to deliver services
- Vouchers

■ Many communities allow public employees to compete with the private sector for government work.

■ Developing well-planned competition is a multi-step process that begins with self-analysis and ends with building continuous improvement into competitive arrangements.

■ An organization's ability to improve is limited by the effectiveness of its distributors and suppliers.

Planning and competition can be combined only by planning for competition, but not by planning against competition.

— Friedrich A. Hayek,
Nobel laureate in economics

It is a central tenet of our society and economy that businesses must continually improve their products and services, else they will lose business to competitors and eventually perish. In this manner, competition creates a compelling need to improve. By custom or law, many government businesses are free of competition, which explains in part their failure to keep up with changing customer demands and private sector performance standards. Lately, there has been a healthy push toward injecting competition into the public sector, mostly through calls for privatizing government services.

However, our experience is that privatizing public assets and services does not guarantee healthy competition, nor does healthy competition always mean you have to privatize. Improvement Driven Organizations have many alternatives for injecting healthy competition into their operations, which we will discuss in this chapter.

SO WHAT'S NEW ABOUT PRIVATIZING?

Through most of United States history, private organizations delivered much of what today is done by governments. For example, privately run toll roads between cities were normal in the eighteenth and nineteenth centuries, and almost all city fire battalions were private, nonprofit organizations. In some cases, several such fire battalions competed for business and occasionally fought each other for the privilege of extinguishing a blazing building (a few houses turned to cinders during these heated debates). This was certainly competition, albeit a bit misguided.

At the start of the twentieth century, reformers throughout the world wanted to reduce what they viewed as the negative effect of market forces on public services. Then, governments took over some previously private operations like fire battalions and toll roads; they also introduced government-owned industries that competed with private sector counterparts. Some governments outside the United States nationalized entire industries, such as railroads, creating public-run monopolies instead. At the very extreme, communist governments brought their entire economies under public sector control, thus eliminating capitalist competition.

More recently, this private-to-public trend is reversing itself. Virtually every public service has been contracted out in whole or in part, by some government, somewhere. Four out of five local governments in the United States contract for vehicle towing and storage, while most of the taxpayer money spent for state and local social services goes to private and private, not-for-profit agencies. A few small towns and villages operate all services via contract, keeping only a small staff of contract administrators as public employees. Many communities contract out their police functions, albeit to neighboring jurisdictions, not private companies. Dozens of privately run correctional facilities have come into being since 1980. About the only service that has not yet been let out for bid in this country is military service—we still feel citizen soldiers fight better than mercenaries, and we trust them more with guns.

Privatization is not about public versus private, but monopoly versus competition.

— William F. Weld,
Governor of Massachusetts

From Privatizing to Competition

Given the ubiquity of public arrangements with the private sector, is the current trend toward reintroducing market forces to the public service anything new? Yes, because we finally understand that governments need more *competition,* not just more private delivery of government services. Indeed, privately held monopolies like utilities and transit systems have no more incentive to improve operations than do their government-run counterparts.

We are at the beginning of an important, creative movement in the U.S. economy—a shift toward competitive approaches to public services no matter who provides them. It is a bipartisan movement, found at all levels of government. For example, one Executive Order issued in 1992 under President George Bush's Republican administration requires all federal agencies to permit and encourage private investment in federally assisted facilities. Democratic President Bill Clinton's National Performance Review reports are replete with the word *compete,* while a Republican-controlled Capitol Hill urges privatized solutions for government. With capital budgets inadequate for major infrastructure projects like roads and operating budgets strained to the max, governments are becoming increasingly amenable to new joint arrangements with the private sector.

For many public officials, it is no longer a matter of *whether* they will introduce competitive approaches to service, but how and when. That is why planning for healthy competition is so important.

COMPETITION OPTIONS

Governments have a wide range of alternative arrangements for introducing competition to the public service. We show them in Figure 11-1 and discuss each in detail below.

Operations are characterized as:		
Totally Private	**Private/Public**	**Totally Public**
Abandoment		Commercialization
Asset sales		
Corporatization (free-standing nonprofit)	Corporatization (partial government control)	Corporatization (total government control)
Franchise (business)	Contracting out	
	Outsourcing	Franchise (interagency)
	Vouchers	
	Grants and subsidies	
	Consolidation (nongovernment entity provides service)	Consolidation (government entity provides service)
Management buy-out	Public/private competition	

Figure 11-1
The Spectrum of Competition Options in Government

Abandonment

The most extreme way of introducing competition, aban-donment means that a government reduces or abandons a service, allowing the private sector to step in and do the job. Abandonment usually occurs when a service is not central to an agency's mission, citizens do not care who provides it, and there is ample private competition. Also, the services shed usually benefit only a small number of citizens or private groups. For example, Massachusetts's state government at one time mediated disputes over automobile purchases. Now, the American Arbitration Association runs the program, charging consumers a fee for services.

Asset sales

Asset sales can mean a sale in which ownership title of a government property or business is transferred to another entity. This transfer removes the cost of maintaining the asset from the government, which receives revenues from the sale. Some forms of asset sales include long-term lease (maintenance and operation of the facility or service are spelled out in the lease), sale-leaseback (the government leases back a property it sells, using the revenues from the sale to provide services), and sale- or service-leaseback contract (the purchaser agrees to furnish services for a specified period, as with a waste water treatment plant). Many governments use these arrangements for transferring utilities to the private sector or obtaining funding for capital projects.

Commercialization

This approach involves introducing user charges, private enterprise accounting, and revenue-related performance objectives to a public sector activity or asset. It is used to make government services self-sustaining and to segregate them from the general fund budget. Gas, electric, and waste water treatment utilities, airport operations, golf courses, and other recreational facilities are examples on the local and regional level.

A variation on this is the *revolving or enterprise fund system.* Most government agencies that provide support services to other agencies operate under annual appropriations. Not having to depend on the customer for revenues, the supplier agency has little incentive to improve its operations or become more responsive to customer agencies.

Revolving or enterprise fund systems establish a single operating cost fund for support agencies. When a customer agency contracts to buy a service, it uses money appropriated to its budget. This money is transferred to the revolving fund, which pays the funds out to the seller agency according to an agreed-upon schedule based on delivery or project completion. Such an arrangement makes the supplier agency more dependent on the customer agency, which promotes competition, especially if the customer has other choices. Support organizations in the Department of Defense, such as industrial operations and depots, run their businesses under such a system, called the Defense Business Operating Fund (DBOF).

Corporatization

A step further than commercialization, corporatization involves the transfer of public assets to a legal entity such as a nonprofit, public benefit corporation owned in whole or part by a government. The best candidates for incorporation already have their own sources of funding outside the appropriations process, such as rents, fees for service, or payment for goods received from citizens, private companies, and other government agencies. Examples include utilities, stadiums and convention centers, public hospitals, transportation services, and housing or development authorities. In the federal sector, corporations include such well known organizations as the Federal Deposit Insurance Corporation (FDIC), the Tennessee Valley Authority (TVA), the National Railroad Passenger Corporation (Amtrak), and the Corporation for Public Broadcasting. As of this writing, Washington is full of serious talk about corporatizing the air traffic control system of the Federal Aviation Administration.

At first glance, corporatization seems the answer to many problems. It separates a service from strict government control, which can mean less cost to taxpayers and more management flexibility. Often, corporatization introduces competition to a service, which should improve quality and price. Corporations are by their nature more independent of the political process, which is why some politicians like them and some don't.

There's a downside, though. A corporation that holds a monopoly may be no more efficient or responsive to the public than a government agency with the same advantage. What happens then? Well, corporations are less responsive to the political process, so when they do not satisfy customers, there are fewer political remedies possible. Also, there is the financial balance sheet. When you run a revenue-generating service within a government, all the revenue comes to the government. When you corporatize, all or most of the revenue goes to the corporation. However, the government's costs do not always go completely away. For example, a public corporation may still require appropriations funding if it operates at a loss. Also, there is some expense involved in government oversight of public corporations, and neither these entities nor their customers are interested in paying for this cost directly.

While corporatization may be a good alternative for many revenue-generating government services, it is not a panacea. Incorporating an agency or service simply to make it more efficient and responsive is not sufficient reason to go this route. Unless your government is so hopelessly mired in bureaucracy that a corporation is the only way out, think first about making the agency or service more efficient and responsive. At the very least, make sure that you are not transferring existing regulatory, structural, and managerial problems to the new corporation—after all, you own it.

Contracting out

Contracting is the most frequently used system for introducing competition in government. Contracting out has these characteristics:

- Contracts are usually for less than two years.

- They result in the delivery of a defined product or service.

- The customer sets and controls product specifications, delivery, and acceptance.

- The vendor is solely responsible for delivering a product according to agreed specifications, time frame, and costs. In other words, the vendor usually takes most of the risks. The exceptions are found in some types of R&D contracts in which the outcome is uncertain, in which case the customer assumes part of the risk.

- The product or service may be used by and even alter a customer's internal processes or functions, but does not replace them.

- There is no expectation by customer or vendor that their relationship will last beyond the current contract.

Hiring a private firm to conduct a one-time study, build all or part of a weapons system, pave a stretch of road, or build a facility is contracting out.

Outsourcing

In the broad sense, outsourcing means to transfer selected functions or services, along with their daily management, to third-party vendors or suppliers. Usually, these functions or services are not vital or mission-critical to the customer's most important core business processes. Instead, they are non-core functions and processes, ranging from running a computer center to internal financial audits to building maintenance. However, parts of core business processes may be outsourced to obtain technical expertise. Figure 11-2 is a good example of the types of internal support services that are typically outsourced.

Figure 11-2
List of
Potential
Functions
and Services
for Federal
Franchising

- Alternate dispute resolution

- Personnel

- Budget preparation

- Printing and reproduction

- Employee health care

- Procurement

- Engineering

- Quality assurance

- Facility management

- Security

- Finance and accounting

- Training

- Information technology

- Travel

- Logistics

- Worker's compensation

- Payroll

Source: *Franchising: Essential Information,* National
Performance Review.

Some of the characteristics of outsourcing that make it different from contracting out include the following:

- The contract calls for ongoing delivery of a service, versus one-time delivery of a product or completion of a single project.

- The contract is long-term, usually five or more years.

- Customer staff may transfer to the supplier.

- The longer the contract term, the higher the risk to the customer that costs will rise to an extent that offsets expected savings from outsourcing. The shorter the contract term, the higher the risk to the vendor that it will not recover up-front investments and start-up costs. This is why the customer and vendor form a vendor partnership in which both share goals, objectives, benefits, and risks. Vendor partnerships are discussed later in this chapter.

Many governments outsource their internal functions or services to our firm, Coopers & Lybrand. In some cases, these services are vital to our customers' core business processes, such as when we staff the information system center of the Government National Mortgage Association. In others, our services are not part of a core business process but are still necessary for sound stewardship of public funds. For example, we provide the internal audit function of one state agency concerned with the way that its grantees (mostly local organizations) handle and account for these funds. For the Defense Finance and Accounting Service, we review major payments to defense contractors to find overcharges; this has resulted in the return of tens of millions of dollars to the U.S. Treasury.

In *management and operations contracts (M&O)*, a form of outsourcing, governments hire commercial companies to manage programs or public assets such as facilities and lands. The U.S. Department of Energy hires M&O contractors to run several of its research and defense weapons facilities. In Massachusetts, the state government uses M&O contractors for its public ice skating rinks, which has lengthened the skating season, improved services, and bolstered surrounding businesses.

An emerging practice in the federal government called *interagency franchising* is a form of outsourcing, as opposed to the private sector franchising discussed next. In federal franchising, line managers of an agency have the choice of purchasing support services from their own organization or another federal agency that offers better, more cost-effective service. This creates competition to improve among all support services. Figure 11-2 shows the functions and services covered under this federal arrangement.

Commercial Franchising

In this agreement, the government gives a private company the right to provide a service such as garbage collection, cable television, or food vending at a park or public facility. The company collects its fees directly from users. Sometimes, this is a monopoly right so that the government has to create a rate board or oversight function to ensure cost-effective service to citizens.

Vouchers

Here, governments pay for services in advance and give people redeemable vouchers that they can take to their vendors of choice. This promotes competition among the vendors. Vouchers are now being promoted as a way of introducing competition to public education. In communities such as Minneapolis, Minnesota, some parents are given vouchers equivalent to the state's normal contribution to local public education. They can use the vouchers to pay their children's tuition at the public or private school of their choice (parochial schools cannot participate). The voucher system is intended to have schools improve their operations by competing for students. The roots of the education voucher concept go back to the GI bill immediately after World War II, when the federal government agreed to pay trade and academic schools for educating veterans.

Voucher systems also can be used to reduce the cost to the government of providing services. One example is the rental voucher system, where local governments issue poor people vouchers that they use to pay their rent to public housing or private landlords. Often, this system frees the government from building public housing or from operating a more complicated rental reimbursement system. The U.S. Department of Agriculture food stamps program is another voucher system, designed to replace the older, more cumbersome surplus commodity foods distribution program.

Grants and Subsidies

When the market will not support all the costs of a service, a government may make up the difference with direct grants or subsidies to the commercial or nonprofit group that provides the service. Many privately owned transportation systems, zoos, and museums receive these types of funds. In some cases, the subsidies save the government money, because it does not have to provide the service itself. However, such subsidies may perpetuate poor management habits by the recipient.

Consolidation

A government may elect to consolidate a service with other related services that operate in a more competitive environment. Another form of consolidation is when two governments merge one or more services into a single operation run by one of them or by a separate entity they establish. Examples include regional jails, battered women's shelters, and public safety training facilities.

Mixing and Matching the Alternatives

Governments "mix and match" these alternatives in creative ways. For example, in build-to-transfer agreements, private companies receive long-term franchises to provide a service in return for investing in developing, operating, and maintaining it. At the end of the franchise (twenty to fifty years is usual), all property and improvements revert to the government. In a hybrid form of outsourcing, Pennsylvania's state travel office operates with public employees working alongside employees of an experienced private contractor that, as a recognized travel agency, can receive rebates from airlines (and turns 70 percent of the amount over to the state). The benefit of these forms of competition is the value added that bidding companies offer for the franchise or contract.

DIRECT COMPETITION BETWEEN THE PUBLIC AND PRIVATE SECTORS

As noted earlier in this book, private companies and public agencies in Phoenix and Indianapolis compete for government contracts to provide services such as garbage collection and road maintenance. These municipalities divide their jurisdictions into districts and run competitions in each area separately. In Massachusetts, the approach is used to give agencies a choice between government-owned and outside suppliers of printing and vehicle maintenance services. The U.S. Navy has allowed its aviation depots and shipyards to compete with private companies for contracts to overhaul and refit aircraft and vessels. The federal A-76 process (named after the Office of Management and Budget [OMB] Circular A-76) permits federal agencies to run competitions between internal groups who provide a service and outside contractors.

Ohio AFSCME Employees Win Against the Private Sector

Members of the American Federation of State, County, and Municipal Employees (AFSCME) in Toledo and Huron County, Ohio, have proved to be the cost-effective alternative for services that many jurisdictions job out to private companies.

Toledo. When a contractor wasn't doing a speedy job of demolishing condemned houses, Toledo AFSCME workers persuaded the city to let them try. Costs dropped 23 percent per house, and response time is "absolutely" better, according to the city's manager of demolitions. Now, union workers do all the wrecking, using more efficient, purchased equipment, where contractors spent $8,500 in bulldozer rental.

Huron County. AFSCME members in this county have cut the costs of repairing bridges down to 40 percent less than contractors wanted to charge, averaging $30,000 for labor and costs involved in fixing a twenty-foot span versus private sector bids of $50,000. Process improvements were the reason: transferring snow removal and roadside mowing employees to bridge work during their slow seasons, buying instead of renting equipment, and buying steel in bulk for eighteen cents a pound (contractors charged forty to sixty cents). The public employees move faster than contractors, too—a decided plus because the county has two hundred bridges to fix.

Source: *The Public Innovator,* December 29, 1994 (See Appendix A)

Public Employees and Unions

If an outside supplier wins a contract to provide a service now handled by public employees, then most of public employees will no longer be needed in that service. Even when an in-house group competes and wins against an outsider, it has done so by cutting costs that often include labor made unnecessary by process improvements. Either way, a government that engages in competition must be prepared for painful personnel decisions and political resistance by unions.

There are no easy answers here. Perhaps the best way to avoid these problems is to allow public employees and managers the chance to improve their services before facing competition. Just as nothing improves a person's focus as much as being an hour away from execution, so does the imminent prospect of privatization foster a search for process improvement by management and labor. A next best alternative is to allow public personnel to join in a competition, as happened in Toledo and Huron County in Ohio (see box: Ohio AFSCME Employees Win Against the Private Sector).

The key to success in these cases is to provide employees with methods for discovering improvements in existing processes, such as the procedures discussed throughout this book (see box: Competition and Cost Accounting in Indianapolis, Indiana on pages 297-8). If these approaches are handled fairly, unions and employees will actively participate in them to the point of reducing labor costs in order to become more competitive. If you decide not to allow internal units to compete, a third alternative is to require that outside suppliers hire key in-house staff and give preference to hiring everyone else already on the staff.

Management Buy Out

In industry, sometimes a private organization will permit

managers and employees of a non-core operation to establish a separate company whose business it is to provide a once-internal service. This is called a management buy out (MBO). The new company benefits from an initial outsourcing contract with the original organization, which helps it keep going while finding other business in the marketplace. The original organization benefits because the MBO company has little or no learning curve, and key staff members are familiar to organization managers.

This arrangement works fine for a private business, where a company can give contracts to whomever it pleases, within the bounds of its stewardship of owners' funds. It may be harder for governments to handle, given procurement rules that specify open and fair competition for contracts, with no favoritism or "revolving door" situations where people who help arrange contracts end up working on them. Still, an MBO is worth considering, so long as discussions and arrangements are open and demonstrably fair.

CHOOSING WHAT TO PRIVATIZE

There are several schools of thought on what types of services and internal processes are best for privatizing. For example, Tom Peters suggests that private companies should subject their non-core functions to this simple test: "Could their output be sold on the open market?" he says. "If not, subcontract their work to firms that specialize in each function, which will almost certainly do it better and more cheaply." Here, Peters is applying a quality test: if no one else would buy an internal operation's output, then the organization that owns the operation is being shortchanged. Also, he is saying that many internal operations are only sideline business and do not benefit from top management's interest and investment in keeping the organization competitive. Such operations should be outsourced to organizations where they are the core business, not a sideline, concludes Peters, because top management there will invest in keeping them competitive.

Peters' rule is a good one, and you should consider it. However, it requires a bit of modification for some government services and operations. For example, there may be no other private providers of a public service, and thus no private market for it. Also, in some cases security or public safety require that an operation be done in-house. Finally, a particular service or operation may be a valuable asset to your identity with the public. In this section, we will outline decision frameworks for privatizing public service and operations. In the next section, we will discuss steps to introduce competition to operations, whether through privatizing or other means.

Centrality to Mission

In Chapter 7, we outlined a value classification system that evaluated processes by identity, priority, background, and mandate, according to their status as asset, liability, or value neutral. In Figure 11-3, we apply this classification to the decision to privatize a process. Note that a case exists for privatizing most processes, except for identity processes that are assets. The case becomes progressively stronger for priority, background, and mandated processes. All value-neutral processes are candidates for privatizing, if this will save costs, increase efficiency, or relieve administrators of the burden of overseeing them.

There are many exceptions to the decision criteria just mentioned. The closer a service is to being central to an agency's primary mission, the less desirable it is to privatize the service. In a law enforcement agency, apprehending criminals is a core business process, but issuing parking tickets may not be. Most internal support services fall in the non-core category.

There can be exceptions to this rule, because each situation is unique. For example, maintaining public roads is a key identity process of a highway department and an asset when department employees do world-class work. However, if

Value Classification

Type of Process	Asset	Value Neutral	Liability
Identity	Keep in-house, continuously improve.		Take strong measures to rapidly improve the process, such as through reengineering, if necessary. If sufficient improvement cannot be gained in-house, then privatize the process if this will meet customer or stakeholder demands.
Priority	Privatize if this will increase competitive advantage.	Privatize if this will save costs, increase efficiency, or reduce administrative attention.	Privatize or greatly improve in-house operation.
Background	Privatize if this will save costs, increase competitive advantage, or change a background process into a asset identity process.		Same as above. These are very strong candidates for privatizing.
Mandate	Mandated processes can never be assets.		Same as above. These are the strongest candidates for privatizing, if it will relieve the liability.

Figure 11-3
Process Value
Classifications
for Privatizing

there are many private companies that can provide this service with equal effectiveness, then public/private competitions still may be in order.

On the other hand, processing medical tests is definitely a background operation for a health department and may seem a prime candidate for privatizing. Yet Coopers & Lybrand recommended to one state health department that it not outsource medical lab tests, even though there were several excellent private laboratories that could do the work. The reason? To a public health department, testing for contagious disease demands stringent quality control, plus the flexibility to test, retest, and test yet again, no matter what the cost. For that state, an in-house laboratory is the best way to assure quality and flexibility for this background process.

Finally, some governments mandate that public personnel be trained about avoiding sexual harassment in the work place. The training could be contracted out to a private organization, but it may be more effective if delivered by executives and managers. In short, there are no clear-cut, cookie-cutter guidelines for privatizing.

Process Performance and Available Market

Another way of considering a privatizing option is to contrast your current performance in a process to performance in the external market that provides the same process. Figure 11-4 shows the steps in this procedure when considering privatizing. Through methods discussed below, you determine if the existing process performs as well or better than similar processes elsewhere, or could be made to do so. In either case, you are or could be a world-class supplier of this process, so there is nothing to be gained from privatizing it. If the process cannot be improved to make it world class, then privatizing is a viable option if there is a competitive market that can take on the job.

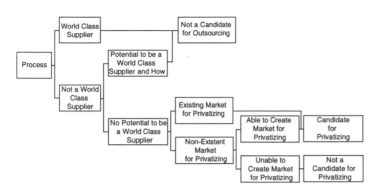

Figure 11-4
Privatizing,
Process
Performance,
and Available
Markets

Is there is an opportunity to *substantially* improve the service by allowing several entities to compete for it?

If you set out to gain 10 percent improvement in services or cost savings through contracting out for a service, chances are you will not realize any benefits. This is because even the best estimates of competitive benefits are based on assumptions that may not be altogether accurate. However, if you set the decision-to-compete threshold at improving by 25 to 35 percent, then even if your assumptions are off a bit, you will still make significant gains. If you only need a 10 percent gain in effectiveness or savings in order to satisfy customers and stakeholders, try continuous improvement methods instead.

How can you determine if a substantial gain is possible? Methods include the following:

*   **Market studies, comparative analyses, and performance benchmarking.** Use these studies to research the performance of other organizations that carry out the same or similar services. Documenting that someone else does the service substantially better is good evidence that you can achieve the same result, either by contracting out, improving internal operations, or a combination of both.

- **Consult experts.** Consultants and trade associations who specialize in a service are aware of leading-edge performance in it.

- **Consult potential vendors.** Invite potential vendors to study the process and give you their opinions on how they would improve its operations.

Chances are you will learn that others have improved on your process. You can incorporate these improvements into the in-house process, or use them when creating a request for proposal (RFP) or quote (RFQ) for a contract.

Is there an established external market with at least two or three viable competitors?

By this, we mean external to the agency that needs the service, which might include private vendors and other public agencies. With a viable market, an agency will always have leverage over the incumbent contractor. Without one, the reverse is true. To find out if such a market exists, you can do the following:

- Solicit capabilities statements. This involves making it known that you are considering contracting out for a service and that you wish to review the capabilities of private contractors who might bid on the work.

- Contact experts and trade or business associations. This may be as simple as calling the local chamber of commerce or the director of a trade association.

- Contact your neighbors. Usually, someone in your government will know if a neighboring jurisdiction contracts out for a service.

If the market does not precisely fit what you need, then consider modifying the need a bit to fit the market. If you can do this without sacrificing the basic integrity of the process or service, chances are the benefits of competition will exceed the value of continuing to operate it without competition.

STEPS FOR DEVELOPING COMPETITION

Listed below are steps to take when planning for competition. These steps by no means encompass all the procedures for private contracting or asset sales, but, in general, they relate to cost effectiveness, flexibility, and reducing the risk of a wrong decision.

1.   Understanding What Is Being Competed for

To ensure successful competition, a government must identify and map the processes and boundaries of an existing service, taking care to understand the number of people involved and their location in the system, resources consumed, and other factors. By doing this, an agency may discover information that will shift the balance of decision toward or away from privatizing. At the least, doing a high-level process map of a service will show what will go away once it is privatized, including administrative and other support resources devoted to the service.

2.   Reviewing Competition Issues

In this step, you answer the following questions. (Often, you will need to include customers and stakeholders, as well as managers and employees, in arriving at the answers.)

Is the cost of competition reasonable?

This includes the cost of locating potential vendors, setting up a competitive award system, contract administration, and oversight. If the initial cost of doing this is great and the payback period is long, then competition may not be cost effective when compared with other quality improvement methods. A related question is, *"Will competition result in less administrative burden?"* The net effect of competition should be that government administrators will be free to focus more attention on other services and issues. This means that the performance of the competed service can be easily monitored and managed.

Will it be economically and legally feasible to reverse the decision?

Over time, some private companies move support services such as market research and advertising back and forth between in-house and outside suppliers. The reasons for this flexibility include cost, control, and politics (just like in government). Regardless of the reason, it should never be so difficult and costly to take back in-house an outsourced service as to prevent you from doing so. Some things to consider include the following:

- Selling public assets outright to a private company is the most difficult decision to reverse, which is why many governments prefer to lease them.

- All contracts and franchises should have termination clauses that are favorable to the buyer.

- An agency that contracts out for an important service should consider retaining a few staff who know the intricacies of the service. They can monitor contractor performance and, if it is necessary to take a service back in-house, they can plan how to do this.

3. Competing for a Service

Define desired results

A major mistake is to start out by thinking of a service or asset solely in terms of its outputs. Unfortunately, too many governments use spending or output measures to define a service, instead of its results. This mistaken approach increases the risk of perpetuating the status quo, as governments contract out services that are based on false assumptions or ineffective designs. Then, contractors end up doing the wrong things faster and cheaper.

A simple example of this problem is to spell out in a contract the number of hours mechanics are to spend in repairing government vehicles. They may consume the hours, ask for more, and still not do an effective job. A better definition would be the number and type of repairs expected; contractors can bid on this amount of work and have an incentive to be cost effective. The best definition of the work expected might be effective, full maintenance with minimum downtime for all vehicles in a specified fleet. This puts more risk on the side of the contractor and motivates performance.

Less simple examples include educational and social services, which are subject to many variables, some of which are outside the control of a service provider. However, stating clearly a desired result, such as "increasing the number of preschoolers with developmental problems who successfully enter primary school," is much better than simply listing the number of hours required of special education teachers (see Figure 12-4 for an example of this).

Cost accounting and the level playing field

The level playing field applies to public/private competitions. As discussed in Chapter 13, most governments' cost accounting systems are not adequate for good financial decision making, much less for competition. For example, the New York Mayor's Private Sector Survey in 1989 found that of over two thousand performance measures for mayoral agencies, less than 2 percent showed the cost of work done in specific functions and activities. Given this situation, plus other problems outlined in Chapter 13, how can a government do a fair cost comparison (the level playing field) of in-house and outside service delivery options? (See box: Competition and Cost Accounting in Indianapolis, Indiana.)

Complaints from private sector contractors about this problem perennially plagued Navy shipyards and the aviation depots that competed against them for overhaul and refit work. Only when the government facilities adopted better cost accounting methods did the complaints subside. (Interestingly, the new methods helped the shipyards and aviation depots develop better, more competitive bids.) We recommend using the ABC system discussed in Chapter 13 to arrive at accurate internal costs.

Procurement regulations

Procurement regulations often add significant amounts to the cost of contracting out or running competitions between in-house and outside suppliers, making these alternatives less affordable. We could write another book about procurement reform but will content ourselves with saying that, the more you contemplate competition, the more reason you have to fix an unwieldy procurement system.

4. Contract Administration

Performance measurement

Because a government is responsible to citizens for the quality of services, it must have sufficient control over competed services to affect the factors that have the greatest impact on quality. The details of this control must be spelled out in the contract. This includes having a good set of performance measures for both the operation of the service and its outcomes. Also, an agency often will need to develop an independent customer feedback system, in which it proactively solicits customer and stakeholder satisfaction and expectation information.

Preventing disruption

The essence of competition is that incumbent service providers run the risk of losing their business if they cannot perform as well as competitors. This means that, from time to time, a government will have to adjust to a new supplier. Thus, a system must be in place to minimize the disruption of services provided to citizens or of internal operations that depend on a competitive service. Other disruption problems include severe political or community opposition and difficulties in employee dislocation or other transition issues. To deal with these problems, some agencies require that contractors hire certain public employees whose knowledge and experience is critical to the continuity of service performance. Finally, in some cases, two internal departments will have worked together effectively to provide a service. Contracting out the work of one of these departments can cause problems in creating a new synergy, which must be

---

Competition and Cost Accounting in Indianapolis, Indiana

In 1992, Stephen Goldsmith was elected mayor of Indianapolis with a strong promise to reform local government through marketplace competition. He directed the city's Department of Transportation to set up competitions between city road repair crews and private contractors. He also made it plain that "gaming" the numbers would not be allowed; auditors would check the city bids before they were submitted.

DOT managers knew their direct costs, but actual "full cost" figures were distorted. This distortion was due to the traditional accounting practice of evenly allocating indirect or overhead expenses, usually by putting a multiplier on direct labor hours. This allocation approach to overhead overstated DOT's costs and made it difficult to discover what caused them.

DOT found the answer in ABC (ABC, see Chapter 13). Among other things, ABC traces the relevant costs, both direct and indirect, of operating an activity or producing a unit of output. It also helps you understand what factors or events drive those costs, so you can identify their root causes. Said Mayor Goldsmith, "Activity-based costing has to come in front of competition because we can't

---

even get our own folks into a bid mentality until we know how much it costs to provide a service."* Once they got into that mental set, though, city employees became hard-nosed businesspersons, and they have won most of their competitions. Indianapolis won, too, because the cost of road repairs dropped by as much as 60 percent.

* Stephen Goldsmith, "Moving Municipal Services into the Marketplace," No. 14 in a series of papers by Carnegie Privatization Project. New York: Carnegie Council, November 20, 1992.

dealt with in the legal terms of a contract.

Technical administration of contracts

If an agency has no experience in contracting out for a service, then it faces a definite problem in contract administration. Ideally, the government manager in charge of a contract will be both knowledgeable about the service area and proficient in contract administration. Most of the time it is not hard to find technically knowledgeable people; a senior manager in the service organization that has been competed usually remains to oversee the contract. However, managing the contract requires a whole different set of skills than those required for managing the service itself. Training in contract-managing skills is a critical prerequisite to successful competition.

Continuous improvement between competitions

You want a service to improve all the time, not just before a competition, when incumbents and their competitors hastily enhance their services and bids in order to win. A government can ensure this ongoing improvement within its internal operations. But how do you do it for outside contractors? We will address this now.

CHANGING RELATIONSHIPS WITH DISTRIBUTORS

In government, distributors are organizations that receive resources from funding agencies and give them to the final beneficiaries. For example, local and state food stamp and Women, Infants, and Children (WIC) programs are distributors for the U.S. Department of Agriculture. Local community health clinics are distributors for federal- and state-funded health care resources. This relationship exists even under a block grant arrangement, because the donor government has certain management expectations of the distributor, including that the distributor will:

- Exercise sound stewardship of the funds received from the donor;

- Use the funds to deliver high-quality services to the beneficiaries; and

- Continuously improve the processes that benefit the beneficiaries.

One model for distributor relations is the detailed and inflexible procedures manual combined with massive documentation. The other is the grant that has few controls attached to it. Neither model is satisfactory, because neither does anything to promote better management practices among the distributors. A new model is emerging.

Enabling Distributors to Create Their Own Quality Systems

Each year, the Department of Education gives or guarantees billions in grants, loans, and work-study assistance to college students. It depends on thousands of schools to help administer the various financial aid programs. Once, the predominant department strategy for working with the schools included prescriptive regulations, massive documentation, after-the-fact inspection, multiple process check-points, and minimum standards and quotas.

The new strategy for Title IV student aid programs is to deregulate the process and give the schools the authority to determine on their own how best to accomplish financial aid program objectives. And instead of quotas and minimum national standards, the effort pushes for continuous improvement. The department exempts schools in its Institutional Quality Assurance Program from some federal regulations that prescribe in inflexible detail how to verify student application data before awarding financial assistance. Instead, the schools can design their own verification programs. In return, the schools develop a formal quality system that includes management self-assessment, error measurement, corrective action management, and monitoring. The department trains and consults with the schools in setting up these systems.

According to an evaluation of the program, most schools find that the new system helps them manage their financial aid offices better. In addition, the system consistently identifies chronic problems, which lets the schools target corrective action at process improvement, not individual mistakes.

VENDOR PARTNERSHIP

Vendor partnership is a term for a formal system of dealing with companies that sell you goods and services. The advantages of this approach have been proven repeatedly in industry and include improved product quality, reliable delivery performance, reduced lead times, increased vendor service, extended technical capabilities, and lower product cost.

Traditional	Vendor Partnership
Multiple vendors for the same types of products: The reasons for this are leverage in price negotiations and an assumed protection of the flow of supplies.	**Number of vendors minimized:** This creates a vested interest in the mutual success of both customer and vendor. It also allows the vendor to increase the level of specialized services to a customer.
Ignorance of the vendor's quality system: As a result, an organization must use incoming inspection to determine quality. The relationship between customer and supplier becomes one of blame versus assistance for achieving quality.	**Specific quality systems requirements:** The customer requires proof that vendor processes are in control. No incoming inspection is needed. Both parties combine problem-solving resources.
Poor communications of standards and specifications: The arms-length posture between traditional organizations and their vendors means that the vendors cannot become involved in the setting of standards and specifications. The results are confusion and frequent change orders in contracts to correct these mistakes.	**Mutual agreement on standards and specification:** Customers and vendors work together to set standards and specifications. There are no misunderstandings.
Short-term contracts: Contracts are for a few months or years.	**Long-term contracts:** Contracts are for several years; commitments are even longer.
Emphasis on price: Particularly in government, price becomes the overriding factor in selecting vendors. The quality of vendor products and vendor reputation often take a back seat to price.	**Emphasis on value:** The customer considers the overall value of vendor products, customer service, and vendor participation in the production process.

Figure 11-5
Traditional
Versus
Vendor
Partnership
Relations

A vendor partner's prices tend to be lower than open-market prices, because the vendor is guaranteed a large portion of an organization's business for a long period. True cost is also lower because these products and services can be designed to fit a customer's processes precisely, and the customer receives better service. Figure 11-5 compares traditional relationships with vendors with the vendor partnership approach.

Vendor partnership may at first seem an alien concept, given government acquisition regulations. Perhaps the major barrier remaining to vendor partnerships in government is the legal requirement for open competition to all qualified vendors and contractors. Private companies are under no such obligation, and those that practice vendor partnership tend to give their business to vendors with whom they have long-term relationships. They do this as long as the vendors maintain commitment to quality and continuous improvement and offer a fair market price. It is only natural for such vendors to help customers set standards and specifications for purchases and plan projects that will result in business for the vendors. This information is a closely held secret in most government agencies, until requests for bids are made public.

Despite these differences in the private and public sectors' procurement environments, vendor partnership has many features that work well in both. Among these are the up-front work customers do to improve buying practices, teamwork with vendors, and certifying vendors.

Starting Vendor Partnerships

An organization begins a vendor partnership program by forming an internal cross-functional procurement systems team of high-level managers. This team provides program direction and resources and evaluates and resolves issues that arise. The procurement systems team then sets up several commodity teams, which focus on particular categories of purchased products and services. The commodity teams establish goals and objectives for vendors, coordinate vendor improvement activity, and report progress to the procurement systems team. Internal users of products serve on the commodity teams, provide pertinent data, and assist in evaluating vendors.

Commodity teams identify improvement opportunities in current purchasing practices and products for their areas. They work with vendors to identify causes of, and potential solutions for, problems and measure and evaluate results of vendor improvement. The purchasing department is responsible for introducing the vendor partnership program to vendors and works with them to implement continuous improvement practices.

Vendor representatives form vendor partnership teams with an organization's personnel. They work on common issues and problems and are available to participate on improvement teams when the need arises.

Vendor partnership is appropriate only when you buy a large volume of a particular product or service or when a product is critical to operations. Exceptions to this are commonly available raw materials, paper, and so forth. The higher the percentage of the vendor's sales to you the better, because the vendor becomes dependent on your business and will be more motivated to meet your expectations.

Selecting Vendor Partners

You select vendor partners on the basis of their historic performance in quality, delivery, and price; ability to produce the needed volume; attitude toward quality and continuous improvement; expertise; use of statistical process control, if appropriate; proximity; stability; and financial solvency. You would place potential vendors into three categories, based on audits and vendor documentation:

- **Certified vendor.** The vendor's quality system is accepted and has a history of deliverying value and service. The customer need not inspect goods and services from certified vendors, because they are assumed to meet standards and specifications. This saves the customer time and money.

- **Approved vendor.** The vendor's quality system is acceptable, and quality, delivery, and value are under review. The customer inspects samples of goods delivered.

- **Additional vendors.** The vendor's quality system is unknown or under review, and product quality, delivery, and value are under review. The customer increases inspection until reducing it is justified by results.

This classification scheme is much like the Navy's red-yellow-green system for its vendors, with green being the equivalent of approved vendors and yellow the same as additional vendors. The Navy's red category indicates a vendor with a history of poor performance. Adding requirements for quality practices to the Navy system (parts of which are already on the Department of Defense's books and have been introduced at NASA) would create the top category of certified vendor and make this arrangement come very close to being a true vendor partnership.

Contracts and Trust

Contracts are definitely part of vendor partnerships. The difference is that for U.S. private industry these contracts tend to be for longer periods than in the past. However, industry's definition of short-term contracts is usually six months to a year, and a long-term contract is often only two years. Government contracts tend to be longer. This is especially true for large and complex buys such as weapons systems, data-processing systems, and facilities support.

The very-long-term relationships between customer and vendor under this approach are based on trust, not contracts. Each party in a vendor partnership has a degree of commitment to the other (and to the end user) that goes far beyond the typical arm's-length buyer/seller arrangement. This is why great thought must be given to selecting a vendor partner and why vendor attitudes toward quality and continuous improvement are so important.

ISO 9000: GUIDELINES FOR VENDOR QUALITY SYSTEMS

Organizations that want guidelines for vendor quality would do well to look at those adopted by over seventy countries, including the United States. In Europe, they are called the International Organization for Standardization 9000 Series of Standards, and almost everyone refers to them as the ISO 9000 standards. Identical standards in the United States are called the American National Standards Institute/American Society for Quality Control Q90 Series of Standards. The original idea behind ISO 9000 was to promote standardization in quality systems for organizations engaged in international commerce. Today, ISO 9000 has become the basic benchmark in over one thousand U.S. companies, in nearly all the states.

ISO 9000 includes standards for quality management, assurance, and control. Although certification in the standards is voluntary, many corporations, such as Chrysler, Ford, and General Motors, require their vendors to be certified. Both the DoD and NASA have approved the use of ISO 9000 as acceptable quality standards for contractors.

Certification means that an *accredited, independent auditor* has reviewed an organization's quality systems and found them to meet one or more of the ISO 9000 series of standards. Auditors receive their accreditation from the Registrar Accreditation Board, which is affiliated with the American Society for Quality Control (ASQC, see Appendix A). Having passed the audit, the oranization receives a registration certificate used to prove to customers that its quality systems meet international standards. This relieves customers of the need to conduct a separate quality assurance audit of the vendor.

Understanding and Applying the Standards

ISO 9000 was originally designed to be applied to all industries, but sometimes people misunderstand how the standards apply to their operations. One result has been a bumper crop of hundreds of ISO seminars, books, and software, the prices of which range from a few to many thousands of dollars. In addition, there are hundreds of consultants available to assist you, some of whom only heard about ISO 9000 yesterday. Here are a few suggestions to aid you in getting smart about ISO 9000 and applying it to your best advantage.

Background information

To obtain the ISO 9000/Q90 series, contact the American Society for Quality Control. As of this writing, we think that *The ISO 9000 Handbook,* 2nd edition, is the best background guide because it is both encyclopedic and includes suggestions for implementing the standards. To order these documents, see Appendix A.

Assessing existing quality systems

The best application of ISO 9000 is using it to conduct an analysis of the gap between existing quality systems and those outlined by the standards. Eliminating the gap is the goal for improving the systems.

Uses of the standards. If you are a government contractor, using ISO 9000 to guide internal quality assurance and control may be an excellent idea. If you are a government agency, the standards can become part of your contractor quality assurance audit guidelines (you might see a few hints for internal improvements, too). If you are a government organization that sells its services to other public agencies or to the public, consider adopting the standards as part of your own quality assurance system.

Develop glossaries. In Chapter 8, we mentioned the glossary as a tool of process improvement. Glossaries are lists and definitions of terms that may refer to steps or parts of a process or, in this case, a definition of the scope and meaning you apply to the requirements of an ISO standard. If you are a contractor, such a glossary will help managers, employees, certification auditors, and customers understand your interpretation of a standard.

Avoid overdevelopment in the wrong areas. ISO 9000 standards focus on quality control and quality assurance, so it is possible to focus too much on these areas instead of quality improvement. In some cases, companies have set up their quality control systems so tightly that it is difficult to introduce improvements. You have to find a balance between quality control and flexibility in meeting the intent of continuous improvement.

Documentation as side product, not purpose. The effectiveness of an ISO 9000 quality system is measured by its results, not massive volumes of quality manuals, procedures, and training materials. As a seller, you will need to focus on developing the processes that assure quality and to record the results along with the processes. As a buyer, you must be concerned with how a supplier applies ISO 9000 standards, so look for documentation of use, not plans to use them.

Alternatives to ISO 9000

Some buyers, such as Motorola, require their vendors to apply for the Malcolm Baldrige National Quality Award. This award, which we indicated in Chapter 4 is similar to many federal, state, and local quality awards, is more comprehensive than ISO 9000 and aims at improvement, not just quality assurance and control. The reason for the requirement is that the buyer uses the Baldrige criteria to improve its own operations and wants vendors to do the same. The issues and outcome are similar for both ISO 9000 and the Baldrige: both buyer and seller strive to improve products and services.

INFRASTRUCTURE
DEVELOPMENT

Chapter
12

MEASURING PERFORMANCE

■ Performance-based governance is a new, results-oriented management method that includes defining an agency's mission and goals, developing plans tied to the mission, and using performance measures to improve program results.

■ Results-oriented measurement demonstrates the link between agency action and desired outcomes, promotes innovation and creativity, and facilitates flexibility in management approaches.

■ Governments face problems when introducing results-oriented measures but have overcome them.

■ Success in measuring operations performance depends on knowing customer expectations, identifying ingredients of customer satisfaction, determining internal indicators of this satisfaction, and discovering what causes these indicators to vary over time.

■ Performance measurement systems must be dynamic to reflect changes in customer expectations and environment and to allow for continuous improvement.

What gets measured, gets done.

— Anonymous

We spend too much time producing performance measures to send in to headquarters. I hope they use them, 'cause we sure don't.

— Government manager

Our second quotation makes it clear that what gets measured *does not always get done*. Whatever that government manager was measuring—spending, unit cost, on-time deliveries—he was not using the information for process improvement. Having good measures is a critical factor in successful government service, but it is only part of the equation. In this chapter, we will present several comprehensive approaches to creating *and using* performance measures.

PERFORMANCE-BASED GOVERNANCE

The problem of unused measures is reduced by performance-based governance or results-oriented public service. According to the U.S. General Accounting Office, "Results-oriented management of an organization involves the articulation of its mission and goals, the development of plans and measures tied to the mission, and the use of performance information to improve program results." The operative word here is *result*. In performance-based governance, you measure more than inputs (funds from the legislature), outputs (the amount of work done or services provided in a period), and efficiency (inputs divided by number of outputs produced). This new approach assumes that it is more important to measure the *outcomes* or *results* that come from government action, such as the percentage reduction over time of the number of children growing up in poverty.

Type of Measure	Description	Examples
Input	Resources used to carry out a program over a given period	Number of full-time employees, amount of equipment or materials used, dollars spent
Output	Amount of work accomplished or services provided over a given period	Number of welfare applicants processed, number of workers' compensation claims paid
Efficiency	Cost of labor or materials per unit of output or service	Cost per client served, equipment costs per square mile, or brush cleared
Outcome	Extent to which program goals have been achieved or customer requirements have been satisfied	Percent reduction in teen pregnancy rate, customer satisfaction with taxpayer services

Source: *Managing for Results: State Experiences Provide Insights for Federal Management Reforms,* U.S. General Accounting Office, December 1994.

Figure 12-1
Types of
Performance
Measures
Used by
Government

At the federal level, the movement toward performance-based governance includes the Government Performance and Results Act of 1992 (GPRA). The GPRA requires agencies to develop strategic plans that include mission statements, goals, and plans to achieve goals. Agencies are to report progress toward goals with results-oriented performance measures. The act also calls for testing performance budgeting in some agencies, whereby the agency shows the direct relationship of proposed program spending to expected program results.

Governors of several states worked with the National Governors' Association to develop a conceptual model of performance-based governance, shown in Figure 12-2. According to this model, the driver of performance-based governance is the need to achieve results through cultural change (both inside and outside government) and continuous improvement. This process of change has four guiding elements:

1. It begins with citizens and government leaders developing a shared vision of what they want a state to look like in the future.

2. Leaders set measurable strategic goals or targets that, if achieved, will make the vision a reality.

3. Leaders and agencies develop strategies to achieve the goals and results-oriented performance measures to monitor goal attainment.

4. Governments develop budgets tied to achieving the goals, as gauged by results-oriented process measures.

Much like the PDCA and Improvement Driven Organization frameworks, performance-based governance is a circular model, indicating the opportunity (and the need) to repeat its processes to achieve continuous improvement.

Figure 12-2
A Strategic
Framework
for
Performance-
Based
Governance

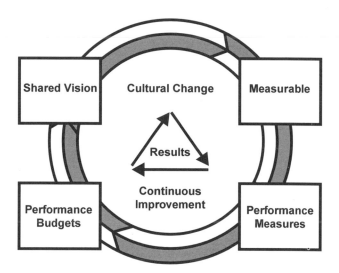

Source: *An Action Agenda to Redesign State Government,* National Governors' Association, 1994.

A good example of the performance measurement element of this model comes from the Texas Commission for the Blind. One goal of the agency is to assist blind or visually impaired people to live as independently as is consistent with their capabilities. A 1995 objective of the goal is to

increase by 66.2 percent the number of visually handi-
capped people who achieve their independent living goals.
One strategy to reach the objective is to provide services
that equip blind high schoolers to make the transition from
school to working. In turn, the performance of these services can be measured by the numbers and types of people
served, service outcomes, and efficiency measures such as
the cost per person served.

BENEFITS OF MEASURING RESULTS

This approach to performance measurement has several
advantages over older input/output measures, such as the
following.

Demonstrates Causality. To leaders who control the public
purse strings, the most important question is, "If you spend X
amount of dollars on program Y, what do citizens get back?"
Variations on this question echo down through every layer of
an organization, posed alike to managers asking for expensive
new information systems and employees who want personal
computers. Focusing on results makes it possible to develop a
causal link from an outcome to the processes that effect it.
Thus, goals are linked to core business processes to simple
processes to tasks within the processes. In this manner, everyone from leaders to line employees understands how his or
her work is related to the desired results. We will return to
this point later in the chapter.

Promotes Innovation and Cooperation. A results-oriented goal prompts out-of-the-box thinking and interorganiza-
tional solutions. An employment agency may have thought
of its work as simply helping place people in available jobs,
as measured by the number placed. If a goal is to increase
high-wage employment, the agency is more likely to look
for ways to cooperate with other agencies and businesses to
attract such jobs to an area and ensure that job seekers have
appropriate training for them. If your funding and career

depend on gaining a specific result, you'll be motivated to explore all reasonable means of achieving it.

Facilitates Flexibility. A focus on outcomes also makes clear a need for flexible management. For example, in 1991, the Florida Governor's Commission for Government by the People noted that the state's "personnel and budget systems often concentrate on inputs and ignore outcomes. [These systems] limit a manager's flexibility to move resources as needs change, hide the true costs of programs, and encourage managers to waste money." Such systems often were put into place precisely because an agency could not define and measure desired results, leaving the agency open to micro-management by lawmakers through budgetary and administrative processes. In Florida, legislators are now pilot testing flexible personnel and budget requirements in some agencies, in part because the agencies can produce results measures. The underlying motivation, according to an adviser to the state's governor, is that legislators are finally hearing community leaders and citizens who say, "What are you talking to me about these programs for? Tell me what's happening to people."

CREATING RESULTS MEASURES

Results measures answer the question, How do we know we are getting where we want to go? As shown in Figure 12-2, developing results measures begins by creating a vision of a future desired state, which can be obtained by achieving certain goals. These goals may be expressed as measures such as those in Figure 12-3, from the state of Oregon's Benchmarks system.

Customer and Stakeholder Driven. Creating such measures requires a clear understanding of customer and stakeholder expectations. In Oregon, the measures were arrived at by citizen steering committees and participation by over two hundred organizations and individuals statewide. The

Years of Measurement	1970	1980	1990	1992	1995	2000	2010
Examples: Benchmarks for People							
Percentage of babies whose mothers received adequate prenatal care		77%	75%	77%	100%	100%	100%
Percentage of kindergarten children ready to participate successfully in school				65%	80%	95%	99%
Percentage of fifth graders who achieve established skill levels in math			77%	81%	86%	91%	99%
High school graduation rate			73%	76%	83%	93%	95%
Percentage of adults completing at least one year of postsecondary schooling		39%	52%	56%	70%	80%	85%
Examples: Quality of Life Benchmarks							
Percentage of Oregonians living where the air meets government ambient air quality standards	33%	30%	89%	50%	100%	100%	100%
Acres of Oregon parks and protected recreation land per 1,000 Oregonians			157		160	160	160
Percentage of Oregonians with work commutes during peak hours other than by single-occupancy vehicle				29%	29%	33%	38%
Rate of index crimes per 1,000 people		64.1	63.1	57.8	44	28	22
Percentage of Oregon households that can afford the median-priced Oregon home			47%		50%	50%	50%
Examples: Economic Benchmarks							
Oregon's real per capita income as a percentage of the U.S. real per capita income	96%	99%	90%	92%	95%	100%	100%
Oregon's ranking among states in workers' compensation costs			8th	WP	20th-25th	20th-25th	20th
Major international cities served by direct, nonstop flights from any Oregon airport		1	4	5	6	8	11
Real per capita capital outlays for infrastructure maintenance and improvement (1990 dollars)	$426	$525	$330	$432	$597	$651	$758

Figure 12-3
An Oregon Benchmarks Sampler

state legislature then adopted the measures as its yardstick for legislative proposals. Other governments have used surveys and focus groups of citizens to help set such goals.

Within an organization and at the process level, internal results measures can be developed simply by talking with internal customers and suppliers about their needs and priorities. Organizations that provide services to other agencies can do this, too. Take care, though, to align these measures with the strategic results goals of the organization and the government.

Logical. Another important element of the measurement development process is to define precisely a program's purpose or mission. The outcome measure must align with that purpose, which means the two are logically related. Figure 12-4 shows how this relationship might be displayed in a comprehensive measurement report of the Prince William County, Virginia Parent-Infant Education Program for at-risk infants and toddlers. The outcome—percentage of toddlers requiring no special education services when discharged—is logically linked to the purpose of the program.

Understandable. Every performance measure has a primary audience: the people who will read and act on the information it provides. This audience may include you and your staff (who control a process, program, or agency), general citizens (their action is to vote), legislators (they control budgets), or the next process in line (its operators need confirmation of the quality of your output, which is their input). It is especially important that all parts of your audience understand and agree on the meaning of a results measure. One reason is obvious: it is the ultimate yardstick of your performance. Another reason is that a results indicator often spawns a host of smaller, more immediate measures used at different points in a program or process. Confusion about the result measure will cascade into the rest of your measurement system.

Program Definition

To help at-risk infants and toddlers attain maximum development and to enhance the capacity of their families to meet their special needs.

Program Performance Measures

Outcomes: Percent of children served who require no special education services when discharged.

FY 94:	16%
FY 93:	10%

Inputs:

Staff	FY 94:	14.4 FTE*
	FY 93:	14.8 FTE
Total Dollars	FY 94:	$675,359
	FY 93:	$678,745

Outputs:

Children and families served	FY 94:	374
	FY 93:	400

Efficiency:

Cost per client	FY 94:	$1,746
	FY 93:	$1,688

Quality: Percent of families satisfied with service (client survey)

FY 94:	90%
FY 93:	90%

*FTE: Full-time equivalent. A measure of labor hours; one FTE is equal to about 1900 labor hours.

Source: "Measuring Performance: A Prince of a System," *The Public Innovator* 15 (October 27, 1994): 4.

Figure 12-4 Selected Performance Components of Parent-Infant Education Program, Prince William County, Virginia

Comparable. Results measures should, insofar as possible, be comparable with the same or similar measures in other organizations, jurisdictions, states, or even countries. This allows you to benchmark your performance against an outside standard. Such knowledge will sometimes help you develop realistic targets for performance. More important, it will alert you to the opportunity to study how another organization or government with much better results than yours managed to get there.

Reliable Over Time. Because results measures reflect the purpose of a program, they tend to be needed for years and even decades. During such long periods, they may lose their sensitivity to changes in the phenomena they purport to measure. For example, infant mortality rates (the ratio of deaths among infants less than one year old to the number of live births in the same period) are good measures of health status in developing countries and poor communities. However, as health care availability and income increase, these death rates become less sensitive to changes and are less useful. This is why "low birth weight" is a better long-term measure in developed countries. Like infant mortality rates, low birth weight is associated with factors such as "month of pregnancy in which prenatal care is first received" and "cigarette-smoking status of mother." Both these factors can be measured over time, usually with increasing degrees of accuracy, to determine the success of prenatal care programs.

Available. Results measures should be readily available from outside sources, or you should be able to easily generate them yourself. Spending inordinate amounts of time and money developing results data probably means people either are heading in the wrong direction with their measurement or just haven't bothered to look around for secondary sources. Oregon has managed to find or develop over two hundred fifty high-level results measures, without breaking the bank.

Credible. Whether you collect the data yourself or find it in published sources, you must show people it is credible. You demonstrate the credibility of your data by explaining the underlying logic of your measurement plan, showing that you followed the plan, and documenting the sources of your data.

Problems in Introducing Results Measurement

Three major problems confront governments that select the results-oriented route to measurement: degree of control, political acceptance, and culture. Each problem can be solved but sometimes only with a new paradigm.

Degree of control

Often, an agency has only a mild influence over a major results measure. Teen pregnancy is a good example. A county health department charged with lowering the teen pregnancy rate has only a small degree of influence over the rate and confronts powerful societal forces outside its control that affect the rate. Two options are available to help the county better deal with this problem. The first is to use another results measure that better fits the narrow scope of influence of the department; for example, the department might seek to lower the rate among patients who attend county-run clinics. The second option is to become a community catalyst and educator. In this alternative, the department expands its scope to affect the measure through more comprehensive programming and alliances with other organizations. This is one of the key points of the National Performance Review's "steer more, row less" philosophy of government.

Political acceptance

Elected officials must use a results-oriented measurement system; otherwise, the system will rapidly fall into disuse or not even get off the ground. For example, both Minnesota and North Carolina tried to introduce performance-based budgeting in their agencies, including results measures. However, legislators and legislative staff were not happy with the performance information and did not use it. According to evaluations, state executives did not consult with state legislators and their staffs about their needs for performance information, establish the reliability of the measures, or present them in a format acceptable to this group of users. Both states have gone back to revise performance measurement approaches, this time with the active participation of the lawmakers. Florida and Oregon took this involvement step and did not have the same problem.

Culture

Remember, what gets measured does not always get done. An agency can have a culture that ignores any form of measure-ment, much less one that clearly targets results. If your orga-nization does not use performance measures now, then it will not automatically adopt results measures in the future (or any other type, for that matter). Here, the paradigm must shift from subjective to objective judgment based on facts. Such a change occurs through working on the following factors:

- **Leadership.** Agency leaders must begin to make deci-sions based on results measures. As in the case of the Minnesota and North Carolina legislators, if the leaders do not use the information, no one else will.

- **Infrastructure.** The agency must develop a system for obtaining and distributing performance measures. Often, this requires major changes in management information systems.

- **Participation.** Managers and employees must partici-pate in the development of the measurement system in order to fit it to their needs and to feel ownership for it.

- **Training.** Users of the measures must be trained in how to collect, analyze, and apply objective measurement information.

- **Reward.** People must be rewarded both for achieving results targets and for using the measures.

So much for performance-based governance. Now, let's look at how to drill down into an organization to measure performance in its daily operations.

MEASURING OPERATIONS PERFORMANCE

If you agree with the following statement, please read on; if not, please stop reading and give this book to someone else. *The only reason to measure operations performance is to take action to maintain and improve good results or solve problems that cause bad results.* Here, the key word is *action*, because if nobody does anything, there is no point to measuring.

Most organizations have internal performance measures and some way of getting feedback on customer satisfaction. Rarely, however, do the performance measures tie in with processes; neither are they collected, analyzed, or used by process operators. That's the first disconnect between measurement and action. Even more rare is the organization that links its process performance measures to achieving customer satisfaction. This second disconnect means that process operators cannot take appropriate action because such action is ultimately determined by customer expectations.

Measuring for Process Improvement: Four Steps to Success

To create a link between process performance and customer satisfaction, managers and employees must see evidence of a cause-and-effect relationship between the two. Gaining

this viewpoint is a four-step process of (1) identifying customers, (2) learning their expectations and levels of satisfaction, (3) finding and measuring process outcomes that cause
satisfaction to vary, and (4) using measurements to discover
root causes of this variation. This is a team project and produces the best results when the team includes members of
the processes being studied.

We'll walk you through this measurement process, with the
intent of showing some basic concepts. However, our summary does not include the fine points and subtleties of the
process, which we cannot address here for lack of space.
For more information on it, please consult the monograph,
Customer Service Measurement, listed in Appendix A.

Identify customers

As we said in Chapter 3, often organizations do not understand clearly who their customers are, so simply asking
people to list customers can be confusing. However, most
managers and employees know their outputs, so start with
having them identify these outputs. If you are looking at
measurement from an agency-wide perspective, begin with
the final outputs that go to external customers. If your outputs are only used inside your organization, then look at
those that go to internal customers.

Make a list of these outputs, and write a definition of each.
Next, using a worksheet such as that shown in Figure 12-5,
write down the name of the customer of each output. Some
outputs may have several, so you will need to repeat them
on the worksheet. If you cannot match an output with a customer, then it is simply part of a process and has no importance in initial measurement. (Sometimes, these
pseudo-outputs are prime candidates for elimination.)
Finally, list the process or group that produces the output
for a particular customer next to that customer's name.

CUSTOMER IDENTIFICATION WORKSHEET

Process Name Group   Customer   Output Received

Figure 12-5
Customer
Identification
Worksheet

Now you have a complete list of customers, the outputs they use, and the processes that produce the outputs. But ask yourself this: "Is every customer the same, or even equally important?" You may need to stratify your customers, or group them into different categories. Some categories of interest include the following:

• **Type of output used**. If you produce several types of output going to different customers, then each customer set probably has different expectations.

• **Importance**. All customers are important, but some use your services more than others or are more critical to your agency's mission. For example, you may have a mandate to work with certain types of customers, but you may also have some customers who do not fall under the mandate. Likewise, your strategic plans may identify top priority customers; you should focus more attention on them.

- **Demographics**. If you serve many individuals, then you may need to break them out into groups according to sex, age, income, or location. The same is true for local versus non-local organizations you serve, if this makes a difference in the way you serve them.

Define and describe each group in detail. Circulate your lists and definitions of outputs, customers, and processes among process operators and managers to ensure that everyone agrees on them.

Learn customer expectations and levels of satisfaction

In this step, you learn (1) what your customers expect from you and (2) how well you satisfy those expectations. There are many ways to get this information, but we believe the simplest and most reliable is a survey. We don't mean a long, complicated survey like those used in commercial product research but instead a simple questionnaire form such as that shown in Figure 12-6. You may need a more complex survey procedure than this, but every survey should include customer expectations, priorities, and levels of satisfaction. Also, such systems must be based on clear objectives that answer the questions "Why do we need this information?" and "What will we do with it?"

Figure 12-6
Customer
Interview
Form

CUSTOMER INTERVIEW FORM

Importance (1 – 5)	Expectation	Satisfaction (1 – 5)

What types of expectations should you include in a customer survey? You can start out with an open-ended question, "What are your expectations?" and list the responses on a form like that in Figure 12-6. If you have many customers, its a good idea to ask this of a sample of them, then print the most likely expectations on the form, with blank spaces for others. At a minimum, though, you need to ask internal customers about cost, responsiveness, accuracy, and working relationships. Be sure to clearly define these expectations in writing so that customers and process operators alike understand them.

Once customers list their expectations, ask them to set some priorities: which expectation is most important, which is least? This allows you to focus measurement and improvement on the most important expectations. In the form in Figure 12-6, customers rate the *importance* of their expectations for a product or service on a scale of one to five (one is least important, five is most important). Next, customers rate your *performance* on an expectation, again rating this on a one-to-five scale with five being the highest rating.

By summing and averaging the responses, you can develop tables and charts such as those shown in Figure 12-7, which is an example of the results of a government supply group's survey. The table "Results of Customer Interviews" shows the average importance and satisfaction responses for each expectation. It is used to construct the "Improvement Opportunity Window" grid chart at the bottom of the figure. In the window, the most important customer expectation is "supply availability," defined as parts and materials being available when the customers need them. Unfortunately, customers indicate that they are, on average, least satisfied with the supply group's performance in meeting this expectation.

Figure 12-7
Charts for
Displaying
Customer
Survey
Results

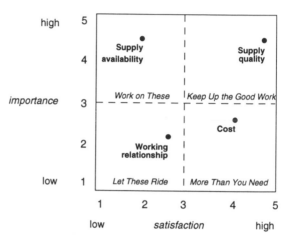

RESULTS OF CUSTOMER INTERVIEWS

Expectation	Importance	Satisfaction
Supply availability	4.6	2.1
Physical quality of supplies	4.8	4.5
Cost of supplies	2.5	4.0
Working relationship of customers and supply staff	2.1	2.5

By plotting expectation and satisfaction level of all four
expectations on the chart, the group sees that it should work
on "supply availability" first. Supply quality is not a problem, and although working relationships with customers
may be wanting, customers do not consider that a priority
problem. Finally, some of the management resources devoted to controlling costs might be redirected to ensuring
supply availability.

Find and measure process outcomes that cause satisfaction to vary

Now, you want to find cause-and-effect relationships
between process performance and customer satisfaction. To

create this link, you answer the questions: "What does a specific customer expectation mean in terms of a specific work process?" and "What measurable indicators can be used to determine the outcome performance of the process?" In our supply example, the group defined a desirable process outcome measure as "completeness of orders." Its outcome measure, they decided, was "the percentage of orders delivered on time with no missing items," as determined by information on copies of the packing slips sent along with orders.

PROCESS OUTCOME

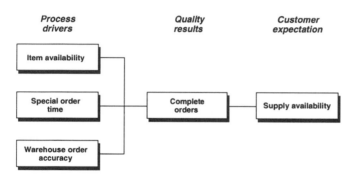

Figure 12-8
Causal Links
in Process
Outcomes

Through process analysis such as that described in Chapter 7, the group then determined that three *process drivers* might have the most effect on variation in the percentage of complete orders. As shown in Figure 12-8, these were:

- **Item availability,** or that a normally stocked item was in inventory when ordered. Its measure is the percentage of time that items on the stock list were not in inventory when ordered.

- **Special order time,** defined as the time between customer orders for items not normally stocked and final delivery to customers of those items.

- *Warehouse order accuracy,* or the percentage of order forms with wrong or missing item codes, because these errors caused delays or incorrect deliveries.

To verify the cause-and-effect relationship, the group measured outcome performance (complete orders) against the three possible process drivers. This verified that, when measures of item availability and warehouse order accuracy went down and special order time went up, order completeness measures went down in a predictable way (if you look ahead to Figure 12-11, you will see this relationship in run chart form).

Use measurements to discover root causes of problems

However, what was causing these process drivers to vary? Data on Period A in the run chart in Figure 12-9 showed the group that, over time, warehouse order accuracy went up and down in a predictable manner. A few questions identified one root cause of this trend. Supply clerks received a new inventory list four times a year, but the list was quickly outdated as items were added or dropped or vendors changed. The group solved the problem with weekly updates to the inventory list.

Figure 12-9
Trends in
Warehouse
Order
Accuracy

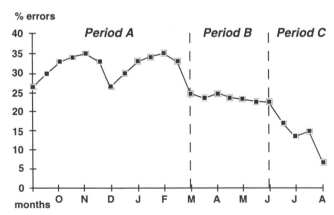

WAREHOUSE ORDER ACCURACY

As you can see in Period B in the run chart, this change stabilized error rates but at an unacceptably high level. Even with up-to-date inventory lists, clerks sometimes misidentified parts and materials when preparing an order. Better training helped solve this *root cause* problem. The result was a downward trend in errors during Period C, a trend that continued as the group discovered other root causes and corrected them. Figure 12-10 is a tree diagram that shows the various cause-and-effect relationships involved in this continuous improvement effort.

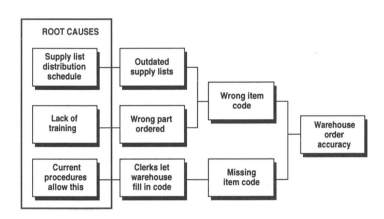

Figure 12-10
Tree Diagram
of Cause-
and-Effect
Relationships
in Warehouse
Order
Accuracy

A complete picture of cause-and-effect relationships is shown in Figure 12-11. As the trends in measures of the three process drivers improved, so did the process outcome measure of complete orders. Also, note that customer satisfaction with supply availability went up over the same period. This is a final indication of causality.

Figure 12-11
Cause-and-
Effect
Relationships
in Supply
Availability

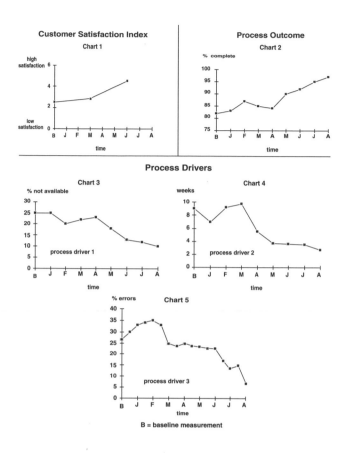

Measurements such as those shown in Figure 12-11 are useful to all parts of an organization. The chief executive will want to monitor customer satisfaction, while the supply chief pays close attention to the completeness of orders. Employees responsible for maintaining supply inventory or special orders have ready measurements of their process's performance. Clerks get quick feedback on warehouse form accuracy, for which they are primarily responsible. Further, the clerks understand the link between warehouse form errors, overall supply group performance, and customer satisfaction. Being aware of these connections is a powerful motivator for improvement.

CONTINUOUS MEASUREMENT MEANS
CONTINUOUS IMPROVEMENT

Performance-based governance and the operations measurement system just outlined have this in common: They are dynamic. Figure 12-4, which shows that target results in the Oregon Benchmarks system change over time, illustrates this dynamism. When they meet each target milestone, agencies will likely need to do different things to reach the next higher milestone. Also, the environment in which agencies, their customers, and society as a whole exist will change over the years. Technology and advances in science will offer new and different means of reaching the targets. Finally, citizen expectations (and therefore, political requirements) will change, resulting in different priorities and considerations for service delivery.

At the operations level, as one set of customer expectations is satisfied, the expectations become the status quo. Customers accept improved service as the norm and turn their attention to another set of expectations (no one is ever completely satisfied).

Given all this dynamism, performance measurement systems must be dynamic, too. Over time, what they measure and how they measure it must change or else these systems will lose their usefulness.

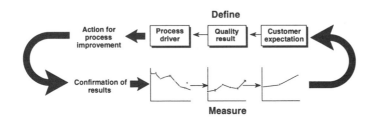

Figure 12-12
The
Continuous
Improvement
Measurement
Cycle

Just as continuous improvement is exemplified by the PDCA cycle discussed in Chapter 8, there also is a cycle for measuring for continuous improvement. We show this cycle in Figure 12-12. The top part of the cycle, which begins with customer expectations, involves the defining of customer expectations, outcome measures, and process drivers, and their causal links. This step leads to action for process improvement, then confirmation of results through continued tracking of measures of performance. Periodically, or whenever needed, this cycle loops back to redetermining customer expectations, which will inevitably change over time. Perhaps the healthiest thing in the world for both agencies and their customers is that this loop starts another cycle of continuous improvement.

Chapter
13

PROCESS MANAGEMENT AND COST

■ Traditional methods of cost accounting and budgeting are not suitable for process management. In fact, these older methods frequently mislead managers into making the wrong decisions.

■ Activity-based costing (ABC) is a managerial cost accounting method that accurately accumulates costs by process, product, or service.

■ ABC is ideal for estimating the costs of cross-functional processes, something nearly impossible to do with traditional accounting.

■ Cost-of-quality (COQ) is an analysis method that groups processes into four categories (prevention, appraisal, internal failure, and external failure) and sums the cost of each category.

■ COQ can be used to discover ways to reduce the costs that arise from poor quality practices.

Activity-based costing has to come in front of competition because we can't even get our own folks into a bid mentality until we know how much it costs to provide a service.

— Stephen Goldsmith,
Mayor of Indianapolis, Indiana

Mayor Goldsmith points out a major problem in public management: most public managers do not consider cost in making program decisions. Yes, some will think about their budgets, but traditional budgeting only looks at "spending," or the amount of resources that flow into an organization. Few government budgets or managerial accounting systems let you know how much money it takes to produce a unit of output or whether the money is used effectively. This is why Indianapolis and other local, state, and federal organizations are switching to activity-based costing. ABC, as it is called, is a set of process-based management information and accounting methods used to identify, describe, assign costs to, and report on the operations in an organization.

Some government organizations apply another process management tool when looking at costs and budgets. Called cost-of-quality (COQ), it identifies money that could be saved if processes produced the right thing the first time. Later in this chapter, we present a case example of COQ drawn from a Swedish government organization.

PROBLEMS WITH EXISTING BUDGETING AND ACCOUNTING METHODS

Here's the bottom line: government cost accounting practices and line-item budgets do more harm than good. They hide rather than reveal costs, encourage functional instead of cross-functional thinking, and send the wrong signals to managers. Want a simple test to prove this is true? When was the last time your cost accounting information (assuming you have any) or office budget gave you clues about how to improve a process?

Accurate Cost Information

For example, Figure 13-1 compares an IRS Center's traditional line-item budget with the same information presented in an ABC report format. If you wanted to reduce costs in this center, where would the traditional budget line items tell you to start? "Reduce staff" would be the obvious answer from many ax-happy budget cutters: "Tell every department head to come up with a plan to reduce personnel by 25 percent." This directive says nothing about making operations more cost effective. The result, according to another government ABC user at the U.S. Navy's shipyards, is that "you transform large, bloated, and inefficient bureaucracies into smaller, bloated, and inefficient bureaucracies. You end up still too fat in some areas, but dangerously thin in others."

Traditional Line Items		New Way: ABC	
Salaries	$500,000	Prepare work plans	$30,000
Telecommunications	100,000	Facilities and personnel planning	30,000
Enforcement expenses	50,000	Mail receipt and sorting	50,000
Facilities	30,000	Document and data preparation	180,000
Travel	20,000	Data entry	40,000
		Document and security control	130,000
		Data reconciliation	90,000
		Taxpayer file maintenance	110,000
		Refund requests/ correspondence	40,000
Total	**$700,000**	**Total**	**$700,000**

Figure 13-1 Traditional versus Activity Views of Costs, IRS Cincinnati Service Center— Processing Division

However, look at the ABC information on the right side of the figure. It breaks costs out into processes: preparing work plans, data entry, maintaining taxpayer files, and so forth. You can readily see that "document and data presentation" is the most costly process—a logical place to start looking for process improvements that will yield major cost reductions.

Most government budgets are useless for optimizing the return on taxpayer dollars, and, in fact, make managers less aware of the cost consequences of their decisions. Dr. Dale R. Geiger studied the effect of cost awareness at IRS district offices[1]. In the study he found that managers greatly underestimated their staffs' salaries and wages because they were never asked to consider dollar costs. Instead, they only focused on keeping the number of employees within budgetary limits. However, under that rule, $18,000-per-year employees "cost" a manager as much as $55,000-per-year employees. There was no incentive for managers to learn their employees' salaries and ask if the cost of some equaled the value they created.

ABC showed the managers that highly paid professionals were doing standard, routine work better suited to paraprofessionals and even clerks. Armed with ABC information, the managers are moving toward using more paraprofessionals and fewer professionals.

Another problem with traditional cost accounting is that it mistakes indirect or overhead costs. These costs include administrative, support, maintenance, facility, and other expenses that most government organizations *allocate* to products, services, or cost centers as an addition to direct labor hours. Allocating means you use a formula to assign

---

[1]. Dale R. Geiger, "An Experiment in Federal Cost Accounting and Performance Measurement," *The Government Accountants Journal,* Winter (1993/94): 39-52.

these costs, such as multiplying direct labor costs (hourly wage plus fringe benefits) by some percentage that reflects overhead. For example,

- If indirect or overhead costs are forecast to be $1 million during a year, and

- Fifty thousand hours of direct labor are forecast at $20 an hour, then

- Each direct labor hour ($20) is assigned an additional $20 of indirect cost ($1 million divided by fifty thousand hours), for a total cost of $40 per hour.

This calculation is accurate only if your organization produces only one output that consumes the same amount of resources each time you make it. If you produce several services, then uniformly allocating overhead costs to them is less accurate, because some require more overhead support than others. In a make or buy decision, this could give an outside contractor an unfair advantage over an in-house group that is burdened with more overhead than it actually consumes.

In addition, because they are not set up to track process costs, traditional accounting systems tend to mask the downstream costs of decisions. For example, engineers might view their decision to make a new engineering drawing as costing only $95 for drafting. However, each new drawing triggers indirect activities such as inspection ($15), data processing ($25), quality control ($80), keeping stock ($20), and ordering parts ($40), for a total cost of $275[2]. If the engineers understand the effects of their decisions, they

---

[2.] H. Thomas Johnson, "It's Time to Stop Overselling Activity-Based Concepts," *Management Accounting,* September (1992): 26-35.

will be more open to reusing an existing drawing instead of creating a new one.

ACTIVITY-BASED COSTING CONCEPTS

Processes are the core of an ABC system. As shown in Figure 13-2, the two central concepts of ABC are that:

• Processes consume resources and cost objects consume processes, and

• Cost drivers affect resource consumption, which in turn affects process performance measures.

Figure 13-2 Central Concepts of ABC

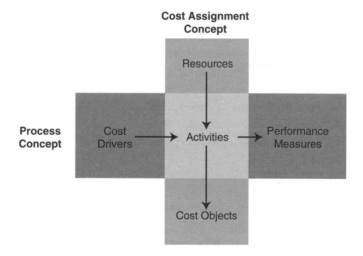

Processes Consume Resources and Cost Objects Consume Processes

In the process in which you now work, what is the cost of producing a single unit of output? When they try to answer this question, most government organizations fall back on a crude form of unit costing that basically divides all spending in an organization or department by the number of units of output produced. You already have seen that that form of measurement is inaccurate.

ABC's cost-finding method is to first *trace* all costs in an organization to the specific processes that consume these resources. This method requires identifying all processes in the organization, usually through *activity dictionaries* and *cost models* by identifying the costs of each process in it.

To assign costs to the processes, you then identify and quantify all inputs or resources that flow into them. For example, you could ask all personnel in a work unit to estimate the percentage of their time spent doing a particular process during a year. If you multiply each person's annual salary and fringe benefits by that percentage, you have a good picture of labor costs. Material and supply costs can be directly traced to each process or estimated in much the same way as labor costs. You would do this same type of calculation for line, administrative, and support departments or work units.

Next, you identify the outputs of each process. These might be reports, services, actions, physical products, or other forms of work-in-progress or final output. If all the outputs are the same for a process, then the unit cost of output is simply the number of outputs produced divided into the total cost of the process over a period. This is the cost of cycling through a process once. (Sometimes a process requires more resources to produce the same type of output. We will discuss this below under "Cost Drivers.")

Now, you have a more accurate cost picture of each individual process and the unit cost of its outputs. But to understand the cost of producing final outputs, you must have a way of linking the processes involved. ABC organizations do this by expanding the concept of final outputs into cost objects, which are the reasons that a process exists. Cost objects can be products or services, programs, projects, or groups of customers. For example, a repaired bridge is a cost object whose processes include all those that fall within the production stream that repairs the bridge. An extended-day program in a school is a cost object of all processes that operate and support the program. A neighborhood is the cost object of processes that collect and analyze information on crimes within its boundaries. ABC organizations use top-down flow charts and other process mapping tools to establish the links among processes and specific cost objects.

A final step is to determine how much of a process is consumed by a cost object, using *process* or *activity drivers.* Process drivers are factors that affect the demand for output. For example, the cost object "one mile of water stream monitored for pollution" may involve the processes of planning, collecting, analyzing, and reporting the findings of ten water samples. Collecting and analyzing are *unit drivers*, because they are done each time a sample single is produced. In other words, ten cycles of the collecting process must occur to monitor the stream. Planning and reporting are *batch drivers*, because only one cycle of each must occur to monitor a stream, no matter how many samples are collected. The total cost of monitoring a mile of stream is ten times the cycle costs of the collecting and analyzing processes and one times the cycle costs of planning and reporting.

How would you handle indirect or overhead costs for these processes? By direct tracing or using estimates, you can assign each process the time the testing department supervisor spends on it, the costs of the organization's information system it uses, a portion of the personnel costs of each employee who operates it, and so on. This still leaves administrative costs, such as the time of the organization's executive department. These, too, can be traced or estimated or, if the costs are relatively low, simply allocated according to traditional accounting practice.

With adjustments made for cost drivers (see below), it is now possible to calculate the total cost of a cost object—that is, the cost of the outputs of each process in the production stream that the cost object consumes. This is why ABC states that processes consume resources and cost objects consume activities.

Cost Drivers Affect Resource Consumption, Which in Turn Affects Process Performance Measures

As noted earlier, sometimes an output can consume more than the average amount of resources. ABC adjusts for this situation with *cost drivers* to estimate the amount of difference. A cost driver is a factor that causes process performance to vary in a way that results in the process consuming fewer or greater amounts of resources. For example, cost drivers of the process of monitoring a stream would include the types of tests that are required, because some will cost more than others. Cost drivers for the process of evaluating competitive bids include the number of vendors who submit bids and the number of people who must review the bids. More bids and more reviews mean higher cost for this process; fewer mean lower costs. The source of an outside inquiry (i.e., from citizens, the media, or elected officials) may determine the amount of resources devoted to responding to it. A cost driver for providing health services to citizens may be their geographic location (urban or rural). ABC organizations use such cost drivers to adjust their estimates on the amount of resources a process consumes, assigning more costs to complex outputs than to simple ones.

Understanding cost drivers is important for process improvement, because they are the causes of changes in the amount of resources a process consumes. For example, the number of errors in a document drives the cost of the task of correcting errors (in this sense, errors also are process drivers). If you can prevent the errors, then the need for the task of correcting them will disappear, and the total cost of the report writing process will be reduced. If "type of contract vehicle" is a cost driver of the "preparing purchase orders" process, then shifting more purchases to less costly types of contracts will reduce the cost (and probably the time) required for this process.

An organization can have structural and cultural cost drivers, too. For example, the number of management layers (structure) a decision must pass through before it is approved increases the cost and cycle time of the process of gaining approval. These factors are the chief reason that many organizations have pushed decision authority to lower levels. A cultural example is when people believe that they will be severely reprimanded for minor mistakes and so spend more time avoiding them than in accomplishing the main goal of their work.

Process Centers for Cross-Functional Processes

In 1994, one federal department announced that it was going to halve the staff in its personnel office. Will this reduce the department's total personnel administration costs by half? No, and it may increase the amount of time other offices must spend on personnel administration. Why is this so? Because personnel is a cross-functional process, and reducing personnel office staff may be sub-optimizing the process. How can ABC help? Please read on.

Most organizations divide their operations into *cost centers*: work units or departments that do specific types of work. Examples include print shops, a planning unit, and in our current example, a personnel office. Although ABC can generate accurate cost information for these cost centers, it is often more revealing to look at *process* or *activity centers*. These "centers" do not necessarily physically reside in an office or department. Instead, they are reports—yes, simply reports—on cross-functional processes that may be spread across an entire organization. Thus, a report on the cost of a cross-functional personnel process center includes resources consumed within the personnel office plus related processes in other offices. These other processes include those that people outside the personnel office do to prepare background information for job descriptions, requisitions to hire new staff, employee performance appraisals, special leave requests, and so on. Often, these other processes take longer and cost more than those inside the personnel office. If your objective is to reduce the cost and cycle time of all personnel processes and improve their outputs, then the process center concept is better than the cost center concept. This is because a process center will let you study the entire cross-functional process of personnel administration.

ACTIVITY BUDGETING

Most government systems are based on statute and show a unilateral view of spending. Spending is not the same as cost. Spending is the amount of money an organization expends over the course of a period. Cost is the amount of resources actually used to produce outputs. There is more than a subtle difference between the two—agencies often spend more than the actual cost of their outputs.

ABC budgeting gives you several different views of an organization. These include process, product or service, customer or customer group, and strategic views. When you have digested and used these different views, they fold back into the usual line-item budget format. Best of all, this is easy information to generate if you practice ABC.

Different Budgetary Views

Activity budgets are simply large-scale organizational and cost models based on past resource usage, projected demand, and assumptions about improvement, technology, and other factors. Using process centers, they can focus only on core business processes or go all the way down to the lowest process level. They show what resources a process consumed during previous periods and what consumption will be in the future. They also identify the exchange of inputs and outputs in a proposed reconfiguration of a cross-functional process, so that executives can understand who will be doing what for whom and for how much.

This type of budget includes process-level performance measures, cost drivers, process drivers, and the cost of products, services, and serving different customers. With this information, executives and managers can ask questions about performance improvement and the impact of changes in work load or technology and receive immediate answers.

Product budgets show the proposed cost of an organization's products and services. They are created by identifying which activities will produce these outputs and the amount of resources they will consume doing it. This process allows cost comparisons with benchmarked products and services.

Customer budgets show proposed costs of providing services to individual customers or groups of customers. Such analysis helps executives determine if a disproportionate share of resources is being devoted to any one customer or group and the reasons why. By using activity centers such as "customer support services," these budgets lead to questions about how such costs can be reduced.

Strategic budgets show resource usage by processes linked to an organization's long-range plans and operations strategies. These budgets can relate to core business processes, capital investment, and changes in basic strategies for serving the public.

Flexibility in Budgeting

For every view above, budgets can be disaggregated into different categories, such as "environmental protection," "training," and "facilities maintenance." All you need to do is create a process center to show which processes these categories will involve and how their resource consumption will change under your proposals.

The sources of change in resource consumption during a budget period can be more easily identified with ABC than with traditional accounting's budget variance reports. If major changes occur, their impact on the total budget is easier to understand with activity and cost models geared to that budget.

According to a financial officer in Indianapolis, "We have a better way for managers to look at a budget. That's because the core of our budgetary process are the organizational and cost models built from everyone participating in process mapping and costing. We still prepare line-item budgets required by statute, but we use an activity-based budget."

COST-OF-QUALITY

Cost-of-quality (COQ) is another way to find process improvements. It is not as detailed as ABC, but it provides a good starting point for understanding factors that drive up costs without improving performance. Not an accounting method, but simply a technique used in analysis, COQ is the dollar cost of ensuring that customers get top service and the consequences when they don't. For most organizations, the bulk of COQ goes for inspection, mistakes, rework, repairs, waste, warranties, and customer refunds. Few spend more than a token amount of revenues to prevent these problems.

Experts calculate a typical private company's COQ to be between 20 and 40 percent of gross sales, which means this quality "tax" costs businesses billions a year. But most business leaders say it's 10 percent or less of gross sales, or just don't know, according to surveys by the American Society for Quality Control and Gallup.

Why this disparity? Executives aren't blind, but they tend to focus only on the most visible costs of quality—the "tip of the iceberg" in Figure 13-4. This limited way of seeing is why COQ analysis can be so effective: it shows the hidden costs. The good news? Total COQ can be lowered to less than 10 percent while increasing productivity and reducing cycle time.

Figure 13-4
The COQ
Iceberg

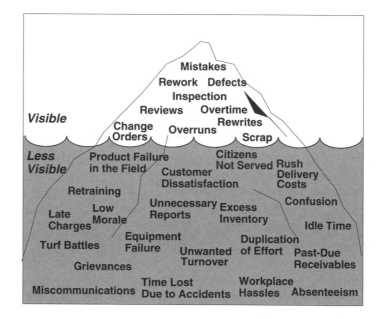

COQ Results as Shock Therapy

In 1988, Sweden's postal service knew it had problems. Market research showed that more and more customers complained of late deliveries and long waiting lines. Business customers especially thought that Sweden Post neglected them—and these customers accounted for most of the organization's revenues. It was no wonder that private competitors were gaining market share in the postal service's major product lines.

Despite this, no one was eager to take decisive action, although Sweden Post was not meeting some of its own official standards. Improvement, said the organization's board of directors, could only come from massive capital investment and hiring more employees—and the money just wasn't there.

One Sweden Post executive had another idea. "Some of us wanted to challenge the traditional idea that there is a trade-off between quality and cost," said the head of the Letter Department, who also was the organization's quality manager. "Quite the contrary. We wanted to show where costs could be reduced by better quality."

To prove his point, this executive had his people conduct a COQ survey of Sweden Post's operations costs. In COQ analysis, a company identifies and adds up its operations costs for error/defect prevention, appraisal (i.e., inspecting for errors), and internal and external failure (see Figure 13-5). Sweden Post added a fifth category to its COQ classification, called *image costs,* which is not shown in Figure 13-5. These are opportunity costs usually associated with a private business. They include sales forgone due to dissatisfied customers, such as lost business associated with missent, late, never delivered, or damaged mail. If your organization's success depends on payments by your customers, an image cost category may be useful in COQ analysis.

The following COQ categories are based on Sweden Post's system and a COQ manual prepared by Coopers & Lybrand for the U.S. Postal Service.

Figure 13-5 Cost of Quality in Mail Delivery

Prevention costs. Associated with preventing errors and defects.
- Employee training programs for job skills and quality improvement tools and methods
- Preventive maintenance on equipment
- Collecting and analyzing data on performance

Figure 13-5 (Continued)

- Time executives, managers, and employees spend on improvement projects

Appraisal or inspection costs. Traditional quality control—after-the-fact, postproduction inspection.
- Postal inspectors
- Appraisal by supervisors
- Sorting controls
- Inspections by quality control departments and branches
- Test mailings for quality control

Internal failure costs. Mostly rework needed for errors that happen before delivering mail to customers.
- Tracking misdirected or missing mail
- Rewrapping or resorting parcels, letters, and flats
- Planned manual resorts in response to destination complaints
- Extra transportation due to misdirected mail
- Forgone revenues when mail is delivered with insufficient postage
- Corrective maintenance after equipment breakdowns, and unplanned downtime for machines, vehicles, and computers

External failure costs. Rework done or refunds made after delivery to customers.

- Remailing misdirected or mis-sent mail
- Cost of claims paid to customers
- Refunds to customers
- Cost of handling customer complaints

Only a few examples of mail service COQ costs are listed in each category. If fact, there are hundreds of other costs that can fall into the four areas, depending on the industry. Also, quality costs can be categorized and quantified in administrative and overhead functions as well as line operations. Errors in paychecks, employee accidents, delays in hiring needed

Sweden Post chose to limit the COQ survey to a rough estimate of twenty cost elements thought to be major quality
costs. These included factors such as sorting errors and
incorrect addresses. To collect cost data, Sweden Post
examined accounting records and performance reports and
interviewed managers and workers. They found that cost of
the twenty elements added up to 9 percent of total costs, or
roughly U.S. $180 million. Of this amount, 6.5 percent was
for internal and external failure, 1.5 percent for appraisal or
inspection, and 1 percent for prevention.

According to the executive who initiated the survey, "Once
these costs were made visible, it was clear that many of the
problems causing them could be solved through low-cost
management improvements in work systems. Savings from
reduced COQ costs could be passed on to customers and
used to buy advanced processing equipment."

Confronted with these facts, Sweden Post's leaders felt they
had to take responsibility for drastic cuts in what was essentially pure waste. That's what a COQ analysis does to top
management: it shocks them into action.

Taking action based on COQ

In a pilot project aimed at reducing COQ, one Swedish
postal region used both top-down and bottom-up approaches to improvement. Regional managers selected seven team
projects that resulted in one hundred thirty improvement
recommendations. For example, one team developed a new
process that reduced by 75 percent the time needed to
respond to customer complaints. In addition, employees and
supervisors working on their own identified many improvement opportunities. Regional payroll assistants used to
spend 20 percent of their time correcting incoming payroll
data; this cost about $150,000 a year. They developed new
work routines that saved most of this money by reducing
incoming error rates. Both improvements are now in operation throughout Sweden Post.

After the project, workers were enthusiastic about the new management approach, because none of them had ever been asked before to participate in any kind of intellectual activity concerning their work. That was the good news.

The bad news was typical of first efforts to introduce new management approaches—middle manager resistance. Regional managers in the pilot region felt they already knew what issues to address and how. They paid little attention to most team recommendations, and seemed to see no advantage to increased employee participation in problem solving.

"We concluded that although workers and managers had the skills to use quality management, managers lacked the motivation," said the executive. "We needed a more comprehensive approach that motivated managers, or else the quality management effort would go nowhere."

COQ budgeting and quality audits as management motivators

The motivators included a regional COQ budgeting system and quality audit. Sweden Post developed a COQ budgeting system for regional managers that required them to review their operations for specific, measurable types of quality costs and to report on this review and on their improvement activities to executives. The criteria for the system were that it:

- Be based on customer needs,

- Have a limited number of costs,

- Be easy to measure,

- Be comparable over several years,

- Be easy to check for accuracy,

- Promote desirable action, and

- Gain high acceptance by managers and employees.

Sweden Post integrated the system into the regular budget procedure, focusing on twenty-five cost elements in eight core business processes. Each region calculated its 1990 quality costs in these eight processes, arriving at a total of about $68 million for all Sweden Post. Then, they set out to reduce the costs 10 percent by 1991 and 30 percent by 1993. No allowance was made for inflation.

Top leaders instituted a formal quality audit to ensure that regional managers worked on improvement issues in a structured way. The audit looked at each region's activities and progress in areas such as quality management, quality systems (i.e., checks and balances, COQ budgeting, quality assurance in production), improvement and development issues, market research, and customer service. The audit is somewhat similar to the Malcolm Baldrige National Quality Award self-assessment, discussed in Chapter 4.

Thus, Sweden Post created a comprehensive operations improvement system that identified quality costs (the COQ budget system), provided a method for reducing them (quality management), and ensured that managers used both (the quality audits). This approach generated the desired results: cost savings plus improved customer service.

Results measured in lower COQ, and much more

The program costs of implementing the new quality management approach have been less than $1 million per year since 1989. The cumulative effect of the many resulting improvements is beginning to pay off, and faster than expected.

Cost savings. Though the target was 10 percent, by 1991 the regions reduced by 29 percent the quality costs measured in the 1990 COQ budget system baseline. This reduction meant measurable savings of U.S. $19 million—*despite about 10 percent inflation in the general economy.* However, Sweden Post estimates that true savings are much higher than 10 percent. This is because the measured quality costs are in core business processes, and reducing them requires improving other non-measured, non-core areas that affect the core. Why not track all the savings? Sweden Post thinks such a move would create a "measurement bureaucracy."

Improved customer service. Errors and defects delay mail processing, which angers customers. Because its COQ savings meant fewer errors were occurring, Sweden Post made these gains:

- In 1989, 94 percent of first class mail was delivered overnight. In 1991, this rose to 96.6 percent.

- In 1989, 88 percent of economy mail was delivered in three days. In 1991, this was 95.0 percent.

- In 1989, one postal region received complaints on 14 percent of its forwarding agreements. This fell to 2 percent in 1990.

Profits. Despite inflation, Sweden Post made a 10 percent profit on 1990 revenues of over U.S. $3 billion.

Most organizations start to use COQ analysis in much the same way as Sweden Post, by calculating a rough estimate of quality costs in one or more core business processes. The results become inputs for executive decision making and corporate strategic plans for improvement. Many organizations set up department and business unit COQ budgeting systems. This gives managers a new way to look for improvements, set priorities, and track progress.

Improvement teams use COQ analysis for the same purposes. Thus, everyone from the board room on down has the same language and approach for cost and quality issues.

COMBINING ACTIVITY-BASED COSTING AND COST OF QUALITY

Most organizations initially can get enough COQ information with rough estimates, but remember that ABC cost data can readily be converted into highly accurate COQ reports. To make this conversion, simply code each process in an ABC business or cost model according to its COQ category: non-COQ, prevention, appraisal, internal failure, or external failure. Usually, however, it is not cost effective to use ABC merely to produce COQ information, so you have to plan to use the ABC information for other purposes as well.

Figure 13-6 ABC and COQ in a University

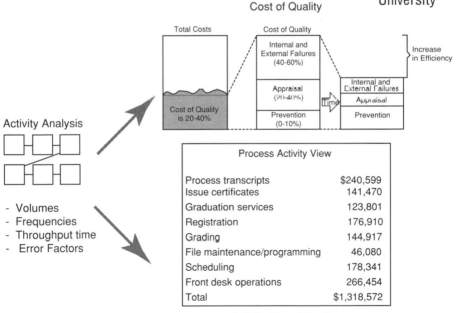

Activity-Based Costing

Figure 13-6 shows how process analysis followed by activity costing helped in a COQ assessment of a university's administrative and support departments. Extra benefits from using activity costing and management with COQ include the following:

- It associates the cost of nonconformance with specific activities within a process.

- It captures all the costs associated with these activities, which shows the true cost of nonconformance.

- It lends itself to additional research, such as value and cost driver analyses.

A LEXICON OF VALID, PSEUDO-, AND NON-APPROACHES TO RESTRUCTURING GOVERNMENT

For both background information (and your amusement), please review this lexicon before reading Chapter 14.

Centralize: (Valid approach in some cases) To gather services, programs, or functions into and administer them through one decision-making structure. *The agency centralized the personnel functions of its line departments into a single new human resources department.*

Consolidate: (Valid in some cases) To unite or combine different agencies, programs, or services that do the same thing. *The town consolidated its police agency and the county sheriff's office.*

Decentralize: (Increasingly valid and desirable) To break up centralized or consolidated structures and move the decision making to local, line, or operating unit groups. *"It is not possible for a society to de-massify economic activity, communications, and many other crucial processes without being compelled to decentralize government decision-making as well."* — Alvin and Heidi Toffler

De-layer: (Valid, but often used as a pseudo-approach) To remove one or more levels of management in a hierarchical organization. *The agency eliminated its deputy director positions to enhance communication among directors and line managers.*

Devolve: (Valid in some cases) The transfer of power, a program, or a service from a central government to a local government. *The federal government devolved its welfare programs to the states, leaving it up to them to figure out how to run and pay for the programs.*

Downsize: (A non-approach) To make an agency smaller by reducing the number of its staff, usually through layoffs, early retirement, or shedding services. Downsizing does not imply improvement or other changes. *The county executive ordered agencies to downsize their staffs by 10 percent.* According to Peter Drucker, dean of American management experts, "Downsizing has turned out to be something that surgeons for centuries have warned against: 'amputation before diagnosis.' The result is always a casualty."

Entrepreneurial government: (Valid) According to David Osborne and Ted Gaebler, who coined the term, this means public institutions that constantly use their resources in new ways to heighten their efficiency and effectiveness. We have no example sentence, because entrepreneurial government covers just about everything positive about reinventing government. However, note our example of Orange County, California, in Chapter 15; the entrepreneurial approach can be risky.

Lean and mean: (A non-approach) Refers to an organization that has been repeatedly downsized to the point that it can barely meet its mission. It is the result of a macho, meat-ax approach that leaves the survivors feeling not lean, but certainly mean. *Across-the-board budget cuts left the agency dangerously lean in some areas and still too fat in others.* In industry, *lean production* (valid approach) refers to a management system characterized by flexible processes with fast cycle times and little waste, cross-trained and self-managed workers, vendor partnership, and continuous improvement.

Privatize: (Valid in some cases, sometimes pseudo- and non-valid) To move a public service or asset into the private sector (see Chapter 11 on competition). *The city privatized waste water treatment by selling its treatment assets and powers to a group of private investors.*

Redesign or reengineer: (Valid when the situation calls for it) To completely reconfigure a process, changing nearly every component of it to gain a quantum leap in performance (see Chapter 10). *By establishing new processes and using information technology, the city, county, and state governments reengineered customer contact processes in several agencies to consolidate them into a single-point-of-contact system.*

Reinvent: (Always valid) To fundamentally question the mission and methods of government, with the intent of restructuring it to focus on outcomes desired by citizens. *By selling its public housing assets, issuing rental vouchers for the most needy, and providing tax credits and other assistance to private developers, the city reinvented the way it ensured low-cost housing for poor citizens.*

Rethink: (Always valid) Peter Drucker says rethinking goes beyond reinventing, because the rethinking asks, "If we were not already doing this, would we now go into it?" He's referring to an agency's basic mission, not its operations. Rethinking leaves open the alternatives of completely eliminating agencies with outmoded missions or agencies that have not produced desirable results for reasons no one can determine. *"If no rational rethinking of government performance [occurs], it is predictable that the wrong things will then be cut—the things that perform and should be strengthened."* — Peter Drucker, *The Atlantic Monthly,* February 1995.

Reorganize: (Pseudo- and often non-approach) As it is most commonly practiced in government, this means to shift around the boxes in an organizational chart, without changing anything else. *After severe criticism for ineffective handling of a crisis, the agency director published a reorganization plan that put the work units involved in the crisis under the control of the deputy director in charge of crises, a newly created position.*

Rightsize: (Pseudo-approach) To adjust the size of the work force until there is a balance between the work to be done and the number of people available to do it. Usually synonymous with downsizing, because it does not include process improvement. *The agency rightsized its work force to meet capacity needs.*

Streamline: (Valid, if you use our definition; pseudo if you don't) To change a process by minimizing non-value added work steps and maximizing value added steps. *The agency streamlined its procurement process by eliminating unnecessary sign offs and paperwork and raising spending authority limits.*

Chapter
14

STRUCTURE

■ Most organizations structure themselves around functions
and departments, but their work is cross-functional. This
can create problems:

- Slow communication and decision making
- Excessive numbers of management layers that add cost
  but not value
- Poor or no management accountability for final outcomes and results

■ Few organizations can completely do away with departments
and functions, because these serve a valuable purpose.
However, even functionally organized agencies have alternatives that will improve their structures.

■ The alternatives, none of which is mutually exclusive,
include structuring operations around:

- Core business processes
- Projects, products, or services
- Key customers or customer groups

■ Successful restructuring requires changes in an agency's
concept of its individual employees and managers.

In reality, many of our state and local agencies stand as great monuments to themselves, sustained and protected by their internal rules and hierarchies. They often stifle the creativity that is so desperately needed, putting one obstacle after another in the way of new ideas and energetic leaders. Innovation tends to become an accident when it could easily be the natural result of reconnecting chief executives, employees and concerned citizens.

> — Hard Truths/Tough Choices:
> An Agenda for State and Local
> Reform, The First Report of the
> National Commission on the
> State and Local Public Service

Governments are no strangers to reorganization. Just about every new administration engages in some reorganizing of its major departments and agencies, as does a newly appointed chief executive in a single agency. At its best, this is a more or less logical reordering of functions and creation of new agencies to handle emerging issues. More often, it is simply an attempt to gain control of operations. At its worst, reorganizing is a way to get rid of a rival, by eliminating or drastically reducing his or her internal department. Whether motivated by logic, politics, or ambition, these types of reorganization miss the point: form follows process. Simply shuffling boxes on an organization chart does not create a process-oriented organization.

Further, as the quotation above indicates, the basic problem with government agencies (shared by many private companies that will not survive the millennium) is that they are seldom structured with the goal of enabling constant change, the outcome of creativity and innovation. If there is a twenty-first century truism, it will be: *Organizations whose structures hinder constant change are doomed to constantly fail.*

In this chapter, we will outline how to restructure an agency using the principles and some of the methods of the Improvement Driven Organization. We are going to do this without promoting as panaceas any of the valid, pseudo-, and non-approaches listed in our lexicon of restructuring in the mini-section that precedes this chapter. Instead, we want you to understand what the Improvement Driven Organization structure looks like and how you can build it into any valid approach to organizational structure.

WHAT IS RESTRUCTURING?

Restructuring means to reconstruct an organization from the point of view of the whole rather than any single part. The "whole" includes processes, personnel, infrastructure, relationship with outside groups, and culture. Most organizations consider only one or two of these parts or none of them if they follow one of the pseudo- or non-approaches to restructuring. As a result, they fail to achieve the maximum benefit of restructuring and often simply fail. Changes to any one of the parts usually require adjustments in all or most of the others.

Making the fundamental transformation from a traditional organization to an Improvement Driven Organization means major changes in all parts. Let's look at the first two parts, processes and personnel, in this chapter, and examine the others in subsequent chapters.

Problems with Traditional Structures

Most companies and agencies organize as in the chart shown in Figure 14-1. As we said back in Chapter 2, this arrangement evolved from industrial and railroad company models in the nineteenth and early twentieth centuries. It is a functional model: each box on the chart is tied to a specific function such as planning, production, and distribution. Some functions hire experts in a professional specialty, and most people rise through the ranks of their profession. This structure also is a chain-of-command management model: except for the lowest boxes, where the actual value added work gets done, each level of the hierarchy is a layer of management designed to foster command, control, and communication.

Figure14-1
Traditional
Organizational
Chart

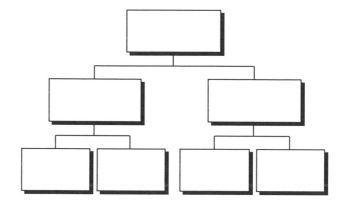

Silos, Ping-Ponging, and Elevator Management

Functional silos

A traditional, hierarchical structure poses problems to contemporary management approaches. An organization's core business processes usually are cross-functional. In a traditional hierarchy, processes and people are trapped inside functional silos—tall, thin structures with walls that prevent communication and cooperation.

Ping-Ponging

In this silo structure, a need is recognized in one department, summarized, and then passed on to another for planning, to another for execution, another for inspection, another for distribution, and several others for documentation, accounting, and other types of control. It is a slow process, and doesn't permit any one manager to be held accountable for the result. When inter-silo communication is poor, work-in-progress can bounce back and forth between the departments like a Ping-Pong ball.

Elevator management

If a problem arises during cross-functional work flow, people who encounter it at the bottom of the functional silo summarize the problem and send it up the chain of command to higher layers of management. At one of these higher layers (the height depends on the seriousness of the problem and the rigidity of the organization), a silo manager contacts his or her peers in other silos. They discuss the problem, solve it (most of the time), and send their decisions back down their respective silos for implementation. This is *elevator management*: problems always are traveling up and down the hierarchy, instead of being handled by those who first encounter them. Elevator management inevitably slows down and garbles decisions.

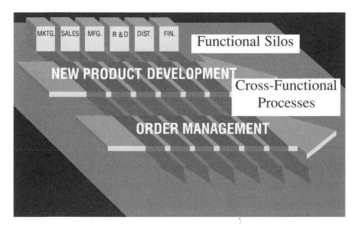

Figure 14-2 Functional Silo versus Cross-Functional Operation.

Should Functional Departments in an Organization be Eliminated?

Some organizations have proposed doing away with their internal functional departments entirely, which would eliminate the silos. Instead, all their staff would form teams organized around core business processes, products, or customers (we will discuss this in a moment). Each team would have its own production, accounting, personnel, planning, and other functions—a micro-image of an entire organization. This is a seductive alternative, but right now it still has serious problems for many organizations.

Functional departments as learning organizations and homes for specialists

In some Improvement Driven Organizations, specialists—accountants, engineers, personnel experts, systems planners—live in their functional departments but work in cross-functional teams. This arrangement has three advantages. First, the specialists stay abreast of advances in their specialties through interaction with peers and formal training inside their departments. Second, they have a place to come home to once a project is over or a process is reengineered so that it no longer needs them. Third, their functional departments offer career ladders in their specialties. In an increasingly specialized world, these are all important benefits of functional departments.

In the long term, most functional departments should shrink in size

However, there are subtle changes afoot that may alter the role of the department of the future. With each passing year, technology automates more routine operations, and most of the operations in many departments are routine. Also, network systems, data base technology, and artificial intelligence now give many line workers both the information and the tools to make and act on decisions once handled by functional specialists. These innovations, process improvements, and competition cause (or should be causing) many functional departments to shrink, without causing other functions to grow as a result. If this is not happening in your organization, you have or will soon have serious problems competing with service providers who have mastered the art of growth in capability without growth in numbers.

So, if you have to maintain functional departments, how do you structure an organization in a way that avoids the problems they can cause? Below, we offer some examples.

RESTRUCTURING AROUND PROCESSES

Improvement Driven Organizations structure along the lines of their core business processes. This structure can be made a formal part of the organization chart or simply a way of running the organization (even though the chart remains as before). Either way, the intent is the same: to operate in a structure that follows the flow of operations, regardless of how many functions are involved.

In the following section, we present a stepped approach to determining how best to restructure an organization along its core business process (Figure 14-3). We also offer two variations of the core business process approach: organizing by product and by customer. The approach assumes major restructuring based on a revised mission, which is the focus of steps 3 through 5. Steps 1, 2, and 6 through 11 can be used for lesser restructuring efforts, although we advise that you invest at least some time in every step we outline, no matter what your restructuring goals.

There are several tasks done in parallel with the eleven steps, and they are so critical to ongoing success that we will explain them now. They are (1) building information, improvement, and control systems into the new structure and (2) managing the change to a culture of process management.

Figure 14-3
Steps in
Restructuring

1. Form a restructuring team of top executives

2. Identify products, services, and the customers who use them

3. Rethink purpose, mission, and strategy

4. Review products and services in light of revised mission

5. Consider alternate ways of delivering products and services

6. Identify core business processes

7. Classify all processes according to their relationships with core processes

8. Streamline processes

9. Review personnel and management structure

10. Select product or service delivery structures

11. Create competition

Parallel Tasks in Restructuring

Build in information, improvement, and control systems

Manage organizational and cultural change

Build in Information, Improvement, and Control Systems

Leaving these tasks until last will at best create more work and at worst jeopardize the new structure:

Control systems

Throughout this and other chapters, we have stressed the need to push process control down through the organization to process operators. Also, we have outlined the need for decentralizing operations, less traditional management communication and control, and more self-management. In making these changes, you have to develop new financial and risk control systems—the need for them does not go away. In Chapter 15, we discuss in detail how to determine the types of control systems you will need. Plan on how you will build them into the new structure as you go along.

Improvement systems

Primarily, these are systems for continuous improvement, including training managers and employees in process improvement methods, benchmarking, performance feedback, and so on. Chapters 7 through 11 discuss the several methods of improvement. Some structural changes may require modifying improvement systems, so it is best to be aware of them at the outset.

Information systems

Information systems developed for a new structure should support the communications, control, and improvement objectives of the organization. A flatter, decentralized organization that uses self-managed teams requires that much more information be integrated and made available to all employees. In such a structure, electronic information access and sharing becomes a primary means of achieving control over operations. Often, information technology will enable you to organize your structure in innovative ways, so it is best to include information specialists in discussions of restructuring. We will discuss this more in Chapter 15.

Manage Organizational and Cultural Change

An organization's structure says much about its culture. Think about what a many-layered structure with lots of functional "boxes" indicates about an organization. It means an old-style command-and-control culture that stresses avoiding risks in its lower echelons, advancement only through managerial ranks, and a functional myopia that prevents cooperation. A flatter, decentralized structure indicates a culture of routine sharing of information, appropriate risk taking at all levels, advancement through management or professional ranks, and a "big picture" attitude toward serving customers and improving processes.

Problem is, you can't overlay the old culture on the new structure and expect the new structure to work or somehow evolve its own culture. Thus, the restructuring team, working with top executives, must develop plans for managing the changeover from the old to the new culture. We discuss this changeover at greater length in Chapter 18.

With these parallel tasks in mind, let's start the restructuring sequence.

Step 1: Form a Restructuring Team

A restructuring team has the same basic composition as one of the issue management teams discussed in Chapter 15 on strategic planning. It includes a senior executive, who is the champion, and senior managers. Due to the gravity of restructuring, we recommend that the chief executive head this team. The team should be charged with rethinking the purpose of all functions and operations during their investigation, to avoid any halfway thinking or patchwork reorganizing.

We recommend that the team take a "green fields" approach to restructuring. This means starting with the assumption that, like the builders of a new factory, the team looks out on a green, empty field—the future factory's site. The only constraints are those inherent in the processes nature of the work the organization plans to do. Sure, there may be some regulatory and nonprocess design constraints, but many can be overcome or modified *so long as the team does not accept them as givens at the outset.*

Step 2: Identify Products, Services, and the Customers Who Use Them

Using the same basic system described in Chapter 6 on measuring performance, the team identifies and describes the organization's products and services, then matches them to the customers who use them. Great care must be taken to clearly define these outputs, so that everyone will understand and agree on the descriptions. The tool for this is a glossary that also specifies the customers who use the products and the expected results from this use. If evaluation information is available on a product or service, it should also be included.

Step 3: Rethink Purpose, Mission, and Strategy

Looking at the list of products and services, the team must rethink the organization's purpose and mission. Peter Drucker's approach, outlined in the February 1995 *Atlantic Monthly*, is to ask these questions: "What is the mission?" "Is it still the right mission?" "Is it still worth doing?" and "If we were not already doing this, would we now go into it?" The answers to these questions can lead to decisions to abandon some services, which will have major implications for the structure of the organization. Often, though, Drucker says the answer will be "Yes, we would go into this again, but with some changes. We have learned a few things." The outcome of this consideration should be a redrafted mission and purpose statement, which should be reviewed and approved by top executives and, if possible, by customers and stakeholders. Even if an organization does not change its mission statement, the statement should still be reviewed by these outsiders.

Step 4: Review Products and Services in Light of Revised Mission

When rethinking its products, the team needs to think in terms of results. We discussed this in Chapter 12 on measuring performance. As noted in that chapter, results-oriented governance develops strategies and structures to achieve results desirable to customers and citizens. There always are several strategies for achieving results, and the team should list and evaluate them before going further. This evaluation can be done in part by reviewing the list of existing products and services in light of the revised mission statement. Do they fit with the new mission? In the past, have they delivered the results required by the new mission? Are new products and services needed to produce the desired results? The outcome of this review should be a revised list of products and services. At the least, the team must redefine some old products and services in light of changes in customer demand, new technology, and other external changes.

Step 5: Consider Alternate Ways of Delivering Products and Services

This step guides the restructuring process. In it, the team asks, "What alternatives do we have for making the products and services that deliver the desired results?" Some alternatives include:

- Forming cooperative relationships with other organizations, including those in the private sector, to produce a result;

- *Devolving* all or part of a service to state or local organizations or to citizens;

- *Privatizing* a service by completely turning it over to the private sector, such as through asset sales or abandonment (see Chapter 11);

- Combining process redesign and information technology to transform a service;

- Refocusing services on a different group of customers;

- Expanding the organization's role to include other services; and

- Specializing in what the organization does best, and contracting out other services it does not do well.

Exploring these alternative strategies includes studying other organizations that use them to accomplish the results envisioned in the revised mission. Performance benchmarking is a good tool for doing this, although a great deal of detail is not needed at this point.

At the end of these first five steps, the team will have a list of the products and services that will be produced by the restructured organization. Top executives, customers, and stakeholders should review and approve the list before the team goes forward. This review process can take some time and may involve public hearings and much legislative consultation.

Steps 3 through 5 are for major restructuring based on a change in mission. The following steps apply to that situation or to lesser restructuring brought about by budget cuts, reengineering, or the desire to have a more productive organization that produces essentially the same products as before.

Step 6: Identify Core Business Processes

Working with the most senior executives in the organization, the team identifies the few core business processes that produce products and services that customers value most. If you have revised your list of products, then do this step for the new list, not the old one.

For example, the senior executives of one Navy shipyard identified the core business processes in Figure 14-4. This list is now used by all shipyards, whose basic and largest service is overhauling or refitting surface vessels and submarines (some also refuel nuclear vessels). Their processes are organized around this basic service.

Figure 14-4
Shipyard
Core
Business
Processes

Provide material support
Define, estimate, plan, schedule, and forecast work
Provide administrative and general management support
Manage work execution at the waterfront
Manage and maintain equipment, facilities, and tools
Manage training programs
Administer information systems
Manage safety and environment

In another example discussed in Chapter 3, in 1992 the IRS's top executives, in an off-site meeting, divided all its business into five core business systems (CBS): **managing accounts, informing and educating, ensuring compliance, resourcing, and value tracking** (see Figure 14-5). The three CBS in boldface are considered "customer touch" operations, and the other two are support operations. This arrangement recognizes the primacy of the "customer touch" operations and the fact that many, if not most, IRS front-line personnel often work in cross-functional processes. It reflects how work gets done in the field, at service centers, and at headquarters.

Step 7: Classify All Processes According to Their Relationship with Core Processes

Working with managers in line and support functions, the restructuring team aligns all processes in the organization with the core business processes. This is best done through the process mapping methods and process center concept discussed in Chapter 13 (on ABC). Some processes will be closely related to core processes, others only tangentially or not at all. Also, some processes fit into many core business processes.

IRS CORE BUSINESS SYSTEMS   Figure 14-5

Managing Accounts	Informing and Educating	Ensuring Compliance	Resourcing	Value Tracking
Receiving Accessing IRS Receive returns/docs and payments Deposit payments **Maintaining** Review/perfect doc/payments Correct account, create entity, or return to customer Process unprocess- able payments Post to master file Reconcile Account settlement **Providing** Provide account data Create compliance cases External reporting **Assisting (External)** Responding to account inquiry Responding to tax law and proced- ural inquiry	**Planning** Legislative planning Policy planning **Developing** Develop products and procedures – internal – external Test products and procedures – internal – external **Distributing** Analyzing Determining Distributing **Enabling (Internal)** Training and communication Design training/ communication tools Test/verify effectiveness of training/communi- cation	**Identifying** Measure compliance levels Identify cases of potential non- compliance Identify strategies and Improve compliance **Compliance Planning** Establish inventory Determine level of resources to apply to cases Assign inventory **Determining** Determine case potential Gather/analyze information and evidence related to case Work case **Collecting** Contact taxpayer Alternative action Enforcement action	**Planning, Funding, and Assessing** Servicewide Performance Determining Measuring Acquiring Linking and managing Assessing **Managing Human Resources** Determining Acquiring Developing and delivering Maintaining and using **Managing Assets** Planning Acquiring Managing Disposing	Provide value-added assessment of each core business system process as gathered from customer and employee surveys **Primary activities include:** Obtain customer information about products Research taxpayer and employees to identify product values Identify new product opportunities

If you revised your list of products and services, at this point it will be evident that some smaller processes do not fit into the new core business processes. These can be eliminated, once you understand their boundaries and operation. Also, you may discover that you do not have some of the processes needed to produce a new or reconfigured service. These will need to be built into your new structure.

Step 8: Streamline Processes

Restructuring is your best opportunity to streamline all processes within your organization. The effect on your finances will be the same as a downsizing, except that downsizing reduces staff but not work, while effective streamlining reduces work.

To streamline the right way, you need *value analysis*. Value analysis originated in an older industrial method that carries the same name. For decades, industrial engineers in factories have classified as value added those tasks that change the physical properties of materials. Raw materials have value added to them by the processes that form them into finished products. Moving, storing, and inspecting do not change the physical form of material, so they do not add value to it. Besides using these industrial classifications, our approach to value analysis asks, "Would the customer for the service made by this process be willing to pay for a specific task in the process?" If the answer is no, then it is very likely that task would be called non-value added. Such a task would either be eliminated or, if this were not possible, drastically curtailed.

Value classifications

There are two basic classifications of value shown in Figure 14-6. The word *customer* here refers to any external recipients of the outputs of a process or activity. Value added activities should be targeted for continuous improvement or reengineering. Non-value added activities should be targeted for elimination if an organization can survive without them.

Figure 14-6
Value Analysis
Classifications

Value added

- Work that is absolutely essential to making and delivering a product or service the customer needs

- Work that changes the fit, form, or function of the final output delivered to customers

- Any work that increases the net worth of the output (quality, value) as perceived by the customer

Non-value added

- Any work or other resource used beyond what is absolutely essential to delivering the product the customer needs

- Work that can be eliminated with no deterioration of performance of value added work

- Any work that does not transform inputs into outputs, such as supervision, reviewing work products, inspection, and rework

- Any work that can be eliminated if a previous task or activity is done right the first time

"Non-value added" is not a judgment of the inherent worth of an activity or a reflection on the people who do it. Not all non-value added work can or should be eliminated. For example, inspecting reports for errors is something you may want to eliminate through process improvement. Inspecting components of the space shuttle is not. Likewise, training programs that increase basic skills are non-value added but still important to an organization's success. In summary, any non-value added activity that produces benefits in excess of its costs should be retained until that activity is no longer necessary.

Benefits of value analysis

Here are some benefits of value analysis as reported by different government organizations.

Reduced costs. Teams conducting value analysis at one government facility found that more than 50 percent of its support resources were being poured into non-value added activities. It didn't take long to take advantage of these new insights. As one facility executive put it, "The magnitude of these activities showed us that we could easily expect to get at least a 20 to 25 percent reduction in support costs." Improvements included simply eliminating activities or reducing the resources devoted to them.

Reduced cycle time. Removing a non-value added work step almost always speeds up a process. At a government facility's purchasing office, buyers found out that getting serial approvals for buys wasted time without adding value to the purchase process. The buyers sped up the buying process by revising it to include parallel instead of serial reviews. Ultimately, they eliminated most approvals by raising spending authority levels.

Cleaner closets. Every organization has rules, procedures, and activities that you *think* have to be done but that are really self-created extra work or legacies of another era. For example, there are always so-called mandated non-value added activities. These include complying with the endless rules, regulations, and procedures demanded by lawmakers and regulatory organizations. Until you can get some relief from these activities, you have to do them, even if customers are not even remotely interested in paying the bill.

Our experience is that you should be vigilant about these mandates. "Validating them is critical," said one government manager. "In many cases, what we always thought were external requirements were actually self-imposed. We could eliminate these requirements without higher-level approval."

Organization-wide process mapping, activity-based costing, and value analysis during restructuring

As they prepared for reduced work loads and, in some cases, closure, six of the eight Navy shipyards mapped the processes of their support functions, which are staffed by thousands of personnel. Each shipyard had dozens of support departments, including those for personnel, planning, engineering, security, accounting, and administration. Few of these departments had mapped their processes, and shipyard executives did not know where and how to reduce and restructure them.

In this situation, most organizations simply assume that departments are all "too fat," do across-the-board budget and personnel cuts, and leave it to managers to decide where to slim down. As one shipyard executive noted, "The result of this attitude is to transform large, bloated, and inefficient bureaucracies into smaller, bloated, and inefficient bureaucracies. You end up still too fat in some areas, but dangerously thin in others."

Using ABC principles (see Chapter 13), the shipyards developed top-down flow charts of all processes in their support functions, then integrated the maps into their eight core business processes, which are shown in Figure 14-4. Also, they determined the costs of processes, using ABC methods. Among the discoveries they made were the following:

Work location. Many of the departmental processes were part of larger cross-functional processes that transcended department boundaries. For example, the executives expected to find that most job order planning occurred in the planning department. Instead, over half this function took place outside the planning department. Had they simply reduced or reconfigured the planning department, they would have missed the opportunity to completely restructure the job order planning process.

Non-value added activities. More than half of the resources devoted to support functions went to nonmandated, non-value added work. Said one executive, "The magnitude of this showed us we could expect to substantially reduce the costs of support functions by eliminating non-value added activities. This meant less work, which was fortunate since we were going to have fewer people around after downsizing."

Rational centralizing and decentralizing. ABC data revealed that support departments were spending too much time on tasks such as travel vouchers, W-2 forms, savings bonds, and so on. One shipyard decided to centralize these into a one-stop-people-shop, where all employees could come with questions and get forms and assistance. ABC analysis of future work load requirements helped to figure out the shop's staffing level and equipment needs and verified the types of processes required to support it. The result was better, more accurate service because the staff were specially trained in their work. Fewer staff hours were needed in this centralized set-up than when the work was done in the departments.

All six shipyards used a common classification and coding system during their activity analysis, which gave their headquarters (NAVSEA 07) the opportunity for centralizing support services. Eight teams of shipyard representatives (one for each of the eight core business processes shown in Figure 14-4) determined the amount of support services required for the forecasted number and type of overhauls expected over the next several years. Using data developed while mapping and analyzing their processes, the team then reviewed support functions to see which could be done at a remote site and which had to be done locally at a shipyard.

They found that in many cases more than half of a support process could be done off site. Said a headquarters manager, "This means we can achieve some economies of scale at a central location. For example, if a yard now employs fourteen engineers in a support activity, we might move six to a central location to do specialized work and planning for common processes, and leave two generalists on site to work on daily problems and needs. The other six would not be needed, due to reduced work load and to reuse of products such as engineering drawings. When we need to plan and estimate the cost of a specific overhaul, a team from the central and local sites can meet face-to-face or electronically to do the work."

Appropriate staffing. Activity data were used to calculate the staffing requirements of a restructured administrative services department at one shipyard. In reviewing the data, executives found that the pay grade of most of the department's employees was higher than normally required for the work they did. The restructured department now has fewer people and at lower salary levels.

Politics. ABC data helped executives to circumvent the usual politics involved in restructuring. For example, some astute managers with good lobbying skills had positioned themselves to get more job slots than their departments needed. One manager demanded eighty more people if his department were to take on new responsibilities. Top management pointed to data showing that he had too many people shuffling papers already and hinted that he could transfer them to other departments to do some real work. That ended that.

In summary, ABC and process analysis helped Navy ship-yards to better understand their support functions and to make wise decisions about their restructuring. Now that support processes and activities are visible, mapped, and measured, it will be easier to apply process improvement methods to them.

Step 9: Review Personnel and Management Structure

When you restructure around processes, and improve them while doing so, it is a certainty that you will have to do some restructuring of the roles and responsibilities of work-ers and managers. We will discuss this restructuring now.

A new type of worker

In Chapter 17, we outline the foundations for enabling employees to control and improve their processes. Restructuring an organization is a good opportunity to establish these foundations, along with systems to promote employee innovation. These new foundations and systems help create a new type of worker who will be a source of continuous improvement.

Restructuring processes often creates a need for employees who can carry out several roles. As discussed in Chapter 18 on teams, an employee who handles a single task requires training just for that task. Put the employee in a self-man-aged team, and chances are he or she will need to cross-train in new skills in order to be able to shift from position to position on the team, as the need arises. Also, this employee will need training in team skills—group dynamics and using team tools—to be an effective team member.

You need this multi-skill ability if you switch to a case management system or single-point-of-contact system, where one employee is in charge of all aspects of a single case or customer query. Although most employees can work on teams, some do not have the instincts and ability for these systems. You have to test for it, and this testing must become part of the new process.

One place to start is by cutting back on the number of formal job descriptions in your organization. Besides taking time to develop and maintain, such descriptions limit agency and employee flexibility by spelling out in minute detail the single-skill tasks a worker is to perform. Recently, Florida's Department of Transportation had one thousand seven hundred eighteen job classes across all its positions. Today, there are ninety-six.

Some people say that managers are an endangered species; after all, since 1980 over 1.5 million management positions have disappeared from private industry. This elimination of management positions is starting to happen in government, too, which is why many public managers resist restructuring and new management approaches. Most of those approaches advocate de-layering or flattening organizations, which means removing managers. Proponents of *de-layering* government point to low manager-to-employee ratios, such as the current one-to-seven ratio in the federal government, and the number of levels between employees and the top executive, which sometimes exceeds the high teens.

However, simply increasing the manager/employee ratio and eliminating layers are both simplistic solutions. Instead, you need to examine each management layer (and sometimes each position) and ask, "What do these managers do?" and "Do we want them to continue doing it?" Below are some of the issues we urge you to explore when making this investigation.

Communication. Earlier in this chapter, we discussed the problem of elevator management, which is a communication and control issue. Today, it is usually the worst way to manage. Information technology enables the capture of data at their source and their instantaneous analysis and communication throughout an organization. Likewise, orders from on high can be quickly transmitted to everyone who needs to know them. This efficient flow of information drastically cuts back on the need for cadres of managers to send and receive reports up and down the hierarchy and is the key reason that Coopers & Lybrand only has four layers in its hierarchy: associate, senior associate, managing associate, and partner.

If you look closely at the work of many managers, you will find that much of their time is spent in communicating in the old style. When restructuring, consider how a modern communication system would reduce the need for this outmoded management task.

Control. A government manager waggishly told us that the span of control concept originated in ancient Egypt. "Groups of workers moved huge stone blocks to build the pyramids, and each team had an overseer," he said. "Group size depended on how far the overseer's whip could reach. Management hieroglyphics of the time indicate this averaged ten workers, five on the left and five on the right."

If your restructuring includes enabled workers, self-managed teams, and network technology, then the amount of time some managers will need to control employees and lower-echelon work units will be reduced. So you can subtract from current managerial labor much of the time spent in giving orders, planning and scheduling routine work, and reviewing work-in-progress. This time saved, along with reduced management reporting needs, translates into fewer managers.

Professional versus managerial work. Many so-called managers don't spend much time in communications, control, or any other management function. They are really professional workers who have a few people reporting to them. The reason they are labeled managers is to allow them advancement and wage increases when the only career ladder is through management ranks.

So another area to look at is how much time managers spend doing the same work as their employees. When managers stop replicating the work of their employees, they can use the time gained for communication and control matters.

At the same time, consider building a dual-career path into your organization. Some government organizations have done this by allowing professional employees to advance in salary to just below the top management level. Often, these professionals already were at that salary level but with the fictitious label of "manager" or with real managerial responsibilities that they neither wanted nor did well.

Planning for and managing systems issues. In Chapter 2, we discussed the 85/15 maxim: 85 percent of an organization's problems and opportunities lie in systems and 15 percent in employee performance. Working on systems issues—probably the most valuable thing that managers can do—includes the following types of activities:

- Developing objectives and plans to meet organizational goals;

- Working with other managers to coordinate and improve cross-functional processes;

- Reviewing process performance and benchmarking that performance against the best practices of other organizations;

- Removing barriers to improvement, such as unneeded rules and lack of resources;

- Looking for new technologies and other process enhancements;

- Talking with customers and suppliers to understand their requirements, complaints, and suggestions; and

- Asking employees for their suggestions on improvement and putting those ideas into action.

One objective of restructuring should be to give managers more time and training to work on these systems issues; in the Improvement Driven Organization, this is true management.

Coaching individuals and teams. The managerial coaching role goes beyond participative management, in which managers simply involve employees in business decisions. One objective of employee empowerment is to enable workers to make business decisions by themselves, with guidance from managers. Like a sports coach who can't take the field or call in every play, a successful coach/manager prepares his or her team for self-management. This includes the following:

- Training workers in new job skills and improvement methods;

- Supporting individuals and teams through advice and obtaining needed permissions and resources;

- Counseling people on ways to improve their work and advance their careers;

- Directing teams to work on priority process issues; and

- Facilitating team meetings, when needed, to foster excellent group dynamics.

When reviewing how managers spend their time, look for those types of activities. The more time spent in them, the more likely that a managerial position will need to be maintained. In that vein, you have to be honest about your labels.

A coach is a manager, and a management layer made up of coaches is still a management layer.

Managing change. A final job for managers is to help manage the human and organizational aspects of change, which includes the following types of activities:

- Studying how managerial and technical changes will affect process and employee performance and drawing up plans to facilitate employee acceptance of new ways;

- Communicating about change to employees and sharing their concerns with executives;

- Ensuring proper training in new skills;

- Monitoring how changes are made in order to ensure that they are fully adopted and effective; and

- Encouraging an atmosphere of continuous learning, which both accelerates and facilitates positive changes to processes.

In an Improvement Driven Organization, managing change is a critical job, because constant improvement means constant change. It can start while you restructure, with managers carrying out the just-listed tasks as you make the transformation. This is one area in which most organizations need to increase management time investments.

At the conclusion of this analysis, you will probably want to shed those management layers that exist primarily for control of and communication about daily operations. Also, if you move toward self-managed teams, then logic will force you to thin the ranks of managers who directly interact with workers. Although you might need one first-line manager for one small work unit, only one manager/coach is needed for several self-managed teams.

In summary, the modern agency does not need to be—indeed, cannot afford to be—structured into a many-layered, function-oriented hierarchy. To survive in an ever-changing world, you need newer, flatter, and more flexible structures.

Step 10: Select Product or Service Delivery Structures

There are three process-oriented models for restructuring. The first is a pure core business process approach, and the other two, product- and customer-oriented, are variations of it. We will discuss the advantages of each now, keeping in mind that you may want to use all three, each for a different part of your organization.

Pure core business process structure

The IRS's structure is based around its CBS, which are core business processes. "This structure," according to one IRS manager, "allows us to begin to blend the jobs and skill sets of people while we start merging the processes from different CBS. For example, a tax case used to move from functional department to functional department, with many delays and hand-off errors. Now we're successfully trying out case management in which one agent handles all aspects of a single case. You can't do that in an organization with rigid functional boundaries."

Another IRS manager added, "We've made it clear that the 'customer touch' CBS call the shots for support CBS. For example, our old marketing research group had its own agenda, without sponsors from the rest of the IRS. They would say, 'Here, look at this. Isn't it great? Why don't you do something with it?' Now all our market research has sponsors from our internal customers."

"We are, of course, doing some more visible restructuring, such as going from seventy telephone inquiry centers to twenty," said a senior manager. "Also, our automation and telecommunication projects are making fundamental changes to the way we do business. What you don't see is that these physical changes are being guided by the way our CBS structure forces us to look at processes."

Organizing around services or projects

As discussed in Chapter 16 on teams, the 653d Communications-Computer Group reorganized its structure around specific types of services it provides to customers. These include mainframe computer, Xerox 3700 copier, and personal computer support. Each service is handled by a mixed-skills team that includes functions such as hardware operations, programming, customer relations, and customer service. In industry, this is called a product or service management structure.

This structure is fine for a small support group, some may say, but what about extremely complex operations that require input from many, often super-sophisticated functions?

Few government operations are more complex than over-hauling a modern Navy vessel. An overhaul and refit of an aircraft carrier may cost upwards of $100 million and involve millions of parts and components and thousands of people. A few years ago, the direct labor of overhaul work at the shipyards was controlled by the heads of functional departments or shops such as pipefitting, welding, electrical work, carpentry, and so forth. Each department head decided what types of workers, and how many, to send to a job. Work often occurred out of sequence. For example, electrical components were installed that later had to be removed to do other tasks. The number of workers a department head sent to a job frequently corresponded to the number of people without any work to do at the time. The result usually was too many hands for too little work.

Then, the shipyards restructured their operations around the individual ship overhaul, or project. In the new system, a single project manager has responsibility and authority for all operations of overhauling a vessel from the time it is planned until it returns to the fleet. These managers "rent" from the departments the type and number of specialists and equipment they need for jobs and control these specialists on the job. One project manager told us, "I want nothing more or less than the resources I need for a job, and I'm constantly looking for ways to do the work for less. This starts at the planning and estimating stage, when we figure out a project budget and work plan. My team and I do the planning, and we live with the results. You had better believe I am motivated to make improvements and save money."

Our own firm, Coopers & Lybrand, also is organized around projects, which we call client engagements. On paper, our organizational chart shows a central headquarters and geographic regions with hub offices; professional specialties such as accounting and management consulting; and industry specialties such as financial services, utilities, and government. In real life, the only structure that matters is the individual client engagement, which may use people from many regions, professions, or industry specialties. Each engagement has a partner-in-charge who, by both policy and custom, can command the resources of any part of our U.S. firm of sixteen thousand five-hundred people. This type of flexible structure allows Coopers & Lybrand to constantly shift resources to meet client requirements.

Organizing around customers

Like the shipyards, the 46th Test Wing of the Air Force Development Test Center at Eglin AFB, Florida once was organized around line and support functions. This caused complaints among its customers, who are in charge of developing new combat weapons systems. Each customer had to interact with several functional departments in order to complete a single test project, which often caused delays and confusion.

To solve the problem, the Test Wing formed teams dedicated to each major customer. Like the 653d Communications-Computer Systems Group, each team has members with functional specialties. Like the shipyards, each "rents" services from support functions. Customer satisfaction has increased, along with employee morale, because each team member can see or take part in the full cycle of a project. The Test Wing, which four years ago gave itself low marks in a quality self-assessment, is a 1995 finalist for the federal President's Award for Quality.

Again, Coopers & Lybrand is a good example of a firm that organizes around customers. Our industry groups focus on the needs of customers in specific industries and act as resources and learning centers on related subjects for the rest of the firm. Each major, long-term client has a partner-in-charge assigned to it, who coordinates all work of any kind done by the firm for this customer and is ultimately responsible to the customer for the results.

Organizing into customer teams is a viable and flexible alternative for many agencies and support departments whose role is to serve other agencies. The result is a single-point-of-contact for each customer and a customer/team relationship that increases the value of services provided.

Step 11: Create Competition

As we discussed in Chapter 11, the team should look for ways to inject competition into all operations. This can include privatizing some services or engaging in public/private competitions.

CONTINUOUS RESTRUCTURING

If the above sounds like a lot of work, consider the alternative: a stagnant, rigid structure that impedes instead of encourages progress. But even if you go through the steps just outlined, are you finished? No, you have just begun.

In an Improvement Driven Organization, you can never finish the job of restructuring, because processes, environment, technology, and other elements will change. To be sure, this change will happen at a slower rate than a major restructuring, but change is relentless. To avoid wrenching, painful restructuring every couple of years, you need a system of continuous restructuring that is resilient and robust enough to evolve with changing needs. We discuss this in Chapter 18 on organizational culture.

Chapter
15

INTERNAL CONTROLS AND INFORMATION SYSTEMS

■ Many internal controls and information systems create rework, delays, and other barriers to progress. Such systems focus on the wrong things, and they waste time and money better spent on preventing catastrophes.

■ An Improvement Driven Organization sees internal controls as a strategic, integrated framework of objectives and components to be built into operations, not tacked on.

■ The chief executive officer owns and is accountable for the internal controls system.

■ Most governments isolate management information in data base islands. An Improvement Driven Organization uses strategic information plans to bridge the islands.

■ Installing new technology but not changing processes results in inflexible systems that "pave the cow paths" of inefficient operations.

■ The first years of the new Information Age have been marked by high cost and much waste—and costs will rise even more.

To be great, to be a person of stature, a man must have character, judgment, high intelligence, a special aptitude for seeing his problems whole and true—for seeing things as they are, without exaggeration or emotion—and above all the ability of decision, the right decision, of course.

— Bernard Law

As an Improvement Driven Organization pushes authority down the hierarchy and decentralizes decision making, it becomes increasingly critical that managers and employees are capable of independent action and judgment. This independence will not occur without effective internal controls and information systems, which are part of an organization's infrastructure. In this chapter, we will examine how to build these systems so that they do what they were intended to do: help achieve agency missions, alert people to trends, inform decisions, communicate, improve processes, and guide sound stewardship of public resources—*without creating an unwieldy infrastructure of "money police."* As you read, you will discover that character and intelligence are more important to these systems than rules and technology.

PROBLEMS WITH INTERNAL CONTROL AND INFORMATION SYSTEMS

Here are a few examples of the outcomes of poor control and information systems:

- Municipal, county, school district, and special district organizations deposited $7.4 billion in tax receipts in a joint investment fund run by the Orange County, California government. For a while, the fund enjoyed above-average earnings, because large amounts were invested in high-risk financial securities tied to derivatives whose value depended on stable interest rates. In 1994, interest rates went up, the fund lost $1.7 billion, the county went bankrupt, and investors scrambled to cut budgets and lay off hundreds of public employees. Belatedly, everyone realized that heavy investment in risky derivatives was not—indeed, had never been— appropriate for the conservative portfolio of the fund.

• The U.S. General Accounting Office (GAO) says that although federal agencies invested $200 billion in information management systems in the last ten years, the agencies still lack critical information needed to analyze programs, control costs, and measure results. Information system projects are often late, fail to work as planned, and cost hundreds of millions more than expected.

• A large Northeastern city called in Coopers & Lybrand after losing hundreds of thousands of dollars in misappropriated funds, including illegal overtime and disability payments. We found that the problem lay with the government's culture and management structure, as well as with its financial controls.

• At one federal facility we worked with, over $150 million in inventory was unrecorded and thus not available to other facilities because it was not on the books. Why? The supply system was so bad that facilities could not depend on getting supplies on time, so their people "squirreled away" extras.

Each of the above failures occurred because an adequate internal control or information system did not exist, did not perform as intended, was not used, or was thwarted by criminal intent. Most people are honest, so the chief cause of internal control problems lies with control systems and control culture. Causes of poor information systems are myriad: piecemeal development, the automation of inefficient processes, and failure to consider the needs of users. We are going to discuss internal controls first, because they can and often do shape an effective management information system (MIS). Our expanded definition of internal controls, given later in this chapter, shows why.

Built In   Added On

Figure 15-1
Effective
Control and
Information
Systems Are
Built In, Not
Added On

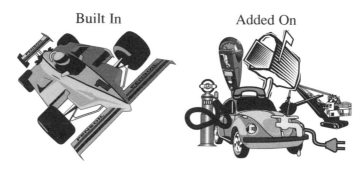

WHAT MANY INTERNAL CONTROL SYSTEMS DO (AND DO NOT DO)

Many control systems create massive paperwork, redundant reviews, and barriers to progress. Too often, such systems focus on the wrong issues, gobbling time and money that could have been spent to prevent crises. In process terms, many are just post-production quality control activities, and add no value.

Consider the following example of travel expense reports, which are part of internal controls. We were asked to help a federal facility improve its operations and reduce costs. During the project, we found two clerks whose only job was to ensure that *draft* travel expense reports complied with regulations (inspection), attach all receipts (rework), re-add figures to verify accuracy (inspection and rework), and type reports on a five-carbon form (rework). They sent the forms to another office that re-checked them (inspection and rework) and authorized payment; then the bursar's office checked them again (inspection and rework) and issued reimbursement checks to the travelers. The reason for the two clerks, said their supervisor, was that expense checks had been delayed because of errors in travel reports and illegible copies of the form (you have to press down very hard to get that fifth carbon copy).

In the meantime, poor internal controls in other parts of the facility allowed the waste of public funds totaling a hundred times more than the entire travel budget. Sitting in warehouses was new, uncrated equipment, worth millions of dollars, that no one was trained to operate, while other machines sat idle for lack of spare parts. Core business processes were full of bottlenecks and rework that caused cost overruns, and angry customers were taking their business elsewhere. Today, the facility is targeted for permanent closure. Its epitaph: *No one ever complained about our travel expense reports!*

The saddest part of our little travel example? There are thousands more so-called internal control systems just like it, affecting every aspect of government. But there is a better way. Not perfect, but easier and more effective. We will discuss it now.

AN INTEGRATED FRAMEWORK FOR INTERNAL CONTROL

In an attempt to improve similar situations in the private sector, the Committee of Sponsoring Organizations of the Treadway Commission (COSO, see box on next page) developed a fresh approach to internal controls, one ideally suited to Improvement Driven Organizations.

> **The COSO Report: Internal Control—Integrated Framework**
>
> In 1987 the National Commission on Fraudulent Financial Reporting, known as the Treadway Commission, recognized the seriousness of control problems in the private sector. The commission's sponsors include five major accounting and financial operations organizations in the United States: the American Accounting Association, the American Institute of Certified Public Accountants, the Financial Executives Institute, the Institute of Management Accountants, and the National Association of Accountants. The commission formed a Committee of Sponsoring Organizations (COSO) to integrate and reconcile conflicting internal control concepts into a common framework. In 1991, Coopers & Lybrand was retained to conduct the COSO's study and wrote the final report, *Internal Control—Integrated Framework* (see Appendix A). Since then, C&L has used the COSO framework as the basis for our In Controls Service, which assists companies, nonprofits, and government organizations to establish better internal controls.

Internal Controls Redefined

Ask members of different professions the definition of *internal controls,* and their answers will vary. To elected officials, they are systems that provide evidence that agencies are effectively pursuing appropriate goals set by the officials. To agency executives and line managers, controls include policies, processes, and actions that ensure operational effectiveness and that enable them to respond quickly to changing conditions. To financial personnel, they include checks and balances on spending authority, audits, procedures for preparing and evaluating financial reports, and other sound stewardship practices. To regulators, internal controls are the means to ensure that agencies comply with rules and regulations.

The COSO definition of internal controls shows that these different meanings must be combined for an integrated approach:

> **Internal controls:** A *process,* effected by an entity's *board of directors,* * *management, and other personnel,* designed to provide *reasonable assurance* regarding the *achievement of objectives* in the following categories:
>
> - Effectiveness and efficiency of *operations,*
>
> - Reliability of *financial reporting,* and
>
> - Compliance with *applicable laws and regulations.*
>
>   * To make this definition work for government, substitute "elected officials" for "board of directors."

Because internal controls are processes, they benefit from all the process control and improvement methods discussed throughout this book. Because they involve people, the processes can be affected by changes in an organization's culture. Thus, every other subject in this book, from strategic planning through ensuring continuous improvement, relates to internal controls processes. Conversely, deploying strategy and ensuring continuous improvement requires effective internal controls.

Do You Have Effective Internal Controls?

Considering the COSO definition, answers to this question require more than a formal review or audit that compares existing controls with established standards. Such audits tell you little about your culture and processes, which are key to successful internal controls. The COSO report shows a formal assessment method that gives you the whole picture of your current control system and points the way to building a better one.

Form steering committee

Any organization-wide assessment of internal controls should be done by a senior management steering committee led by the chief executive. This committee's purpose is to evaluate how the existing internal controls system is purported to work, how it actually works, and how it should work considering current and future requirements for sound controls.

The job of the steering committee head should not be delegated to the chief financial officer or auditors, because the chief executive officer, not they, owns the internal control system. However, some managers, auditors, and consultants can give staff support to the committee, while all personnel can help the evaluation by joining in discussions of control policies, procedures, and effectiveness.

Review objectives for internal controls and establish new objectives

One of the committee's first jobs is to understand the objectives of the existing internal control system, weigh them against requirements, and (usually) establish new objectives for a revised system. There are three categories of objectives in the COSO internal controls framework: operational, financial reporting, and compliance.

Operational objectives concern an organization's ability to achieve its mission and strategic goals. They aim at controlling and improving the ability of processes to meet customer and stakeholder requirements. Although the specific operational objectives for internal control will vary with mission, goals, and environment, they always address the following factors:

- Timely performance measurement information that is appropriate, useful, and used for process control and improvement at all levels of an organization.

- Information on how resources are invested to meet routine operations and strategic goals.

- The accuracy, value, and use of information gathered to learn about customer requirements, changes in external environment, best practices, new technology, and related subjects.

- The capability of an agency's people and processes to respond to changes in demand or external environment.

- Assurance that the organization protects the public's trust.

- An MIS that ties together information related to these objectives and the others listed below, along with other information needed for sound and timely decisions.

Sound operational objectives for internal control are tied to the strategic plans discussed in Chapter 5, because gaining the objectives is part of achieving strategic goals.

Financial reporting objectives relate to ensuring reliable published financial statements. For government, external users of the statements include parent, treasury, audit, oversight, and budget organizations, as well as elected officials, stakeholders, and the general public. The federal government and some state governments have started to require major public organizations to provide annual audited financial statements, which would be included in this category of objectives. We would include budget proposals, too, because they are a primary means of controlling public agencies.

Other financial reporting objectives include that internal controls should provide fair presentations of financial status that:

- Conform with appropriate accounting principles and statutory requirements;

- Are informative of matters of concern to the users of the statements; and

- Reasonably reflect transactions and events in ways that present financial position, results of operations, and cash flows.

One area of difficulty for many governments is to produce financial information that presents a fair estimate of the unit cost of products and services so that this information can be compared with costs of alternative sources. Chapter 13 discusses costing systems that will help overcome this problem.

Compliance objectives concern how an organization conforms to applicable rules and regulations. For an Improvement Driven Organization, internal controls objectives for compliance include ensuring the following:

- People understand and have the means to comply with rules and regulations that apply to their processes, positions, and responsibilities. People might need training, time, information, special equipment, and other resources.

- When possible, the organization builds into its processes the tasks of following compliance requirements and documenting compliance activities and events.

- People promptly identify compliance problems inside
  and outside their processes, and report them to the proper
  person inside (and sometimes outside) the organization.

- The organization takes immediate and appropriate
  action to remedy a compliance problem and prevents its
  recurrence by eliminating the problem's root causes.

Government organizations probably are subject to more rules
and regulations than any other part of the economy. This is
a good reason for rule-making bodies to keep their requirements to a minimum so that they can focus on issues important to sound governance, safety, health, and well-being.

Figure 15-2
Components
of Integrated
Internal
Controls

Components of Integrated Internal Controls

The steering committee needs to understand the effectiveness of the components of existing internal controls, using
the framework shown in Figure 15-2. This can be done

through interviews with employees and managers, surveys such as the Culture Climate Survey discussed in Chapter 4, review of the organization's written policies and procedures and the extent of its compliance with them, and identification of unwritten practices. Starting at the base of the control pyramid, internal controls include the following:

Control environment

The foundation of effective internal control is people: how they behave and are organized and managed. This environment is intimately associated with an organization's culture, which we discuss in Chapter 18. The control environment thus includes the following:

- **Integrity and ethical values** include expected standards of behavior and how they are communicated, exemplified, and enforced through executive word and deed, rewards, and sanctions. Certainly, incentives and temptations for questionable or even criminal behavior have to be removed or minimized by, for example, segregating duties in areas that provide the opportunity to steal or conceal poor performance and strengthening internal audits. Also, executives must be vigilant in exercising their oversight responsibilities.

- **Commitment to competence** means that an organization ensures that all employees have the requisite knowledge and skills to do their jobs effectively. Otherwise, processes will become unstable and will not operate as expected.

- **Management's philosophy and operating style,** including the types of business risks it finds acceptable, attitudes toward financial reporting, and attention to internal control objectives, must be clearly understood.

- **Organizational structure** must be appropriate for mission, processes, and effective control and communication. In Chapter 14, we discussed how layered, functional hierarchies cause control problems.

- **Assignment of authority and responsibility** includes how individuals and teams are enabled and held accountable for controlling and improving their processes (see Chapters 16 and 17) and the limits set on their authority. This component relates to competence and structure. As we said earlier, the more an Improvement Driven Organization pushes authority down the hierarchy, the more critical it is that employees are capable of independent action and exercising sound judgment. This component also relates to the effectiveness of management monitoring of process and employee performance.

- **Human resource policies and practices** include hiring, orientation, training, evaluation, counseling, promoting, compensation, and rewards and sanctions. These policies and practices should be geared toward fostering competence and reinforcing integrity and ethics.

- **Audit and oversight groups independent from management** must be made up of people competent to render opinions on agency operational, financial, and compliance controls.

Risk assessment

In excusing his part in the financial disaster that devastated Orange County's multi-billion dollar fund, the official in charge said that he did not know that investing heavily in derivatives was so risky. The government facility with the incredible travel expense report system minimized the risk associated with use of travel money while ignoring the risk of wasting millions of dollars in other areas. Both organizations failed to address *appropriately* the risks associated with their operations.

As shown in Figure 15-2, risk assessment is a basic component of internal controls, resting just above control environment. Risk assessment includes identifying, analyzing, and ranking internal and external factors that could imperil performance. It does not include the management actions taken to reduce risk by removing or minimizing the effects or causes of risk, although internal control systems should monitor the implementation and performance of risk reduction activities.

Figure 15-3
Process Risk
Assessment
Matrix for
Internal
Controls

Probability

	Severe	Moderate	Minor
High	Strong controls	Strong controls	Moderate controls
Medium	Strong controls	Moderate controls	Light controls
Low	Moderate controls	Light controls	Very light or no controls

Negative Consequences of Process Failure

All processes in an organization should be subject to some level of risk assessment, but a reasonable balance is necessary to avoid paralyzing operations or wasting time over minor risks in non-core processes. This means weighing the seriousness of consequences against their probability, as shown in Figure 15-3. Serious consequences with medium or high probability receive more analysis and action from executives and senior managers; minor consequences with low probability receive little or no attention from them. Finally, the costs of internal controls activities must be compared with their benefits. It makes little sense to spend a million dollars to avoid the potential waste of one-tenth that amount, but we have found many instances of this sort of reasoning in government agencies.

Comprehensive risk assessment is arguably most important to an organization's future when it focuses on strategic goals. Also, it is critical when making changes required to respond to new customer or stakeholder requirements, new technology, and competitive pressures. Thus, risk assessment is a continuous, iterative process in an Improvement Driven Organization.

Control activities

One product of the steering committee's risk assessment will be a ranked list of serious risks to core business processes and total organizational effectiveness. Items on this list are the chief focus of control activities, which include *policies,* or management directives that control and reduce risk, and *procedures* for carrying out the policies. For an Improvement Driven Organization, some of the most important control activities include the following:

- **Performance measurement and management** of control objectives, including how management uses the measures to identify, report, and correct problems;

- **Information processing** activities that check accuracy, completeness, and authorization of transactions and that follow up on exceptions and problems. Information systems also can automate applications controls such as documenting compliance with rules, resource use, and process performance;

- **Physical controls**, such as securing and periodically conducting inventories and counting equipment, securities, cash, and other assets, and comparing these counts with control records;

- **Dividing and segregating duties** to reduce the risk of error, fraud, or other inappropriate action; and

- **Top management reviews** of performance of core business processes, other major initiatives, and progress toward strategic goals. Actions that follow these reviews should, in turn, be reviewed.

Such actions can be built into processes, such as reconfiguring a process to reduce hand-offs of work-in-progress, using cross-functional teams, and putting one manager in charge of a core business process. These actions reduce miscommunication and delays and ensure a focal point for management responsibility and authority that often is missing from government.

Information and communication. Information and communication systems hold together the other components of the internal controls structure, so they are shown on the sides of the pyramid in Figure 15-2. In reviewing how these systems meet an organization's control needs, the steering committee evaluates the systems' appropriateness in the following areas:

Information

- Collecting internal and external information to provide performance reports to management;

- Providing the right information at the right time to the right people, in sufficient detail to permit them to take appropriate actions; and

- Determining how systems development is tied to and enhances progress toward an organization's strategic goals, how this development is guided by a strategic plan for information systems, and how management supports information strategies with resources.

Communication

- Effectiveness of communication with employees about their duties, control responsibilities, and reporting of problems (including possible improprieties);

- Management's response to employee suggestions for improvement (see Chapter 17);

- Adequacy of cross-functional communication, including in design, daily operations, and core business processes;

- Openness and effectiveness of external communications channels with customers, suppliers, stakeholders, regulators, and the general public and how management responds to this communication; and

- The extent to which external parties are made aware of an organization's ethical standards.

Monitoring. Because internal controls are processes, they must be monitored and evaluated over time to ensure that they remain appropriate and effective, given changing requirements. *Ongoing* monitoring includes routine review by management of the effectiveness of internal controls, as evidenced by these controls' ability to identify and report problems and concerns. Also, internal and external auditors routinely review the controls and recommend ways to improve them. Regularly discussing controls policies and procedures with managers, employees, and suppliers helps assure effectiveness and identifies problems and opportunities for improvement. Finally, documenting internal controls activities is critical. Because an Improvement Driven Organization is constantly evolving to meet new needs, special attention is needed to ensure the effectiveness of ongoing monitoring activities.

Separate evaluations include reviewing all or certain internal controls objectives and components to align them with major changes in structure, strategy, mission, or management approach. Also, these evaluations periodically confirm the results of ongoing monitoring with audit data, physical counts, reviews of customer complaints, and other information. For the Improvement Driven Organization, separate evaluations are an opportunity to benchmark internal controls processes against those of outside organizations known to have excellent systems. Finally, a monitoring component needs to include a process for reporting deficiencies in controls to the appropriate person or group and for starting and tracking management action to correct deficiencies.

Flexibility in Developing Internal Controls Systems

Although the same generic standards may apply to a range of internal control activities, such activities are different for large, decentralized agencies and small, centralized agencies; those that work in high-risk areas are different from those used in another type of setting. Central governments need to recognize these differences and give their agencies flexibility in developing internal controls.

The State of New York gives its one-hundred-plus agencies latitude in developing their internal controls, so long as they meet recognized standards. Most of the agencies are small and cannot afford (and likely do not need) sophisticated controls evaluation and design. The state developed a simple four-step process, driven by questions and forms, that helps agencies (1) identify functions, (2) assess risks and vulnerability, (3) review existing controls against the risks, and (4) design corrective actions. Nearly half the state's agencies now use the process as their internal control review system. Key to the approach is preparing a written plan for internal controls that can be used by internal and external auditors. The plan must include steps to be taken to correct deficiencies.

There are alternatives to the COSO integrated internal control framework. These include hiring hordes of people just to watch over every activity in your organization, or "flying blind" without internal controls in key areas. Most agencies do both, and you read the scandalous results in the headlines or in cost overrun reports. If you build internal controls into processes with the intent of making the processes more effective, there will be far less need for non-value added "work watchers" and no reason to fly blind—because everyone will participate in maintaining internal control.

INFORMATION SYSTEMS AND TECHNOLOGY

Most of the internal control objectives just listed can be built into core business processes and individual work processes and thus into an MIS. For example, the operational objective of timely performance measurement information applies to every process. Building in feedback mechanisms for process operators answers this objective. Developing cost tracking systems geared to individual process cost and volume drivers enables managers to report accurate operations cost information, which helps satisfy both operational and financial reporting objectives. Linking this information into an effective MIS serves all three categories of objectives.

We will not repeat the many internal control purposes of a MIS, except to reemphasize that it should give people feedback on process performance. Instead, here are additional, non-control (or not-necessarily-control) issues.

Statewide MIS in Texas Supports Strategic Planning

Not long ago, Texas state government used its MIS primarily to report costs by program. Today, reports the GAO, the information system includes the missions, goals, objectives, strategies, and progress measures of state agencies' strategic plans. The MIS also links budgets, accounting, and performance information and is tied by computer to the state's comptroller, governor, and legislature.

Management Information Systems

Because an Improvement Driven Organization's structure and decision making are often decentralized, it needs tight horizontal and vertical communication linkage among all processes. Trying to establish this linkage through coordinators or "elevator management" is wasteful and causes delays, so it is better to enable the different processes to handle their own coordination.

Such coordination requires a system for sharing knowledge that is now isolated in "information islands" throughout your organization. The knowledge includes customer expectations, strategic goals and objectives, schedules, supplies, product and service descriptions, the capacity of different processes, costs, and other vital data. The islands are data bases in work units or functional departments, existing in many formats and often on different hardware. One objective for an MIS is to give people quick and easy access to information in a meaningful format and to enable them to reconfigure it to satisfy their needs. Advanced organizations often include their external customers and suppliers in this loop.

You cannot link the islands without a strategic plan for information systems and technology. Otherwise, systems development will be helter-skelter, ineffective, and more expensive than you could ever dream. Such a plan sets and monitors progress toward results-oriented goals of information integration.

You will need expert help in plan development, but don't let information experts alone develop and execute goals and strategy. Include line managers and employees, who know their information needs best. Also, the plan should be built around your organization's core business processes, aiming first at optimizing information flows to improve their operation and results. Planning around core business processes helps avoid focusing on secondary processes like travel expense reports while mainline operations like producing services for external customers go wanting.

However, don't think that simply linking information islands will do the trick. At a minimum, the groups that capture and store data for the islands will have to change what information they collect, and how, to make it available to the rest of your organization. We will discuss the reasons for this in the next section.

Now that we've automated, we do the wrong thing faster.

Applications Technology

Most of the examples of new technology in this book are called *applications systems,* because they are designed for specific types of work. These include the IRS's system for paying taxes with touch-tone telephones, Riverside County's law enforcement information system, computer kiosk systems that enable citizens to transact business with their governments, and the use of automated teller machines (ATMs) to dispense welfare payments. None of these systems simply automated existing processes. Instead, their processes were radically altered to take advantage of the new technology, and the technology selected was appropriate for achieving the desired results. We discussed the need to do this in Chapter 10 on reengineering, but we want to reemphasize the point with some additional examples.

The reason many government applications systems fail is noted in James Martin's *Information Engineering*: "The first motorcars were called 'horseless carriages' and were the same shape as a carriage without a horse. Much later it became recognized that a car should have a different shape. Similarly, the first radio was called 'wireless telegraphy' without the realization that broadcasting would bear no resemblance to telegraphy. Today we talk about the 'paperless office' and 'paperless corporation,' but we build [information] systems with screens and data bases that duplicate the previously existing organization of work."

For example, a few years ago a military facility decided to test a work planning and information system. This kind of application system combines process changes and new technology to smoothly regulate the flow of work and materials, saving time and money. We advised the facility that the best way to start was to improve the processes before installing the system. While doing this, a facility team found changes that would greatly increase quality, reduce cycle time, and save $1 million (enough to pay for the system). The improvements were available without the new system and later helped to speed up its installation.

Another military facility installed the same type of system but made no real attempt to streamline procedures or at least alter them to fit the system. Instead, everyone insisted on continuing the old way of working. The result? Only minor improvements occurred, everyone hated the system, and it was scrapped.

The second facility's mistake is repeated throughout government and industry. When agencies design systems to exactly fit their existing processes, they usually end up doing the wrong things faster. This approach also creates expensive, inflexible systems, which are barriers to continuous improvement. It is better to adapt processes to flexible, robust systems that do critical tasks with excellence and that are satisfactory at everything else.

Hidden Cost Issues

Finally, here is the greatest puzzle of the late twentieth century, and let's hope that someone finds the answer soon. The cost of information technology is plummeting at a rate such that today it is virtually a commodity good. In contrast, the cost of owning information systems continues to skyrocket. For example, *Business Week* recently reported that a $250 computer game due for release by Nintendo in 1995 has the power of a 1985 computer that cost $14 million. Such power is great if you can harness it, but that can be expensive. Gartner Group, Inc., the market researchers, estimates that the five-year cost to operate a typical MSDOS-based corporate personal computer is $40,000— ten times its $4,000 purchase price, which includes software; that estimate covers things like training, technical assistance, installing extra memory, and electricity. Corporations are certainly entitled to get more than an $8,800 a year return on their investment (some do, some don't, *most don't know*).

In short, we are not yet out of the budget-buster woods when it comes to information technology and systems. This fact is scary when you think about the hundreds of billions of taxpayer dollars already spent on such systems, the waste within that investment, and the additional hundreds of billions that governments are going to be spending as we continue our journey through the early part of the Information Age. All the more reason to integrate process improvement with information technology in order to maximize the returns on both investments. Finally, such high costs mean that you must continuously improve the way you work with information systems—that, too, is a process.

ORGANIZATIONAL PROCESS ALIGNMENT

Chapter
16

PROMOTING TEAMWORK

■ Improvement Driven Organizations use team-based management at all levels, starting with top executives.

■ Benefits from teamwork range from breaking down organizational barriers to leadership training. The greatest benefit is harnessing everyone's ability to contribute to improvement.

■ Teamwork is a management *system*, not a management *style*. Like any other system, it must be planned, introduced as planned, and supported with subsystems. These sub-systems include training, group facilitation, and management assistance.

This story is told of Wernher von Braun, pioneer of America's space program. Someone once found him lying on the beach at Cape Canaveral, staring out at the waves, and asked, "What are you thinking about, Dr. von Braun? Are you dreaming about an innovation in space flight, or how to solve some problem?"

"No," he replied. "I am thinking about something much more important: my team."

Teams are critical to the success of the Improvement Driven Organization. They are the key to unlocking the potential of all personnel, from the top executive to the lowest paid worker. Guiding and supporting teams are the most serious business of most new management approaches and the most rewarding aspects of the jobs of many managers.

WHAT IS AN IMPROVEMENT DRIVEN ORGANIZATION TEAM?

In an Improvement Driven Organization, a team is a group of people, each affected by the same process or processes, working toward a common goal and using common methods. The team may include executives, managers, supervisors, employees, external customers, vendors, and other agencies.

You can expect to see teams at work throughout an Improvement Driven Organization, from a top management executive team down to natural work groups or self-managed teams of employees. Let's look at several roles that teams can play inside an Improvement Driven Organization. This overview also will illustrate the benefits of teamwork listed in Figure 16-1.

• Teams maximize skills and insight.
• Well-managed teams promote discipline and structure in the search for improvement.
• Teams offer a way to include people who are not normally part of a group.
• Teams break down barriers.
• Team-based organizations facilitate top-down, bottom-up management.
• Teamwork increases acceptance of change.
• Teamwork is the new leadership training.

Figure 16-1
Benefits of
Teamwork

Process Improvement

Administrators at the Florida Department of Transportation (FDOT) estimated that quality management helped them save Florida taxpayers $28 million in 1989, and the savings continue to grow. Every branch of the department uses TQM, from the director to the lowest-paid employee; many FDOT contractors do, too. Most of the savings come from teamwork.

For example, a team of managers and employees in FDOT District 5 found they were spending $21,940 per mowing season to manually service roadside grass-cutting equipment. They surveyed other mower operators to find out why.

They expected the big-time wasters would be breakdowns, flat tires, and equipment repairs, but the greatest cause surprised them. Plotting their findings on a pareto chart, they found that 45 percent of the manual work was cleaning grass and dirt from mower decks with shovels and brooms, which took each crew thirty minutes at the end of each day.

The solution to the problem came in a structured brainstorming session: an $80, gasoline-powered leaf blower. "We gave one crew a blower and tracked their effectiveness," said a team member. "The trial crew was able to clean up in five minutes. They used the time saved to mow two more acres a day."

The increased productivity saves the district $2,600 a year per three-mower crew (this does not count the other six improvements the team developed). Sound insignificant? The FDOT has *hundreds* of mowers.

Team benefit #1: Teams maximize skills and insight

One aim of teamwork is to maximize insight into how to make improvements. Traditional organizations usually put individuals in charge of improvement: specialists and managers. The Improvement Driven Organization does not deny the skills of specialists and managers, but it realizes their natural limitations. Specialists tend to have a narrow range of skills, and managers often see things only in terms of their units or are removed from day-to-day operations. Teaming them with employees overcomes these limitations.

Team benefit #2: Well-managed teams promote discipline and structure in the search for improvement

Note that the FDOT mower team followed the Plan-Do-Check-Act cycle described in Chapter 9, conducted surveys to gather objective data, and used tools and techniques such as pareto charts and brainstorming, which were discussed in Chapter 8. This is a disciplined approach to teamwork, which gives structure to improvement activities.

Client/Contractor Relationships

NASA's Johnson Space Center includes contractors on the working groups that carry out fundamental planning tasks, such as the strategic planning support team, the technology support team, and the contractor incentive working group. The center director also holds periodic meetings with contractor executives to share information on NASA and center strategic plans. "We have about fifty contractor organizations at Johnson Space Center, and we have to have a structured system to use their expertise," said a management chief. "Like employees, contractors perform better when they understand how they contribute to the big picture. How can they do that if you don't give them the big picture?"

Team benefit #3: Teams offer a way to include people who are not normally part of a group

Most organizations do not have ways of involving contractors in planning. Indeed, many would consider this an unwarranted breaking of the old "arm's-length" rule of client/contractor relationships. Because of their flexible nature and because you can establish specific ground rules for each, teams offer a way to assemble any type of working group.

Cross-Functional Improvement

A few years ago, employees of the 653d Communications-Computer Systems Group at Warner Robins Air Force Base were organized by function, such as programmers, machine operators and technicians, and customer representatives. When the group wanted to reorganize around thirty-eight major process lines, it formed cross-functional teams of employees directly involved in the processes to figure out how to carry out the reorganization. For a year, the employees remained in their formal functions as they analyzed their processes and planned for restructuring. During this time, they met regularly as cross-functional teams to manage the group's processes. Then, they helped to realign the group around its major service lines, instead of by function.

Employees on the cross-functional teams say that their team experiences enabled them to make better decisions about which organizations and specialties should be grouped together in the new structure. Despite a 40 percent reduction in staff, the group now provides better service to its customers as measured by on-line computer time, service delivery time, and accuracy and timeliness of reports.

Team benefit #4: Teams break down barriers

Before this experiment in cross-functional teamwork and management, computer programmers, program operators, and customer service representatives had not worked together and thus did not understand each other's requirements. A year's worth of teamwork broke down this barrier and was the foundation for a new, team- and process-oriented group.

Top-Down, Bottom-Up Management

In Chapter 2, we described how self-managed teams of road maintenance workers in the Oregon Department of Transportation (ODOT) make and carry out what are normally management decisions. But is the highway the only place you will find such high performance teams in the ODOT? Hardly. In Oregon, teams are hard at work at the department, region, district, and work crew levels. Figure 16-2 shows how this is an interlocking system of teams, with members of higher-level teams serving as team leaders of the next level down. Such a system is essential for top-down, bottom-up management, in which policy directives flow down through an organization and policy-related issues, concerns, suggestions, and needs flow upward.

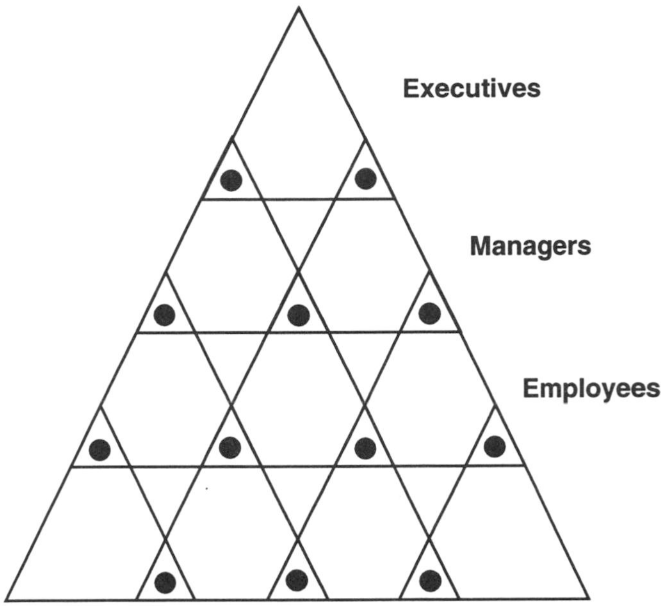

Figure 16-2
Interlocking
Teams

ODOT has a consensus, team-based management style that starts with the department director's Management Team, which makes policy decisions about the structure and reporting relationships of major organizational units. The department is divided into regions, and each region's manager formally reports to the ODOT deputy director. However, region managers also serve on the director's Management Team, which is led by the director. The region managers are encouraged to bring organizational issues to the Management Team meetings, which assures an upward flow of ideas and concerns. On the other hand, region managers are responsible for taking department policy to their regions, which is a downward flow of issues requiring work.

This team does not make the daily, routine decisions of the department or handle emergencies. Those are the jobs of individual managers. Instead, the director's team focuses on long-term plans to improve operations. It's an important point: team-based consensus takes time and is not suited for immediate decisions.

At the next level down, each region has its own management team made up of the region manager and district managers. This team works on improvement projects and on implementing department policy. The district managers bring their suggestions, concerns, and issues to the regional team meetings; if these cannot be dealt with locally or through regular channels, the regional manager will take them to the next director's Management Team meeting.

The districts have their own teams, consisting of a district manager and area managers. Together, the area managers form a team, and each area manager serves as the coach of several self-managed crews. According to the ODOT, the seven area managers in Region 5 were the most significant players in the implementation and operation of the pilot test of self-managed road crews. One of the most important jobs of the area managers was to carry the issues, concerns, and suggestions of the road crews upward to the next level in the system.

Team benefit #5: Team-based organizations facilitate top-down, bottom-up management

As you can see by this system, some of the road crews' issues and suggestions will reach the very top of the organization—through the interlocking teams of the ODOT. This bottom-up flow of information keeps top managers in touch with reality. Top-down information flow is enhanced because the people in charge of implementing policy, such as the region managers in ODOT, participate in forming it, so they understand the issues involved. This means they are better able to communicate the policy to other parts of the organization.

Such systems of interlocking teams also can be used to create written policy implementation plans at every level of an organization. Sometimes called *policy deployment*, this approach is based on a Japanese system called *hoshin* planning. For example, a top management team will establish critical goals such as reducing cycle time, improving service for key customers, or reducing costs. The executives and managers on that top team will go to their own management teams to write objectives on what their groups can do to help meet the goals. Lower-level teams prepare written plans for meeting those objectives, indicating the resources and other assistance they will need. The objectives, plans, and resource needs are then taken back to the top management team for review and approval. In this way, all managers can participate in policy planning as well as implementation. We discuss this system more in Chapter 5.

Change Management

Executives and managers in organizations like ODOT reach consensus on policy before deploying it to the groups they lead. This helps ensure that they will support and enforce the policy. Such support does not automatically occur in a traditional government organization, because some executives and managers have their own power base—they do not have to listen to top executives, especially political appointees who will not be around in a couple of years.

People do not resist change, they resist *being* changed. No matter how logical, rational, and beneficial a change in operations is, they will resist it if it is imposed from without. When people affected by a change participate in planning and introducing it, the change will be more acceptable to them. Teams are a way of ensuring this participation.

Team benefit #6: Teamwork increases acceptance of change

Leadership Training

Reflect for a moment on how, in the team examples given, employees were engaged in making management decisions and managers were forming executive policy. How can this help but benefit their organizations?

Well-managed teams are training grounds for future managers and executives. As one consultant noted: "Every team has a team leader, someone responsible for scheduling meetings, conducting them, and keeping the team on target. This is valuable experience in group management and leadership. That this happens in a controlled setting using top-notch decision tools is a plus. The team leader learns the right way to lead, which is more than can be said for how many managers learn this."

> *Team benefit #7: Teamwork is the new leadership training*

TEAMWORK AS A SYSTEM

As a system, Improvement Driven Organization teamwork has several components. These include the teams themselves, their internal structure, team management, and team support.

Internal Structure of Teams

All teams have a leader and members. Often they have a facilitator and may be helped by other specialists

The *team leader* is responsible for calling meetings, making task assignments, and keeping to the schedule. A team leader might be an employee or a manager; sometimes managers are team members and their employees team leaders. In self-managed teams or natural work groups, leadership may rotate among members.

Team members are people who are directly or indirectly involved in a set of processes or in a problem area. They may include the people who operate or manage the processes; sometimes, team members include internal or external customers, suppliers, and partner organizations.

Many organizations use *team facilitators* trained in problem-solving methods and group dynamics. They help in selecting and using problem-solving tools, often train members in their use, and help guide discussions. Special facilitators are most frequently used during the early development of an Improvement Driven Organization. Later, most managers and some employees assume this role.

Types of Teams

Figure 16-3 shows the types of teams you might consider using. Each will now be discussed, except product and service design teams, which are covered in Chapter 9. Please note that the lines between different types of teams are often blurred; some may share responsibilities or do the same types of tasks.

Types	Membership	Focus
Management teams	Executives and managers	Manage quality activities
Executive steering committee	Top executives	Guide the organization
Issue management teams	Top and middle managers	Work on key issues of the strategic plan or other special issues
Unit management teams	Top and middle managers	Guide and support quality progress in their units and work on systems issues
Improvement teams	Anyone, including customers, vendors, distributors, and partner organizations	Conduct improvement projects
Self-managed teams	Employees and first-line managers	Manage and improve their specific processes

Figure 16-3
Types of
Teams

Top executive teams

The key tasks of a top executive team are to develop an organization management style, philosophy, policy, and strategic plan and to identify major improvement projects. This team also monitors the progress of introducing major change and the key performance indicators of the organization. Finally, it works on major systems issues that require top management consideration and often takes the lead when working on quality and improvement issues with partner organizations or high-level appointed or elected officials.

Sometimes this team will form a council made up of its own members and others inside and outside the organization. This council may include other managers, union representatives, and top support contractors. This larger body will assume some specific tasks involved in introducing management approaches, such as TQM, or serve as a "board of directors" for the organization's quality effort.

Management teams

Management teams are charged with management and oversight of quality of work and improvement activities for the units they represent. They act on higher management directives, solicit suggestions for improvement from managers and employees, and may be in charge of the formal suggestion programs in their units. They also maintain contacts with customers, vendors, and other organizations to obtain information useful for planning improvement actions. As needed, they pass this information up the line to executives or down to employees.

Another important job of these teams is management of change. Using such techniques as force field analysis, they form strategies for overcoming obstacles to introducing innovations to their units and the organization. These obstacles may include unneeded rules, "turf" issues, and departmental barriers.

Management teams review feedback from any source in the organization. There will always be many opportunities for improvement (if there are not, something is wrong), so the team must systematically separate the significant from the trivial. Methods such as pareto analysis help to do this.

Unit management teams work on systems issues within their units. When doing this, they may follow a procedure such as PDCA from start to finish. If they find issues specific to one or a few processes within their units, they may create an improvement team to work on it. They also may ask other management teams to help form a cross-functional team when an issue requires this approach. Finally, they establish any self-managed teams in their unit processes.

A management team ensures that lower-level teams have the resources they need for their projects. This includes training, meeting time and space, and access to information. Sometimes the management team or its leader must counsel supervisors and middle managers to allow employees to participate in teams.

A management team monitors lower-level teams, asking for periodic progress reports. If some technical or procedural problem arises that is beyond the ability of the lower-level teams to solve, management must come to their assistance.

Managers must follow the rules, too. Do not think that somehow executive and management teams can gloss over the normal process improvement procedures and still do their work right. Whenever they do, both their solutions and their instructions to lower-level teams are usually suboptimal. Also, if they skip steps, so will their lower-level teams. Teamwork is a *management* approach, and managers should follow it.

Another mistaken notion is that a team of managers will be immune to group dynamics problems. As one government quality manager pointed out, "Managers are used to having 51 percent of the vote or following the directions of a senior manager. Put them in a team situation where everyone is equal, and you can imagine the struggle."

Improvement teams

Improvement teams focus on specific projects or issues and tend to be temporary. They can include anyone in the organization and representatives of outside groups such as unions, vendors, distributors, customers, or other government agencies. Each team member is closely associated with a particular process or small group of processes, either working in it or serving as an internal customer or supplier. Together, the team members represent all processes or subprocesses that are the targets of their improvement project.

In selecting projects for improvement teams, consider the criteria given to us by the Fresno IRS Service Center, presented in edited form in the box below.

Improvement teams meet over several months until they complete their project. Usually, these meetings take place once a week for one or a few hours. The exception is where management needs faster action on a critical process, in which case the team will meet more often. Teamwork is part of the members' jobs, and they should not be expected to put in after-hours time.

A Guide for Selecting Improvement Team Projects

Team projects should be:

Important. Only those few vital projects that will result in significant benefits—achieving an organization's mission, improving services for customers, or reducing the cost of quality—should be selected as team projects.

Chronic. If several attempts to solve a problem have failed, the problem will probably benefit from using a team approach to get to root causes.

Systemic. Issues selected usually should not be limited to a few people, cases, or situations. For example, if all employees face the same problem or make the same error, the root cause is probably systemic. A few isolated problems *may* have systemic causes; if their negative consequences are severe, this may justify a team approach.

Customer oriented. Management goals are important, but team issues should focus most often on meeting customer expectations. This means learning first-hand what customers want.

Measurable. The problem or issue, and the changes made to it, must be measurable—"good feelings" about results are not enough.

Source: Adapted From the Fresno, California IRS Service Center.

Many organizations have mistakenly equated the progress of their quality management initiatives with the number of improvement teams in operation. Even worse, some have assumed that these types of teams *are* quality management. In fact, improvement teams of the type just described are only one part of a comprehensive effort to reform an agency's management style. Because they are only a part, these teams are subject to imperfections in the whole of the agency's systems. For example, many improvement teams in government successfully go through the PDCA process and develop good solutions, but management, although applauding the effort, does not implement the teams' recommendations. That's one reason for managers to form their own teams before forming improvement teams of employees.

Cross-functional teams

Cross-functional teams consist of managers, key employees, and often outside suppliers and customers from several different functions working on an issue that involves all of them. The chief of statistical methods at the Watervliet Army Arsenal explained: "We have executive/middle manager teams working on several fundamental cross-functional systems. We call one of these 'acquiring,' or how we obtain the external inputs we need. The team includes managers from such departments as engineering, product assurance, manufacturing, procurement, and accounting. Each of these departments affects and is affected by the 'acquiring' system, so the members of the team are at once customers and suppliers to each other. If we limited this team, say, to the procurement department, we could not deal with the whole system of 'acquiring.'"

Natural work groups

These are small groups of employees and managers who operate a single process or small group of processes, with most operations happening within their work unit. Such teams act in much the same manner as the self-managed teams we discuss next, with this exception: they are managed by supervisors and managers, instead of by the team itself. The benefit of the natural work group system is that it organizes people around their processes, instead of by function or profession. Some examples include:

- Multi-skill work crews for facility maintenance operations. These groups would include people with skills such as carpentry, plumbing, and electrical work;

- All managers and employees of a small document reproduction or print shop; and

- Grant administrators in a specific subject area.

Self-managed teams

Self-managed teams consist of a line supervisor or lead employee who is the team leader, and all other employees who work on a specific process or major task (sometimes, the team elects its own leader). The team is responsible for operating and monitoring the process, coordinating with adjacent processes, and making improvements.

These are some of the characteristics of self-managed teams:

- They are found in complex processes. They are not usually found in processes where everyone uses simple repetitive motions (i.e., a simple assembly line).

- The teams are supported by management teams.

- The team leader is more of a coach than a boss. He or she trains the team in problem solving, scheduling, and other methods, helps them make decisions, and carries their concerns and suggestions to management.

Forming self-managed teams. Making the shift to self-management requires:

- Defining a team's processes, including their boundaries, and developing process performance measures;

- Providing special training in improvement and management tools and procedures for team members;

- Briefing and gaining support for the self-managed team concept from middle and upper managers in the unit where the process is located;

- Establishing rules, procedures, and other guidelines for team operations; and

- Developing incentive plans that reward both group and individual effort in the team.

At one time we believed that the transition to self-management teams should occur on a unit-by-unit basis, after each unit had management teams, experience with several improvement teams, and at least a few pilot self-managed teams. We still hold this opinion but must report that several organizations have gone straight to self-management and had good success (they also had strong leadership commitment).

QUALITY CIRCLES: A LESSON IN HOW NOT TO RUN A TEAM

The American model of quality circles came into vogue during the 1970s and 1980s. These were small groups of employees engaged in similar work who met once a week, often after hours on their own time, to discuss improvements. Sometimes they were led by facilitators.

Although hundreds of thousands of quality circles started in this country, almost all have died out. This is in distinct contrast to the experience in Japan, where quality circles began and where millions of these teams thrive today. The reasons for their demise in this country provide a valuable lesson in how not to run a team:

- **For employees only.** U.S. quality circles were limited to employees, and managers were often told to keep hands off. As a result, quality circles did not have management support, nor were they seen as part of management systems. The Japanese quality circles have always had supervisor and management participants. (In Japan, there are also quality circles for supervisors, managers, and top executives. These are analogous to the management teams described earlier.)

- **Management resentment and fear.** As the chief of statistical methods at Watervliet Army Arsenal noted, "Quality circles did what managers were supposed to be doing, which ticked off the managers." His counterpart in the city government of Wilmington, North Carolina said that this management feeling went even deeper: "Quality circle members made long lists of problems. Most of these were problems of the system, and managers saw themselves as being blamed for them."

- **Lack of training.** Most quality circle members did not receive adequate training in problem-solving tools and procedures. They took short cuts, which led to poor and insupportable recommendations.

- **Nature of problems addressed.** Many quality circles focused on quality-of-work-life issues. They did not address problems that directly affected the performance of their organizations. Also, because they were limited to employees, the circles could not address problems that needed management input, so their efforts were never taken very seriously.

- **Voluntary participation.** Said a manager at the Defense Industrial Supply Center, "I think one reason the quality circle program did not work optimally is that it was seen as voluntary. If volunteers handle a task, then it is not always seen as that important." Japanese quality circles were never "voluntary" in the sense we think of the term. Instead, management asked a supervisor to form a circle with his workers, and you can bet he persisted until they "volunteered."

The quality circle concept is not wrong, and there are some well-run quality circles in this country today. But the way the concept usually was executed in America weakened it. Japanese experts point out that quality circles are the last component to be installed in their quality systems, while here they were the first. Thus, the U.S. circles had no foundation.

TRAINING AND FACILITATING TEAMS

Figure 16-4 outlines the characteristics of successful and unsuccessful teams. Success requires management support, which includes training and guidance in using tools, following procedures, and group dynamics.

Training

The crucial part that training plays in teamwork cannot be overemphasized. People have to learn new ways of approaching problems and issues, unfamiliar terms and techniques, and how to conduct themselves in a meeting. The what, how, when, and who of team training are somewhat different from formal classroom instruction.

Successful Teams...	**Unsuccessful Teams...**
Are focused. The more the issue has been defined for the team members before the start of a project, the less chance they will get off the track.	**Are unfocused.** Teams spend much effort trying to narrow the scope of the issue, and often head out in the wrong direction.
Have the right members. People on the teams represent the processes involved and the skills needed to address the issue.	**Do not have all the right members.** The team does not have representatives who come from key processes or have the right skills. Any solutions they develop will be less acceptable to the organization.
Have time to work on the issue. The issue does not require an immediate solution.	**Must look for "quick fixes."** The team is pressured by management to look for quick solutions or to "firefight" a problem.
Make teamwork a priority. Teamwork is at the top of the team members' "to do" lists and is seen that way by management.	**Feel pressure to do other things first.** Team members feel that other things are more important, and may be pressured by their superiors to put other tasks first.
Are backed by committed management. Management sets high expectations for the team; instills confidence; provides oversight, guidance, and recognition; and demands excellence.	**Have little management commitment.** Management does not make demands on the team or provide it with support and guidance.
Have excellent communication. Team members communicate well in meetings, and with management and other parts of the organization.	**Work in isolation.** Team members do not get along and work in isolation from management and the rest of the organization.
Have good information. The team has enough information to deal with an issue, or the skills and resources to gather this information.	**Have little information.** The team does not have hard facts on an issue, nor can it obtain this information. Any solutions are based on guesswork.
Follow the improvement cycle. The team uses the appropriate tools in the right sequence to address an issue.	**Skip steps in the cycle.** The team does not follow the cycle; results do not get to root causes.

Figure 16-4
Successful
and
Unsuccessful
Teams

Curriculum

For employees and managers alike, the key subjects of training are the improvement cycle (PDCA or some variation of it) and how to use the basic improvement tools discussed in Chapter 8. Every member of a team, and eventually all employees from the top executive down, should be familiar with these tools. More specialized training includes in-depth study of statistical process control, quality function deployment, and advanced tools. Training also should cover group dynamics, in order for teams to understand how best to run their meetings.

Beware of canned courses. A host of companies will sell you standard, off-the-shelf courses on quality management, self-managed teams, and other improvement approaches. Their trainers (who are simply trainers) will deliver these by rote to your personnel. The effect will be neither satisfactory nor long lasting. Everything taught should reflect the mission and situation of an organization. Instruction need not be tailored from scratch, but it does require some customizing.

Materials

Just as they adapt courses to their needs, most of the organizations interviewed for this book customize training materials obtained from outside groups. These materials are roughly divided between workbooks for team members and those used by team leaders and team facilitators. The materials contain examples relevant to the organization, often drawn from previous teamwork.

Timing

The consensus among the people interviewed was that training for teams needs to be just-in-time. That is, teams should receive training as they need it and must apply it immediately. In no more than three weeks, some estimated, team members start to forget what they learned.

As discussed in Chapter 8, most training should be on the job, using actual data from the process under examination. The only way people understand team tools is to use them, and they understand the tools best when applying them on a process with which they are familiar.

Instructors

When it comes to tools and procedures, managers and supervisors should be the principal instructors of their employees. This not only ensures that everyone has a common language and understanding, it also sends a clear message to employees: this is important.

If managers do not have the knowledge and skills to act as instructors, special internal instructors can be used. Most of the organizations interviewed for this book started with outside consultant trainers, but only as an interim step while they trained their own. The exceptions are advanced courses in highly specialized methods. Many organizations certify managers and instructors as qualified to teach improvement methods.

Instructors tend to give their own interpretation of their organization's approach to process management and improvement. There is nothing wrong with this when it simply reflects the style of the instructor. But people can stray from the basic messages, so certification and periodic refresher courses help keep them on track.

The ideal instructor also can perform the job of facilitator, which is discussed below. However, at the start of introducing the Improvement Driven Organization approach to management, you may have to use different people to serve as instructors and facilitators.

Facilitators

If the idea of an outside facilitator for a team meeting seems alien to you, consider how meetings are run in your organization right now. Does everyone contribute freely to them? Do the meetings stay focused? And do they always produce results? If so, send us an application form—we want to work there, too! If not, you will need facilitators, because people are not used to the structured team style called for by most new management approaches.

The best team facilitators know how to use the right tools, follow the appropriate improvement procedures, and handle the dynamics of group meetings. They attend team meetings, observe the group dynamics, recommend ways to help teams work more effectively, and advise the team leader on how to get individual members to work together. Facilitators stay in the background if things are running smoothly and come forward to help when they are not. (Keep these qualities in mind: they are how you want all your managers to manage.)

Choosing facilitators. A person from outside a process area who has no vested interest in an issue makes the best facilitator. He or she will bring an objective view to team meetings. All the organizations interviewed for this book had several facilitators that they assigned as needed to different teams. Many of these facilitators were managers or had management experience.

Some of these organizations use full-time facilitators selected from among their staff, while others use part-timers who hold other internal jobs, or a combination of both. It is also common to use outside consultant facilitators during the early phases of introducing team-based approaches. A few organizations use permanent outside facilitators.

Training facilitators. Many people interviewed report that the early training they gave to their internal facilitators lacked balance: they concentrated too much on the tools and procedures or too much on group dynamics. Facilitators need both sets of skills. Several organizations require that their internal facilitators be certified in both by outside consultants.

Instructor and facilitator roles as management norm

Eventually you want to do away with special instructors and facilitators. All of your managers and key employees should learn to handle both roles, both in assisting a team outside their units and in their day-to-day management of subordinates. This is true participative management.

Chapter
17

ROLE OF THE INDIVIDUAL

■ In an Improvement Driven Organization, employees have the means to control and improve their processes.

- They understand organizational goals, priorities, principles, ethics, and their place in the system.
- They receive appropriate training in their jobs and in process improvement.
- They receive performance measurement feedback on their processes.

■ Innovative ideas from employees are critical to the success of an Improvement Driven Organization. Generating high volumes of these ideas requires management to take a comprehensive, systematic approach to promoting employee innovation.

To us, *empowerment* is one of the most irritating and confusing terms in contemporary management. A popular
notion is that it means "managers authorize workers to
make decisions." First, we think that the term reinforces a
we/they attitude between management and labor, with the
former being the source of power. In an Improvement
Driven Organization, power derives from individual and
collective understanding of customer expectations and
processes, plus the skills to control and improve operations.
Neither management nor labor has a monopoly on that
power.

Second, empowerment says nothing about the capability of
an organization as a whole to make wise decisions, when its
systems often prevent wise decisions. Everyone, from the
chief executive to the front-line worker, needs training and
disciplined use of specific types of information, skills, and
tools for those decisions. Every system must be designed
for enabling wise decisions.

That's why we use the term *enable* instead of *empower.*
Enabling people is much different from empowering them,
starting with the notion that everyone already has the intrin-
sic power to control and improve their lives and process. If
they do not, then why did you hire them?

In this chapter, we will discuss three factors that relate to
enabling employees to make maximum contributions to
your organization. Next, we'll discuss employee suggestion
programs, which right now are the shame of most U.S.
organizations.

Before that, here's why many organizations support the
move to enabling employees.

WHY ENABLE?

In industry and government, modern information technology is reversing a century-long trend of breaking work down into small, discrete activities done by low-skill workers. Office "assembly lines" that involve, say, paying vendors or handling customer inquiries are being rapidly replaced by solo operators aided by computer data bases and algorithms. This new, highly skilled worker has the basic tools to make decisions that were once bounced up to first-line supervisors and managers: whether to guarantee a loan, which supplier to use, whether to issue a permit, and so on. Even when work is not data-intensive, employers are setting up self-managed teams of employees such as those discussed in Chapter 16 to control and improve daily operations in their work processes.

What the solo operators and teams have in common is that they have been enabled to make decisions once entrusted to managers. Here are factors that ensure this works.

Three Foundations of Enablement

1. Develop goals, principles, ethics, and process understanding.

As every manager knows, no computer algorithm or policy manual can provide all the information needed to make every decision. For starters, empowered employees must know their organization's goals and objectives in order to steer toward achieving them. We have some objective data to support this observation, developed during Coopers & Lybrand's 1994 survey of the best management practices of three hundred private and public organizations (see Appendix B). We asked survey respondents to rate their organizations on whether employees who are most affected by change understand what is required of them to support the change. One of the factors that correlated strongly with high scores on this rating was that employees understand the link between their work and the organization's strategic plans and goals.

Also, employees need a set of principles that guide daily decisions, such as "First, find out what the customer wants," "Use hard data in making decisions," and "Look at the operations plan for guidance." Figure 17-1 is an example of the guiding principles of the Army's Tank-Automotive Research, Development, and Engineering Center, which won the federal Quality Improvement Prototype award in 1994. Managers teach these principles best by example—by walking the walk as well as talking the talk.

Figure17-1 Principles of the U.S. Tank-Automotive Research, Development, and Engineering Center

Guiding Principles

- Customers are the focus of everything we do

- People are our most important resource

- Professionalism and integrity are the foundations of our work

- Teamwork is essential

- Innovation is our business

- Quality is our cornerstone

Management Concept

- Operate as a business with a corporate plan

- Focus each business center's activities with operating plans

- Achieve mission through concurrent engineering teams composed of all required technical and functional experts, including customers and suppliers

- Seize the initiative

- Fully satisfy our customer needs

- Continuously improve

- Ensure that pricing structure reflects true product cost

Ethics is another area of increasing concern. As employees gain more discretion in decision making, they need more than just a written code of ethics. Many organizations now give everyone from executives to line employees formal training in ethics, with refresher discussions at regular intervals. We discuss this in Chapter 15 on internal controls.

Finally, unlike managers who put blinders on workers, confining their vision to the job at hand, managers using the enablement approach educate their employees about the entire business process in which they work. Thus, employees understand the impact of their daily decisions on others, and vice versa. One way to do this is to have employees participate in process mapping, from the start of a process to its finish. This mapping should include identifying customers, suppliers, and their expectations.

So, you must put in place the foundation of enablement long before you begin authorizing workers to act independently. When you develop goals, principles, ethics, and understanding of processes and customer expectations, you create the base for all that follows. If you skip this step, expect failure in the rest.

2. Provide training and education.

You cannot empower an untrained, uneducated work force—they cannot handle the responsibility. Formal training in how to do a specific job ensures that employees understand it enough to do more than simply march along in lock step. Instruction in job skills and cross-training in different jobs adds depth and insight to a worker's search for the right decision. Training in work analysis and decision-making procedures gives employees the tools they need to improve their own work processes, which is the ultimate benefit of enablement. Finally, training also must show workers how and when to consider company or unit goals and principles in decision making.

It is not unusual for organizations that embrace worker enablement to spend as much as 5 percent of operations costs on employee training and education. This is money well invested when you consider that the best competitive advantage is a work force able to change and grow with new challenges.

3. Give frequent, routine feedback on process performance.

In most organizations, performance measurement data flow uphill to the bosses but not back to employees who do the work that generates the numbers. As we said earlier, this is like police having radar guns and cars not having speedometers—unfair, and certainly confusing. People are not truly enabled unless they can get information on how their process performs—and get it in sufficient time to keep operations on a normal or constantly improving trend line.

As discussed in Chapter 12, employees often can collect and analyze their own performance data. Management's job is to help them link this information to the bigger picture of process operations, corporate goals, and customer expectations.

Finally, managers need to compel the use of measurement data by asking for it. For example, an employee of the Air Force 653d Communications-Computer Systems Group said, "If I go to the colonel with a status report without the numbers, he tells me to go back and get the facts. 'You can't manage what you can't measure,' he always says."

Without these three foundations, *enablement* is a buzzword just like *empowerment*. With them, you do not need to do much more to achieve a basic level of enablement. That's because everyone will understand what they do, why they do it, and how it is best done.

However, baselines are only starting points. Now, let's look at high performance enablement, as measured by employee innovations.

PROMOTING EMPLOYEE INNOVATION

Suppose that over the last four years, your agency's benefits package and salary increases have raised labor costs by $2,000 per worker. That's a modest amount nowadays, given the inflation of health insurance, workers' compensation, and other benefits, plus normal cost-of-living adjustments. What does that do to your ability to meet your mission? The answer is easy: you either cut back on labor, start trimming benefits and salary, or invest in labor-saving technology.

There is a fourth way, less costly than the rest in money, morale, and ability to serve citizens: improve your employee suggestion system. According to a 1994 Coopers & Lybrand "Trendsetter Barometer" survey of America's four hundred fastest growing businesses, eight in ten have an ongoing program to solicit employee recommendations on improving business operations. And those that find their programs most valuable—some two thirds in all—have higher growth rates and higher anticipated growth rates than their peers. "Employee participation programs appear to play a significant role in growth company development," said C&L's national director of entrepreneurial advisory services. "By the end of 1994, only 13 percent of the four hundred fast-growth companies will lack a program."

In this section, we'll examine how such programs increase the flow of ideas from workers.

Employees' Participation Is Essential for Innovation

In our 1994 best practices survey, we asked respondents to rate the strength of their organizations' reputation for innovation. Then, we looked for a relationship between "reputation for innovation" and other management practices. Of the three best practices that were most highly correlated with strong innovation, two spotlighted the role of employees:

- Concepts for new products or services originate at many levels of the organization.

- Innovative ideas from employees are readily accepted by management.

Indeed, the success of an Improvement Driven Organization depends on a steady, high-volume flow of excellent improvement ideas from employees. Now, we will describe why workers in some organizations generate twenty times or more the average number of innovative ideas.

WHAT MOTIVATES AN EMPLOYEE SUGGESTION?

What is the greatest employee incentive to make a suggestion for improvement? If you answer "Cash for the idea," you're dead wrong. Some companies pay up to $150,000 for a single suggestion, but the number of ideas they get from employees is woefully small. Yet, a few others pay only token amounts, and nearly every employee contributes dozens of ideas for improvement a year.

Their secret? These latter organizations have a "yes" bias and accept up to 90 percent of employee ideas. This attitude naturally encourages employees to make suggestions, because the greatest employee incentive to make suggestions is to routinely have them accepted. This was the number one reason given by a 1990 national survey of employees by the American Society for Quality Control and the Gallup organization.

Unfortunately, the average North American employer has a "no" bias toward employee ideas. A survey of member organizations of the National Association of Suggestion Systems showed that, on average, they rejected two-thirds of the ideas submitted through formal employee suggestion programs. Those unfriendly odds are the chief reason that the average suggestion program delivers only thirteen to fourteen ideas per one hundred employees per year, with only about four or five being adopted.

After all, why should a worker risk such a strong chance of humiliating rejection? According to one government manager we interviewed, "My first experience with participative management was as a field office employee. I submitted a suggestion through the channels, and it ultimately went to Washington. [Officials there] bounced it back with a reply that made me wonder if they could understand English. So I wrote it up again. This time someone in Washington called me—and chewed me out for forty-five minutes for wasting their time. That was eleven years ago, and I haven't submitted a formal suggestion since then." Another government manager told us that an increase in employee suggestions would bog him down: "It takes me half a day to fill out the paperwork on an employee suggestion. I don't have time for that." He doesn't have to worry—with his existing suggestion program's bureaucratic barriers, we doubt that suggestions will ever come pouring into his office.

These are *typical* management reactions to employee suggestions, backed up by data and anecdote. Yet, every organization espouses the principle that employees are encouraged to contribute ideas for improvement. The darker interpretation of this contradiction is that many organizations are hypocritical; we feel, however, that the answer lies more in an organization's innovation infrastructure: the systems that guide, encourage, accept, and reward employee ideas. Here are steps you can take to increase the flow of these innovations.

Figure 17-2
A Twelve-
Step Program
for Super
Suggestions

1. Everyone knows what is important to organizational success.

2. Employees know where they fit in the system and how they can contribute to it.

3. Everyone is trained in his or her job and in how to improve it.

4. Everyone knows the customers' expectations.

5. Teamwork is practiced throughout the organization.

6. Management reacts quickly to employee ideas.

7. Tracking systems are in place to monitor suggestion program performance.

8. Managers are proactive in seeking employee ideas and have a bias toward accepting them.

9. The number of acceptable ideas is what counts.

10. Quality of work life suggestions are valued.

11. Everyone receives the right recognition and rewards.

12. Management frequently emphasizes the importance of employee innovation.

A Twelve-Step Program for Super Suggestions

To find out how the best organizations handle employees' suggestions, we interviewed three Malcolm Baldrige National Quality Award winners, three federal Quality Improvement Prototype winners, and executives at two U.S. factories with exceptionally high suggestion rates (up to nineteen suggestions per employee, compared with the aver-

age rate of thirteen to fourteen *per one hundred employees*).
Below, we call them the "high performers," and here are the
twelve factors behind their success. We present the factors
in the approximate order in which you would implement
them—a true twelve-step program.

1. Everyone knows what is important to organizational success.

We discussed this principle earlier as part of the first foundation of employee enablement, but it bears repeating.
Often an employee's idea may be wonderful, but it just does
not fit what the organization needs at the time. The high
performers let employees know priorities, so they can focus
their search for improvements on what is most important to
the organization.

For example, if an agency faces a tight budget, employees
know to concentrate on ideas to reduce errors, rework, and
waste. But if the goal is faster delivery, employees know to
look for ways to reduce cycle time without sacrificing cost
or quality. Among the high performers, you will often see
specific corporate and lower-level goals and objectives posted on all bulletin boards and hear them discussed at nearly
every management and employee meeting.

2. Employees know where they fit in the system and how they can contribute to it.

This awareness also is part of the first foundation of
employee enablement. Consider, for example, workers on
the P3-C line at the Jacksonville, Florida Naval Aviation
Depot, where individual and team suggestions helped cut 40
percent off the labor needed to refit these antisubmarine aircraft. Each employee has a flow chart of work processes
both upstream and downstream from the work he or she
does. Thus, the employee can readily see how the changes
he or she suggests will affect the entire work flow.

3. Everyone is trained in his or her job and in how to improve it.

We discussed formal training in job skills and improvement methods in the second foundation of enablement. All the high-performer organizations invest heavily in training, and many encourage employees to cross-train in other work skills. This adds depth and insight to a worker's search for improvement.

High performers teach employees to recognize specific opportunities for improvement. For example, employees may see waste as simply the way things are supposed to be done. With training, they learn that waste may be going to get a tool that should be at their work station, unpacking supplies that should arrive presorted and ready to use, correcting avoidable mistakes in a document, and so on. Being able to recognize waste, they can develop ideas for removing it.

4. Everyone knows the customers' expectations.

High-performer employees routinely visit their internal customers—the people next in line in the production process. These meetings focus on clarifying internal customer needs for information, input, and method and timing of delivery. Then, the employees return to their work with new insights to guide their search for improvement.

Also, some high performers arrange periodic employee visits with end users, so workers discover first hand how what they do affects external customer satisfaction. For example, at some organizations every employee is required to visit at least one external customer a year, where they see their products and services being used. These visits give workers a new perspective, and motivate them, too.

5. Teamwork is practiced throughout the organization.

In our 1994 survey, we asked organizations to rate the extent to which employees are active in improving processes. One factor that was strongly correlated with highly active roles was that employees participate in team activities to evaluate product development or service quality. High performers have many teams—natural work groups, self-managed teams, and improvement teams. The group dynamic of well-trained teams generates many ideas, then helps employees focus on those ideas with high priority and high payoff. Further, the teams know how to logically review and test ideas before suggesting them to management.

We worked with one government organization, for example, whose formal suggestion system delivered sixteen ideas per one hundred employees in 1990, with only one-third of them accepted. In five weeks, a trained natural work group of ten employees generated twenty-six new ideas, most of which are being implemented. This translates to an annual rate of two thousand five-hundred ideas per one hundred employees. As we will show later, such rates are not at all unusual among high performers.

6. Management reacts quickly to employee ideas.

High performers act on nearly all employee suggestions in days, not weeks or months. They can do this because managers and line supervisors at the lowest level have the authority to approve most employee ideas. Fast turnaround is probably the second most important factor in a high-performance suggestion program, because it shows workers that management values their ideas enough to give them immediate attention.

7. Tracking systems are in place to monitor suggestion program performance.

These systems keep track of employee ideas to ensure that none are lost and all receive attention. They also generate key performance measures: number of suggestions per employee in a unit, percentage accepted, average turn-around time for management handling of suggestions, percentage of eligible employees who participate, net value of the ideas, and awards given. Executives use this information for unit and manager performance appraisals. Such tracking need not be complex or costly; high performers use everything from simple logbooks to computer registers to do the job. If it does not create such a system, management is making a clear statement of how little it values employee innovation.

8. Managers are proactive in seeking employee ideas and have a bias toward accepting them.

In high-performance organizations, managers do not sit back and wait for employees to slip suggestions under the office door. Instead, they constantly ask employees for ideas and insights on issues important to their processes and the organization as a whole. Managers do this at team meetings and in informal contact with individual workers.

What if a manager does this, and gets back what he or she thinks is the wrong response (i.e., no ideas or the wrong ideas)? Then it is the manager's responsibility and challenge to find out why and take corrective action. In a high-performance organization, a low rate of acceptable suggestions is a symptom of corporate infirmity—or of managers who aren't doing their jobs.

9. The number of acceptable ideas is what counts.

Occasionally, you read a news story about a government employee whose suggestion saved millions of dollars. That's a home run, and such success should be valued and praised. But do home runs always win a game? Mostly, the scores come from base hits.

For example, the late John Franke, former assistant secretary for administration at the U.S. Department of Agriculture, said when he was director of the Federal Quality Institute: "At USDA we had an employee suggestion campaign and were pleased that we got 2,700 suggestions in one week and put 2,300 of them into effect. Then I learned that Toyota implements 5,000 employee suggestions *per day*." That's a lot of base hits.

To understand the effect of volume on the value of a suggestion program, let's compare the typical North American and Japanese systems. The value of the average North American suggestion that is accepted by management is $8,000, nearly sixty times greater than the Japanese average of $140. But the typical Japanese company accepts about seventeen ideas per employee per year, and American companies only about 0.4 suggestions per worker. If we subtract the costs of running the program (about 10 percent of the value of the suggestions), the net economic benefit of employee innovations to a Japanese company of one thousand workers is $2,200,000 per year. An average North American company of one thousand gets only $300,000 in net benefits from its program—seven times less than a Japanese firm.

Don't think that only fanatical Japanese workers can do this. You will find similar numbers in Japanese-owned plants in the United States—Honda and Canon, for example, or the General Motors/Toyota NUMMI plant in Fremont, California. At the NUMMI plant, the suggestion rate is nineteen ideas per employee per year, with 90 percent accepted. American-owned high performers such as Miliken, another Baldrige winner, have the same or better results (Miliken estimates their rate to be twenty ideas per employee). Simply put, many small ideas beat a few big ones.

> *I think there is a tendency for managers not to see their employees as capable of making suggestions to improve things. We tend to forget that employees manage their families and are community leaders. If they use their brains to solve community and family problems, then they can certainly do this at work.*
>
> — Assistant commissioner for administration, U.S. Patent and Trademark Office

10. Quality of work life suggestions are valued.

Often managers disparage quality of work life suggestions: more parking spaces, redecorate the cafeteria, and so on. High performers understand that such suggestions may have a relation to safety, productivity, and efficiency that is not always readily apparent. For example, managers at one government organization we work with at first dismissed as a frill the suggestion of putting water coolers on loading ramps. A closer look showed that ramp workers were using productive time to get water somewhere else and that some workers risked heat exhaustion.

Even when such ideas have no direct economic merit, they deserve attention. According to a manager at one Baldrige Award-winning company, "Management that is bothered by quality of work life suggestions needs to examine its priorities. If employees feel management does not care about these ideas, they think, 'Why should I try to improve the system?'" And remember, the higher the percentage of all good ideas accepted, the more ideas get generated.

11. Everyone receives the right recognition and rewards.

Another factor leading to employees taking an active role in process improvement is that their contributions are recognized and rewarded, according to our 1994 best practices survey. Our interviews with high performers reveal how these organizations show their appreciation to employees.

Most high performers offer cash for ideas, but generally only token amounts. Other incentives are actually more powerful motivators. Along with cash, high performers use frequent non-cash awards, ranging from pins, T-shirts, and coffee mugs to dinner with the boss to site visits with customers. They have many formal and informal award and recognition ceremonies, where employees have the chance to talk about how they came up with their good ideas. Perhaps more important, their managers take the time to give workers one-on-one recognition by listening to and acting on their ideas. These organizations understand the need to make recognition part of the daily lives of their workers, thus reinforcing the positive behavior of searching for new ideas. We discuss this more in Chapter 18.

12. Management frequently emphasizes the importance of employee innovation.

We put this step last because it is so often listed as one of the first ones in traditional suggestion programs. In an organization that takes the previous eleven steps, management can honestly say that it values employee innovation. It can put a dollar figure on that contribution or use other measures such as decreased cycle time or increased customer satisfaction, and this is extremely important.

Why? Because our 1994 best practices survey showed that the factor that has the greatest influence on active participation in an organization is that employees believe that their jobs affect the change and quality initiatives of the organization. It is management's job to show them how and why this is so, with hard data on their contributions, not vague and vacuous pronouncements.

A "yes" bias to employee ideas cannot be created by executive order. Both employees and managers must get better at suggestions before they can expect the results of our high performers. Making that happen is a leadership job—it starts at the top, but not with a proclamation. Instead, an organization's leaders must establish systems in which employees can do the following: learn about the ideas the organization needs most, analyze ideas correctly, and present and implement them in a manner acceptable to managers. Also, leaders must work with managers to ensure that they search for, use, and reward employee suggestions.

Chapter
18

CHANGING CORPORATE CULTURE

■ Corporate culture is the set of formal and informal beliefs, norms, and values that underlie how people in an organization behave and react to change.

■ An organization can learn to treat its culture as a set of manageable variables that can be modified to fit the requirements of mission, goals, and strategy. The tools for doing this include:

- Leadership
- Training
- Rewards systems
- Organizational structure
- Budget practices

■ A primary cultural objective for an Improvement Driven Organization is to become resilient, or capable of reacting quickly to changes in its environment.

One of the greatest challenges is to make lasting change. The culture of government lives on from one administration to the next with little change through the civil service system. Reshaping the cultural values of career public employees will leave a legacy well beyond any political cycle.

> — *An Action Agenda to*
> *Redesign State Government,*
> National Governors' Association

What makes your organization's environment different from any other's? Answering that question is like looking at an iceberg. Only a small part of an agency's individuality is visible: its official organization chart, rules, regulations, and other public pronouncements. The other, larger part is unofficial, yet it is common knowledge to people inside an organization: values, habits, ways of thinking, and unofficial operating principles. Together, the official and unofficial views constitute an organization's *culture.*

Figure 18-1
The
Organizational
Culture
Iceberg

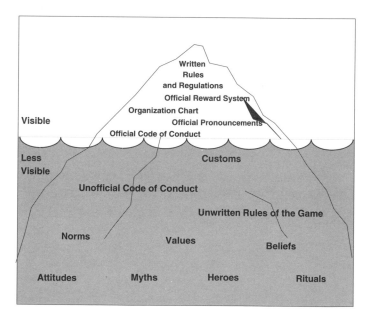

WHAT IS CORPORATE CULTURE?

Like the culture of a society, an organization's culture is so deeply ingrained that it is taken for granted. You know what your agency's culture is, because you live and operate in it every day. But to define the elements of culture, you may need to step back and isolate the beliefs, policies, and practices that shape it.

For example, who are your organization's *heroes?* Are they "Lone Rangers"— people who single-handedly save the organization from crises? Or are they team members who work together to prevent crises? Do you tell new employees "war stories" about how these heroes overcame crises, with the implied moral being, "That's how you get ahead in this agency"? To anthropologists, those stories are your organization's *myths.* If an employee finds a critical problem in a highly visible project, will he or she report it, or keep quiet because managers shoot messengers who bear bad news? The employee's decision will be based on his or her *beliefs* about management's reaction, and the reaction reflects management's *values.* Does your organization value risk takers? Not if the norm is to avoid risks. The answers to these questions start to describe an organization's culture, and you don't need Margaret Mead to explain what they mean.

Why Change Your Culture?

The relationship of an agency's culture to continuous improvement is reciprocal. Striving to become an Improvement Driven Organization creates cultural change by introducing new practices and new ways of thinking. Yet the *lasting* success of an Improvement Driven Organization depends on how firmly these cultural changes take root. When managers and employees adopt values that support continuous improvement, striving for excellence becomes an organizational way of life.

You don't have to completely transform your organization's culture to sustain continuous improvement, because some of the culture already reinforces sound improvement practices. Otherwise, your organization would have disappeared long ago. But you can— indeed, must—modify some parts of your culture, if only to align it to Information Age business requirements.

Can You Change Culture?

Can you really change something as complex as culture? The answer lies with that same complexity, which offers many variables that can be modified to achieve cultural objectives. Figure 18-2 lists some of the variables, each of which can be modified by management to reinforce individual behaviors that become the habits of an improvement driven culture.

As you look at Figure 18-2, consider this: nearly all the listed variables already exist in your organization and effectively define your culture. For example, you have decision methods, whether or not they are always fact based. You have training and education policies that may or may not encourage continuous learning in subjects that are critical to organizational effectiveness. The jobs in your organization may be broadly or narrowly defined, but they do have scope. Thus, many of the tools for cultural change are readily at hand, so you might as well use them to create a culture appropriate for twenty-first-century public service.

Cultural Objective	Variable	Example of how the variable is modified in an Improvement Driven Organization's culture
Common vision, goals, and objectives.	Strategic Planning	Executives reach consensus on the organization's vision of the future, and they deploy this vision along with goals and objectives to all personnel.
Teamwork is valued.	Reward Systems	Promotions, salaries, bonuses, awards, public recognition, and performance appraisal tied to successful teamwork.
Focus on processes.	Organizational Structure	Restructure based on core business processes.
Focus on customer satisfaction.	Customer Contact	Opportunity for employees to talk with internal or external customers or to observe them using a process's outputs.
Improvement ideas come from all levels of the organization.	Employee Input	Enhanced team or individual suggestion programs; monitoring how managers use employee ideas for improvement.
People are accountable for controlling and improving their processes.	Performance Measurement	Tie performance measures to customer requirements; information systems that give people quick feedback on their process's performance.
Continuous learning.	Training and Education Policies	Training for jobs, process improvement, and basic reading or math skills; support for participation in trade and professional groups; paying for outside education.
Decisions are based on facts.	Decision Methods	Training managers and employees in fact-based decision tools; requiring that they use the tools.
Flexibility is valued.	Job Scope	Broaden job descriptions and work responsibilities; cross-train people in the different skills needed in a process.

Figure 18-2
Selected
Variables
That Can Be
Modified to
Achieve
Cultural
Objectives

467

WHAT DOES AN IMPROVEMENT DRIVEN CULTURE LOOK LIKE?

Because each government agency is unique, no one improvement driven culture will ever exist. Our experience is, however, that the cultural objectives shown in Figure 18-2 are critical to continuous improvement. In turn, continuous improvement leads to an *adaptive culture,* a term used by Columbia University professor W. Warner Burke to stress the value of organizational flexibility. In an era of chronic future shock, adaptive culture is the only lasting competitive advantage.

Resilience, the hallmark of adaptive culture, is the ability to quickly respond to changes in customer requirements or to the environment in which an organization exists. Consultant Daryl Connor, who, along with Burke, works with us on many change management projects, identifies five attributes of resilience. According to him, a resilient individual, group, and organization is:

- **Positive.** Views life as challenging but filled with opportunity, and accepts that disruption is the natural state of a changing world.

- **Focused.** Has a clear vision of what must be achieved. This vision acts as a guidance system to reestablish perspectives following major disruptions.

- **Flexible.** Believes change is manageable, has a high tolerance for ambiguity, and challenges and modifies assumptions when necessary.

- **Organized.** Has and applies structures and methods to help manage ambiguity.

- **Proactive.** Engages change instead of evading it, investing energy in problem solving and teamwork.

These attributes do not imply that change is always comfortable to a resilient organization or that it engages in change for change's sake. Rather, such organizations have successfully adapted to a world in which the only constant is change, change, and more change.

LEADERSHIP AND CULTURE

When executives do not follow the principles they espouse, managers and employees know that the organization is in a business-as-usual mode. People imitate what they see their superiors do, because they know this is the road to personal advancement. Thus, no single aspect of management support is more important than leadership for cultural change. Managers provide this leadership in many ways, such as the following:

- Recognize and embrace cultural change when it is needed.

- Create a vision for the new culture, and communicate it.

- Make or allow process changes that support the new culture.

- Stay actively involved in the change process, including directing and monitoring it.

- Walk the walk by offering a personal example of the new culture's ethics, principles, and values.

Not all executives are willing or able to assume this change leadership role. It should be obvious to you (because it certainly is to them) that they prospered under the old culture, else they would not be at the top of the heap. That's why successful cultural change must always be led by the chief executive officer—it is a duty he or she cannot delegate. Only the CEO has the power to overcome resistance by other executives, should this become a barrier.

Management by example makes for success. At the Philadelphia Veterans Affairs Regional Office and Insurance Center, the director, assistant directors, and division chiefs were the first to receive quality management training. Then several division chiefs became the trainers for the next level of management. Top managers also made up the first improvement teams. "We believe it's important for top management to get its hands dirty to show everyone that we're serious," explained VAROIC's assistant director.

We are continually astonished by the power of direct contact between a CEO and line supervisors and employees. What the CEO does during that contact can set the tone of a culture for years to come. According to the director of the Orange County, Florida Corrections Division, "I met with every employee for about two hours in a small group setting. We have one thousand five-hundred people, and it took me about six months, but I wanted every one of them to hear from me personally what it was I wanted us to do and how I wanted us to be." Four years later, his division had grown by 18 percent, despite reducing its budget by 6 percent, and was able to invest $800,000 in new programs without asking for additional money.

Symbolic acts help to set the tone at the top. Time and again, we hear employees say how impressed they were when their CEO dropped in on an improvement team meeting just to listen or came into an office to informally but personally thank someone for a good suggestion. Combined with the CEO's daily oversight of the change process, these symbolic acts create the heroes and myths of the new culture.

MANAGING THE CULTURAL TRANSFORMATION

Advanced organizations understand that they must plan for cultural change. In Chapter 6 we discussed change management at length and showed how to use the Improvement Driven Organization framework for introducing an innovation. This framework also applies to cultural change:

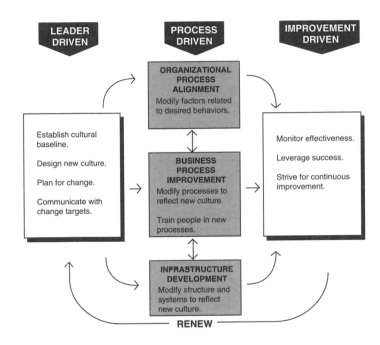

Figure 18-3 Improvement Driven Organization Framework Applied to Culture Change

The Leader Driven Phase

Assessing the cultural baseline

How much cultural change does your organization require? How do managers and employees feel about continuous improvement? What is their perception of your organization—and of their work place environment? To direct successful cultural change, planners need the answers to questions such as these.

Cultural change cannot be planned in a vacuum. It begins by understanding the type of culture that an organization requires in order to achieve its mission, vision, goals, and objectives. For example, if you plan to introduce self-managed teams, both managers and employees will need to behave in ways that can be defined as cultural attributes. Cultural attributes for the team members may include teamwork, flexibility, customer focus, and willingness to be accountable for results. Managers' attributes may be a change in management style from supervisor to coach and facilitator. These attributes become the objectives of cultural changes related to self-managed teams. So you can't just look over a list like Figure 18-2 and say, "Those sound good. They'll be our objectives." Instead, there must be a clear connection between what your organization must do to succeed and the culture that will support that success.

Next, you need to determine your cultural baseline, which is the as-is culture your organization has now, and compare it with the new culture you envision. Many organizations use cultural surveys to do this; Chapter 4 discusses them in detail. Such surveys often include questions similar to those used in our 1994 best practices survey (see Appendix B). For example, they may ask, "To what degree are improvements in your work unit driven by customer needs and expectations?" Employee and manager responses to this question help reveal the strength of customer focus in an organization. Analysis of such responses often uncovers the link between culture and performance. When we asked a similar question of the three hundred organizations in our survey, those that were the most innovative also strongly agreed that customers drove improvement. Those that said they were not innovative were much less likely to agree with this idea.

Cultural survey results often hold surprises for organization management. At the Defense Industrial Supply Center (DISC), for example, a baseline survey showed that values and perceptions differed substantially among staff at different levels of authority. Although top management was highly receptive to a new quality management initiative and gave DISC high marks as a work setting, the degree of enthusiasm dropped at each successive level on the organization ladder. "By our second survey, we'd made some progress, but supervisors still had major concerns about the managerial style of their middle management superiors," DISC's quality coordinator recalled. "As a result, middle managers became a high-priority target in our efforts to change attitudes and behaviors."

Other means of assessing your culture include reviewing the results of existing management practices. For example, if you feel your organization already emphasizes teamwork, how many team awards were made in the last two years, and what were they for? If you feel you value employee suggestions, how many were made in the past year, and how many implemented? Answers to questions like these help portray the reality of organizational values. Not being able to answer them at all because the necessary data does not exist indicates management does not consider such cultural traits to be worth measuring, and therefore not worth managing.

Planning for cultural change

Armed with assessment information, you plan logically to change culture. Without the information, every action you take will be a shot in the dark, more likely to confuse and anger managers and employees who feel that their culture "is just fine the way it is, thank you."

Involving people in the change process. Information alone, however, won't be enough to prevent that type of reaction. People are not like Pavlov's dogs, which could be conditioned to respond to the experimenter's tinkling bells. People must be involved in planning and implementing something as fundamental as a change in their culture, else they will feel manipulated and used. This is why you must include representatives from middle management and employees on teams and task forces that address culture change. Besides keeping executives honest about both assumptions and intent, these representatives probably know your culture better than top management.

Culture change means process change. As you recall from Chapter 7, improvement is not the result of working harder to do the same thing. It is working differently, in a process that has changed in some positive way. Likewise, management cannot simply say, "We want more teamwork," without changing processes related to forming, training, coaching, and rewarding teams. If such processes do not exist, they must be created.

You begin planning for changes to culture-related processes by identifying those associated with a cultural objective. For example, processes associated with fact-based decisions include those that gather, analyze, and distribute information about customer requirements, process performance, and other internal and external factors. Related processes include those that govern how executives and managers monitor and enforce the use of this information in decision making. Having identified processes, you can then apply to them the various approaches to process improvement discussed in Chapters 7 through 11. (We include Chapter 11 on competition because it can be a variable for several cultural objectives, such as customer focus and flexibility.)

Culture change should produce results valued by customers. In planning changes to culture-related processes, take care that you understand the link between these processes and the ultimate goal of producing goods and services valued by customers. The more you can demonstrate that link, the greater the acceptance of cultural change by all members of your organization.

Timing. One of the best times to transform culture is during major changes to core business processes or when new management approaches are being implemented. Then, you can build culture-related processes into new or reengineered systems. An organization that schedules a series of such major changes, to take effect in different work units over time, can gradually expand its new culture along with operational improvements.

Perhaps the worst time to attempt major culture change is during major layoffs and downsizing. No one is going to be interested in a new culture if they think they will not be around to enjoy it. However, when the layoffs are over, making a cultural transformation is perhaps the best way to start the survivors down the road to recovery. Ideally, the cultural change will occur at the same time that operational processes are being improved to bring work load back into equilibrium with the smaller number of people available to do it. Instituting the change at this time reinforces the value of the new culture.

What to do first. Every organization has to develop its own unique sequencing of the implementation of cultural changes. Some factories and offices have literally changed all their major culture-related processes over a weekend when they switched to self-managed teams. However, such conversions were comprehensively planned, understood, and applied by everyone. Naturally, everything did not go 100 percent as planned, but people's commitment to change eased them over the rough spots.

More usual is a gradual transition that cascades down through the ranks of the organization. As noted earlier in the VAROIC leadership example, executives are the first to adopt the new culture; they teach and exemplify it to managers, who in turn work with employees to make the transformation. Also, organizational leaders change culture-related processes *before* they exhort people to adopt the new culture, so that everyone can successfully follow the new way.

Other than that, there is no hard and fast sequence of actions that guarantee success. However, our experience is that government agencies sometimes put the cart before the horse by doing the following:

- Forming employee teams to develop new award systems for process improvement when an agency is still in the beginning stages of introducing improvement methods.

- Changing culture-related processes that depend on managers' cooperation without winning over the managers first.

- Assuming that managers and employees understand the compelling need for cultural change and want to embrace the new culture.

Communication

If your CEO announces that your organization is about to change its culture, expect blank stares and not a few snickers. Most people do not think about any of the many cultures in which they exist: their church, community, social clubs, families, circles of friends, and work place. Instead of expounding on culture, the CEO needs to talk about the specific ways people are going to behave in the future.

As with any sound change management plan, a cultural change plan must include a communication component. We recommend that such communication include a strong message about compelling need and many, many illustrative examples of the desired behaviors of the new culture. You or anyone in your organization could probably write a book about your existing culture, replete with such examples. Your challenge is to rewrite that book and to make sure everyone reads, understands, and believes the new version.

Take care, though, that you do not communicate empty propaganda. Resist putting up a lot of banners and slogans. Most traditional productivity or efficiency campaigns begin this way, and you do not want people to confuse your new effort with them. Should some of your leaders push for this, you might tell them that most experts suggest putting all the banners and slogans in executive meeting rooms— but nowhere else.

The Process Driven Phase

In this section, we will review some of the most important tools and variables in cultural change and show how to use them during the Process Driven phase.

Training

Training is often the starting point of cultural change. It raises awareness about improvement principles and gives the skills needed to succeed in a participative, cooperative environment. The training experience brings people with diverse roles together to work on constructive tasks exemplifying the ethic it teaches. Job-related training also can help institutionalize an organization's emphasis on improvement. Employees need the proper skills and instructions even to begin doing a quality job.

"Before, our 'training' was one worker telling another how the job had always been done, which often institutionalized methods that never should have existed," a Naval Publications and Forms Center manager told us. "We knew training was important, but in the press of everyday business, training schedules often fell behind. Now, every

Tuesday we shut down the operation for forty-five minutes of training. Each department designs its own training plans, and our training coordinator finds the expertise. We also require certification of competency, which shows our commitment to doing the job right."

Deming emphasizes this point frequently: An organization that uses formal job-related training ensures that people know how to "do it right."

Making organizational and regulation changes that support flexibility and continuous improvement

Just as form follows function, so the structure and rules of an organization should promote and reinforce its cultural values. Some changes made by organizations that we interviewed for this book point the way to a new framework for improvement.

Restructuring individual work processes

The U.S. Patent and Trademark Office increased the continuity of its work processes by reformatting lines of responsibility. Now one employee or one team owns a discrete, start-to-finish process. This restructuring enhances both accountability for quality and job satisfaction. As management expert Tom Peters says, "Quality begins with emotional attachment."

Flattening the organization chart

As discussed in Chapter 14 on structure, Improvement Driven Organizations tend to reduce the number of management layers between leadership and employees. "Making participative management work had been complicated by too many levels of supervision," a quality coordinator at NASA's Lewis Research Center recalled. "The structure really got in the way of communication between upper

management and employees. We solved the problem by
cutting out one supervisory layer.

"Naturally, people at first viewed the move with suspicion
and fear, especially those directly affected. But we
addressed concerns by beefing up our dual career program,
which allows some classes of employees to receive supervisory grade levels without holding supervisory positions."

Cutting down on red tape

Externally imposed regulations often are barriers to quality.
For example, the U.S. Forest Service recognized that
enabling its units to get the job done meant freeing them
from traditional bureaucratic controls. As a pilot test, three
national forests and a research station received full authority
to change or eliminate any process.

According to a manager interviewed in Tom Peters's film,
Excellence in the Public Sector, "Prior to the pilot we relied
heavily on our manuals and handbooks, and it was easy for
some managers to deal with that. If it wasn't in the manual,
it was an easy answer: 'No.' Now 'no' is a forbidden
word."

The Forest Service found that lifting the bureaucratic bur-
dens freed staff to spend more time "on the ground." New
projects developed, customer service improved, and the culture now reflects an ethic of faith and trust in the employee.

Redesigning individual performance appraisal and monetary reward systems to reflect new principles

Nothing sends a clearer message to managers and employees than the rewards they receive and a superior's evaluation of their performance. The measures an organization
chooses to evaluate should show its real priorities—because
they are the expectations people will try to meet.

- **Executive and manager rewards tied to results.**
Most public agencies reward management for either sticking to procedures or putting out the fires that break out when procedures don't work. Adopting a long-time private sector practice, many governments have started paying for results instead. For example, in cities like Houston, Texas and Philadelphia, Pennsylvania school superintendents' salaries or bonuses are pegged to improving student achievement, parent and community participation, and diversity in staff or curriculum. If the superintendents in cities like these do not meet their goals, they face pay cuts or a job search.

  It is not always easy for a government to reward results, because some are hard to define, and the connection between agency action and a result may be tenuous. Yet, if a government wants to be improvement driven, it must find ways to reward its executives and managers for improvement results.

  Along with this accountability must come a new type of authority, in which an executive becomes a leader instead of a rule-bound caretaker for his or her organization. In a National Association of Governors' publication, Oklahoma Governor David Walters said that "for far too long, we have believed that agency heads, if given any flexibility to manage, will abuse their power unless every operational detail is legislated. Thus, we not only take away their ability to serve public needs, we tie their hands and feet and then demand that they run faster."

- **Employee compensation and reward based on improvement principles.** Many organizations are still struggling to develop incentive systems compatible with improvement driven principles. They know their old way is not having the desired effect. Deming states the reason: "The effects [of evaluation by performance,

merit rating, or annual review of performance] are dev-
astating—teamwork is destroyed, rivalry is nurtured.
Performance ratings build fear, and leave people bitter,
despondent, and beaten." Here is insight for aligning
your reward and compensation approach with an
improvement driven culture.

- **Individual performance appraisal.** The following list
  of questions is from *A Study of Performance
  Management Systems Compatible with Total Quality
  Management,* a study that Coopers & Lybrand helped
  design and manage for the Naval Industrial
  Improvement Program. The researchers looked at the
  appraisal methods of eight private companies and four
  government organizations that apply continuous
  improvement and reviewed the methods against quality
  principles. In deciding how to handle performance
  appraisals, you might ask some of the study's questions
  about your existing method.

  - **Does it do what it is supposed to?** What an
    Improvement Driven Organization "is supposed to
    do" is to gain continuous improvement in meeting
    customer expectations—which is different from
    rewarding people for sticking to rules, fire fighting,
    or just making managers happy. Such an evaluation
    system also would be closely tied to an organiza-
    tion's strategic goals and objectives and would
    reward people for helping to achieve them.

  - **Does it consider the 85/15 rule?** As you recall
    from Chapter 2, 85 percent of problems (and there-
    fore potential improvements) are caused by systems
    issues beyond the control of individual employees.
    Individuals in such systems can solve only 15 per-
    cent of the problems (or create 15 percent of the
    solutions). In this case, appraisal based on individ-
    ual results does not consider the system barriers to

good performance. "We take the approach that deficiencies are not the mechanic's fault," said a foreman at the Norfolk Naval Shipyard. "Instead, we look for defective material, bad processes, inadequate training, or poor instructions. When we examine the process, we see that most of the time the mechanic has done a 100 percent job of doing what he's supposed to do. If what he's supposed to do is wrong, whose fault is that?"

- **Is it annual or continuous?** Most annual performance appraisals usually are rituals that come too late to help employees. Appraisal should be continuous, with frequent discussions between managers and employees over issues, personal goals, and individual progress. This is called management.

• **Individual versus team rewards.** *Beyond the Bottom Line: Measuring World Class Performance* is a joint Coopers & Lybrand and National Association of Public Accountants study of five Coopers & Lybrand private industry clients. Part of the book looks at performance appraisals of self-managed teams. The authors suggest that rewards to such groups should be based on total performance improvement against a series of indicators that measure process results. The indicators might be cost, cycle time, on-time delivery, defects or errors, or some other customer-oriented measure.

Individuals should be rewarded for improvement in personal knowledge, say the authors. This improvement should take the form of new skills and the ability to perform new tasks that contribute to group performance. Much of this new knowledge should come from cross-training in the skills of other group members. Cross-training creates the flexibility needed in an Improvement Driven Organization; it is also a form of job enrichment.

This method creates a "competition-cooperation" tension that is healthy for the individual and the group. The competition promotes individual knowledge, the reward for which is advancing in pay grade or classification; the knowledge gained by individuals helps the group.

- **Gainsharing.** Because employees help an organization achieve results, they should share in the rewards given for that achievement. For example, some federal facilities that do projects for other agencies follow the practice of gainsharing, in which a portion of the difference between the estimated and actual cost of a project is distributed evenly to all employees. In Oklahoma, the state government instituted a pay raise system similar in spirit, if not method, to gainsharing. Employees with satisfactory or better performance evaluations could receive additional pay, but the money had to come from agencies' current personnel budgets. Both systems create an incentive to seek out and eliminate waste. Likewise, every employee in an agency that meets or exceeds its goals for results should share in bonuses distributed for this achievement.

The need for hard data. The recommendations of both the just-cited studies assume adequate data on process, group, and individual performance. Collecting these data is discussed in Chapters 12 and 13, under performance indicators and ABC. Obviously, if you are going to use any of the methods just described, you will need to collect this information. Setting up your compensation system is one more reason to add these valuable measures.

Changing budgeting and accounting practices. Because money is power, the way an organization's budget operates paints a telling picture of its priorities. Changing budget practices to support a continuous improvement environment can be a powerful tool for reorienting organizational values, as DISC has learned from experience.

The foundation of a continuous improvement budgeting system that will create culture change is to make visible the link between spending and results. According to the National Governors' Association, Texas's state budgeting system is a solid attempt to do this, because strategies from state agencies' strategic plans became the line items in their budgets, and strategic performance measures are included in their appropriations bills. This arrangement compels the agencies to focus on results.

Internal to an agency, ABC makes visible to managers the actual costs of producing goods and services (see Chapter 13). This cost consciousness on the part of managers gives them a starting point for controlling costs, because ABC-based budgets and cost information are directly linked to specific processes.

Because flexibility is one of the cultural objectives of an Improvement Driven Organization, budgets must reinforce this objective. "Your budget structure has to follow your organization's structure and promote its goals," said DISC's comptroller. "We now develop flexible budgets, based on business volume. To promote interdepartmental cooperation, we've removed many fences that had existed between various 'pots' of money. To foster participative management, we began to delegate budget authority to the departments. We removed budget limitations and centralized review. Our central staff now provides budget support rather than oversight."

The Dallas Regional Office of the Social Security Administration has piloted giving its field offices more control over operations budgets. "Keeping the budgetary decisions as close to the point where services are provided and relying heavily on the judgment of employees providing the services will ensure more service value for the dollar spent," said the regional commissioner.

The Improvement Driven Phase

Most people can be won over to an improvement driven culture through actions such as those discussed in this and other chapters. Even the most committed executives, managers, and employees, however, can slip back into the old ways. Also, teamwork and participative management can degenerate into ritualistic behavior—all form, no substance. *An improvement driven culture is not self-sustaining.* It must be revitalized constantly.

The quality coordinator at the Cincinnati IRS Service Center compared the social change needed to create a continuous improvement environment with the behavior change needed for weight loss: "People make enormous changes, they beat the difficulties, and they lose weight. But unless they work just as hard at keeping the weight off, normal human backsliding puts them right back where they started."

Monitoring is important

Culture must be constantly monitored. Top management must review performance measures of culture-related processes, conduct periodic surveys, talk to employees and managers, and otherwise keep a finger on the cultural pulse of the organization. Based on the information they gather, managers can take action to sustain (and continuously improve) their culture.

Leveraging cultural change

We won't go so far as to say that you can develop a culture that loves to change. Most people are not going to go out of their way to find new ways of behaving. However, you can use a successful cultural change in one area to smooth the path toward other changes. Successful teamwork among managers can be used to encourage more teamwork among employees (the reverse is usually not true, though).

Success in developing a culture that supports continuous improvement within an organization can be used as the platform for launching similar changes among key suppliers.

Future culture

What kind of culture will be needed for organizational success in the future? On the horizon, it is clear that customer focus, teamwork, self-management, and flexibility will be primary variables in effective culture. Beyond the horizon, there are potential innovations in technology, bioengineering, and the social sciences that, if past is prelude, will alter organizational culture in ways we do not yet anticipate, much less understand. Because of these unknowns, we must learn how to change our culture to adapt to new circumstances.

PART IV

THE IMPROVEMENT
DRIVEN PHASE

Chapter
19

PROMOTING CONTINUOUS IMPROVEMENT

■ Even if it has many breakthroughs, without continuous improvement an organization's performance will inevitably begin to decay.

■ With continuous improvement, performance will always rise to the highest level of process capability, at which point a breakthrough will be needed.

■ The structure of continuous improvement is the result of the successful execution and integration of previous phases of the Improvement Driven Organization framework. However, over the long term, continuous improvement will depend on:

- Leadership
- Monitoring improvement progress
- Training people in improvement methods
- External searches for improvement ideas

■ Best practices benchmarking means comparing your performance with the highest level attained by outside organizations and then adopting and adapting their best practices.

Now here, you see, it takes all the running you can do to keep in the same place. If you want to get somewhere else, you must run at least twice as fast as that.

— Lewis Carroll, *Alice in Wonderland*

Public servants should empathize with Alice—no matter how fast your organization changes, it must change even faster just to keep up with increased pressure from budget cuts and rising citizens demands. Most people would prefer a series of short sprints, but in today's world there is no time to rest between races. It's a combination sprint/marathon, and the only way to keep winning is through continuous improvement.

How do you create an organization where everyone pressures him- or herself to constantly improve? How do you maintain a steady flow of outside ideas that stimulate innovation? Finding the answers is critical to long-term success. In this chapter, we will examine these questions, in order to to bring to a conclusion our discussion of the framework of Improvement Driven Organizations. We will begin by briefly outlining the rationale for continuous improvement.

WHY CONTINUOUS IMPROVEMENT?

We said that most people would prefer improvement programs to be like a sprint—a breakthrough hundred-yard dash, followed by a time of resting on one's laurels. Unfortunately, if a process is left alone between breakthroughs, its performance will inevitably decay, both *absolutely* and *relative to* customer requirements and competitors' performance. Let's look at both types of performance problems now.

Absolute Performance

In Chapter 6, we said that, in physics, entropy is a measure of the amount of energy unavailable for work during the operation of a natural process. This quantity increases in a system undergoing spontaneous change. Work processes also tend to change spontaneously. For example, equipment in a process may be poorly maintained and so may break down frequently. The breakdowns mean that less of the process's energy is available for work, as its operators sit idle or repair the equipment. If an employee lacks training in a process, he or she may use a nonstandard shortcut that saves some time but causes the process to vary in its operation. This variation eventually causes problems, which require labor and money—energy, in other words—to correct; this energy is not available for productive purposes.

As shown in the top graph in Figure 19-1, after a breakthrough in performance, these spontaneous changes, both good and bad, accumulate and cause performance to fall. Processes with this problem require frequent breakthroughs in order to increase their performance. Unfortunately, most of the breakthrough-performance increase dissipates due to entropy.

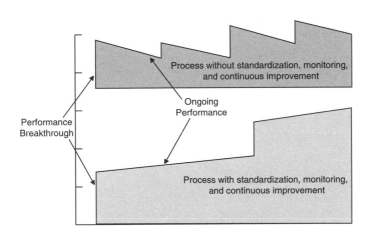

Figure 19-1
Effect of
Continuous
Improvement
on Process
Performance

To reduce the entropy, you can train process operators in standard work procedures, monitor performance measures, and follow a regular maintenance schedule for equipment. If the process is hard to standardize, you can at least monitor its performance and correct problems when they become visible. These practices reduce performance decline.

However, the practices cannot not totally prevent decay in absolute performance. If you are forced to reduce staffing due to a budget cut, and you do not adjust your processes to this event, then quality and cycle time performance may go down as fewer people try to do the same work. Also, increases in the price of labor, supplies, travel, and equipment can cause cost performance to fall. So, no matter what you do, absolute performance is bound to fall in an unimproved process.

Relative Performance

When competitors raise their performance or customers change requirements, the effect on your processes is the same as in the top graph in Figure 19-1—at least in the eyes of customers and the elected officials who fund your organization. Although your processes may maintain close to the original level of absolute performance, they decline relative to what customers want and competitors can deliver.

With continuous improvement, you gradually raise ongoing performance beyond the original standard of excellence set by a breakthrough, as shown in the bottom graph in Figure 19-1. In economics, a constantly rising standard creates constantly higher barriers to entering a market. This means competitors will have to stretch harder and spend more money to surpass your performance and win away your customers. Thus, continuous improvement is one of the best defenses against privatization or losing your programs to other public organizations.

Ever-increasing customer requirements also require constant process improvement. This is especially true for public organizations that serve other agencies of their government, because these agencies are themselves straining under the burden of increased demand and funding limitations. They want your services to be better, faster, and less costly because that is what their customers require of them. In addition, customer agencies are changing their processes and require your organization to modify its operations to integrate with these changes.

With continuous improvement, your performance will look like the bottom graph in Figure 19-1: breakthroughs (the sprints) followed by more gradual increases (the marathon). When performance constantly increases, you will not need as many breakthroughs to keep up with demand. Although breakthroughs are good, they tend to be expensive, so the fewer you need, the lower your costs. In general, the many minor and moderate gains of continuous improvement are virtually free, because they provide quick returns on investment.

WHAT DOES CONTINUOUS IMPROVEMENT LOOK LIKE?

Throughout this book, you have seen the *components* of an Improvement Driven Organization, such as leadership, process improvement methods, determining customer requirements, performance measurement, and motivating employees to make suggestions. Taken individually, these components produce a bare minimum of benefits; management must integrate them to produce continuous improvement.

In the following case study, we show how one management team integrated the three dimensions of Process Driven improvement—Business Process Improvement, Organizational Process Alignment, and Infrastructure Development—to create continuous improvement. Although the example is industrial in nature, its lessons apply to every type of government enterprise. For some public organizations, the emphasis given to competition will be particularly relevant.

Compelling Need

A few years ago, the Jacksonville, Florida Naval Aviation Depot faced a critical problem. Using process improvement methods to prepare the proposal, it had won an open competition with private industry to refit aircraft. But when work began, the depot found it was using too much labor to stay within budget. The depot had to act quickly because the contract was for one year, with up to four follow-on years if the winner performed well. To have delayed, according to the commanding officer (CO), would have meant "people going out of the depot gates—permanently." *That* is a compelling need faced by more and more government organizations every day.

Today, the depot completes planes with 50 percent less labor than originally planned and is still improving. At record quality levels. Without new automation. The result: millions of dollars saved for the Navy and taxpayers. Let's examine how the depot used continuous improvement to achieve this victory.

Business Process Improvement

In a weekend meeting, a team of managers, supervisors, and employees developed a better sequence of installing the one hundred modification work kits used to refit an aircraft. This change trimmed more than five hundred labor hours per plane—the depot soon matched its bid amount. It was a breakthrough gain in productivity, and usually a one-time occurrence in labor intensive work such as this.

This would be a single-dimension change (Business Process Improvement) if the depot only altered the sequence of its work processes. Instead, management took a planned, controlled approach to continuous improvement by also making changes that fell in the categories of Organizational Process Alignment and Infrastructure Development. The changes included work process tracking, a new management structure, and a proactive program to get suggestions from workers and customers, which generated a constant stream of new ideas for improvement, which were put in place in a rational, controlled manner.

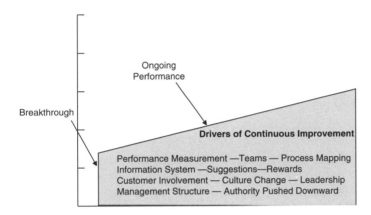

Figure 19-2
Continuous
Improvement
at
Jacksonville
Naval
Aviation
Depot

Infrastructure Development

Structure designed to promote improvement

Structure includes how managers and employees are organized to do their work. At Jacksonville, the structure was deliberately set up to drive continuous improvement.

Front-line management changes. Many managers complain that they cannot find the time to plan beyond the immediate tasks of the day. To give them time to plan for improvement, Jacksonville assigned routine tasks done by first-line supervisors, such as tool control, minor leave requests, and work assignments, to work leaders in charge of small teams of employees. According to the chief supervisor, "This is the first time in my twenty-four years of work that I've actually been able to manage instead of just doing paperwork and putting out fires." When he and other supervisors started concentrating on process improvement, so did the employees.

Employee teams. Before, a group of employees did the same task on all aircraft, which caused delays when one group was off schedule and the others had to wait for it to finish. This functional structure caused some of the sequencing problems, when a group installed a modification kit that had to be removed to install another that should have gone in first. The depot restructured employees into small multi-skill teams, each of which is responsible for all aspects of the refitting of a single aircraft. Besides helping to solve schedule and sequence problems, this approach fostered a sense of ownership—no one wanted his or her aircraft to have any faults.

Process-oriented information system

Depot managers' first priority was to ensure that their processes stayed in control. A new information system allowed them to measure and monitor quality, schedule, and cost, producing data vital for controlling daily operations. Using computerized work flow chart graphics, the depot tied its process performance reports to the breakthrough sequence of installing the one hundred work kits. Now people could link the reports with specific processes and tasks, which helped diagnose problems. Computer graphics also made it easy to revise, print, and distribute new procedures to workers. With fresh print-outs in hand, workers could follow these changes just hours after they were made.

Organizational Process Alignment

Alignment means to unify people around a cause. In an
Improvement Driven Organization, the cause is continuous
improvement in meeting customer and stakeholder requirements. The following changes in Jacksonville brought
about this alignment.

Involvement

Information sharing empowered workers and customers to
find improvements. Instead of keeping the performance
reports, managers sent them swiftly to front-line personnel
and discussed them with customers. Combined with the
computer graphics, the reports made it easy for supervisors
and workers to spot and solve problems early and see where
new improvements were possible. Managers and supervisors went over the reports with customer representatives
and asked for their improvement ideas, too.

Suggestions encouraged. Jacksonville actively encouraged workers to think of new ideas in several ways. For
example, team leaders met with each of their team members
at least once a week to solicit improvement suggestions, and
they helped organize informal competitions to generate
ideas. "We usually have two teams doing the same thing on
different planes," said one work leader. "If one team is
faster or better, it wins a contest, sometimes for baseball
caps and jackets, but usually for the pride of teaching the
other teams what they did to win. This makes improvement
fun." Workers also are motivated by the fast turnaround
management gives to their suggestions. As noted earlier, a
depot employee's new idea can be introduced to the system
within hours of its discovery.

In some industries, most innovations are initiated by customers, so managers and supervisors met with customer
representatives almost daily to gain their ideas on improve-

ment. Also, the depot invited the representatives to spot check quality at any time, not just during mandated inspections, because managers understood that a problem discovered is an opportunity for improvement.

Innovation

As you can see, workers and managers at Jacksonville had all the tools and resources needed to make creative improvements. They also received training in how to identify problems and isolate their causes, then develop innovative solutions. Management's encouragement unleashed the workers' natural, human desire to innovate, but creativity would not be possible without the right tools, resources, and training.

Alignment

Leadership. However, managers would not have dared to fiddle with "the system" were it not for the forceful example of the depot's CO. When work was delayed because of too few lift platforms, the CO said, "Why don't you rent them? Sure, it may cost some, but not having the platforms causes bottlenecks that cost us much more time and money. Think about the big picture, not its parts." When procurement hassles delayed the arrival of a refrigerator for refit materials, the CO moved his headquarters' icebox into the work area instead. Managers quickly got the message: do whatever necessary to improve core business processes, and do it now! That message cascaded downward to managers, who channeled it to employees and customer representatives.

Design for culture change. Jacksonville's high performance culture did not happen by chance. Management's conscious goal was to change a risk-averse, command-and-control, business-as-usual culture into a risk-taking, improvement-driven culture. Although the CO's leadership set the tone and got things rolling, it was management's conscious planning of the many other changes in

Organizational Process Alignment and Infrastructure Development that created this continuous improvement culture. It was the only way to survive.

"This may be difficult for some people to understand, but the truth is we simply can't stop getting better," said one depot manager. "When you structure an operation with the goal of improving it, there are no brakes on the quality train." Would your employees complain about this relentless drive to improve? As one depot worker said, "The pressure to improve doesn't come from our bosses. We put it on ourselves."

Woody Flowers of the Massachusetts Institute of Technology summed up the emotional side of this pressure when he said, "Creative activity is one of the few self rewarding activities. Being creative is like being in love!" If you can develop the environment of the Jacksonville depot, then both your people and your customers will love continuous improvement.

ENSURING CONTINUOUS IMPROVEMENT

Although continuous improvement is absolutely critical to long-term success, promoting it is the task most often overlooked. Some reasons for this include the following:

- A century of management theory and practices has hard-wired into our brains the notion that the most desirable state for an organization is consistent, unchanging operations. Continuous improvement means constant change, which is counter-intuitive. For example, whoever heard of rebuilding a jet plane while it is in mid-flight? Yet that is exactly what Improvement Driven Organizations do: they constantly change operations without taking processes off-line or reducing performance.

- Most organizations' cultures divide personnel into "thinkers" (managers) and "doers" (workers), and most thinkers want to keep it that way. A continuous improvement culture is one in which all are both thinkers and doers.

- Most organizations like their work to be easy, with much of it running on automatic pilot. Continuous improvement is the *hardest* work an organization must do, especially at first, and, while it is sustainable, it *never* becomes automatic.

Despite these difficulties, the benefits of continuous improvement far exceed the costs of introducing and maintaining it, as the people in Jacksonville discovered. Here are some guidelines for making the shift from the Process Driven phase to the Improvement Driven phase, then for sustaining continuous improvement over time.

Figure 19-3
Drivers of
Continuous
Improvement

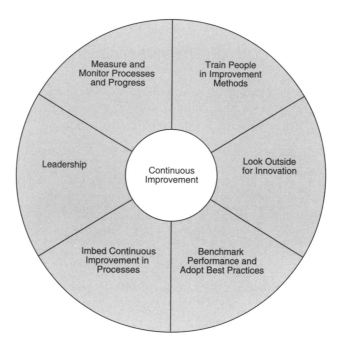

Continuous improvement depends on leadership. As just noted, continuous improvement does not fly on automatic pilot. It needs real pilots—executives and top managers— to keep things on course. Establishing visions of excellence and goals for achieving them is only part of what leaders must do. Their longer term, more important task is to monitor how managers are carrying out the work of promoting continuous improvement, both in the ranks of managers and among employees. This is why leaders must review improvement trends in key processes and then reward or sanction managers based on improvement results.

Imbed continuous improvement in processes. If you plan to lose weight, the healthiest thing you can do is to determine in advance how you will keep it off permanently. Likewise, when planning process changes, consider how you will continuously improve them after making the changes. Any planned innovation is flawed if you cannot develop ways to (1) give process operators performance information on their part of the innovation, (2) enable the operators to adjust their part to internal or external problems or changes in environment, and (3) monitor whether they take successful action in continuously improving the innovation.

Measure and monitor progress and processes. Measure what counts the most. What to measure will depend on your mission and organization, but in general it includes customer expectations and satisfaction, process performance, and results. A system of continuous measurement *to which management gives its attention* is a baseline requirement for continuous improvement.

Train people in improvement methods. As noted in earlier chapters, Improvement Driven Organizations teach their people methods for continuous improvement. These include some form of Plan-Do-Check-Act (PDCA, Chapter 9), management planning, suggestions programs (Chapter 17), and others. Each method requires formal training, so that systems must be in place to provide this instruction. We will discuss this more in the next chapter.

Look for innovations outside the organization. After awhile (especially if they are good at what they do) some organizations develop a "not invented here" attitude. This is the road to ruin, because more good ideas are available outside an organization's walls than inside. Without these external ideas, your agency is like a stagnant pool of water, which evaporates without replenishment. Instead of waiting for rain, start opening channels to outside stimuli and thereby promote continuous improvement. Ways to do this include the following:

- Encourage and permit job rotation among talented managers and employees, allowing them to work in all parts of your organization, with customer or supplier agencies, and with other types of governments through temporary intergovernmental transfers;

- Encourage and support your people's participation in trade and professional associations, conferences, and seminars;

- Make it more important to read trade journals than to know what's in your internal newsletter;

- Invest in training and education to ensure that everyone stays up to date on the latest developments in your business;

- Send people on site visits to customers, who, as mentioned earlier, often are a major source of innovative ideas; and

- Constantly compare your performance with that of the best outside organizations, and adopt and adapt their best practices.

This last area—best practices comparison—is part of what is called benchmarking, which we will now discuss in detail.

BEST PRACTICES BENCHMARKING

For the past several years, private companies have found that one of the most productive ways to discover new ideas is to *benchmark* the best practices of outside organizations. Benchmarking is a process in which an organization compares its performance with the highest levels attained by other organizations and then acts to close whatever gaps exist. The objective of benchmarking is to achieve and sustain best-in-class performance.

Benchmarking is not the same as conducting comparison studies. Just about every federal, state, and local agency has conducted (or been subjected to) some comparison of its services with those of other organizations that do the same thing. However, almost all those studies are now gathering dust on a shelf, because the officials who commissioned them lacked the commitment and means to act on their results.

Origins of Modern Benchmarking

Xerox is recognized as one of the premier practitioners of benchmarking, or using other people's ideas for improving one's own work. How Xerox benchmarks is a good introduction to this subject.

Several years ago, the chairman of Xerox was shocked to see an ad for a rival's copying machines with prices lower than what it took Xerox to build comparable copiers. Customers saw the ads, too, and Xerox soon began losing market share. Part of the problem was that Xerox had a "not invented here" culture. After all, the company's founder had invented xerography, and it led the world in sales. Now, the compelling need to quickly surpass new competitors stimulated Xerox to start comparing its products and processes with those of competitor and noncompetitor organizations.

Competitive and industry benchmarking

A joke in the copier industry is that a company can always be sure of two sales for new models—to its own headquarters and Xerox. Xerox tests nearly all copiers made by other companies. If a rival copier works better than its own comparable model, the rival becomes Xerox's benchmark, or goal for improvement.

Competitive benchmarking means looking at the products or services of direct competitors who are generally regarded as the best at particular segments of their operations. *Industry benchmarking* means analyzing trends in performance among organizations in the same or similar industries. For example, in competitive benchmarking a municipal waste disposal department might compare its costs and services with those that of a local private company. In industry benchmarking, the department might look at national trends in both public and private organizations that collect, transport, and dispose of waste products; bill customers for these services; and otherwise operate the same or similar processes. Such comparisons are good when they provide a benchmark or reference point measuring an organization's performance. However, they rarely can do more than just provide the measurement, for the following reasons:

- **Low to medium accessibility to direct competitors' benchmarking data.** An organization does not give this data to its competitors; finding it out takes special studies.

- **Low likelihood of discovering innovative practices.** No competitor wants you to know its secrets, so they are hard to get. But chances are the practices are already fairly well known to people familiar with their field.

Trade journals, conference speakers, vendors, consultants, and informal contacts usually talk about them.

- **Meeting competitor and industry performance is not beating it.** You have to perform better than competitors to win against them; using their current performance as a standard does not compel you to look for breakthroughs to surpass it.

Competitive and industry benchmarks are important; you are at a severe disadvantage if you do not know your industry's standards or how your competitors are performing. You are in even worse shape if you do not think you have any competitors.

Best-in-class benchmarking

Xerox benchmarks more than copiers, which is the secret of its continued success. For example, the company has hundreds of thousands of customers located around the world. It must quickly ship spare parts from warehouses to these customers, or else they will be irate at copier downtime. Wanting to improve logistics and distribution functions, Xerox turned to L.L. Bean. What can a copier manufacturer learn from a catalog sales firm? Plenty, because L.L. Bean has about the world's best distribution system for small items.

The genius of Xerox's benchmarking approach was to see that much of L.L. Bean's distribution system, even though it was designed for moccasins and tents, could also work for them—spare parts are small items, too. The Xerox team in charge of this task did not limit their search to other copier companies, but instead looked for the generic *best practice* of small item distribution.

Xerox's Business Products and Systems division used lessons from L.L. Bean to help win the 1989 Malcolm

Baldrige Award. More important, the company's combined benchmarking and continuous improvement approach meant recovering earlier market share losses to competitors, and gaining new markets. Today, Xerox is still the world leader in its industry.

Best-in-class or best practicing benchmarking has the following characteristics:

- **High accessibility to benchmarking data.** There is no reason to keep this information secret from a noncompetitor.

- **High likelihood of uncovering innovative practices.** The further away you go from your own industry, the greater the chance of finding totally new solutions. This is because people in dissimilar industries often approach similar problems from different perspectives.

This type of careful and objective study can uncover the absolutely best practices, resulting in the ideal type of competitive advantage: your competitors may not have a clue why your performance has suddenly increased. While they figure things out (and overcome their own "not invented here" skepticism), you win kudos from citizens and legislators for world-class performance.

Internal benchmarking

You can also benchmark internal processes against other internal processes; for example, you could compare the performance of several field offices in certain operations and then have all field offices adopt and adapt the practices of the one with the best performance. Often, this is a good way to get started in learning the benchmarking process we describe later in this chapter. Eventually, though, you want to begin using external comparisons whenever possible.

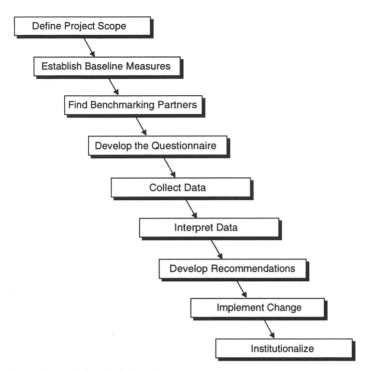

Figure 19-4
Coopers &
Lybrand's
Benchmarking
Methodology

Benchmarking Methods

A best practices benchmarking project has several steps, as shown in Figure 19-4. Some of the steps in the figure, such as Define Project Scope and Establish Baseline Measures, are similar those in other process improvement methods such as reengineering and PDCA. Below, we will focus more on the parts that are unique to benchmarking.

Define project scope

Your first objective is to understand the needs of the person or group who wants the benchmarking study, such as a need for better accuracy, cost savings, or cycle time. Narrow your study's focus to the customer's most critical information needs in order to avoid collecting useless data on other factors.

Next, make sure you are focusing on root causes of the customer's needs, not on symptoms. A need for better accuracy is a symptom. You want to focus on deficiencies that cause problems in specific processes that cause inaccuracy.

Establish baseline measures

Having identified the right processes, create top-down or detailed flow charts of them and learn about their operation. Most of the time, you will find ways to simplify or improve the processes, such as by eliminating non-value added steps. *It is critical to improve the processes before you collect baseline data on their performance.* Otherwise, you will mistakenly believe that some high-performing external processes have a marvelous innovation you want to adopt, when they are just simplified, more efficient versions of your own internal processes. You don't need a benchmarking study to tell you that. However, if you find external processes that beat the socks off your *improved* internal processes, then you know you are on to a breakthrough.

After improving the processes, you measure their current performance to create a baseline for comparison with external benchmarks. Also, you need to know the drivers of the processes: what factors cause changes in their volume, quality, cycle-time, or cost of goods or services produced? Process drivers are essential for developing the criteria for identifying comparable processes for benchmarking. For a discussion of volume and cost drivers, see Chapter 13 on activity-based costing.

Find benchmarking partners

Benchmarking partners are organizations that agree to share information about their processes. In best practices benchmarking, your partners' processes have the same criteria for success as yours. These criteria are the key characteristics or drivers that determine or constrain the way a process must be done; if you changed them, your business would change, too.

For example, an airline wanted to benchmark its process for servicing planes between flights. The criteria for comparison with other organizations included the following:

• Some regularly scheduled things had to be done every time, such as refueling;

• Some things simply had to be checked and replenished if needed, such as magazines;

• Some random maintenance might be required due to unanticipated damage;

• The operation had to be done as quickly as possible; and

• Several people with varied skills had to work on different parts of the planes.

The airline found that a race car pit crew had the same criteria for its processes, so the crew was an ideal benchmarking partner. Interestingly, in a separate benchmarking project a hospital operating room staff found that it also had much in common with a pit crew.

The cost of operating a process, technology, customer requirements, and time constraints are not criteria for selecting benchmarking partners. Instead, they are constraints on the way that you might adapt the best practices of benchmarking partners to your operations. Therefore, do not state in your criteria that an external process must cost a certain amount or that it must use a specific type of equipment you already own. You are looking for the best possible practices, not just those that exist within the parameters of your organization's limitations. Even if you do not have the budget to buy all of the technology of a external process, you can still adopt at least part of it and perhaps use the partner's performance to justify future investment.

Having established criteria, you begin searching for potential partners. This requires research such as the following:

- Talking and brainstorming with employees, managers, customers, and suppliers about organizations they know of that have the same criteria as the processes being benchmarked;

- Library data-base searches for published material;

- Government, industry, trade, and professional periodicals, associations, and meetings;

- Relevant departments and professors at universities and professional schools;

- Chambers of commerce and their literature, professionals, and volunteers;

- Promotional material and annual reports from outside organizations; and

- Analysis of the products and services of outside organizations.

As you do this research, be sure to collect background information on the latest trends in the processes you are studying. This will help you to understand the processes and to refine your criteria before you begin talking with partners. The matrix in Figure 19-5 is a way of displaying information about the candidate organizations you initially select. You can quantify the information in the matrix to help you narrow your search to the most likely candidates.

Criteria	Candidate A	Candidate B	Candidate C
Similar Drivers	No	Yes	Yes
Similar Customer Satisfaction Measures	Yes	No	Yes
Similar Product or Service Characteristics	No	Yes	Yes
Ease of Data Collection	Hard	Easy	Moderate
Reputation for Excellence	High	High	High
Level of Cooperation or Interest	Mild	Strong	Mild
Innovative Practices	Yes	No	Yes

Figure 19-5
Benchmarking
Criteria Matrix

Develop the questionnaire

The benchmarking questionnaire is the primary instrument for collecting data for the project. It also serves two other important purposes:

Study organizer. The questions correspond to the key information you need to prepare a benchmarking report.

Sales tool. World-class organizations—the kind you want to benchmark—often are inundated with pleas to become benchmark partners and are forced to reject many of them. A sound, narrowly focused questionnaire that proves you have done your homework is a good way to convince such organizations to work with you. This means trying to answer as many questions as possible about a potential partner by using published information, which saves time and shows you are serious.

Collect data

During this part of the study, you use the questionnaire to collect information from benchmarking partners. Forming a relationship with a benchmarking partner means that you should both abide by the following rules:

- Both parties agree to share information on the selected processes. This means you must answer your partner's questions about your own processes.

- Treat all information collected as confidential, and avoid questions about sensitive or proprietary information.

- Agree in advance on a protocol for the study, and be open and honest throughout the research.

You initiate contact with potential partners by phone call or letter and follow up with phone or in-person discussions about the nature and purpose of your study. Use these contacts as an opportunity to screen candidates to ensure they meet your criteria and will cooperate. Also, be clear about the time that you will require of the partner (a good rule is to do a first estimate of the time, then double it).

Although you can collect much of the information you need over the phone and by mail, an in-person site visit will produce the best results. Your visiting team should take extensive notes and try to obtain all relevant written documents. In some cases, it may be a good idea to photograph or videotape some of the activities being benchmarked. Other information to be collected includes:

- The names, model numbers, and manufacturer contact information for any equipment that seems essential to the best practice. This goes for supplies, too, when they are markedly different from those used at home;

- Instruction, training, or quality assurance manuals related to the process;

- Information on performance indicators used and on how they are collected and analyzed;

- Job descriptions of people who work in the process; and

- Process maps or flow charts and related material.

By the end of the visit, team members should be able to sketch out at least a preliminary work flow diagram of the benchmarked process. They should understand all its components, as described in Chapter 3 on customers and processes.

Remember to exchange telephone numbers with managers from the benchmarking partner, and make an effort to build these professional relationship. They will profit both individual team members and your organization long after the benchmarking project is over.

Interpret data

Your interpretation and analysis of the collected information should focus on the following topics:

- Confirming that benchmarking partners and their processes are in fact comparable to your organization and its processes;

- Identifying what the partners do in their processes that is different from your processes; and

- Establishing who, among all the partner organizations, is the best of the best.

Develop recommendations, implement change, and institutionalize

These are the last three steps in the benchmarking process. Your recommendations will focus on adopting and adapting to your organization the best practices you discovered. This always requires some modification of your partners' processes.

Depending on the nature and magnitude of improvement you introduce to your organization, you can follow the appropriate improvement and change management procedures discussed in other parts of this book. For example, a minor or moderate change confined to a few processes would be ideal for PDCA, while more extensive change might require a reengineering approach. As always, in order to institutionalize the innovation in your organization, pay attention to all of its dimensions. Use the measures developed during the benchmarking project to monitor ongoing performance of the improved processes.

Making Benchmarking a Permanent Part of Continuous Improvement

One of the best ways to ensure that your people will, at the least, pay attention to outside best practices is to require them to compare internal performance with that of external organizations that do the same types of things. Don't let your people get away with saying, "Well, the data show that we are above average." Insist that they discover and measure best-in-class performance, because this is the only comparison that matters for your most important processes. Then, always require that they begin closing the gaps between internal and external performance. If you do not require action for improvement, there is no reason to look for benchmarks (or for internal performance measures either, for that matter).

Use your initial benchmarking projects to refine your approach to this improvement method. Create your own benchmarking methodology, and promote it throughout your organization. The keys to its success are the same as those for all continuous improvement activities:

- **Planning.** Careful planning of improvement objectives, approach, timing, and resources.

- **Senior management commitment.** A high level of commitment by executives and top managers to benchmarking and continuous improvement.

- **Proper mind set.** An organizational disposition that favors improvement and change, recognizes the value of outside examples, and is confident in the benchmarking process.

- **Appropriate resources.** Ample time, money, and other resources for conducting improvement activities.

- **Coordination.** Coordination of all improvement activities, including benchmarking, and the routine communication of their progress and results to employees, customers, suppliers, and stakeholders.

PART V

DEVELOPING IMPROVEMENT DRIVEN ORGANIZATIONS

Chapter
20

BECOMING AN IMPROVEMENT DRIVEN ORGANIZATION

■ The first and most important step in becoming an Improvement Driven Organization is to secure the enthusiastic commitment of your CEO and other executives.

■ A temporary agency-wide improvement team will be needed during the first two years to make the transformation to an Improvement Driven Organization.

■ During this early period, devote the majority of resources to improving core business processes, using management planning and special project teams to do the work. Let these improvements guide changes in other parts of your organization.

■ Use these projects to develop your approach to improvement (methods, courseware, tools). Then, use cascade training, natural work groups, and suggestion programs to introduce the new way of doing business throughout your organization.

How to win a boat race

Recruit and train the captain and crew.

Don't fall out of the boat.

Don't hit any other boats.

Get to where you are going.

Get there as fast as you can.

— Anonymous

Becoming an Improvement Driven Organization is a lot like a boat race, which is why we start this chapter with a sailor's basic instructions for winning. Note the first caution in those instructions: we include it because some organizations *think* they have an excellent crew of executives to guide and support this improvement initiative, when in reality that support is lukewarm at best. Our precautions about not falling out of the boat or hitting other boats have to do with surviving the transformation period and gaining the cooperation of pre-existing improvement campaigns. Getting to where you are going implies that you know where that is and that you complete one phase of the transformation so that you can build on its results during the next phase. The final instruction is about the speed at which you can do all this development work and get results. Our experience shows that, if you plan the race right, you can get solid results from the very beginning, but full development can take years.

In this chapter, we will present ways to transform an agency or entire government into an Improvement Driven Organization. Our approach to transformation is, once again, the Leader Driven, Process Driven, and Improvement Driven phases of the IDO framework. We will start at the agency level.

Let's be clear about what is meant by this race. Applying a particular tool or method to radically change your agency does not make you an Improvement Driven Organization. For example, you are not improvement driven when you use activity-based costing (ABC) to do a major downsizing or restructuring; you are when you commit to using ABC afterward to continually monitor the cost effectiveness and performance of processes. You are not improvement driven when you set up self-managed teams; you are when you commit to training, enabling, and rewarding the teams for making continuous improvements.

Borrowing a Tom Peters idea, you can become excellent overnight when you commit to acting that way, no matter what barriers people erect. The tough part is to follow excellent business practices forever. That is why we insist that you build a firm foundation for your Improvement Driven Organization—because this race never ends.

LEADER DRIVEN PHASE

Figure 20-1 shows the IDO framework as a two-year Gantt chart with a series of milestones that, if achieved, will establish a firm foundation for an Improvement Driven Organization. The amount of time it will take to gain the milestones will depend on the scope of the effort and on your agency's resources, commitment, and culture.

However, you don't have to wait two years for results. In fact, if you have not made some significant gains within a few months after committing to excellent management, chances are you never will. That's because you need early results to sell the idea of the Improvement Driven Organization to everyone in your agency. Below, we take you through the first two years of the framework, showing how to get results while building a solid foundation.

Figure 20-1
IDO
Implementation
Plan

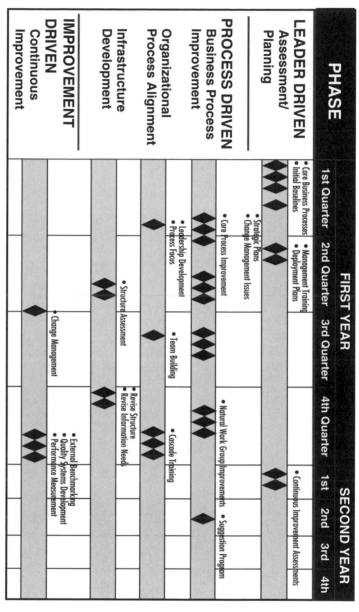

Success and speed depend on scope, resources, commitment, and culture.

Recruiting and Training the Captain and Crew: Educating and Winning Over Executives

Your first challenge is to gain top executive support for becoming an Improvement Driven Organization; otherwise you will not be able to even start the race toward improvement. Your objectives are to:

- Develop several champions for the initiative and get at least the tacit backing of the majority of elected executives, political appointees, and careerists;

- Have these champions use the management practices of the Improvement Driven Organization from the very start of the initiative; and

- Form an executive steering committee to guide the initiative.

Expect resistance. As you recall from earlier chapters, nearly all career executives scaled the functional hierarchies of your organization by becoming masters of Taylorism and other aspects of traditional management. *Why should they abandon the management practices that gave them so much success for a new, unproven (in their eyes) approach?* Answering that question to the satisfaction of most executives will be hard, and some will never see a reason for change. Here's how you approach the problem.

Secure support from the top executive

Your CEO must be the first sponsor of agency-wide management improvement. Otherwise, you reduce the chances of success by more than half. To gain the CEO's support, consider the following actions:

- If you are not an executive, then get an executive ally with enough influence to make the case to the CEO;

- Understand the CEO's immediate pressures, or his or her compelling needs. Are they related to results? Costs? Speed? Poor customer satisfaction? Align your arguments with these pressures, and the CEO is more likely to listen to you;

- Use some of the assessment methods discussed in Chapter 4 to do a few small internal studies that indicate the need for substantial improvement, and present the results to the CEO, along with suggestions for how to enhance the results;

- Educate the CEO through briefings, site visits to model Improvement Driven Organizations, and discussions with experts;

- Present information from outside organizations you have benchmarked, showing the gaps between their performance and your agency's, with reasons for the gaps;

- Encourage and arrange for your chief to discuss Improvement Driven Organization practices with his or her peers in other agencies; and

- If your central government is mandating change, show how following improvement practices will comply with that mandate.

All the leadership tasks of making the transformation will require a major time commitment by the CEO. This can be as much as two-thirds of his or her time to do such things as working with direct reports to educate and win them over, meeting with small groups of employees, participating in strategic planning, monitoring progress, and acting as the most enthusiastic supporter of the initiative.

A CEO can reduce this to about a third- or a half-time responsibility by delegating some of the work to an improvement champion, a position we discussed in Chapter 5 under horizontal deployment of strategic goals. However, for the challenge of completely transforming an organization, the improvement champion, if one is used, needs to be exceptionally able and must have the full support and trust of the CEO.

Start winning support from other executives

Your CEO is the best person to start educating and motivating other executives to support the agency-wide improvement initiative. At a minimum, this means the CEO will discuss the initiative with each executive, include it on top management meeting agendas, and be present at executive training sessions on improvement practices.

Executive briefings, seminars, and training sessions. Invite outside experts to speak to your executives on the benefits of improvement practices and how to introduce them. The expert can be an executive from a world-class organization that qualifies as improvement driven or a respected consultant who specializes in management. Ask some executives to attend outside seminars on improvement and to report back their findings. With a little help, in a few days you can develop exercises or mini-studies that executives can carry out on their own, using improvement tools such as those discussed in this book. This experience helps them learn about the tools and their benefits.

Literature and videotapes. There are many excellent articles, books, case studies, and videotapes about organizations that have succeeded in making improvement part of their culture. Such materials are most effective when accompanied by a note from the CEO that says, "This looks good. Let's talk about it."

Forming the agency-wide improvement team

As discussed in Chapter 5, the agency-wide improvement effort requires a special team led by senior executives and executives and managers. This team does not have to meet as a separate body. Its business can be conducted as an item on the agenda of regular top executive meetings. However, that item *always* has to be on the agenda, and the CEO must take the lead in discussing it. As individuals, each committee member must be a champion for change to the new way of management and must start modeling the behavior of the improvement-driven executive.

Supporting the team

The agency-wide improvement team will need staff support for planning and implementing changes. We recommend that you use a mixture of outside and internal personnel to meet this need.

External consultants. During the first two years of the initiative, it is a good idea to acquire the services of an experienced outside management consulting group. This can be a private firm or, if your government offers it, experienced managers from a central support organization or managers on loan from another agency.

The consultants can help you plan the transformation; design training courses; instruct and facilitate executive, management, and employee teams; or coach executives and senior managers. Such consultants should be flexible in regard to your unique situation but still have the backbone to be frank with executives who veer off course.

You absolutely must insist that the consultants transfer their knowledge and skills to your people; this should be part of the contract with them. Such transfer is best done by having the consultants train your internal support people while working alongside them. If you do not do this, then when the consultants leave you will not have the capability to run the effort on your own.

Internal support staff. During the first couple of years, you will likely need a small group of managers to be change agents and to do training and team facilitating, to gather progress information, and otherwise to support development. These individuals should report to the chairman of the agency-wide improvement team, and at least a couple of them should be full-time at this job. They will need appropriate employee and clerical support, also.

However, do not build a large, full-time support staff, because then you are setting up an specific office that will become responsible for improvement when you want everyone in your agency to be responsible. Use as many part-timers from all over your organization from all over your organization as you need, because this is great training.

Don't Fall Out of the Boat, Part I: Plan to Improve Core Business Processes

As you recall, a central premise of the Improvement Driven Organization is that all operations are organized around core business processes—the "get right, keep right, or die" operations. If you do not quickly start to improve these operations, then customers, stakeholders, and elected officials (and probably your employees, managers, and suppliers) will wonder, "Why are they wasting everybody's time on that improvement-driven stuff?" Next thing you know, your CEO will lose interest, patience, or both, or even be fired for taking a risk that does not seem to be paying off.

So, first things first: between 70 and 80 percent of your improvement investments during the first year of the transformation, including for assessment and planning, should be directed at strategic enhancements to core business processes.

That will make everyone more willing to support the expansion of the transformation to other parts of your agency. You will learn what else to improve while working on core processes, and you will also learn the process of making improvements. The rest of your improvement resources should go to developing the internal capability to continuously improve your processes.

Don't Hit Any Other Boats: Align All Improvement Efforts

Several improvement initiatives may already be in place before you commit to becoming an Improvement Driven Organization. One of the worst things to happen is for them to conflict with each other or your use of the IDO framework. This creates ill feelings among people who you sorely need to achieve the goal of becoming improvement driven.

Most often, the initiative is some form of total quality management (TQM), with a few reengineering projects (BPR). You do not want to supplant these efforts with a new management "flavor-of-the-month" acronym called "IDO." If prior improvement approaches are customer- and process-oriented and have been soundly applied, they should integrate with your transformation into an Improvement Driven Organization.

For example, you may already have a well-established initiative called, let's say, Quality Now!, which most work units have adopted and found good. There is no reason to abandon it—simply use the IDO framework to enhance and expand progress to date.

However, if Quality Now! produces no results, then give it a ceremonial burial before using the IDO framework to develop a new improvement initiative. You need to bury Quality Now! so that everyone knows that that phase of corporate life is over and a new one is starting. The burial should be open and ceremonial to show that management honors the intent of Quality First! and the people who tried to make it work and learned some lessons from the experience. Never, ever belittle Quality First!—you will just make enemies of its adherents.

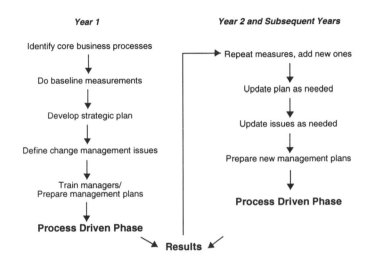

Figure 20-2
Actions for
the Leader
Driven Phase

First- and Second-Year Tasks in the Leader Driven Phase

As shown in Figure 20-2, the first and second year tasks in the Leader Driven phase are interrelated. They include:

- **Core business processes.** The executive steering committee identifies these processes as part of initial assessment (see Chapter 4).

- **Initial baselines.** Using methods appropriate for the situation (see Chapter 4), measure your baseline performance in areas such as customer satisfaction and performance in core business processes. At the start of the second year, remeasure the baselined issues or processes, and expand assessment to new areas or methods.

- **Strategic planning.** Develop strategic plans that focus on core business processes and other important issues (see Chapter 5). Update them in the second year.

- **Change management.** Identify change issues that must be addressed during the first year and also throughout the long-term transformation process (see Chapters 6 and 18).

- **Management training/deployment plans.** Combine the activities of training managers in improvement practices with their developing vertical deployment plans for achieving strategic goals related to core business processes (see Chapter 5). Usually, these are annual plans and so are developed anew during the second year.

These activities flow into the Process Driven phase, where they produce results.

PROCESS DRIVEN PHASE

As you recall, you operate in three dimensions during the Process Driven phase of a major improvement project: Business Process Improvement, Organizational Process Alignment, and Infrastructure Development. The same is true when your actions are directed at becoming an Improvement Driven Organization, as you can see in Figure 20-1.

Get to Where You Want to Go: Early Results From Business Process Improvement

Our experience is that you can start getting results soon after completing your strategic planning. The first of these gains will be executive quick fixes such as removing barriers or time wasters caused by unneeded rules and regulations. Next will be the results of short (one-week to three-month) projects aimed at removing the most obvious and easily solved problems in core business processes (we call these problems "the low hanging fruit"). Starting many short projects is good during the first year because they deliver quick results and involve lots of people, which makes your agency-wide effort more visible.

During this period, it is not a good idea to start more than a few process improvement projects that are expected to last more than three months. There is nothing wrong with long projects, but they do not produce the quick, visible payback needed to give your effort momentum.

Pilot projects and demonstrations

Think of these early efforts as pilot projects and demonstrations. Use them to test different techniques and methods so that you can develop an appropriate improvement tool kit for the future. Pilot projects are your first opportunity to have managers train, coach, and facilitate teams, which prepares them for their new management roles.

When running early pilot projects, avoid the problem of resistance by managers who are not on the project teams. Pilot projects often happen before all the managers in an affected work unit have been trained and gained experience in process improvement. Managers who are not on a pilot team may resent the project because it addresses a problem they should have solved long ago. It will be a serious setback to your improvement initiative if non-team managers refuse to take action on a pilot team's recommendations.

To avoid this resistance, you can do the following:

- Brief all affected managers before starting the project;

- Include as many of the affected managers as possible on the pilot team;

- Have the non-team managers develop the team's charter, including the desired results; and

- Make sure your CEO takes a personal interest in the project, which will send a message to the non-team managers. Your CEO's interest should last at least until the team's recommendations have been implemented.

Core process improvement

During the first year, don't worry about problems over in payroll or travel expense reimbursement; don't start creating new rewards systems; don't train everyone in improvement tools and methods. Just focus on results that matter most to your customers and mission, which almost always come from improving core business processes.

Sound improvement methods and practices used on core process projects will make the first year a positive experience. These practices will contribute to the long-term effort of becoming an Improvement Driven Organization. Likewise, use major projects to install the changes needed to ensure continuous improvement of a core business process (see Chapter 19).

As you maintain this focus in the first year, it will become clear that other things besides the core processes must be improved in order for them to operate optimally. Then, you can work on improving non-core processes with more assurance that the changes will benefit the core processes.

Natural work group improvements

Your second milestone in Business Process Improvement is to start obtaining results from natural work groups, which are small groups of employees and managers who operate a single process or small group of processes, with most operations occurring within their work unit (see Chapter 16). In most organizations, these groups or self-managed teams are the mainstays of gradual improvement.

Each group trains in improvement methods as a team, then applies its new knowledge to the group's processes (we will discuss this training in a moment). A group meets several times a month to identify problems and opportunities that fall within the boundaries of their processes. Their search for improvement is guided by strategic goals, management plans, and issues discovered during core business process improvement projects.

The DO IT program at the Air Force Development Test Center (AFDTC), Eglin AFB, Florida is a good example of using natural work groups to roll out improvement practices to an entire organization. After gaining experience from running several process improvement projects, AFDTC developed a special natural work group training module that included a small set of improvement tools and methods. This training was given to groups in work units where managers had completed their own team building and planning. Most new DO IT teams (as they are called) quickly identified dozens of improvement opportunities. At first, the teams restricted themselves to issues that could be addressed without going outside their processes. As they gained experience, DO IT teams started working together to solve problems that crossed over into other processes.

Suggestion program

At AFDTC, the DO IT initiative became the de facto suggestion program because management wanted to stress team work over individualism for a few years, and so it waited awhile before re-working its individual suggestion programs. You may wish to do the same, or get started sooner; Chapter 17 discusses how to establish high-performance suggestion programs for teams and individuals.

Save the suggestion program for the second year, though. By then, all of your managers should be trained in leadership and process improvement, so that they will be able to respond quickly and appropriately to employee suggestions. Without follow-through, the programs will never get off the ground and will have increased your organization's resistance to change.

Get There As Quickly As You Can: Organizational Process Alignment

The pace of the race to build an Improvement Driven Organization is set by Organizational Process Alignment activities such as leadership development, giving everyone a process focus, team building, and cascade training. The faster you do these activities *effectively,* the faster improvement practices will spread throughout your organization. Also, there is a logical order to these activities; each forms the foundation for the next. Do one out of order, and you will find that the remainder will not work.

Leadership development

Your leaders include executives and senior managers. They will require training and experience in using improvement methods and in modeling new leadership roles and styles. They acquire part of this experience prior to and during the Leader Driven phase, and we discussed some of the training earlier in this chapter. After the strategic plan is prepared, executives and senior managers will require additional training in communicating the plan and new improvement initiatives to their troops, in acting as issue champions, and in motivating people to accept new ways of doing business.

Many organizations ask us to coach their executives during the leadership development period. We meet regularly with individual executives and senior managers to help them plan for how they, personally, will incorporate new leadership roles and styles into their professional lives. Usually, we do this as part of a project in which our consultants provide assistance to the organization in planning and implementing new improvement practices.

Process focus

Most people think of their operations as part of a functional work unit such as a department or office. During the first year, you want managers and employees to start thinking of their work in terms of processes. You can do this in several ways, including the following:

- Educate people about the core business processes identified during the Leader Driven phase;

- Incorporate process thinking into management planning;

- Have the CEO begin requiring reports about cross-functional processes instead of just by department or office; and

- Start using the language of processes in official communications and during management and employee meetings.

Some organizations give all employees a few hours training on process improvement concepts during the early months of introducing this new approach to management. The training is really awareness building and thus helps to reduce any confusion and concern employees may feel. Trainees identify their internal customers and suppliers and may do a high-level process map of their operations.

Team building

Once your managers understand their processes, you can begin building cross-functional management teams. The first of these should be focused on your core business processes and will likely be headed by executives and senior managers. As you broaden and deepen your initiative, you need to form other cross-functional teams for smaller processes.

Team building is a must for these cross-functional teams. Team building takes place in an ongoing series of structured meetings through which members of management-level teams learn each other's needs and expectations and how to work as a team. The sessions require pre-meeting work by facilitators to gain information on the members and their units; this information is used for group problem-solving exercises during the meetings. The team develops objectives to improve its ability to function as a unit and works on those objectives after the meetings. Periodic team building meetings ensure that the members maintain their common focus and understanding.

Quite a bit of team building focuses on customer/supplier relationships within a cross-functional process. Participants in these sessions ask each other, "What do you need from me to achieve this process or team-building objective?" The answers stimulate discussion and clarify what needs to be done to ensure success.

Team building is not just for internal operations or cross-functional processes. It is also useful for developing management teams within a single department, customer/vendor teams, preparing executives for strategic planning sessions, and developing better relations between supplier agencies and customer agencies. Aspects of team building also are used when training improvement project teams, natural work groups, and self-managed teams.

Cascade training

Have you ever watched a small mountain stream trickling down a high cliff, splashing into small pools that brim over and flow down lower cliffs to ponds that spill to still lower lakes? Then you know what we mean by cascading: start at the top and fill up the highest level with knowledge and skill, then work your way downward.

In cascade training, top leaders learn and use improvement methods and teamwork and teach them to their direct reports. These next-level-down managers form management teams and start practicing the methods. After gaining experience on these teams, managers train their own direct reports, who in turn train their subordinates, and so on until employees are trained in natural work groups. In Chapter 18 on change management, we gave an example of cascade training at VAROIC.

Cascading is a highly effective way to train people in a totally new improvement approach, for the following reasons:

- The bosses have to understand the new approach well enough to teach it. This solves a major problem that often occurred when introducing quality management, when managers had no idea what their well-trained employees were doing or talking about during team meetings.

- People may daydream during a training session led by an outsider or peer, but their eyes are wide open when the boss is doing the teaching.

- Cascading is one more way to involve managers in introducing new business practices and to increase their acceptance of the practices.

The best thing about cascade training is that it fits the manager's role of teaching and coaching employees how to use new methods and techniques, which is a plus for organizations that must constantly change in order to improve. However, some executives and managers are not good at this type of training. They can be assisted by another manager, a professional trainer, or an outside management consultant, but they should take part in the sessions, if only to kick things off, ask questions, and summarize at the end. In the future, though, include the ability to give instruction to subordinates in your management evaluations.

For cascading to work, you need the following resources:

- Training courses on new practices that can be customized to meet the needs of each part of the organization;

- A training course in how to train for managers who are not used to doing this;

- Support services for managers during training, such as assistance in customizing their presentations; and

- A system of ensuring that managers present their courses in a correct and standard manner, because what and how they teach is the new management style of your organization.

Cascade training acts as an excellent regulator of the speed with which you introduce agency-wide improvement practices. It keeps you from getting ahead of the organizational learning curve, so although your development pace may be a bit slower, you are more likely to be successful. The downside is that cascading is a slow process. If you need teams to start working immediately on critical issues in key processes, use the pilot project approach discussed earlier.

Other activities in organizational process alignment

Late in the second year and perhaps early in the third, you will be ready to start revising your compensation and rewards systems, skills training, and other aspects of the organization related to human and organizational resource management. We advise holding off until then, so that you can make these revisions with a full understanding of their effect on the improvement practices you developed and on your changing organizational culture. The exception to this timetable is when some existing practice or policy is a barrier to progress; then, you must eliminate the practice and develop a new one.

Infrastructure Development

About midway through the first year you will be able to begin taking a logical, process-oriented look at your agency's organizational structure and supporting infrastructure such as information systems and internal controls. We suggest forming a high-level restructuring team to manage the structure assessment and to recommend actions that will align operations with core business processes (see Chapter 3). Once agreement is reached on a new structure, other teams can use it as part of their blueprints for the new supporting infrastructure.

We recommend that you use value analysis as part of restructuring in order to eliminate or minimize resources devoted to non-value added processes and activities. How much disruption this will cause will depend on the amount of non-value added activity going on in your agency. Whether or not you use activity analysis, if you anticipate major change in structure in a particular work unit, then make the change before you begin training the unit's natural work groups.

IMPROVEMENT DRIVEN PHASE

Chapter 19 discusses in detail the practices needed to ensure continuous improvement after major process changes and shows how to use benchmarking to adopt and adapt the best practices of outside organizations. We will not repeat that discussion here, expect to say that these practices should be a constant, routine part of all major process improvement.

Change Management

About midway through the first year you will begin to understand the type of culture your agency will need to support continuous improvement. At that point, you need to develop a plan for introducing and supporting the elements of the new culture and to incorporate it into your other plans and activities. Chapter 18 provides a detailed discussion on this.

Performance Measurement

Success at gradual improvement depends on the installation of effective performance measures in all processes and the degree to which process managers and operators use the information to control and enhance operations. One of the first assignments for a natural work group should be to map their process to identify key points at which to measure it. At least one of these measures should relate to satisfying the process's customers. If appropriate, one or more other measures can be aligned with strategic goals and management plan objectives.

Quality Systems Development

Your most important quality system is training for improvement. Toward the end of the first year, you will want to have the internal capability to deliver this training to a growing number of people and work units.

Training, coaching, and internal consulting

Temporarily increase the size of the support group of the agency-wide improvement team. For the next several years you may have to continue using a sizable part-time support staff for this team. To do this, you need an internal "train the trainer" program. Combine the instructor and facilitator roles, as discussed in Chapter 17, to create well-rounded internal consultants and coaches. As noted earlier, these people are the "prototype models" of your future management style.

Make training and coaching part of the management role. Start putting your managers and supervisors through these courses. Add training and exercises in participative management, leadership, and change management. Eventually, most of the need for a support staff will fade as your managers routinely perform the staff's functions. Monitor how your managers train and work with people, help them if they need it, and in every other way make this part of management's routine work.

Some topics require special training, such as experimental design and advanced statistical process control. If many of your personnel need this training, develop internal courseware for it. If that is not possible, arrange courses through a community college, send people to outside training, or use a private consultant.

Periodic refresher courses on process improvement methods are good for managers and employees. These may be as simple as "brown bag" lunches or as formal as structured courses.

Install a strong evaluation component in your training, and you will get the feedback necessary to improve it. Send selected managers to off-site seminars and conferences, and you will get new ideas for training.

Monitoring progress

You need an excellent monitoring system to ensure that you are maintaining momentum in the right direction. For the next several years, this will be the job of your agency-wide improvement champion. The champion's staff needs to collect information on team meetings, progress in introducing support systems, complaints about the initiative, and other feedback. This must be done continuously, and feedback on progress should be on the agenda of every meeting of the executive steering committee.

Leadership is the key

Although we divide the IDO framework into three phases, ultimately all improvement is driven by leadership. Leaders must show their commitment to improvement every day of the year, because each day they miss can begin wearing away progress made.

THIS RACE NEVER ENDS

Well, you made it through the first two years. Congratulations! If you kept on course and did all the activities we outlined, you should have both a solid foundation and solid, take-it-to-the-bank results.

So what do you do in Year Three and beyond? Go back to the Leader Driven phase, introduce more sophisticated methods of improvement, and continue to build your capabilities. Never stop doing this, and you will always succeed, because *process improvement is a journey, not a destination.*

References

Alliance for Redesigning Government/National Academy of Public Administration, "A Prince of a System," *The Public Innovator*, No. 15, 27 October 1994.

–"Unions and Taxpayers Win Through 'Publicization,'" *The Public Innovator*, No. 19, 29 December 1994.

David K. Carr and Ian D. Littman, *Excellence in Government: Total Quality Management in the 1990s*, 2nd edition (Washington, DC: Coopers & Lybrand), 1993. ISBN 0-944533-07-8.

David K. Carr et al., *BreakPoint Business Process Redesign: How America's Top Companies Blast Past the Competition* (Washington, DC: Coopers & Lybrand), 1992. ISBN 0-944533-04-3 (see Appendix A).

Clifton Cooksey et al., *Process Improvement: A Guide for Teams* (Washington, DC: Coopers & Lybrand), 1993. ISBN 0-944533-06-X (see Appendix A).

John K. Condon et al., "Cost of Quality at Sweden Post," *Quality Digest*, May 1992.

Council of State Governments, "TQM in State Government: Options for the Future," October/ November 1994. To obtain a copy of this survey of state governments, call the Council at (800) 800-1910.

Peter Drucker, "Really Reinventing Government," *Atlantic Monthly*, February 1995.

Joseph Kehoe et al., *Activity-Based Management in Government* (Washington, DC: Coopers & Lybrand), 1995. ISBN 0-944533-10-8 (see Appendix A).

Young Kim, "ISO 9000—Making Companies Competitive," *Quality in Manufacturing*, November/December 1994.

National Commission of the State and Local Public Service, *Hard Truths/Tough Choices: an Agenda for State and Local Reform* (Albany, NY: The Nelson Rockefeller Institute, State University of New York), 1993. ISBN 0-914341-26-X.

– *Revitalizing State and Local Public Services*, Frank J. Thompson, ed. (San Francisco: Jossey-Bass), 1993. ISBN 1-55542-572-0.

National Governors' Association, *An Action Agenda to Redesign State Government: Reports of the State Management Task Force Strategy Groups*, 1994. ISBN 1-55877-219-7.

New York City Partnership/New York Chamber of Commerce and Industry, *Putting the Public First: Making New York Work Through Privatization and Competition*, a report of the Privatization Task Force, 1993.

Oregon Process Board, *Oregon Benchmarks; Standards for Measuring Statewide Progress and Institutional Performance, Report to the 1995 Legislature,* Oregon Economic Development Department, December 1994.

Vincent M. O'Reilly et al., *Internal Control— Integrated Framework*, Committee of Sponsoring Organizations of the Treadway Commission, 1994 (see Appendix A).

Appendix

A

RESOURCES

BOOKS

Activity-Based Management

Activity-Based Management in Government, Joseph Kehoe, William Dodson, Robert Reeve, Gustav Plato. Washington, DC: Coopers & Lybrand, 1995. 296 pages. ISBN 0-944533-10-8.

A thorough introduction to activity-based costing (ABC) in government, this book shows how to apply the ABC approach in determining the actual costs of public sector products, services, and the processes that make them. Then, the book explains how to apply ABC methods to restructure and manage operations around core business processes, which is called Activity-Based Management. Offers dozens of examples from different levels of government, and from civilian and defense organizations.

Common Cents: The ABC Performance Breakthrough, Peter B.B. Turney. Portland, OR: Cost Technology, 1993. 322 pages. ISBN 0-9629576-7.

An easy-to-read primer on ABC, Turney's is a good first book on both ABC principles and how to introduce ABC to an organization. Besides clearly explaining the technical aspects of ABC, the book outlines the change management aspects of making the transition from traditional cost accounting. This is a must-read. Cost Technology, Turney's company, also publishes several case studies that are worth reading.

Benchmarking

Benchmarking: A Manager's Guide, Meredith Bolon and Amy Weber. Washington, DC: Coopers & Lybrand, 1995. 110 pages. ISBN 0-944533-44-2.

This short, step-by-step guide takes the manager through the entire benchmarking procedure, from defining the scope of the project through institutionalizing the improved process. Authored by Coopers & Lybrand managers who coach government teams in conducting benchmarking projects.

Change Management

Managing Change: Opening Organizational Horizons, David K. Carr, Kelvin Hard, and William J. Trahant. Washington, DC: Coopers & Lybrand, 1994. 284 pages. ISBN 0-944533-12-4.

An in-depth exploration of the art and science of managing change in organizations, this book provides dozens of examples from government and industry. Chapter 11 of this book was based on the methods and techniques presented in *Managing Change.* The authors are partners in Coopers & Lybrand's Washington, DC, and London offices.

Internal Controls

Internal Control—Integrated Framework, Vincent M. O'Reilly et al., Committee of Sponsoring Organizations of the Treadway Commission, 1994.

The methodology described in this set of handbooks is based on a process viewpoint, enabling organizations to build internal controls into their operations, instead of adding them on afterwards. Published by the American Institute of Certified Public Accountants, the COSO report, as it is commonly known, was written by a Coopers & Lybrand team commissioned by the Treadway Commission. The set includes sample forms and scoring criteria for reviewing internal controls. To order, contact:

American Institute of Certified Public Accountants
Harborside Financial Center
201 Plaza Three
Jersey City, NJ 07311-3881
Telephone: (800) 862-4272; Fax: (800) 362-5066

ISO 9000

The ISO 9000 Handbook, 2nd edition, Robert W. Peach, editor. Fairfax, VA: CEEM Information Services, 1995. 688 pages. ISBN 1-883337-31-3.

This is a comprehensive how-to manual on implementing the ISO 9000 quality standards. It includes the full text of the standards. To order, contact:

CEEM Information Services
10521 Braddock Rd.
Fairfax, VA 22032
Telephone: (800) 745-5565; Fax: (703) 250-5313

ISO 9000 Equivalent: ANSI/ASQC Q90

This is a set of guidelines that contain the text of the ISO 9000 standards. It can be ordered from the American Society for Quality Control, listed below under Networks, Alliances, and Resource Groups.

Performance Measurement

Customer Service Measurement, Monograph Series #1, David Wilkerson and Clifton Cooksey. Washington, DC: Coopers & Lybrand, 1994. 72 pages. ISBN 0-944533-08-6.

A handy guide to determining customer expectations and levels of satisfaction, then linking the results to performance measures at the process level. Geared toward government organizations, it contains examples from the public sector.

Survey Assessment, Monograph Series #2, David Wilkerson and Jefferson Kellogg. Washington, DC: Coopers & Lybrand, 1994. 63 pages. ISBN 0-944533-09-4.

This monograph discusses the steps involved in using survey instruments to collect information on customer expectations and satisfaction and on personnel morale, climate, and culture.

Managing Project Expectations, Monograph Series #3, David Wilkerson and Bonnie Brown. Washington, DC: Coopers & Lybrand, 1995. 61 pages. ISBN 0-944533-18-3.

Organizations that carry out projects will appreciate this monograph on the Stakeholder Quality Process used by Coopers & Lybrand to determine the expectations of the firm's customers' expectations, then develop performance measures to ensure that the expectations are met.

Measure Up! Yardsticks for Continuous Improvement, Richard L. Lynch and Kelvin F. Cross. Cambridge, MA: Blackwell, 1991. 213 pages. ISBN 1-55786-099-8.

This easy-to-read, practical overview of modern performance measurement shows the limitations of traditional measures and how to develop a new system that captures all aspects of operations performance.

Process Improvement

Process Improvement: a Guide for Teams, Clifton Cooksey, Debra Eshelman, Richard Beans. Washington, DC: Coopers & Lybrand, 1993. 246 pages. ISBN 0-944533-06-X.

This manual covers how to scope an improvement project, develop baseline data, analyze problems and opportunities, generate and test improvements, and introduce them to operations. Its "tool box" includes detailed instructions on the basic improvement tools discussed in *Improvement Driven Government,* plus other more advanced tools and methods. Designed around the Plan-Do-Check-Act cycle, the manual guides teams through the improvement process and includes a chapter on the dynamics of teamwork. It is designed to be used in teams, so most organizations buy manuals for each team member. All manuals include a computer disk and user guide of software programs for dozens of statistical tools discussed in the text.

SPC Simplified: Practical Steps to Quality, Robert T. Amsden, Howard E. Butler, and Davida M. Amsden. Milwaukee: Quality Press, 1989. 262 pages. ISBN 0-527-91617-X. Supplementary workbook: 362 pages, ISBN 0-527-91638-2.

A practical book on statistical process control requiring no mathematical background. It uses clear, straightforward language to simplify the essentials for monitoring, analyzing, and improving quality through SPC. A supplementary workbook by the same title follows the main text on a module-by-module basis.

Juran's Quality Control Handbook, 4th edition, J.M. Juran, editor. New York: McGraw-Hill, 1988. 1,536 pages. ISBN 0-07-033176-6.

Everything you could possibly want to know about quality and improvement tools is covered in this three-inch-thick tome. It is a handy, comprehensive reference book for someone who designs improvement training or consults with teams on process improvement issues.

Maintenance Management

Uptime: Strategies for Excellence in Maintenance Management, John Dixon Campbell. Portland, OR: The Productivity Press, 1995. 192 pages. ISBN 1-56327-053-6.

Maintenance management is an integral part of the production process. If your organization owns industrial or commercial equipment, this is a must-read book on integrating preventive maintenance into processes.

Quality Management

Federal Total Quality Management Handbook, Federal Quality Institute, Washington, D.C.

This is a series of handbooks, including an introduction to TQM, how to get started, education and training, and other topics. Each handbook can be ordered separately from the U.S. Government Printing Office. Contact:

Superintendent of Documents
U.S. Government Printing Office
Washington, D.C. 20402
Telephone: (202) 783-3238

Quality by Design: Taguchi Methods and U.S. Industry, Lance A. Ealey. Dearborn, MI: ASI Press, 1988. 333 pages. ISBN 0-941-243-05-2.

Ealey presents experimental design in the context of comprehensive quality management. Most of the technical information is in the appendices.

Principles of Quality Costs: Principles, Implementation, and Use, 2nd edition, Jack Campanella, editor. Milwaukee: Quality Press (ASQC), 1990. 140 pages. ISBN 0-87389-084-1.

An ideal book for starting a cost-of-quality (COQ) system in both industrial and service settings. Specific examples and case studies amplify the text's how-to nature. Includes information on quality costs in military specifications.

Malcolm Baldrige National Quality Award

To obtain a copy of the award criteria, write to:

Malcolm Baldrige National Quality Award
National Institute of Standards and Technology
Administration Building, Room A-537
Gaithersburg, MD 20899.
Telephone: (301) 975-2036; Fax: (301) 948-3716

Reengineering

Best Practices in Reengineering: What Works and What Doesn't in the Reengineering Process, David K. Carr and Henry J. Johansson. New York: McGraw-Hill, 1995. 235 pages. ISBN 0-07-011224-X.

The authors base this book on a major survey of organizations that practice business process redesign and reengineering (BPR). They use the results to explain how to select strategic processes for reengineering, get the highest return on process improvement investment, and ensure continuous improvement in redesigned processes.

Business Process Reengineering: BreakPoint Strategies for Market Dominance, Henry J. Johansson, Patrick McHugh, A. John Pendlebury, and William A. Wheeler III. West Sussex, U.K.: John Wiley, 1993. 241 pages. ISBN 0-471-93883-1.

The authors are partners in Coopers & Lybrand offices in the U.S. and the U.K. More technical than *BreakPoint Business Process Redesign*, this book follows the same methodology. It provides more details on global organizations and manufacturing. It's a must-read for any government industrial or technical operation that is considering reengineering.

BreakPoint Business Process Redesign: How America's Top Companies Blast Past the Competition, David K. Carr, Kevin S. Dougherty, Henry J. Johansson, Robert E. King, and David E. Moran. Washington, DC: Coopers & Lybrand, 1992. 206 pages. ISBN 0-944533-04-3.

An overview of BPR, this introductory book shows the relationship of reengineering to information technology, process engineering, quality management, and change management. It presents a methodology for developing, introducing, and sustaining major changes.

All books published by Coopers & Lybrand in Washington, D.C., may be ordered from:

Bookmasters, Inc.
Distribution Center
1444 State Rte. 42
RD 11
Mansfield, OH 44903
Telephone: (800) 247-6553
Fax: 419-281-6883

NETWORKS, ALLIANCES, AND RESOURCE GROUPS

National Performance Review (NPR)

The NPR, central headquarters for reinventing the federal government, has published dozens of reports that are must-read information for federal managers who are engaged in organization-wide improvements. Start with *From Red Tape to Results: Creating a Government That Works Better and Costs Less*, and keeping reading through more detailed initial and follow-up reports on such topics as procurement, support services, privatizing, program design, intergovernmental service delivery, and many more.

Most of these documents can be ordered for free in hard copy from:

National Performance Review
750 17th St., NW, Suite 200
Washington, DC 20006
Telephone (202) 632-0150; Fax (202) 632-0390;
e-mail: rego.news@npr.gsa.gov

Also, you can browse and download the documents, along with a wide variety of reinventing government reports, speeches, newsletters, and other materials, at the following Internet sites:

• World Wide Web: http://www.npr.gov

• Gopher: ace.esusda.gov. Select submenu Americans Communicating Electronically (ACE), then select National Performance Review.

- e-mail: Several e-mail catalogs can be automatically mailed to you. To receive the first flyer on how to obtain these documents, send mail to almanac@ace.esusda.gov with this message: Send NPR catalog. No subject line is required.

Alliance for Reinventing Government

This network was established by *Reinventing Government* author David Osborne and others under the aegis of the National Academy of Public Administration. The Alliance publishes *The Public Innovator,* a twice-monthly newsletter with reports on major process improvements in federal, state, and local government, interviews, meeting announcements, and book reviews.

National Academy of Public Administration
1120 G St., NW
Washington, DC 20005
Telephone: (202) 466-6887; Fax: (202) 347-3252;
e-mail: HN3121@handset.org

The World Center for Community Excellence

Part of the Community Quality Coalition network, the Center promotes the use of quality management methods to improve business, government, and education in communities. This is a good place to start looking for local examples of process improvement because the Center provides lists of community and state quality organizations.

The World Center for Community Excellence
106 State St.
Erie, PA 16501
Telephone: (814) 456-9223

The American Society for Quality Control

With more than one hundred thousand members, the
ASQC is the nation's leading organization devoted to
quality management and control. The society has local
chapters throughout the country and special sections
that focus on particular industries or technical aspects
of quality improvement, including government.
Publications include the journal *Quality Progress* and,
if you join the government special section, *The Public
Sector Network.* Be sure to ask for the Quality Press
book and audiovisual catalog; you get discounts by
joining the society.

The American Society for Quality Control
611 East Wisconsin Avenue
Milwaukee, WI 53203
Telephone: (414) 272-8575; toll free (800) 248-1946

The Association for Quality and Participation

The Association has state and local chapters in many
parts of the country. The annual membership fee
includes the periodical *Journal for Quality and
Participation* and discounts on books, training material
and aids, conferences, meetings, and courses.

The Association for Quality and Participation
801-B West Eighth Street, Suite 501
Cincinnati, OH 45203
Telephone: (513) 381-1959; toll free (800) 733-3310

The Productivity Press

This publisher maintains an exhaustive inventory of
process improvement books, many of which were originally published overseas. Order the catalog to see
what the experts write and read about quality, productivity, and related subjects.

The Productivity Press
P.O. Box 13390
Portland, OR 97213-0390
Telephone: (800) 394-6868; Fax: (800) 394-6286.

Appendix
B

ANALYSIS OF COOPERS & LYBRAND'S BEST PRACTICES SURVEY

In a summer 1994 survey, Coopers & Lybrand found that government organizations recognized as being leaders in quality management scored higher in chief executive leadership and employee training practices than did best-in-industry private organizations. However, these government organizations carried out other quality management practices with less intensity than the private groups. This was true even though the government organizations had had quality management initiatives in place longer.

NATURE OF THE SURVEY

The purpose of the study was to find out what winners do to win in quality management. We generated a short list of desirable outcomes in quality management (high customer satisfaction, high innovation, etc.) and a longer list of "best practices" that would predict these outcomes.

A best practice is any management action thought to be

essential in producing a desired outcome, whether or not the outcome has anything to do with quality management. While the practices we asked about often are associated with quality management, they are really just simple, good management. So it is possible to see this survey as a study of management practices, period.

Also, we probed for factors that provide the foundation for certain types of best practices. Such information helps us develop the Improvement Driven Organization approach to successful management.

To find out this information, we mailed a survey to the person responsible for quality management in about six hundred public and private organizations in the United States and Canada, asking about their quality management practices. We received back three hundred surveys. The organizations we targeted were selected because they were considered best-in-class in their industries. Thus, the sample cannot be projected to all U.S. and Canadian organizations.

The survey does, however, permit an examination of what we call "the winners" are doing in order to be winners. As a study, it is a comparison of best-in-class organizations.

The survey was carried out by our International Survey Center, located in C&L's Arlington, Virginia offices. The Survey Center conducts research for our clients in areas such as customer expectations and satisfaction, organizational culture, and employee readiness for major change.

ABOUT THE SURVEY SAMPLE

The total sample for the survey was drawn from lists of *Fortune 500* and other organizations that had demonstrated superior financial and other performance and were believed to have active quality management initiatives. Also included were several hospitals known to have superior quality management initiatives.

The government sample was strictly federal, and was drawn from lists of President's Quality Award and Quality Improvement Prototype (QIP) award winners, along with a few other federal organizations known to have superior quality management approaches. We received twenty usable responses from our federal sample. We needed twelve to make statistically valid statements about best practices of federal organizations.

RESULTS

Exhibit B-1 at the end of this appendix shows the questions asked in the survey. Questions 1-7 show the percentage that agreed with a specific answer to the questions. Questions 8-66 are the respondents' self-graded score on the degree of intensity with which their organizations carry out a specific practice related to quality management. The numbers shown for these questions are the respondents' average (mean) score of agreement-disagreement with the statements posed in the questions. A score of one on these questions means "Strongly Disagree" with a statement, while a seven means "Strongly Agree."

- **Best.** This is the percentage or mean score of the organizations that reported they had measurable improvements as a result of their quality initiatives (see Question 7) and that strongly agreed that customer feedback showed that their customers are satisfied with the quality of the products or services they provide (Question 10). This includes some members of the government group.

- **Population.** These are the percentages and mean scores of the entire survey population that reported having measurable improvements. This is still a high-performance group, not simply the average performance of all organizations in the U.S. and Canada. All the government organizations are factored into this group.

- **Government.** This is the percentage or mean score of the government organizations in the survey. As winners of the QIP and President's Award, they also are top performers.

The following are summaries of: (1) the overall differences among the three groups and (2) the results in five areas that we think are important for success in an Improvement Driven Organization: leadership, promoting innovation, enhancing employee participation, managing change, and strategies for improvement.

Overall Differences

Note in Question 6 that the government organizations have had quality initiatives in place for longer than the "best" and the total population groups. This reaffirms our belief that some parts of the federal government have been involved in quality management for at least as long as industry. For example, the Navy has been active in this area since about 1982.

The first comparison is level of customer satisfaction (Question 10: "Customer feedback shows that our customers are satisfied with the quality of the products and services we provide."). The "best" group scores a perfect seven on this, the highest possible score, because that is the way we defined this group. The total population group, which includes the "best" group, scores about 22 percent less than that, and the government group 26 percent less. So, if government wants to be the best-of-the-best in serving its customers, it has a way to go.

Now, let's look at differences in several practice areas, shown in Figure B-1.

In Exhibit B-1 you will see three columns to the right of the questions:

Practice	Question(s) Number	Govt. Better than Best	Govt. Better than Population
1. Quality management leadership by the CEO. However, see "Leadership" below for additional comments.	12	Yes	Yes
2. Training of employees (Questions 22 and 24)	22 and 24	Yes	Yes
3. Recognition and reward for contributions to quality improvement	25, 64, 65	Yes for 25, no for others	Yes for 25, no for others
4. Strategic planning	16, 41,44, 54	No	No
5. Management believes it empowers employees	14	No	Yes
6. Employees believe management has empowered them	17, 23	No	No
7. Acceptance of employee ideas by management	30, 31	No	No
8. Employees responsible for process improvement and for quality product/service design	18, 19, 21, 26	No	Yes, except for 19
9. Collection, distribution and use of measurement data on customer satisfaction, cost, cycle time, employee satisfaction, process performance, employee skill development, progress of change initiatives	8, 33, 34, 35, 36, 37, 38, 39, 45, 62	No	No, except that measures of cycle time reduction are more often collected (33), but not as often used (45)
10. Benchmarking	46	No	No
11. Change management (see also below)	52-66	No	No, except 65 and 66

From the data, we might conclude that the best government organizations are ahead of the elite "best" group in CEO leadership, training, and some aspects of reward and recognition. However, they are behind in the other eight areas, all of which are considered important in successful quality management and process improvement. Comparing the government group to the total population, there seems to be room for improvement in strategic planning, accepting employee ideas, measurement, benchmarking, and change management. In the area of measurement, it looks as though the federal Government Performance and Results Act (GPRA) faces a real challenge, because the government group is less prone to measure customer satisfaction and use it to improve operations.

In early surveys of quality management in government, we saw that there was a top leadership gap, which seems to have now closed[1]. Apparently, however, top leadership alone won't get you there anymore. Our reading of these results is that the best organizations in the private sector have been much more comprehensive in their quality management initiatives, and have successfully addressed some basic foundation issues such as measurement and the use of customer satisfaction data in running their operations. Also, the private organizations are doing much more benchmarking and competitor comparisons than the government group. Now, we can understand it when some of our war fighting and intelligence groups don't think they can learn anything from benchmarking or adopting the best

---

[1] These surveys include Coopers & Lybrand's 1989 survey on federal progress in introducing quality management (see "Quality in the Federal Government," by David K. Carr and Ian D. Littman, *Quality Progress*, September 1990, pages 49-52); *Should Total Quality Management be Implemented in Florida State Government*, by Fran Wilber, Florida Department of Administration, November 1991; "Government Quality Needs Assessed," *On Q: The Official Newsletter of the American Society for Quality Control*, May 1992, pages 1-2; and *Quality Management: Survey of Federal Organizations*, U.S. General Accounting Office, GAO/GGD-93-9BR, October 1992.

practices of the private sector. However, all the other government organizations have operations that also are done in the private sector, so they should be studying what's going on outside their gates. Some will be in for rude awakenings if, under privatization, they have to compete head-to-head with private competitors they are not looking at now.

Leadership

Question 2: The single greatest force behind my organization's strategic quality initiatives was...

In our statistical analysis, we found that the answer "our CEO's vision" was the greatest predictor of high levels of customer satisfaction. This relationship was stronger in the "best" organizations than in the population as a whole or the government group.

Question 3: During the past three years, the staff most responsible for building quality awareness and supporting quality-related efforts within my organization has...

Question 4: During the next three years the quality organization will most likely. . .

This refers to the quality management office within an organization. We like to think that the best response to these questions is that the office has or will "become incorporated in the organization's natural work groups and activities." In the three years before the survey, this had not happened as much in the government organizations as it has in the other two groups, but quality managers (the survey's respondents) think it will occur slightly more often over the next three years. However, a higher percentage of the government respondents report that the quality management office has been or will be reduced in size because of cutbacks. This can be interpreted in two ways. First, most private organizations have been downsizing and are likely to continue to do so. However, it seems that their quality offices are less likely than those in the government organizations to undergo similar reductions. Second, twelve out of twenty of our federal respondents are from defense organizations, which are going through major downsizings and won't need as many quality office personnel.

In the following four areas, we used the results of some of the questions as outcomes, and applied multiple regression analysis to identify which other questions' answers seemed to predict or correlate with the outcomes. The assumption to this calculation is that, if you want to get Outcome A, you have to be conducting best practices X, Y, and Z. Our correlations are all statistically significant (at least the .01 level and mostly at the .001 level).

Promoting Innovation

We considered Question 29, "My organization has a strong reputation for innovation," as an outcome, not a "best practice." There were three best practices that were highly correlated with a high score in the answer to this question. They were, in order of the strength of the correlation:

Question 32: "My organization is on the leading edge of technology."

The government organizations were about even with the "best" group on this, and ahead of the total population. This is probably because of the high number of defense and aerospace organizations in our government sample.

Question 30: "Concepts for new products and/or services originate at many levels of the organization"

Question 31: "Innovative ideas from employees in my organization are readily accepted by management."

These were less true of the government organizations than for the "best" and total population groups. Now, you can look at this two ways. First, federal organizations do not need as much input from their employees in order to be innovative (we don't buy that). Second, even the best federal organizations lag behind their private sector counterparts in listening to and using the ideas of their employees (we do buy that).

Enhancing Employee Participation

We used Question 26, "Employees take an active role in improving our processes," as the starting point for this area of inquiry. As you can see, there is not a whole lot of difference among the three groups in their answers to this question. The three questions that most strongly correlated with Question 26 were, in order:

Question 23: "Employees believe that their job impacts the change and quality initiatives of the organization."

Employees in the federal organizations are perceived as less likely to believe this than those in the other two groups.

Question 25: "Contributions to quality improvements are recognized and rewarded."

The government group appears to be better in this area than the other two groups.

Question 21: "Employees participate in team activities to evaluate product development or service quality."

The government group is about even with the "best" group in this area and slightly ahead of the total population.

Managing Change

This part of our study focused on how organizations manage the human and cultural aspects of introducing improvements as part of their quality initiatives. Our outcome variable in this area was Question 53: "Employees who are most affected by change understand what is required of them to support the change." The three questions that correlated most highly with this outcome are, in order:

Question 56: "Employees who are most affected by change understand how the change will affect them personally."

Question 52: "My organization's change initiatives are driven by customer needs and expectations."

Question 16: "Employees understand the link between their tasks and the organization's strategic plans and goals."

For each question, the government group had lower scores than the "best" group and the total population. This was true for all questions directly related to change management (Questions 52-65, with a slight exception in Question 66). We would have to conclude that the federal organizations could be doing a better job at managing change.

Strategies for Improvement

We think it important for organizations to practice "top-down" improvement guided by management as well as "bottom-up" improvement based on what middle managers and employees perceive as requiring enhancement. Because our focus was quality management, our outcome variable for this area was Question 44: "A strategy is in place to ensure that process improvement occurs on a regular basis." The three questions most strongly correlated with Question 44 were, in order of their strength:

Question 51: "Our organization has a system in place for targeting which processes are selected for improvement."

Responses indicate that the intensity of this practice is higher in both the "best" and the government than in the total population.

Question 52: "My organization's change initiatives are driven by customer needs and expectations" (this question was also highly correlated with "Managing Change")

Question 38: "My organization regularly uses process performance data to adjust and improve work processes."

The government organizations carry out these practices with less intensity than the "best" and the total population groups.

IMPLICATIONS OF THE STUDY

Many federal organizations will be facing tough challenges in the upcoming round of budget cuts and, potentially, of privatization. On the budget cut/downsizing issue, many more agencies will have to find ways to expand their capacity to deliver services without expanding their budgets. Most of the best practices discussed above will help them do just that, but only if these practices are carried out with greater intensity.

Budget cuts and downsizing also mean that agencies will have to give much more attention to managing major changes. Right now, the best agencies are not very well equipped to do that; the situation is probably much worse in average agencies not covered in this study.

Regarding privatization and the related practice of outsourcing internal support operations, we think many agencies will be in trouble if they are allowed to compete with private companies for the privilege of providing services. That's because many major private companies want their contractors and suppliers to have active quality management initiatives, and the practices we just described are, in fact, quality management.

Finally, as long is there is a gap in customer satisfaction between the private and the public sector, government organizations are going to be criticized for poor performance. From this survey, we can see that there is such a gap among the best private and public sector organizations. At the least, this gap probably exists to an equal degree among less-than-best private companies and public agencies. Agencies that want to survive, thrive, and do the best thing by their customers have to close that gap.

Exhibit B-1
Survey Questionnaire Results

Best = Scoring in the highest quartile on Question 10 of this survey (n=46).

Population = Average score of all other participants (n=300)

Government = Average score of government participants in survey (n=20)

SECTION 1

For the following seven (7) questions, please select and mark the response that best describes your organization.

1. All participant responses are confidential and only aggregate results will be published in our final report. In this report we would like to include a list of all participants. May we list your company name as a participant in the survey?

	Best	Population	Government
Yes	84.1%	84.9%	85.0%
No	15.9%	15.1%	15.0%

2. The single greatest force behind my organization's strategic quality initiatives was

	Best	Population	Government
our CEO's vision	62.2%	45.3%	45.0%
crises resulting from competitive pressures	17.8%	22.5%	20.0%
crises resulting from changing consumer demands	6.7%	14.1%	15.0%
evolving technology	2.2%	2.3%	5.0%
other	11.1%	15.8%	15.0%

3. During the past three years, the staff most responsible for building quality awareness and supporting quality-related efforts within my organization has

	Best	Population	Government
taken on greater strategic responsibilities	43.5%	41.1%	40.0%
been reduced in size due to cutbacks	6.5%	9.4%	15.0%
become incorporated in the organization's natural workgroups and activities	23.9%	24.1%	15.0%
maintain about the same size with respect to staff and responsibilities	26.1%	22.7%	25.0%
other	0.0%	2.7%	5.0%

4. During the next three years the quality organization will most likely

	Best	Population	Government
take on greater strategic responsibilities	43.5%	37.0%	20.0%
be reduced in size due to cutbacks	4.3%	4.0%	15.0%
become incorporated in the organization's natural workgroups and activities	30.4%	33.7%	35.0%
maintain about the same size with respect to staff and responsibilities	21.7%	24.0%	30.0%
other	0.0%	1.3%	0.0%

5. The senior quality officer of my organization reports directly to

	Best	Population	Government
the senior leader of our organization	66.7%	58.4%	65.0%
the senior board or leadership council	6.7%	6.0%	5.0%
the senior leader of a functional division	22.2%	27.9%	15.0%
other	4.4%	7.7%	15.0%

6. We have had organization-wide quality initiatives in place for

	Best	Population	Government
1 - 3 years	19.6%	27.7%	15.0%
3 - 5 years	32.6%	24.7%	25.0%
5+ years	45.7%	40.0%	60.0%
no organization-wide initiatives in place	2.2%	7.7%	0.0%

7. We can identify measurable improvements in our product or service quality that were a direct result of our quality improvement initiatives.

	Best	Population	Government
Yes	100.0%	83.3%	85.0%
Don't know	0.0%	8.4%	10.0%
No	0.0%	8.4%	5.0%

SECTION 2

Below are items which describe the practices of your organization. Indicate your agreement by choosing the phrase which best represents your opinion.

1 = Strongly Disagree
2 = Moderately Disagree
3 = Slightly Disagree
4 = Neither Agree nor Disagree

5 = Slightly Agree
6 = Moderately Agree
7 = Strongly Agree

The role your customers play in focusing your organization's quality improvement initiatives

	Best	Population	Government
8. My organization collects customer satisfaction information on a regular basis.	6.56	5.95	5.50
9. Customer feedback shows that we understand the needs and desires of our customers.	6.58	5.56	4.85
10. Customer feedback shows that our customers are satisfied with the quality of the products and/or services we provide.	7.00	5.48	5.05
11. My organization frequently uses customer feedback to improve the way in which we perform our work.	6.26	5.52	5.40

The leadership role in your organization's quality improvement initiatives

	Best	Population	Government
12. The CEO is responsible for motivating and leading the organization to improve its quality performance.	5.93	5.57	6.55
13. The senior quality officer is responsible for enabling the organization to produce high-quality products and/or services.	5.26	5.09	4.80
14. Management believe they empower employees with increased responsibility for improving the organization's quality performance.	6.14	5.70	5.75
15. Supervisors in my organization help employees improve their performance.	6.12	5.45	5.10

1 = Strongly Disagree
2 = Moderately Disagree
3 = Slightly Disagree
4 = Neither Agree nor Disagree

5 = Slightly Agree
6 = Moderately Agree
7 = Strongly Agree

Address the role of employees in achieving quality

	Statement	Best	Population	Government
16.	Employees understand the link between their tasks and the organization's strategic plans and goals.	5.26	4.64	4.35
17.	Employees believe that management has empowered them with increased responsibility for improving the company's quality performance.	5.30	4.63	4.00
18.	Employees recognize and act on their responsibility to continuously improve their work processes.	5.58	4.82	4.85
19.	Employees are responsible for ensuring that products and/or services are designed and produced at the level of quality our customers expect.	6.02	5.41	5.35
20.	Individuals in my organization have the opportunity to learn skills which will enhance their ability to improve product and/or service quality.	6.26	5.87	6.05
21.	Employees participate in team activities to evaluate product development and/or service delivery processes.	5.98	5.52	5.90
22.	Employees are satisfied with the formal training they receive to do their job.	4.88	4.61	5.35
23.	Employees believe that their job impacts the change and quality initiatives of the organization.	5.42	4.91	4.75
24.	Employees receive the training necessary to keep up with changes in work processes.	5.37	4.93	5.55
25.	Contributions to quality improvements are recognized and rewarded.	5.30	5.08	5.70
26.	Employees take an active role in improving our processes.	5.74	5.32	5.55
27.	Teams are an integral part of the decision-making process in my organization.	5.60	5.15	5.60
28.	Quality improvement accomplishments are included in employee performance evaluations.	5.40	4.77	5.05

577

1 = Strongly Disagree
2 = Moderately Disagree
3 = Slightly Disagree
4 = Neither Agree nor Disagree
5 = Slightly Agree
6 = Moderately Agree
7 = Strongly Agree

Innovation in your organization

#		Best	Population	Governmen
29.	My organization has a strong reputation for innovation.	6.14	5.36	5.15
30.	Concepts for new products and/or services originate at many levels of the organization.	5.74	5.07	4.95
31.	Innovative ideas from employees in my organization are readily accepted by management.	5.65	4.96	4.75
32.	My organization is on the leading edge of technology.	5.19	4.91	5.05

Use of measurement in quality improvement

#		Best	Population	Governmen
33.	My organization quantifies or measures improvements made in reducing cycle time.	5.44	5.01	5.30
34.	My organization provides accurate product and/or service quality performance information to work groups throughout the organization.	5.53	4.90	4.80
35.	My organization quantifies or measures improvements made in reducing costs.	6.05	5.44	4.95
36.	Cost data are used to drive process improvements.	5.58	5.22	4.70
37.	My organization regularly measures employee satisfaction.	5.07	4.79	4.80
38.	My organization regularly uses process performance data to adjust and improve work processes.	5.05	4.67	4.80
39.	Employee skill development is effectively measured through performance evaluations.	4.63	4.24	3.90
40.	We have changed the way we measure success in the last 3 years	5.60	5.20	4.65

1 = Strongly Disagree
2 = Moderately Disagree
3 = Slightly Disagree
4 = Neither Agree nor Disagree
5 = Slightly Agree
6 = Moderately Agree
7 = Strongly Agree

Address your organization's process improvement efforts

	Statement	Best	Population	Government
41.	The key business processes of our organization are aligned with our strategy.	5.72	5.42	5.15
42.	When processes are changed, we change the organization structure to better support those processes.	5.09	4.72	4.50
43.	Customer satisfaction data are used to drive process improvements.	5.88	5.24	4.45
44.	A strategy is in place to ensure that process improvement occurs on a regular basis.	5.74	5.04	4.65
45.	Cycle-time data are used to improve the organization's business processes.	4.86	4.67	4.60
46.	Our organization uses benchmarking as a tool to improve our key business processes.	5.35	4.72	3.75
47.	Our organization works as a partner with our major suppliers to improve the quality of our supplier materials, products, and or services.	5.47	5.28	4.75
48.	We study how our competitors design, develop, and produce their products and/or services.	5.49	4.97	3.95
49.	Our competitors drive our process improvement and change efforts.	4.16	4.06	3.50
50.	Our customers drive our process improvement and change efforts.	5.74	5.40	4.65
51.	Our organization has a system in place for targeting which processes are selected for improvement.	5.26	4.72	4.95

1 = Strongly Disagree
2 = Moderately Disagree
3 = Slightly Disagree
4 = Neither Agree nor Disagree

5 = Slightly Agree
6 = Moderately Agree
7 = Strongly Agree

Address how your organization manages change in conjunction with your quality improvement efforts

		Best	Population	Government
52.	My organization's change initiatives are driven by customer needs and expectations.	5.88	5.44	4.80
53.	Employees who are most affected by change understand what is required of them to support the change.	5.00	4.50	4.15
54.	The vision and strategies for change are regularly communicated.	5.44	4.97	4.45
55.	Employees understand the compelling need for change from the status quo.	5.49	5.00	4.70
56.	Employees who are most affected by change in our organization understand how the change will affect them personally.	5.21	4.56	4.20
57.	Responsibility for achieving the goal(s) of the change are assigned to a specific individual or group.	4.98	4.93	4.75
58.	Organization structures are aligned to reflect changes in management practices.	5.30	4.99	4.35
59.	Change leaders have a strong internal base of support.	5.44	4.84	4.30
60.	Change leaders demonstrate consistent support for change initiatives.	5.86	5.32	4.45
61.	Changes are implemented at a pace the organization can assimilate.	4.95	4.67	4.10
62.	Metrics are established to measure the progress of change initiatives.	4.30	4.23	3.45
63.	Plans for change are based on realistic expectations of the organization's ability to change.	4.84	4.58	4.30
64.	Success with change is recognized and publicly reinforced.	5.26	4.91	4.30
65.	Rewards and sanctions are used to support the organization's change initiatives.	5.02	4.55	4.25
66.	The organization ensures that employees have the skills they need to accomplish change objectives.	5.05	4.60	4.65

About the Authors

The authors are Partners in Coopers & Lybrand's Government Services Practice in Washington, D.C.

David K. Carr has been with Coopers & Lybrand for nearly twenty years, where he has provided a broad spectrum of advisory services to public and private sector clients. Before joining C&L, he was an analyst with Fairfax County, Virginia and the Central Intelligence Agency. He is the Partner-in-Charge of Coopers & Lybrand's U.S. Quality Management Center of Excellence, and the firm's lead Partner in change management. Mr. Carr's clients include government, manufacturing, university, insurance, utility, and health care organizations, such as the Air Force, Navy, Marine Corps, U.S Postal Service, Tennessee Valley Authority, Federal Home Loan Mortgage Association, AlliedSignal Corporation, Nations Bank, Dunlop Tire, United Airlines, Asea-Brown-Boveri, and New York Life. He is the co-author, with Mr. Ian Littman, of *Excellence in Government: Total Quality Management in the 1990s,* and articles appearing in *Quality Progress* and *The TQM Magazine*. With other C&L professionals, he wrote *Managing Change: Opening Organizational Horizons, BreakPoint Business Process Redesign,* and *Best Practices in Reengineering: What Works and What Doesn't in the Reengineering Process.* He holds a bachelor's degree in political science and a master's degree in public administration, both from Pennsylvania State University.

Ian D. Littmann is the originator of the Improvement Driven Organization concept, which he developed based on his experience in overseeing four hundred plus process improvement projects in more than one hundred government organizations since 1990. A former employee of the state of New York and of a Presidential commission on law enforcement, he has twenty years' experience managing projects involving quality management, change management, business process redesign, contracts and procurement management, logistics, organizational analysis, personnel management, customer satisfaction, benchmarking, inter-governmental relations, instructional design and training, and operations improvement. His clients have included the General Services Administration; Office of Personnel Management; Department of Defense—Defense Logistics Agency, Army, Navy, and Air Force; Departments of Labor, Housing and Urban Development, Interior, Justice, Veterans Affairs, Health and Human Services, Agriculture, Treasury, and Transportation; and the U.S. Congress. He is the author of articles and papers presented in *National Productivity Review, The Federal Times, Government Accounting,* and other national publications. Mr. Littman holds a bachelor's degree from Syracuse University and a master's degree in public administration from The George Washington University.

John D. Condon, a former Marine enlisted man and career Navy officer, has participated in consulting engagements for more than 50 clients, including the Defense Mapping Agency, the Navy's intelligence community and industrial organizations, Air Force, Environmental Protection Agency, Postal Service, New York Life Insurance Company, Convatec/Squibb, AlliedSignal, and Italsiel. He has managed major projects in long-range strategic planning, time-based management, organizational change management, group facilitation, team building, team training, and organizational assessment. Mr. Condon has facilitated senior executive strategic planning sessions for dozens of federal organizations and developed C&L's strategic planning and visioning methodology. Recognized throughout the Americas as an expert in the change management aspects of organizational transformation, he has been a keynote or featured speaker on quality management at several professional and industry conferences and co-authored articles on process improvement in *Mail* and *Quality Digest.* Mr. Condon holds a bachelor's degree in analytical management from the U.S. Naval Academy and a master's degree in national security affairs from the Naval Postgraduate School.

ABOUT COOPERS & LYBRAND

Overview of Coopers & Lybrand L.L.P.

Coopers & Lybrand, founded in 1898, is one of the world's oldest and largest accounting and management consulting firms. Throughout the world, C&L has more than sixty-five thousand partners and staff working in over one hundred countries and seven hundred and fifty offices. In the United States alone, we have more than sixteen thousand staff in all major cities. C&L's Government Services Practice, headquartered in the Washington, D.C. area, has over five hundred partners and staff who provide specialized consulting services to both public and private sector clients. The practice's services include the following:

- **Quality Management.** Providing executive awareness training, assessments, quality planning, methods training, and implementation support.

- **Change Management.** Assisting in implementing technical and human changes in business strategy, organizational structure, and systems.

- **Operations Management.** Creating financial, production, and material control systems, performance measurement, and operational analysis.

- **Strategic and Human Resource Management.** Providing organizational assessment, management, and leadership training, strategic planning and program evaluation.

- **Activity-Based Costing.** Mapping processes and analyzing activities within them to support streamlining process improvements, business process redesign, and cost management.

- **Business Process Redesign.** Planning and training for new technologies to reshape business processes and assisting in re-engineering work processes to meet strategic performance goals.

- **Information Engineering.** Developing strategies to leverage information technology, defining concepts of operations, assessing effectiveness of existing information systems, and creating information, process, and technology architectures to support future operations.

- **Acquisition of New Information Technology.** Defining functional and technical system requirements, performing cost/benefit analysis, and reengineering existing systems to meet changing needs.

- **Systems Development and Implementation.** Designing, developing, and integrating systems, performing systems testing and evaluation, developing and delivering training and documentation, developing user and technical procedures, and providing software quality management services.

- **Private Sector Development Support.** Providing technical assistance to foreign countries in developing new business ventures and infrastructure.

- **Privatization.** Assisting domestic and foreign governments to restructure and convert public service operations and government-owned industries to private ownership.

- **Trade and Investment.** Providing assistance to U.S. firms investigating opportunities in Central and Eastern Europe.

- **Financial Market Development.** Providing assistance on a worldwide basis in the development of capital markets.

- **Government Contract Services.** Working with government contractors on issues such as cost accounting standards, FAR cost principles, cost estimating, pricing, progress payments, and proposals.

For more information on Coopers & Lybrand's services for governments and government contractors, please contact one of the authors at:

Coopers & Lybrand L.L.P.
1530 Wilson Boulevard
Arlington, Virginia 22209-2447
Phone: 703-908-1500
Fax: 703-908-1695

Index